ARGUING ABOUT EMPIRE

Arguing about Empire analyses the most di   ⌐ween Europe's two leading colonial powers fron.   ⌐usm to the post-war era of decolonization. Focusing oı.   ⌐utexts underlying imperial rhetoric, *Arguing about Empire* adopts ⌐   ⌐ approach, treating key imperial debates as historical episodes to be inv ⌐ated in depth. The episodes in question have been selected both for their chronological range, their variety, and, above all, their vitriol. Some were straightforward disputes; others involved cooperation in tense circumstances. These include the Tunisian and Egyptian crises of 1881–2, which saw France and Britain establish new North African protectorates, ostensibly in co-operation, but actually in competition; the Fashoda Crisis of 1898, when Britain and France came to the brink of war in the aftermath of the British re-conquest of Sudan; the Moroccan crises of 1905 and 1911, early tests of the Entente Cordiale, when Britain lent support to France in the face of German threats; the 1922 Chanak crisis, when that imperial Entente broke down in the face of a threatened attack on Franco-British forces by Kemalist Turkey; World War Two, which can be seen in part as an undeclared colonial war between the former allies, complicated by the division of the French Empire between De Gaulle's Free French forces and those who remained loyal to the Vichy Regime; and finally the 1956 Suez intervention, when, far from defusing another imperial crisis, Britain colluded with France and Israel to invade Egypt—the culmination of the imperial interference that began some eighty years earlier.

Martin Thomas is Professor of Imperial History and Director of the Centre for the Study of War, State, and Society at the University of Exeter. He has written widely on the history of European decolonization and French international politics. His most recent books are *Violence and Colonial Order* (2012) and *Fight or Flight: Britain, France, and their Roads from Empire* (2014).

Richard Toye is Professor of Modern History at the University of Exeter, and has been described by the New York Times as 'one of Britain's smartest young historians'. He is a specialist in the history of rhetoric and is the author of numerous articles and several books, including *Rhetoric: A Very Short Introduction* (2013) and *The Roar of the Lion: The Untold Story of Churchill's World War II Speeches* (2013).

Arguing about Empire

Imperial Rhetoric in Britain and France, 1882–1956

MARTIN THOMAS AND RICHARD TOYE

OXFORD

UNIVERSITY PRESS

OXFORD
UNIVERSITY PRESS

Great Clarendon Street, Oxford, OX2 6DP,
United Kingdom

Oxford University Press is a department of the University of Oxford.
It furthers the University's objective of excellence in research, scholarship,
and education by publishing worldwide. Oxford is a registered trade mark of
Oxford University Press in the UK and in certain other countries

First published 2017
First published in paperback 2019

Published in the United States of America by Oxford University Press
198 Madison Avenue, New York, NY 10016, United States of America

British Library Cataloguing in Publication Data
Data available

Library of Congress Cataloging in Publication Data
Data available

ISBN 978-0-19-874919-6 (Hbk.)
ISBN 978-0-19-882048-2 (Pbk.)

Contents

List of Figures

List of Maps

Introduction
Arguing about Empire

'The struggle of races and of peoples has from now on the whole globe as its theatre; each advances towards the conquest of unoccupied territories.'[1] Tempting as it might be to ascribe such inflated rhetoric to Friedrich Nietzsche or Adolf Hitler, its originator was Gabriel Charmes, a disciple of leading late nineteenth-century French republican, Léon Gambetta. In September 1882, Charmes was trying to persuade his fellow parliamentarians that France's recent seizure of Tunisia was ethically imperative.[2] Similar rhetoric could be found across the political spectrum, in Britain as well as in France. In 1888, the Conservative Prime Minister Lord Salisbury described small imperial wars as 'merely the surf that marks the edge of the advancing wave of civilisation'.[3] But if Britain and France both claimed to be the spearhead of civilizing influences, what happened when their interests clashed, and what new arguments emerged to rationalize the struggle for power between rival 'civilized' nations? We may equally ask what happened when their interests appeared to coincide. How did the two countries' respective elites justify their mutual collaboration in the face of challenges from other powers and, increasingly as time went on, from domestic anti-colonial critics and local nationalist opponents too?

This book analyses the most divisive arguments about empire between Europe's two leading colonial powers from the beginnings of the age of high imperialism in the 1880s to the watershed of the Suez crisis in the 1950s. It applies a comparative approach to the specificity of imperial rhetoric—its racial underpinnings and paternalist tones, its ethical presumptions, and the worldviews it enshrined. Were French and British imperial actions justified in ways fundamentally different from concurrent diplomatic interventions beyond the confines of empire? If so, when and why did this begin to change? What part should be assigned to changing international norms as exemplified by the growing influence of transnational opinion-makers—lobby groups, media outlets, and, after 1918, the new regulatory

---

[1] Cited in John Chipman, *France in Africa* (Oxford: Blackwell, 1988), 50.

[2] Charmes' presumptive connection between hierarchies of ethnicity and imperial rivalries also emerged in the writings of another socially conservative republican, Louis Marin. A leading right-wing politician of the Third Republic, Marin's ideas about ethnography are described in Herman Lebovics, 'The Discourse of Tradition in French Culture: The Rightist Social Science and Political Practice of Louis Marin, 1890–1945', *Historical Reflections*, 17:1 (Winter 1991), 45–75.

[3] 'Banquet at the Guildhall', *The Times*, 10 November 1888.

agencies of the League of Nations and its post-1945 reincarnation, the United Nations?[4]

If public statements once served to rally politicians and public to empire projects, from the 1920s onwards the difficulties of sustaining colonial control in the face of increasing global opposition catalysed more diverse forms of rhetorical imperial defence. One of our objectives is to analyse these transitions, the cross-Channel differences between them, and their effectiveness in mobilizing and sustaining support for particular imperial ventures. The cases we examine—most of them historically familiar clashes in the African and Western Asian 'hot-zones' of Franco-British colonial expansion in the late nineteenth and twentieth centuries—reveal instances of acute, but non-violent rivalry, of actual violence, and of imperial cooperation hamstrung by underlying mistrust. Running through them all is the deep-seated conviction that a common Western 'civilizing mission' made the acquisition of empire both ethically justifiable and politically logical. Rooted in enlightenment thought and the new imperialism of the late nineteenth century, the liberal positivism that underpinned this belief in the innate superiority and universal applicability of European cultural and religious norms never entirely crumbled in later decades. Indeed, as we aim to show, the affirmation of colonialism's culturally beneficial impacts withstood the weight of contrary evidence and the violent self-destructiveness of European societies in the world wars of the twentieth century. At the same time, the trends towards deeper democratization and more critical domestic publics in France and Britain drove imperialist politicians to conjure up new arguments to justify empire in terms of material improvements in living standards and even rights protections.[5]

Tracing the derivation of the public political rhetoric of empire yields clues to the unspoken private assumptions and motivational factors that informed it. The highly gendered, often Freudian metaphors of patriarchal imperial family and attendant parental responsibility to infantilized and pathologically unstable subject peoples became a *patois*, a shorthand dialect used and understood by those at all levels of colonial government. Just as such metaphors saturated administrators' self-justificatory language, so, too, they pervaded European imperialist argument at parliamentary and ministerial level.[6] Local opponents of empire increasingly mobilized the same language of familial duties, obligations, and burdens to stress

---

[4] For evaluations of these new factors in the aftermath of World War I, see: Erez Manela, 'Imagining Woodrow Wilson in Asia: Dreams of East- West Harmony and the Revolt against Empire in 1919', *American Historical Review*, 111:5 (December 2006), 1327–51; Eric D. Weitz, 'From the Vienna to the Paris System: International Politics and the Entangled Histories of Human Rights, Forced Deportations, and Civilizing Missions', *American Historical Review*, 113:5 (2008), 1313–43; Michelle Tusan, ' "Crimes against Humanity": Human Rights, the British Empire, and the Origins of the Response to the Armenian Genocide', *American Historical Review*, 119:1 (2014), 47–77.

[5] Alice L. Conklin, 'Colonialism and Human Rights: A Contradiction in Terms? The Case of France and West Africa, 1895–1914', *American Historical Review* 103:2 (1998): 419–42 at 420; J. P. Daughton, 'Behind the Imperial Curtain: International Humanitarian Efforts and the Critique of French Colonialism in the Interwar Years', *French Historical Studies*, 34:3 (2011), 504–7.

[6] For examples from another empire, see: Frances Gouda, 'The Gendered Rhetoric of Colonialism and Anti-Colonialism in Twentieth-Century Indonesia', *Indonesia*, 55 (April 1993), 1–2, 12–14;

the chasm between imperial rhetoric and colonial reality.[7] Particularly notable in this regard were the many anti-colonial nationalists with career backgrounds as physicians. Their scientific training was reflected in their turn to biological and medical language to highlight the endemic weaknesses in the colonial body politic.[8]

Unravelling such commonalities between empires requires comparison. Much as the British and French empires have already been studied in enormous depth, considerable work also compares them explicitly.[9] Of particular note is the work of Véronique Dimier. She has highlighted the interaction between the British and French empires as viewed through two long-term phenomena: the professionalization of the colonial services of Britain and France and the efforts made by members of each to distinguish between British and French styles of colonial governance. Dimier argues convincingly that sustained efforts to distinguish one from the other—for instance, indirect rule and 'light touch' British governance next to the competing French doctrines of assimilation and its more widely applied alternative of association—only made the administrative similarities between the two empires more apparent. Among other things, local resistance and other obstacles to implementation, plus lack of requisite investment, confronted British and French imperial bureaucrats with the same challenges of adaptation and mounting international criticism. However, Dimier's conclusions relate rather more to the colonial services than to government, and further scope remains for comparison at this more overtly political level.[10]

There are many different ways of carrying out comparative history; as John Elliott has suggested, 'the nature of the problem should be allowed to determine the nature of the comparison'.[11] Our problem is that of how far French imperial rhetoric differed from its British equivalent, and also what similarities and differences there were between the start and the end of our period. But our task is not wholly to compare, the better to differentiate. Our story is more of an *histoire croisée*. It is the entanglement of these two empires, and the consequent interrelatedness of imperial rhetoric, that is the object of our study. We are interested not only in 'the circulation of arguments and their reinterpretation according to national context', but also in their recirculation and reinterpretation according to temporal context.[12] Our claim to be offering a novel approach to the comparative

Frances Gouda, 'Languages of Gender and Neurosis in the Indonesian Struggle for Independence, 1945–1949', *Indonesia*, 64 (October 1997), 45–8, 61–3.

[7] Gouda, 'The Gendered Rhetoric of Colonialism', 3–7.

[8] Warwick Anderson, 'Scientific Patriotism: Medical Science and National Self-Fashioning in Southeast Asia', *Comparative Studies in Society & History*, 54:1 (2012), 93–7, 111–13.

[9] Miles Kahler, *Decolonization in Britain and France: The Domestic Consequences of International Relations* (Princeton, NJ: Princeton University Press, 1984); Martin Thomas, *Fight or Flight: Britain, France, and their Roads from Empire* (Oxford: Oxford University Press, 2014). For a broader treatment of Anglo-French relations, see Robert and Isabelle Tombs, *That Sweet Enemy: The British and the French from the Sun King to the Present* (London: Heinemann, 2006).

[10] Veronique Dimier, *Le gouvernement des colonies, regards croisés franco-britanniques* (Brussels: Editions de l'Université de Bruxelles, 2004).

[11] J. H. Elliott, *History in the Making* (New Haven, CT: Yale University Press, 2012), 173.

[12] Michael Werner and Bénédicte Zimmermann, 'Beyond Comparison: Histoire Croisée and the Challenge of Reflexivity', *History and Theory*, 45:1 (2006), 30–50, at 40.

study of imperial rhetoric therefore rests in part on our method of comparison. We examine a series of case studies all of which involved some element of imperial crisis. We are concerned both with how the unravelling of these crises was influenced by rhetoric, and how those crises in turn created shifts in rhetoric.

The principles of selection are that: (a) both Britain and France were directly involved in a given crisis (whether as allies or as rivals); and (b) the crisis concerned generated a substantial volume of public discussion by politicians in both countries. Interaction, even interdependence, between the global expansion and ultimate contraction of the British and French empires from the late nineteenth century to the late twentieth century offers several choices for comparison. Both empires were global and multi-Oceanic, but the conflicts and, paradoxically, the co-reliance between them were perhaps sharper in Africa and, more especially, in Western Asia, than elsewhere. It was here that direct clashes were most frequent, that competition was most embittered, and, at the same time, that the differing costs of conflict versus collaboration were most intensely debated between the 1880s and the 1950s.

In terms of geopolitics, South Asia remained an overwhelmingly British imperial preserve, the proliferation of cosmopolitan imperial cultures and vestigial French settlements in India notwithstanding. Moving eastwards, British colonial interests in South East Asia, hingeing on the port of Singapore, Peninsula Malaya, and the island of Borneo, were matched by French predominance in Indochina. Labour migration throughout South East Asia, whether voluntary or coerced, transformed the political economies and ethno-cultural complexion of the Malay States as assuredly as it did the territories of Vietnam and Cambodia.[13] Imperial competition there certainly was, not least in the fields of export production, the cultivation of client networks, and schemes of administrative redesign.[14] For all that, South East Asia, much like the Caribbean—another Oceanic zone dotted with British, French, and other European colonial outposts—was rarely a site of violent Franco-British colonial dispute. When such conflicts did arise, external challengers catalysed them: Japan in the South East Asian case, the United States in the Caribbean case. Franco-British colonial co-existence, even co-imperialism (a term discussed in detail later in this Introduction) was more typical.[15]

Parallels might also be drawn with vast swathes of sub-Saharan Africa. In much of West Africa particularly, competition persisted between British and French

[13] Sunil Amrith, *Migration and Diaspora in Modern Asia* (Cambridge: Cambridge University Press, 2011), especially chapter 2; David G. Marr, *Vietnamese Tradition on Trial, 1920–1945* (Berkeley, CA: University of California Press, 1981), 23–35, 335–42; Evelyn Hu-DeHart, 'Chinatowns and Borderlands: Inter-Asian Encounters in the Diaspora', in Sunil Amrith and Tim Harper (eds), *Sites of Asian Interaction: Ideas, Networks and Mobility* (Delhi: Cambridge University Press, 2014), 191–215.

[14] Such competition was, for instance, endemic within the colonial rubber industry, see Stephen L. Harp, *A World History of Rubber: Empire, History, and the Everyday* (Oxford: Wiley-Blackwell, 2015), 17–28, 90–1, 118–20.

[15] The idea that shared European interest in the global success of imperialism against local challengers might override particular national interests is not a phenomenon intrinsically limited to the nineteenth or twentieth centuries, see: Stephen Conway, '"Founded in Lasting Interests": British Projects for European Imperial Collaboration in the Age of the American Revolution', *International History Review*, 37:1 (2015), 23–31.

imperialists. This might be over borderlands, waterways, other communications, and the movements of local people across them. It might be within the economic fields of monetary usage, customs, and trade policy, or the social fields of public health, management of epidemic disease, and other service provision.[16] Or it might be in the cultural realms of education, missionary activity, and plural legal systems.[17] Often these overlapped, disrupting the tidy geometry of colonial jurisdiction. For all that, Franco-British co-imperialism was an accomplished fact by the 1890s until its basic credo of co-existence was disrupted by the impact of World War II. These unwritten rules and imagined boundaries to imperial rivalry remained less apparent in Northern Africa and Western Asia, areas in which the fate of the Ottoman Empire and the concomitant interventionism of other imperial outsiders played a distinct and stronger role. So it is on these regions that our study focuses.

Chapter 1 examines the Tunisian and Egyptian crises of 1881–2, which saw France and Britain secure control of new territories in North Africa, ostensibly in cooperation, but actually in competition. Chapter 2 looks at the Fashoda crisis of 1898, when Britain and France came to the brink of war in the aftermath of the British reconquest of Sudan. Chapter 3 considers the Moroccan crises of 1905 and 1911, early tests of the newly established Entente Cordiale, which saw Britain lend support to France in the face of German threats. Chapter 4 deals with the 1922 Chanak crisis, when that imperial *entente* broke down in the face of a threatened attack on Franco-British forces by Kemalist Turkey. Chapters 5 and 6 consider World War II as (among other things) an imperial crisis extraordinaire. As Chapter 5 indicates, the collapse of the Franco-British alliance in 1940 reverberated through the two countries' empires. Indeed, colonial clashes arose almost immediately afterward, causing bitter imperial rivalries to resurface once more. Once again, as Chapter 6 reveals, the harshest confrontations occurred in Northern Africa and the Middle East, confirming the regional pattern evident throughout the book. Taken together, the war years could thus be seen, in part, as an undeclared colonial

[16] For background, see Myron Echenberg, *Black Death, White Medicine: Bubonic Plague and the Politics of Public Health in Colonial Senegal, 1914–1945* (Portsmouth, NH: Heinemann, 2002); Sarah Ehlers, 'Europeanising Impacts from the Colonies: European Campaigns against Sleeping Sickness 1900–1914', in Matthieu Osmont et al. (eds), *Europeanisation in the 20th Century: The Historical Lens* (Brussels: Peter Lang, 2012): 111–26; Moses E. Ochonu, *Colonial Meltdown: Northern Nigeria in the Great Depression* (Athens, OH: Ohio University Press, 2009); Axel Harneit-Sievers, 'African Business, "Economic Nationalism," and British Colonial Policy: Southern Nigeria, 1935–1954', *African Economic History*, 23:1 (1995), 79–86; Gareth Austin, 'Cash Crops and Freedom: Export Agriculture and the Decline of Slavery in Colonial West Africa', *International Review of Social History*, 54:1 (2009), 1–37; Alice L. Conklin, 'A Force for Civilization: Republican Discourse and French Administration in West Africa, 1895–1930', in Charles Becker, Saliou Mbaye, and Ibrahimi Thioub (eds), *AOF: réalités et héritages. Sociétés ouest-africaines et ordre colonial, 1895–1960*, 2 vols (Dakar: Direction des Archives du Sénégal, 1997), vol. 1, 283–302.

[17] Rivalry between missionary groups in sub-Saharan Africa cannot, of course, be understood in national, rather than confessional terms, although the use of language, vernacular or otherwise, often sparked intense argument, see: J. P. Daughton, *An Empire Divided: Religion, Republicanism, and the Making of French Colonialism, 1880–1914* (Oxford: Oxford University Press, 2006), 22, 27, 33–44; Kenneth J. Orosz, *Religious Conflict and the Evolution of Language Policy in German and French Cameroon, 1885–1939* (New York: Peter Lang, 2008), especially chapters 4–5.

war between the former allies, a conflict that was complicated by the division of the French Empire between Charles de Gaulle's Free French forces and those who remained loyal to the Vichy regime. By May 1945, Franco-British imperial enmity in the Middle East was as sharp as it had ever been, the underlying tensions between the two imperial powers expressed in vituperative exchanges between London and Paris over the future of Syria, Lebanon, and Palestine. Moving beyond the World War II years, Chapter 7 analyses the 1956 Suez intervention, when, far from defusing another imperial crisis, Britain colluded with France and Israel to invade Egypt—the culmination of the imperial interference that began some eighty years earlier.

It will be noted that, with the exception of Fashoda and some aspects of World War II, these crises all relate substantially to North Africa and what is now called the Middle East. To reiterate the points made earlier, that is because it was in these areas that the two empires rubbed up against one another with most friction and, in consequence, generated significant volumes of rhetoric. The case-study approach, then, does not provide a complete picture of British and French imperial rhetoric across the period as a whole. But it does have the advantage of allowing us to investigate imperial rhetoric within and between Britain and France as a discrete phenomenon with identifiable rules, codes, and consequences. While each of the episodes chosen is historically familiar, the imperialist rhetoric of the leading political figures involved has not been examined comparatively. Political rhetoric was central to all of them. It was employed instrumentally to justify the scramble for territory and to support imperial business. It was used propagandistically, for instance during World War II, to condemn the perfidiousness of Albion or to highlight the collaborationism of the Vichy state. And it was used reflexively to argue that either Britain or France knew best how to administer colonized peoples. Nor were these mere wars of words. Often, lives were lost and local communities transformed by the actions of the rival colonial claimants. The rhetoric of intense Franco-British rivalry was more than the background hum of global imperial politics. The contestations it exemplified were serious, and they drive our comparative approach. In order to understand how empire operated, it is necessary to engage with the extensive public debate that surrounded it in both countries at moments of tension. Rather than 'laying bare' existing assumptions, the need to arrive at a position on Anglo-French issues forced supporters of empire and their opponents to define their views in relation to each others' arguments. Rhetorical analysis, therefore, offers a valuable, hitherto neglected tool for addressing relations between empires.

This claim of prior neglect might seem surprising, and there are indeed some exceptions.[18] The postcolonial turn in imperial history, associated with the pioneering work of Edward Said, and further developed by the proponents of the

---

[18] Notably: Frank Myers, 'Harold Macmillan's "Winds of Change" Speech: A Case Study in the Rhetoric of Policy Change', *Rhetoric & Public Affairs* 3 (2000), 555–75, and L. J. Butler and Sarah Stockwell (eds), *The Wind of Change: Harold Macmillan and British Decolonization* (Basingstoke: Palgrave-Macmillan, 2013).

so-called 'new imperial history', has placed enormous stress on language or 'discourse'.[19] Durba Ghosh summarizes this long-term analytical trend capably:

> From the generative work of Frantz Fanon, C. L. R. James, and Aimé Césaire in the middle of the twentieth century to the work of scholars such as Edward Said, Homi Bhabha, Gayatri Spivak, and Walter Mignolo near the end of the century, the field of post-colonialism has positioned itself as critical of European colonialism and its role in producing scholarship that depicts non-Europe as backward, uncivilized, primitive, hypersexualized, and violent.[20]

The importance of such scholarship in challenging presumptive historical—and imperial—claims to European civilization's global dominance is incontestable. Yet, perhaps because of its prior concerns with recovering marginal voices and the agency of colonized peoples, there is often less recognition in that scholarship of the heterogeneous and contested nature of discussion of empire among the imperialists themselves. To put it crudely, one sometimes gets the impression that empires were propped up by a somewhat amorphous 'imperial discourse' without recognition of the conflicts between its various protagonists. Much of the work in question is cultural, sometimes literary, in its focus; and the terms 'rhetoric' and 'discourse' are not always differentiated in the way that perhaps they deserve. Thus David Spurr's important book, *The Rhetoric of Empire*, focuses on journalism, travel writing, and imperial administration.[21] In different vein, Frederick Cooper and Ann Laura Stoler's edited collection, *Tensions of Empire*, a beacon of methodological innovation, is rightly acknowledged as a landmark text that places metropolitan and imperial cultures, as well as rival empires, within the same analytical framework. But its primary concern is not with high politics or the rhetorical justifications advanced for colonial expansion.[22]

We, by contrast, approach rhetoric primarily as political historians, and as a result our use of rhetoric is more closely defined. Essentially we view it in a relatively traditional sense as public speech, albeit speech that was often disseminated in written form after it had been delivered, via newspapers, pamphlets, and suchlike. This should not be taken as a sign of methodological conservatism or, we hope, of insensitivity to epistemological problems of colonial knowledge.[23] Quite the reverse: our starting point is that what can be known of the history of empire is

---

[19] Edward Said, *Orientalism* (London: Routledge & Kegan Paul, 1978); Edward Said, *Culture and Imperialism* (London: Vintage, 1994); Stephen Howe (ed.), *The New Imperial Histories Reader* (London: Routledge, 2010); for shifting methodological trends, see Patrick Wolfe, 'History and Imperialism: A Century of Theory, from Marx to Postcolonialism', *American Historical Review*, 102:2 (1997), 388–420.

[20] Durba Ghosh, 'Another Set of Imperial Turns', *American Historical Review* (June 2012), 772–93, at 783.

[21] David Spurr, *The Rhetoric of Empire: Colonial Intercourse in Journalism, Travel Writing, and Imperial Administration* (Durham, NC: Duke University Press, 1993).

[22] Frederick Cooper and Ann Laura Stoler (eds), *Tensions of Empire: Colonial Cultures in a Bourgeois World* (Berkeley: University of California Press, 1997).

[23] See in particular Ann Laura Stoler, *Along the Archival Grain: Epistemic Anxieties and Colonial Common Sense* (Princeton, NJ: Princeton University Press, 2009); George Trumball IV, *An Empire of Facts: Colonial Power, Cultural Knowledge and Islam in Algeria, 1870–1914* (Cambridge: Cambridge

profoundly structured by the concerns of the colonialists. We suggest, in other words, that rhetoric cannot be understood simply as the arrangement of tropes and figures, important though these are. Rather, it is, above all, a social phenomenon:

> Rhetoric cannot be conceived purely in terms of text and language, separate from the technical means by which it is conveyed to listeners and readers. In addition to textual analysis, we need to consider how the 'symbolic ritual dimension of politics' (a term used by the political scientists Alan Finlayson and James Martin) affects what rhetorical messages are produced and how they are received. The 'meaning' of a given set of words cannot be derived purely from an analysis of the text, in isolation from an examination of the circumstances in which that text was delivered, mediated and received. A work on rhetoric that focused on language and ideas to the exclusion of drama, physicality and technology would not be sufficient to understand its functions.[24]

An important consequence of rhetoric's social nature is that it does more than reveal imperial (or anti-imperial) mindsets; it is also part of the process that creates them and forces them to change over time as part of a dynamic process. Here we are at one with J. G. A. Pocock, who observes that the historian who is 'engaged in identifying the language contexts in which speech acts are conducted [. . .] must also be equipped with means of showing how the performance of speech acts not merely modifies language, but leads to the creation of new languages'.[25]

Our focus is primarily on elite rhetoric, with our main sources being newspapers and other contemporary published works, parliamentary debates, and documents that circulated between ministers and officials, as well as material generated by lobby groups and self-styled imperial experts. In the British case, discussion of empire in the national and, on occasion, the local press was well established by the 1880s; the foundation of the *Daily Mail* in 1896 was a key moment in the creation of a mass-market imperialist press. In the French case, too, colonial affairs figured large in the print media, although such press coverage was sometimes subsumed within wider discussion of foreign affairs or regional commercial interests. The minutiae of French colonial administration, in other words, remained a more specialist, quasi-official concern, although empire readily excited mass interest at moments of crisis or, even more so, of scandal.[26] For the latter part of the period,

University Press, 2009); Helen Tilley with Robert Gordon (eds), *Ordering Africa: Anthropology, European Imperialism, and the Politics of Knowledge* (Manchester: Manchester University Press, 2007).

[24] Richard Toye, *Rhetoric: A Very Short Introduction* (Oxford University Press, Oxford, 2013), 4. See also Alan Finlayson and James Martin, '"It Ain't What You Say . . .": British Political Studies and the Analysis of Speech and Rhetoric', *British Politics*, 3 (2008), 445–64.

[25] J. G. A. Pocock, 'The Concept of a Language and the *métier d'historien*: Some Considerations on Practice', in Anthony Pagden (ed.), *The Languages of Political Theory in Early-Modern Europe* (Cambridge: Cambridge University Press, 1987), 19–38, at 29.

[26] William H. Schneider, *An Empire for the Masses: The French Popular Image of Africa, 1870–1900* (Westport, CT: Greenwood Press, 1982); Charles-Robert Ageron, 'Les colonies devant l'opinion publique française (1919–1939)', *Revue Française d'Histoire d'Outre-Mer*, 77:286, (1990), 47; Gilbert Meynier, 'Volonté de propaganda ou inconscient affiche? Images et imaginaire coloniaux français dans l'entre-deux-guerres', in Pascal Blanchard and Armelle Chatelier (eds), *Images et Colonies* (Paris: ACHAC, 1993), 41–8. Although they ranked among France's most 'empire-conscious'

broadcasts are important too. We do not examine popular responses in a comprehensive way because to attempt to do so would present a severe challenge in the space available. It must be remembered, nonetheless, that the politicians with whom we are concerned certainly were concerned with public opinion, although the ways in which they conceived of it and attempted to gauge it changed substantially across time.[27]

In Britain and France there were shifts in the rhetorical landscape as a consequence of the rise of radio, cinema, and television, and the relative decline in importance of the public meeting.[28] At the same time, the concept of 'public opinion' was redefined, from 'opinion expressed in public' to 'the collective private opinions of members of the public'. James Thompson has shown how in pre-World War I Britain, public opinion was seen as 'a product of deliberative debate, emerging organically from the clash of often strongly held beliefs'. He rightly adds: 'Filling in a survey or answering a pollster on the phone would certainly not have satisfied many nineteenth-century thinkers as evidence for the possession of an opinion.'[29] By the time of World War II, however, one of the key pioneers of (quasi-)scientific opinion research viewed public opinion as 'this great conglomeration of private opinions' and took it as axiomatic that 'Public opinion only comes from the minds and the tongues of the people'.[30] Public meetings and (after the 1930s) opinion surveys are therefore relevant to our story, not because they provide a sure guide to what the public really thought, but because a sense of what the public might be thinking conditioned the rhetoric that elite figures produced. As for rhetoric generated within the French and British empires—to include settler criticism as well as that from anti-colonialists and nationalist movements—our principle is to refer to it where it helped shape rhetoric within the metropole.

The degree to which it did so increased over time. The interplay of European diplomacy and interstate conflict during the late nineteenth and twentieth centuries evinced one consistent rule, sometimes broken, but most often tacitly accepted by competing imperial powers. Vital interests within Europe were generally non-negotiable, whereas African interests were, in the final analysis, adjustable. That is not to dismiss the significance of arguments between imperial powers. Far from it: it is, rather, to indicate that imperial rivalry came loaded with the baggage of unspoken assumptions and diplomatic form; in other words, the codes of conduct

newspapers, it was only in the interwar years that the highbrow *Le Temps* produced a weekly colonial supplement, while the more lowbrow *Echo de Paris* published two 'empire' special editions per year from 1929. At much the same time, the emergence of cinema newsreel and the abiding popularity of colonial exhibitions and colonial exotica fed what Elizabeth Ezra describes as the 'colonial unconscious' in French popular culture. See her *The Colonial Unconscious: Race and Culture in Interwar France* (Ithaca, NY: Cornell University Press, 2000).

[27] James Thompson, *British Political Culture and the Idea of 'Public Opinion', 1867–1914* (Cambridge: Cambridge University Press, 2013).

[28] Loic Blondiaux, *La fabrique de l'opinion: Histoire sociale des sondages* (Paris: Presses Universitaires de France, 1998); Daniel Hucker, *Public Opinion and the End of Appeasement in Britain and France* (Farnham: Ashgate, 2011), 8–11.

[29] Thompson, *British Political Culture*, 15.

[30] Tom Harrisson, 'What is Public Opinion?' *Political Quarterly*, 11 (1940), 368–83, at 369.

intended to prevent wars of words from becoming something more. Sometimes such restraint collapsed, and we examine instances of Franco-British colonial conflict around the Mediterranean Basin and the strategic pivots of the Middle East: Anglo-Egyptian Sudan and Suez. It is worth remembering, though, that when it came to territorial revision in Africa, particularly in the latitudes south of the Sahara and north of the Zambezi, most among Europe's political elites were conditioned to prefer negotiated solutions over outright intransigence and the risk of armed conflict between them. The devastating experience of World War I only confirmed that inclination. Reduced to its crudest expression, by 1919 Africa mattered less, and black Africa least of all, next to the more pressing dilemmas of international security within Europe's borders and their southern and eastern margins.

The argument may be taken further still. Faced with mounting internal challenges to the security of their empires, by the 1930s Europe's imperial powers had closed ranks against African challenges to colonial authority. Even when they disagreed, most infamously, over how best to respond to fascist Italy's October 1935 invasion of Haile Selassie's Ethiopia, the quarrel was less about Italian violation of Ethiopia's sovereign independence than about the adverse geopolitical consequences for a Europe dividing into rival blocs.[31] Put differently, the real source of concern for French and British leaders was not the fate of Ethiopia's people or even the consequences for the credibility of the League of Nations as a guarantor of international order. It was, rather, with the looming loss of Italy as a potential counterweight to Nazi Germany and, albeit secondarily, with avoiding blame for the resulting diplomatic mess. Even for the imperialists, Europe came first, Africa a distant second.[32]

An unspoken assumption of Franco-British imperial rivalry, often overlooked in discussion of colonial dispute, is that neither party found it convenient to expel the other entirely. They were, in fact, co-imperialists, co-imperialism being defined as 'the exercise of imperialism as a collaborative project between multiple imperial states; the movement of personnel and translation of expertise between imperial systems; and the geopolitical and environmental circumstances that have invited this phenomenon'.[33] To put this in concrete terms, for all their divisions Britain and France increasingly faced much the same local, international, and transnational threats to their colonial hegemony. As a consequence, each feared the prospect of international isolation—before local opponents or in the court of international opinion—more than the inconvenient presence of their imperial neighbour. After 1945, this international opinion found a new institutional setting within the

---

[31] Ministère des Affaires Etrangères (MAE) archive, Paris, Archives privées (AP) 17, René Massigli papers, vol. 17, Direction politique note, 'France et Italie en Ethiopie', 9 May 1936.

[32] Martin Thomas, 'France and the Ethiopian Crisis, 1935–36: Security Dilemmas and Adjustable Interests', in G. Bruce Strang (ed.), *Collision of Empires: Italy's Invasion of Ethiopia and its International Impact* (Farnham: Ashgate, 2013), 109–34.

[33] 'Co-imperialism' is a major theme of study at the University of Exeter's Centre for Imperial and Global History. The definition above come from the Centre's manifesto, consulted on 11 September 2015: <http://humanities.exeter.ac.uk/history/research/centres/imperialandglobal/about/empires/>.

United Nations organization and gained a new salience in the context of the Cold War, placing new demands on the rhetoric of empire. As past and present imperial relationships were recast in the language of partnership, metropolitan governments expended more energy denying that their policies were 'colonialist' or 'imperialistic'. Imperialism, still in evidence certainly, dared not speak its own name.

This form of linguistic shyness, it should be stressed, was by no means a new development. The great Liberal statesman W. E. Gladstone lambasted the 'imperialism' of Benjamin Disraeli, his Conservative opponent, but when in power (albeit with some reluctance) engaged in imperial excursions himself. Indeed, Uday Singh Mehta has argued that empire was integral to Liberalism.[34] Being sceptical about 'essentialist' interpretations of Liberalism (or any other ideology), we would not go that far.[35] But it is certainly true that Liberal *languages* often proved useful to those who wished to justify imperial interventions, whether or not the people doing the arguing identified themselves as Liberals.[36] Increasingly, Conservatives came to realize this. Indeed, a key purpose of this book is to draw attention to a long-term shift in British Conservative imperial language from a focus on prestige and national self-interest to an emphasis on the need to maintain an ordered, rule-bound community of nations, drawing on an earlier Liberal heritage.

The suggestion that empire and rhetoric were ideationally connected raises the question of how we construct or, differently phrased, how we understand the production of imperialist rhetoric. Gary Wilder, an innovative thinker in French imperial history, gets to the heart of the problem. Scrutinizing the historical discipline's untidy assimilation of its various discursive 'turns' in the past twenty years or so, he warns that the original insights involved risk being oversimplified into broad generalizations about how knowledge is constructed, about the primordial significance of cultural identity, and about moving beyond nation-centred histories to focus on global and transnational processes of change. Wilder's point is a crucial one. Rather than rethinking basic categories of analysis such as 'empire' and 'nation', what he terms this post-turn consensus simply 'promises to do a better job of getting things right by attending to multiple dimensions of social experience at the same time'.[37]

What are the implications for a study of imperialist rhetoric? Rhetoricians, after all, constructed their arguments by playing on ideas of shared cultural identity. And their intended audiences spanned a spectrum from the local to the global. Two points stand out. First is that our primary objects of analysis are leading political

---

[34] Uday Singh Mehta, *Liberalism and Empire: A Study in Nineteenth-Century Political Thought and Practice* (Chicago, IL: University of Chicago Press, 1999).

[35] For a helpful discussion, see Duncan Bell, 'What is Liberalism?' *Political Theory*, published online before print 26 June 2014, doi: 10.1177/0090591714535103. See also Jennifer Pitts, *A Turn to Empire: The Rise of Liberal Imperialism in Britain and France* (Princeton, NJ: Princeton University Press, 2009); Andrew Fitzmaurice, 'Liberalism and Empire in Nineteenth-Century International Law', *American Historical Review*, 117:1 (February 2012), 122–40.

[36] Elías José Palti, 'The "Theoretical Revolution" in Intellectual History: From the History of Political Ideas to the History of Political Languages', *History and Theory*, 53 (October 2014), 387–405.

[37] Gary Wilder, 'From Optic to Topic: The Foreclosure Effect of Historiographic Turns', *American Historical Review*, 117:3 (2012), 723–45, at 729.

actors, overwhelmingly male, overwhelmingly white, and largely of elite background; in other words, the 'big men' who predominated in narrative political
histories for so long and from which protagonists of the cultural and imperial turns
were understandably keen to escape. In our case, though, escape makes no sense.
For one thing, imperialist rhetoric reflected the prevailing articulation of civic
and national masculinities in Britain and France.[38] For another, it articulated
the martial qualities presumed to be intrinsic to each. National crises, wars, and
attendant imperial or national victories and defeats of the late nineteenth and
twentieth centuries altered the ways in which concepts of masculinity, femininity,
and collective sacrifice were understood.[39] So, too, they affected the memories,
images, and examples on which imperialist rhetoric played.

A second point is that our discussion of British and French imperialist rhetoric
might be construed as 'methodological nationalism' insofar as the rhetoricians
frequently played to national audiences, often by invoking the claims and traditions
of their 'home' nation. Even when broader international or global audiences were
addressed, arguments were typically constructed around the particular administrative skills or cultural 'genius' of the imperialist power in question. Set against these
potential limitations are analytical possibilities which make the study of imperialist
rhetoric worthwhile. One is that the chapters that follow explore the connections
between the foundations of colonialist thinking and the global conditions in which
empires took shape. Put differently, the case studies we examine reveal the interplay
between presumptive attitudes about empire and race, the more immediate preoccupations of local politics, and the extraneous influences of international rivalry,
transnational currents of opinion, and particular flashpoints of colonial disorder.
Equally significant is that imperialist rhetoric was intrinsic to the identification of
empire, whether as a political cause, a cultural project, an extractive economic
system, or a plurality of administrative and juridical practices. Again, to put things
more simply, studying imperial rhetoric is fundamental to thinking about—or
thinking through—empire as a category of analysis.[40]

As historian Paul Kramer has suggested, we may learn more by examining
imperial phenomena—in our case imperial rhetoric—as a 'way of seeing', and,
more especially, as a means to compare, not the British and French empires in their
entirety but, rather, particular dimensions of these complex, polyvalent systems.[41]
Rhetoric offers fruitful sources for comparison, in part because its producers were
expressing how they saw the world, in part because their ways of seeing were

---

[38] Robert A. Nye, 'Western Masculinities in War and Peace', *American Historical Review*, 112:2 (April 2007), 417–24, 435–7.

[39] Graham Dawson, *Soldier Heroes: British Adventure, Empire and the Imagining of Masculinities* (London: Routledge, 1994), 11–26; Glenda Sluga, 'Masculinities, Nations, and the New World Order: Peacemaking and Nationality in Britain, France, and the United States after the First World War', in Stefan Dudink, Karen Hagemann, and John Tosh (eds), *Masculinities in Politics and War: Gendering Modern History* (Manchester: Manchester University Press, 2004), 240; also cited in Nye, 'Western Masculinities', 421.

[40] These comments reflect on Wilder, 'From Optic to Topic', 737–8.

[41] Paul A. Kramer, 'Imperial Histories of the United States in the World', *American Historical Review*, 116:5 (December 2011), 1351–2.

substantially affected by rivalry and competition with other imperial powers. As Kramer notes:

> Throughout history, empire-builders have been acutely preoccupied with other empire-builders: networks of modern empire bound rivals together in competitive and cooperative exchange, emulation, and adaptation. These exchanges could occur only where actors perceived a degree of commonality, but they should also be seen as highly charged sites in which ideological accounts of national-imperial difference were born. Indeed, it was often at precisely the places where imperial situations converged and overlapped that actors felt compelled to shore up exceptionalist comparisons that emphasized decreasingly perceptible differences between themselves and others.[42]

The imperial rhetoric we study in this book evinces the rhetoricians' enduring effort to prove what was supposedly exceptional, superior, and particular to British or French imperial governance and the colonial practices that sustained it. For all that, the case studies we examine tend to indicate the exact opposite. What the rhetoricians either cited as evidence of their unique virtues or derided as proof of the vices in other imperial rulers actually underlined the basic similarities between them. The proclivity to assert qualities of imperial difference only intensified as empires encountered equivalent problems. The inverse equation between the assertion of difference and the mounting evidence of similarity was also apparent in the realm of cultural production.[43] The proliferation of domestic commemorations of empire in both Britain and France, plus their domestic publics' shared fascination with colonial exotica and other cultural artefacts of recent conquests, only drove their rhetoricians to more strenuous efforts to identify the imperial differences between them.[44] This was always unconvincing. Supporters of imperial expansion in both countries fell back on the same rubrics of Western rationalism and capitalist modernization, as they did on comparable taxonomies of racial difference and presumptive 'rights to rule'. Equally, the imperial rhetoric of French and British political leaders evinced similar anxieties that colonial violence might escalate, that disorder might expose administrative weakness, and that racial boundaries would be transgressed, causing empires' essential hierarchies of difference to unravel.[45]

---

[42] Kramer, 'Imperial Histories', 1352.

[43] We are not suggesting here that cultural constructions of a British world or a Greater France were reducible to the same imperialist impulse, only that the insistent protestations of difference were belied by remarkably similar cultural practices of commemoration, consumption, and display. For illuminating analyses of such cultural construction, which, nonetheless, make British and French colonial cultures discrete analytical fields, see: Barry Crosbie and Mark Hampton (eds), *The Cultural Construction of the British World* (Manchester: Manchester University Press, 2015); John McAleer and John M. MacKenzie (eds), *Exhibiting the Empire: Cultures of Display and the British Empire* (Manchester: Manchester University Press, 2015); Pascal Blanchard and Sandrine Lemaire (eds), *Culture coloniale: La France conquise par son Empire, 1871–1931* (Paris: Autrement, 2003); Pascal Blanchard and Sandrine Lemaire (eds), *Culture impériale: Les colonies au coeur de la République, 1931–1961* (Paris: Autrement, 2004).

[44] The paradox behind imperialists' insistence on the unique qualities of their own empire is nicely handled in Matthew G. Stanard, 'Interwar Pro-Empire Propaganda and European Colonial Culture: Toward a Comparative Research Agenda', *Journal of Contemporary History*, 44:1 (2009), 29–46.

[45] Ann Laura Stoler, 'Epistemic Politics: Ontologies of Colonial Common Sense', *Philosophical Forum*, 39:3 (2008), 341–69.

Perhaps most importantly, in the context of the non-European societies of Western Asia and North and East Africa that our case studies address, French and British imperial rhetoric, in the epistemological formulation of Ian Hacking and Ann Stoler, 'made up' the colonial peoples over whom it claimed dominion.[46] From the allegedly violent fanaticism of Ahmed 'Urabi's supporters in 1880s Egypt to the supposedly fascistic tendencies of Nasserism eighty years later, such rhetoric thus ascribed distinct, usually threatening qualities and derogatory labels to colonial figures the better to justify imperial intervention against them. This ascription of the dangerous then became a means to rationalize the need for closer colonial regulation, tighter surveillance, and the consequent denial of rights to subject populations.

From the early twentieth century, imperial rhetoric also responded to the spread of what Bernard Bate, in the context of British India, terms 'vernacular political oratory'. This was a call to mass political engagement that eschewed the elitism of proto-nationalist movements in favour of a more populist anti-colonialism.[47] This new-style anti-colonial rhetoric achieved greater prominence throughout much of the colonial world in the immediate aftermath of World War I. It signified less of a radical ideological departure than the adoption of new strategies of opposition to foreign rule, which exploited the singular advantage enjoyed by colonial populations: their strength in numbers. The power of numbers could be mobilized politically to support claims to self-determination and majority rule. And it could be mobilized more viscerally by conjuring the image of an overwhelming, irresistible human tide demanding rights withheld.

The destructiveness of World War I, meanwhile, undermined longstanding European claims of civilizational primacy while, paradoxically, the war's insatiable demands for manpower, resources, and capital built stronger transnational networks of connection between imperial subjects of multiple empires who were called upon to satisfy these demands.[48] The supposition that 'Western civilization' was at best fictive, and at worse oxymoronic, gained greater traction once it became clear that the colonial populations called upon to make sacrifices for their imperial rulers were unlikely to receive much political reward for their contributions. In the realm of political rhetoric, one consequence was the greater prominence achieved by alternative non-Western formulations of cultural attachment, signified in ideas of Asianism, pan-Arabism, and pan-Africanism.[49]

---

[46] Ian Hacking, 'Making Up People', in *Historical Ontology* (Cambridge, MA: Harvard University Press, 2002), 99–114; cited in Stoler, 'Epistemic Politics', 350–3, at 353.

[47] Bernard Bate, ' "To Persuade Them into Speech and Action": Oratory and the Tamil Political, Madras, 1905–1919', *Comparative Studies in Society & History*, 55:1 (2013), 145–60.

[48] David Stevenson, *Armaments and the Coming War: Europe, 1904–1914* (Oxford: Oxford University Press, 1996, reprint 2004), 409; Prasenjit Duara, 'The Discourse of Civilization and Pan-Asianism', *Journal of World History*, 12 (2001), 99–130, also cited in Carolien Stolte and Harald Fischer-Tiné, 'Imagining Asia in India: Nationalism and Internationalism (ca. 1905–1940)', *Comparative Studies in Society & History*, 54:1 (2012), 65–92, at 66–7.

[49] Stolte and Fischer-Tiné, 'Imagining Asia in India', 68–76, 88–91; Israel Gershoni and James P. Jankowski, *Redefining the Egyptian Nation, 1930–1945* (Cambridge: Cambridge University Press, 1995), part I; Amzat Boukari-Yabara, *Africa Unite! Une Histoire du panafricanisme* (Paris: La Découverte, 2014), 55–66, 98–106.

The collapse of the Russian, Austro-Hungarian, and, above all, Ottoman empires amid the fallout from World War I thus compelled imperial rhetoricians in Britain and France to wrestle with the contradiction between their reflexive inclination to equate empire with geopolitical strength and cultural vitality and the mounting evidence that their empires might not withstand stronger local pressure for national self-rule.[50] Nor was this a transient dilemma. The configuration of ethnic minority rights and claims to national self-determination as elements of the Paris Peace Settlement lent a different vocabulary to anti-colonial demands and stirred transnational demands that racial discrimination and political exclusion be addressed within the crafting of a new international system in the wake of World War I.[51] Much as these demands were substantially frustrated in the 1920s, the arguments deployed, particularly through the institutions of the League of Nations and its Permanent Mandates Commission, compelled political leaders in Britain, France, and their mandate territories to come up with more convincing justifications for empire.[52]

Successive interwar French governments responded with a rhetoric that stressed the bargains made and promises to be kept. Colonial populations were expected to submit to the so-called *pact colonial*, a French-imposed bargain that promised economic modernization in exchange for the harsh labour conditions needed to turn agricultural societies into export-oriented economies. This, it was argued, was both a commercial necessity and an educative process that inculcated the discipline of waged work. This belief in the trickle-down benefits of French economic, political, and cultural stewardship, whatever the short-term cruelties of workplace coercion, was by no means confined to diehard imperialists. The liberal conscience of Third Republic republicanism, the *Ligue des droits de l'homme* (League of the Rights of Man), remained firmly pro-empire, despite occasional pangs of collective guilt when chronic colonial abuses were brought to public attention.[53] When, in 1930, the League executive canvassed its local sections about the wisdom of extending citizenship rights to colonial ex-servicemen, numerous replies disparaged the idea in stridently racist language. One section, based in the Seine region, dismissed political concessions to Arab subjects, warning that North Africans were like tiger cubs raised in captivity: manageable at first, but likely to kill their master once they reached maturity.[54]

---

[50] Dominic Lieven, *Empire: The Russian Empire and Its Rivals* (New Haven, CT: Yale University Press, 2001), xiii, also cited in Alan Mikhail and Christine M. Philliou, 'The Ottoman Empire and the Imperial Turn', *Comparative Studies in Society & History*, 54:4 (2012), 737–8.

[51] Erez Manela, *The Wilsonian Moment: Self-Determination and the International Origins of Anticolonial Nationalism* (Oxford: Oxford University Press, 2009); Robert Gerwarth and Erez Manela, 'The Great War as a Global War: Imperial Conflict and the Reconfiguration of World Order, 1911–1923', *Diplomatic History*, 38:4 (2014), 786–800; Weitz, 'From the Vienna to the Paris System', 1313–21.

[52] Susan Pedersen, *The Guardians: The League of Nations and the Crisis of Empire* (Oxford: Oxford University Press, 2015).

[53] As J. P. Daughton notes, the interwar growth of investigatory journalism and documentary-style reportage generated stronger criticism of colonial abuses, if not of colonialism itself: J. P. Daughton, 'Behind the Imperial Curtain', 510–17.

[54] William D. Irvine, *Between Justice and Politics: The Ligue des Droits de l'Homme, 1898–1945* (Stanford, CA: Stanford University Press, 2007), 144–5. As Irvine comments, colonial affairs took second place behind more pressing European concerns in the League's discussions of rights questions.

The proclivity to excuse forced labour, discriminatory legal regimes, and rights restrictions as necessary, if temporary, administrative tools was underpinned by an imperialist rhetoric that claimed to be saving misguided colonial subjects from themselves. According to this worldview, tough working conditions, arbitrary punishments, even military violence and collective punishments did not transgress ethical standards, nor were they the antithesis of freedom.[55] They were the essential precursor to an orderly society in which rights and responsibilities would ultimately be codified to the benefit of all. The tendency among imperialist politicians, journalists, and civil society actors in Britain and France to invoke local examples of massacre, population displacement, and other abuses of minority populations as justification for humanitarian, yet still imperial, intervention was nowhere stronger than in the former Ottoman territories bounding the Eastern Mediterranean.[56] Many of the countries and regions involved—Egypt, Turkey, and the Syrian mandate for instance—fell outside British or French formal colonial control, if not beyond their imperial influence. Seen from the vantage point of imperial rhetoric, this formal empire/informal influence distinction was crucial. Crises and controversy were arguably much more likely to break out with respect to areas that fell outside full-blooded colonial control, where the limits to expansion were more clearly set. The lands of North Africa and the Middle East, by contrast, offer both moments of intense crisis and longer periods of simmering imperial rivalry. These make for especially useful comparisons over time.

The imperial rhetoric we encounter in our earlier case studies mirrored strains of the humanitarian thinking current in the late nineteenth century. Episodic interventions were typically justified in a language of moral uplift and a quest for orderliness, each of them burdens incumbent on the forward-thinking imperialist.[57] With the shock of World War I and the redesign of the international system that followed it, imperialist rhetoric lost much of its earlier missionary inflection, if not its zeal for intervention. Such interventionism was, though, more likely to be defended in materialist, almost technocratic terms—as imposing peace, as assuring good

---

[55] The arguments produced in defence of a particularly egregious use of such repressive means— air power—are analysed by Priya Satia, 'The Defense of Inhumanity: Air Control and the British Idea of Arabia', *American Historical Review*, 111:1 (February 2006), 16–51; see also Daughton, 'Behind the Imperial Curtain', 527–8.

[56] There is a wealth of outstanding recent work in this field, among it: David Watenpaugh, *Bread from Stones: The Middle East and the Making of Modern Humanitarianism* (Berkeley, CA: University of California Press, 2015); David Watenpaugh, 'The League of Nations' Rescue of Armenian Genocide Survivors and the Making of Modern Humanitarianism, 1920–1927', *American Historical Review*, 115:5 (December 2010), 1315–39; Davide Rodogno, *Against Massacre: Humanitarian Interventions in the Ottoman Empire, 1815–1914* (Princeton, NJ: Princeton University Press, 2015); Davide Rodogno, 'The American Red Cross and the International Committee of the Red Cross' Humanitarian Politics and Policies in Asia Minor and Greece (1922–1923)', *First World War Studies*, 5:1 (2014), 82–99; Michelle Tusan, *Smyrna's Ashes: Humanitarianism, Genocide, and the Birth of the Middle East* (Berkeley, CA: University of California Press, 2012); Tusan, '"Crimes against Humanity"'; Weitz, 'From the Vienna to the Paris System'.

[57] Watenpaugh, 'The League of Nations' Rescue of Armenian Genocide Survivors', 1319.

government, or as improving social provision.[58] Claims for empire expansion were subject to closer political scrutiny and more sceptical domestic inquiry. They were increasingly constrained by strategic overstretch and attendant cost pressures, something that emerges strongly in our discussion of the Chanak crisis, the most significant Franco-British imperial clash of the interwar years. And they confronted louder anti-colonial voices at metropolitan, colonial, and transnational levels.

There were competing pressures at the level of international regulation as well. In Western Asia especially, the post-World War I settlements reordered dependent territory to British and French advantage amid the devastating population displacements, widespread hunger, genocidal violence, and ethnic cleansing that accompanied the disintegration of the Ottoman Empire. On the one hand, British and French claims-making about their new Middle East mandated territories rested on the dubious *a priori* assumption that they knew how to administer the region more effectively—whatever that might mean. On the other hand, that administration fell within the ambit of a new variant of imperial governance. Keith Watenpaugh captures this combination of opportunities and constraints perfectly:

> The fact of foreign occupation meant that certain kinds and categories of Western-originated humanitarian projects might now be feasible, certainly more so than in the antebellum Eastern Mediterranean, because of the parallel reduction in Ottoman sovereignty. The establishment of the interwar mandate system in the Arab provinces of the empire extended and institutionalized that subordinate status, opening more possibilities for humanitarian action emanating from the West. Ironically, the most internationalist dimension of the League's larger efforts took place only in the shadow of interwar colonialism; the liberalizing and tutelary agenda of the mandate system created an unprecedented opportunity for the implementation of League initiatives less restrained by questions of national sovereignty because sovereignty itself was held in trust, as it were, by a colonial power and member state.[59]

The League of Nations mandate system as it emerged between 1919 and 1923 was assuredly imperial in its presumption that better-qualified rulers of empires should offer their benevolent guiding hand to peoples previously maladministered by the 'bad' colonial powers, defeated Imperial Germany and Ottoman Turkey. The descriptive labels chosen were hugely significant. Governments in London and Paris led the retreat from the Wilsonian language of self-determination, preferring the fuzzier timetables and wider margins for manoeuvre intrinsic to trusteeship. But President Wilson's self-determination genie was not easily forced back into its bottle. Its implied support for ethnically homogeneous, self-governing polities was widely translated into a political vernacular of national independence.[60] Its legacy lived on in stronger anti-colonial claims articulated in a language of sovereign

---

[58] This is what Keith Watenpaugh describes, in the context of Western humanitarian interventionism in the post-First World War Middle East, as 'organized compassion'. See his *Bread from Stones*, 8.

[59] Watenpaugh, 'The League of Nations' Rescue of Armenian Genocide Survivors', 1320.

[60] Brad Simpson, 'The United States and the Curious History of Self-Determination', *Diplomatic History*, 36:4 (2012), 676–9.

rights, and often by means of travelling delegations and erudite petitions: in short, with all the trappings of diplomatic legalism and Western respectability.[61]

The rhetorical constructions underlying these wars of words had lasting ramifications for the colonial worlds of the Global South. Arguments about the responsibilities of imperial authorities and the presumptive rights of their subject peoples rendered not only mandates, but colonial authority more generally contingent. It did so primarily by connecting the quality and duration of imperial rule to measurable outcomes in living standards, health, education, and political inclusion. To be sure, British governments were, for instance, still capable of pursuing their imperial objectives ruthlessly. But they felt bound to dress the prosecution of illiberal colonial actions, the repression of internal opposition especially, in a language of liberality and good intent.[62] The proliferation of new international regulatory agencies with direct, and often hostile interest in colonial affairs also lent a defensive, self-justificatory tone to imperialist rhetoric as its evolved through the interwar years. By the time another global conflagration engulfed the British and French empires, imperialist vocabulary was expanding once more to embrace concepts of development, social welfare, and even universal rights and respect for international law.[63]

A final definitional problem arises here. What, if anything, distinguished 'imperial' rhetoric from international affairs rhetoric in general? This is a particularly tricky issue given that, as we have noted, after 1945 most politicians in Britain and France were at pains to deploy a more universalist language and to play down the idea that they were acting out of narrow national self-interest. Certainly, the introduction of the concept of 'covert' imperial rhetoric is not without its problems. However, to restrict our focus to cases where rhetoricians spoke about empire *explicitly* would be to miss much of what was actually going on. Given that the rhetorical downplaying of national self-interest took root in many quarters well before World War II, it is clear that overtly 'imperial' rhetoric can by no means always be neatly delineated from other, ostensibly more universalist, ways of talking about international relations. The broader point is that people did not just argue about empire; they also argued about the correct ways of arguing about empire; and therefore what 'counted' as imperial rhetoric was itself a matter of contemporary dispute. British and French views of empire, then, cannot be separated from the rhetorical structures through which they were articulated.

[61] Natasha Wheatley, 'Mandatory Interpretation: Legal Hermeneutics and the New International Order in Arab and Jewish Petitions to the League of Nations', *Past & Present*, 27 (May 2015), 206–35; Andrew Arsan, '"This is the Age of Associations": Committees, Petitions, and the Roots of Interwar Middle Eastern Internationalism', *Journal of Global History*, 7 (2012), 166–88; Susan Pedersen, 'The Impact of League Oversight on British Policy in Palestine', in Rory Miller (ed.), *Britain, Palestine, and Empire: The Mandate Years* (Farnham: Ashgate, 2010), 39–64.
[62] In the context of British humanitarian intervention in Smyrna during the Turkish-Greek War of the early 1920s, Keith Watenpaugh invokes political theorist Jeanne Morefield's description of such action as the 'politics of deflection', see: Watenpaugh, *Bread from Stones*, 22.
[63] Suke Wolton, *Lord Hailey, the Colonial Office and the Politics of Race and Empire in the Second World War: The Loss of White Prestige* (Basingstoke: Palgrave-Macmillan, 2000), 119–48 *passim*; Frederick Cooper, *Citizenship between Empire and Nation: Remaking France and French Africa, 1945–1960* (Ithaca, NY: Cornell University Press, 2014), 4–21.

1
Tunisia, 1881–Egypt, 1882

The early 1880s saw French and British imperial rivalries in Northern Africa transformed. In the space of six months what began as border skirmishing between colonial troops and Khmir clansmen along a disputed land frontier culminated in the occupation of Tunis by a French expeditionary force dispatched eastwards from Algeria.[1] The subjugation of Tunisia's beylical (princely) administration to French imperial will in 1881 was soon followed by a similarly expansive enterprise in Egypt. This time British forces played the lead role; their French adjuncts becoming hostile to the hegemonic designs of their *partenaires anglais*. Two invasions, two colonial prizes seized in the face of unanswered local cries of sovereign rights that were trampled. What historians of empire have long treated as classic exercises in frontier imperialism, evidence of overseas adventurism, and affirmation of increasing strategic competition between Europe's two pre-eminent imperial expansionists were also characterized by violence and rivalry of another sort. For the Tunisian occupation of 1881 and its near-cousin, the Egyptian crisis of 1882, confirmed the emergence of a rhetorical battle of wills between contrasting French and British visions of 'new imperialism'. One was republican and universalist. The other was attuned to the strategic imperatives of free trade. Each claimed to be responsible, liberal, even enlightened in intent. Yet the protagonists on both sides of the Channel decried one another's motives, the better to justify their own.

That this struggle was a war of words, not swords, should not conceal either its immediate significance for French, British, and global politics or its longer-term legacies for Franco-British colonial competition and the African and Asian populations yoked to imperial rule. Indeed, as this chapter aims to show, exploiting the power of imperialist rhetoric became integral to the conflicting strategies pursued by the two imperial powers before home and foreign audiences alike.

French parliamentary and public debate about the annexation of Tunisia revealed a new political elite whose colonial assertiveness masked their uncertain grip on the levers of domestic power in the infant Third Republic.[2] Indeed, the occupation of Tunis was, to a substantial degree, presented not only to French constituents, but to their political representatives as an odd mixture of *force majeure* and *fait accompli*, a combination of Tunisian provocation and initiatives taken by

---

[1] Ali Mahjoubi and Hechmi Karoui, *Quand le soleil s'est levé à l'ouest: Tunisie 1881—impérialisme et résistance* (Tunis: Cérès, 1983).

[2] S. A. Ashley, 'The Failure of Gambetta's *Grand Ministère*', *French Historical Studies*, 9:1 (1975), 108–9.

army commanders subsequently endorsed by a select group of ministry insiders. Sensitive to accusations of stringing the National Assembly along, supporters of annexation used striking rhetorical violence—of anarchic tribal killings and national honour affronted—to stir the press and public into backing imperial adventurism.[3] For British political leaders, more certain of calmer political waters at home, the invasion of Egypt in 1882 was still a crucial moment, not just for the British Empire but for the intra-European imperial rivalries that marked the final part of the nineteenth century. This was the case even though the occupation was supposed to be temporary, and in spite of the fact that Egypt was never formally colonized. In Ronald Robinson and John Gallagher's classic account, the unintended consequence of the affair was the 'Scramble for Africa'.[4] A. G. Hopkins has claimed, by contrast, that 'Egypt played little part' in the calculations that led to expansion elsewhere on the continent.[5]

The domestic contexts in which the contrasting—and competing—rhetoric of the leading political actors in France and Britain took shape between 1881 and 1883 were thus markedly different. For all that, beneath these divergences— whether narrowly constitutional and party political or more broadly social and cultural—there lurked similar motivations. If the impulses behind both invasions remain highly controversial, they were also oddly equivalent. Did France annex Tunisia to impose order along a porous and unruly land frontier with its most precious colony, Algeria? In like fashion, did Britain intervene reluctantly in Egypt to suppress local disorder, an operation essential to defend the Suez Canal and the route to India (the Robinson and Gallagher thesis), or were Britain's substantial economic interests combined with political populism the driving factor?[6] Was the imposition of France's Tunisia protectorate impelled by a public clamour deliberately fomented by the advocates of expansion? Or were French and British actions based on calculations of global prestige: recovering it in the French case; maintaining it in the British?[7] What part was played by local European residents in the disputed territories? Was the small but vocal population of French speakers in Tunis, outnumbered by a faster-growing Italian settler colony, really under imminent threat? And what about the cosmopolitan community of Europeans in Cairo, and more especially Alexandria, in which Britons were matched in number and cultural influence by their French counterparts?[8] Did the imperialist

[3] TNA, FO 27/2492, letter 374, Lord Lyons, Paris, to Earl Granville, 22 April 1881.

[4] Ronald Robinson and John Gallagher, *Africa and the Victorians: The Official Mind of Imperialism* (London: Macmillan, 1961).

[5] A. G. Hopkins, 'The Victorians and Africa: A Reconsideration of the Occupation of Egypt, 1882', *Journal of African History*, 27:2 (1986), 363–91, at 390.

[6] P. J. Cain and A. G. Hopkins, *British Imperialism: Innovation and Expansion 1688–1914* (Harlow: Longman, 1993), 362–9.

[7] Dan Halvorson, 'Prestige, Prudence and Public Opinion in the 1882 British Occupation of Egypt', *Australian Journal of Politics and History*, 56:3 (2010), 423–40.

[8] Mark I. Choate, 'Identity Politics and Political Perception in the European Settlement of Tunisia: The French Colony versus the Italian Colony', *French Colonial History*, 8, (2007), 97–101; Ziad Fahmy, 'Francophone Egyptian Nationalists, Anti-British Discourse, and European Public Opinion, 1885–1910: The Case of Mustafa Kamil and Ya'qub Sannu', *Comparative Studies of South Asia, Africa and the Middle East*, 28:1 (2008), 170.

soldier-administrators of France's African Army drag Paris politicians in their wake, and if so what enabled them to do so? Were the politicians in London lulled into doing much the same by the 'men on the spot' in Cairo, or was Gladstone's government so divided and incompetent that it becomes futile to search out the 'motive' behind what was in fact an irrational act?[9]

We do not attempt to mediate all of these competing claims here. Rather, we seek to show how the arguments about Tunisia and Egypt presented to the French and British publics reflected conflicts within and between political parties and governing blocs as well as between the imperial nations themselves. French supporters of Tunisian annexation denied any expansionist motives, claiming the action was justified by Algeria's security needs.[10] The degree to which the Egyptian question was presented as an 'imperial' one in Britain was influenced by the past history of the 'Eastern Question' as a controversial issue in popular politics. In France, the British rhetoric surrounding the invasion of Egypt fuelled resentments that would at last find their outlet during the Fashoda crisis of 1898, when the British and French came to the brink of war.

FRANCE AND TUNISIA

In a deservedly influential line of interpretation developed in the 1970s, Christopher Andrew and A. S. Kanya-Forstner explained French colonial expansionism in the early decades of the Third Republic as the result of a paradox. France's late nineteenth-century empire-making, beginning in the Sene-Gambian interior in the 1850s, and accelerating after defeat in the Franco-Prussian war of 1870–1, was neither the product of government design nor the outcome of popular imperialism. It was, instead, contingent on the opportunities presented by their absence.[11] Indeed, Andrew went further. He identified the volatility of Third Republic politics as conducive to a kind of decision-making vacuum. Reflecting on the stop-go French colonialism of the early 1880s, he notes, 'Intervention in Tunisia was swiftly followed by refusal to intervene in Egypt; a forward policy in Indo-China was first accepted, then violently rejected; in West Africa Army officers carved out a private empire on their own initiative'.[12] His core conclusion was deceptively simple: in politics, as in nature, vacuums are abhorred. Enthusiasts for empire filled the void left by government indecision, party ambivalence, and wider public apathy.

[9] Alexander Schölch, 'The "Men on the Spot" and the English Occupation of Egypt in 1882', *Historical Journal*, 19:3 (1976), 773–85; John S. Galbraith and Afaf Lutfi al-Sayyid-Marsot, 'The British Occupation of Egypt: Another View', *International Journal of Middle East Studies* (1978), 471–88.

[10] TNA, FO27/2485, FO tel. 440, 7 May 1881.

[11] C. M. Andrew and A. S. Kanya-Forstner, 'The French "Colonial Party": Its Composition, Aims and Influence, 1885–1914', *Historical Journal*, 14:1 (1971), 99–128.

[12] C. M. Andrew, 'The French Colonialist Movement during the Third Republic: The Unofficial Mind of Imperialism', *Transactions of the Royal Historical Society*, Fifth Series, 26 (1976), 143.

So it was that the lack of central government direction in colonial affairs left the way open for an 'unofficial mind' of French imperialism to take shape. More committed supporters of empire in business, academia, the church, the military, and the diplomatic corps aligned with like-minded politicians of firm imperialist credentials. Together, they comprised the French colonialist movement, or *Parti Colonial* (not actually a political party at all). Remarkably successful in the ensuing years before and immediately after World War I, this cluster of elite interest groups arrogated empire-building to themselves.[13] More recently, T. W. Roberts has brought a new twist to this 'unofficial mind'. Focusing on the late nineteenth-century connections between French railway companies and senior politicians, he has suggested that 'empire building was a by-product of the division of economic and political spoils within France rather than an attempt to exploit the resources of tropical Africa'. Cooperation, even collusion, between businesses, financiers, and political leaders over new investment opportunities usually went furthest in consolidating captive markets at home and overseas.[14] Tunisia, in this scheme of things, was viewed as a lucrative adjunct to Algeria's developing railway network, a relatively simple extension of pre-existing plans for railroad construction in the Maghreb.[15]

Historians of the early Third Republic have subsumed arguments about who supported what imperial venture and why within broader debates about the fundamental political and cultural directions that France took after the multiple shocks of 1868–71. Most agree that the violent eclipse of Napoleon III's regime changed France profoundly. Crushing national defeat by Prussia was matched by the ruthless repression of the Paris Commune.[16] But the impact of these traumas on French colonialism is less obvious. The presumption has been that change at home reverberated overseas; hence the tendency to read the emergence of a new French imperialism as the by-product of bitter domestic arguments over how France should be rebuilt in the wake of its cataclysmic experience of war and revolution.[17] Would bourgeois democracy finally triumph after its false start in 1848? Would disciplined political parties at last supplant the older divisions between republicans, monarchists, and Bonapartists? If so, could the Catholic Church and the army be reconciled to a parliamentary system with a republican

---

[13] Andrew, 'The French Colonialist Movement', 143–4.

[14] T. W. Roberts, 'Republicanism, Railway Imperialism, and the French Empire in Africa, 1879–1889', *Historical Journal*, 54:2 (2011), 401.

[15] MAE, 77PAAP2/Dossier C. Charles de Freycinet papers, Tunisie 1880–6, General Mustapha ben Ismail, prime minister, Tunis, to French premier de Freycinet, 22 July 1880, text of railway concession agreement detailing planned French railway construction radiating from Tunis.

[16] Bertrand Taithe, *Citizenship and Wars: France in Turmoil, 1870–1871* (London: Routledge, 2001), chapters 1–3, 9; Karine Varley, *Under the Shadow of Defeat: The War of 1870–71 in French Memory* (Basingstoke: Palgrave-Macmillan, 2008), 25–55, 97–103; John Merriman, *Massacre: The Life and Death of the Paris Commune of 1871* (New Haven, CT: Yale University Press, 2014), 18–38, 241–52.

[17] J. P. T. Bury, *Gambetta and the Making of the Third Republic* (Harlow: Longman, 1973), 171–2; James J. Cooke, *French New Imperialism, 1880–1910: The Third Republic and Colonial Expansion* (Hamden, CT: Archon, 1973), 13–22.

majority?[18] Would France adjust to living with defeat and protracted recession? In short, could France achieve basic constitutional revision, essential economic modernization, and overdue social reforms without turning on itself in the process?[19] The rhetoric deployed during the takeover of Tunisia offers answers.

French designs on Tunisia crystallized in early 1881 thanks in large part to four external—and essentially negative—stimuli. First was the mounting concern among politicians, officials, and missionary leaders about the rapid growth of Italian settlement and commensurate commercial influence in and around Tunis. Linked to this was a second fear, namely that France might lose the advantage of European acquiescence in a French takeover, which was effectively promised at the Congress of Berlin in 1878.[20] Continued delay was expected to mean that not only Italian, but also German and, more especially, Ottoman Turkish objections to French incursion would become harder to ignore. Indeed, as it transpired, both the Italian and German governments turned their frustrations with French incursion into Tunisia into firmer opposition to any further French or British expansionism elsewhere.[21] This raised the third consideration: that the Ottoman sultanate—encouraged by Bismarck—might press its claim to indirect authority over Tunis both to pre-empt French intervention and to drive a wedge between France and Britain over the much greater prize of Egypt.[22] Perhaps unsurprisingly, the French authorities were at pains to avoid justifying action in Tunisia in terms of these three rather self-serving grounds. Instead they focused on a fourth: the abiding problem of disorder along the land frontier between western Tunisia and eastern Algeria.

Contrary to expectations, devising convincing rhetorical arguments for intervention on the grounds of an allegedly 'fanatical' Muslim tribal uprising on the margins of colonial Algeria proved difficult. To be sure, the killing of five soldiers in the disputed Algerian-Tunisia borderland provided the immediate pretext for the formation of a French punishment column. But, as pointed out by the recently founded, and strongly radical newspaper *La Justice*, the mouthpiece of its fiery young editor, Georges Clemenceau, waging war against even some of the Tunisian Bey's subjects surely demanded at least parliamentary discussion, if not a formal vote of approval?[23] Furthermore, the violence of the alleged perpetrators—the Khmir tribal confederation—was motivated more by issues relating to landholding, customary trading rights, and pecuniary gain than by any jihadist

---

[18] Alfred Perkins, 'From Uncertainty to Opposition: French Catholic Liberals and Imperial Expansion, 1880–1885', *Catholic Historical Review*, 82:2 (1996), 204–6.

[19] An outstanding account of these processes in action is Herman Lebovics, *The Alliance of Iron and Wheat in the Third French Republic, 1860–1914: Origins of the New Conservatism* (Baton Rouge, LA: Louisiana State University Press, 1988).

[20] Mary Dewhurst Lewis, 'Geographies of Power: The Tunisian Civic Order, Jurisdictional Politics, and Imperial Rivalry in the Mediterranean, 1881–1935', *Journal of Modern History*, 80:4 (2008), 793–5, 800–1.

[21] MAE, 77PAAP1/DB, Charles de Freycinet papers, Egypte 1882–6, Translation of Declaration by Italian Foreign Minister in Rome Parliament on 12 June 1882, 'La politique italienne en Egypte'.

[22] MAE, 77PAAP1/DB, Charles de Freycinet papers, Egypte 1882–6, 'Note sur la politique allemande en Egypte depuis 1882 jusqu'au début du 3e Ministère de M. de Freycinet, n.d. 1886'.

[23] 'Les retards', by Camille Pelletan, *La Justice*, 26 April 1881, p. 1.

impulse.[24] Moreover, the alleged threat posed by the Khmir soon receded from view once the protectorate was in place.[25] Indeed, Tunisia's beylical administration, in conformity with its numerous international treaty obligations, was remarkably tolerant in its attitude to other faith communities living under its jurisdiction. Tunis in 1881 was neither in cultural nor political meltdown in a manner comparable to Alexandria or Cairo a year later.[26] There was no threat to existing commercial interests, no dispossession of colonists, no massacres of Christians to compare with events in Ottoman Syria or, more recently, Bulgaria. Even if there had been, there were powerful arguments to suggest that other European powers might immerse themselves in Tunisia's affairs at least as much as France. The system of 'capitulations' or referential extra-territorial treaty rights that governed Tunisia's external trade and internal juridical regime had already levered open the door to powerful foreign interests. And, whether classical or contemporary, what traces of European colonization there were came with an Italian flavour.[27]

It was difficult in this connection to challenge Italy's claims to regional primacy when French colonists were so few and far between, and those that had settled in Tunis often forged business connections, social ties, and familial bonds with their Italian counterparts. Perhaps sensitive to his Genovese roots, Léon Gambetta in particular remained loath to antagonize Italy by bluntly enforcing the outright annexation of Tunisia. No longer a government member, his reservations went unheeded. In office since September 1880, Prime Minister Jules Ferry's senior ministers did not share them. Nor, it seems, did they foresee Italy's imminent signature of the Triple Alliance with Germany and Austria-Hungary. In this instance, the rhetoric of restoring affronted dignity in North Africa blinded Ferry's administration to the strategic imperatives of preventing Italy from slipping into the embrace of the Central Powers.[28] As for the danger of Ottoman expansionism, it became increasingly apparent in the early months of 1881 that the sultan's administration, while hostile to French claims on Tunisia, was reacting to events, not driving them. Little wonder that in February 1881 the Bey rejected the first formal offer of a French protectorate for Tunisia to 'save' it from domination by the Ottoman Porte.[29] In this context, the most obvious indicator of an impending crisis was the organization of a French expeditionary force in Algeria, combined with the concentration of naval forces offshore from the Tunisian ports of Tabarka, Sfax, Bizerta, and Tunis itself. Why, the Tunisian royal court and numerous international observers asked, was such crude gunboat diplomacy necessary to punish a tribal insurgency concentrated miles from the coast?

---

[24] TNA, FO 27/2492, no. 33, Paris Military Attaché letter to Lord Lyons, 26 April 1881.

[25] Mary Dewhurst Lewis, *Divided Rule: Sovereignty and Empire in French Tunisia, 1881–1938* (Stanford, CA: Stanford University Press, 2014), 15–16, 28.

[26] Michael J. Reimer, 'Colonial Bridgehead: Social and Spatial Change in Alexandria, 1850–1882', *International Journal of Middle East Studies*, 20:4 (1988), 546–9; TNA, FO 146/2425, Sir E. Malet (Cairo) to Earl Granville, 27 May 1882.

[27] Lewis, 'Geographies of Power', 802; Choate, 'Identity Politics', 97–109.

[28] Bury, *Gambetta and the Making of the Third Republic*, 285–9.

[29] TNA, FO 27/2492: letter 374, Lord Lyons to Earl Granville, Paris, 22 April 1881.

Clues were to be found in three issues that figured large in National Assembly discussion over the weeks and months preceding the final takeover in May. One was the question of further army reform, consolidating legislation originally put forward by Léon Gambetta in the early 1870s in regard to advancement within the officer corps, the scope of general staff responsibilities, and the recruitment and training of conscripts. Anxious to sustain moves to professionalize the army's senior cadres, to make promotions meritocratic, and to improve the usefulness of national service, Gambetta, in particular, was not about to pick another fight with senior soldiers over a colonial matter that might pitch republicans and military men back into conflict.[30] Secularist republicans were, by contrast, already fighting another political battle over state support for ecclesiastical spending with the Catholic Church, various congregational orders, and the anti-republican Catholic bloc led in the National Assembly by former premier, Albert, duc de Broglie. Yet even in this second arena of conflict there was political capital to be made by giving Catholic missionary orders room to expand their activities in North Africa to ease the pain of their marginalization at home.[31]

Central to this project was the close working relationship between Jules Ferry and Léon Gambetta on the one hand and Charles Lavigerie, Archbishop of Algiers and the foremost protagonist of Catholic missionary evangelism in French Africa on the other.[32] Soon to be crowned Cardinal thanks in part to his consolidation of a Catholic 'religious protectorate' in Tunis, Lavigerie's imperial partnership with France's leading republicans gave the lie to any notion that domestic anti-clericalism cut across colonial missionary endeavour. Only when the apparently cheap and easy Tunisian annexation turned sour with the first of several anti-French uprisings in late summer 1881 would Catholic disdain for republican adventurism find its voice.[33] Third and finally was the recurrent problem of budgetary spending on Algeria. On 5 April the Ministry of Interior pleaded with parliamentary deputies to underwrite further investment in state land purchases to encourage settlers to venture into the rural spaces of Algeria opened up by the army's probing southwards and eastwards.[34] Stories of tribal incursion into Algeria's frontier lands were especially unwelcome, creating an image of endemic insecurity in the liminal zones that the Paris government wanted to Europeanize. For all these reasons it was expedient for Ferry's ministers and their parliamentary supporters to force the issue of alleged Tunisian misbehaviour.

French contrivance became clearer still in late April when, after delays caused by adverse weather, landings were staged at the small Tunisian port of Tabarka.[35]

---

[30] Bury, *Gambetta and the Making of the Third Republic*, 356–68.

[31] *Journal Officiel de la République française*, débats parlementaires. Chambre des Députés, 5 and 7 April 1881, p. 763; Perkins, 'From Uncertainty to Opposition', 206–8.

[32] J. Dean O'Donnell, 'Cardinal Charles Lavigerie: The Politics of Getting a Red Hat', *Catholic Historical Review*, 63:2 (April 1977), 191–3.

[33] Perkins, 'From Uncertainty to Opposition', 209.

[34] MAE, Papiers Maurice Bompard, 417PAAP/5, correspondence regarding 50 million franc credit for Algerian colonization; *Journal Officiel*, débats parlementaires. Chambre des Députés, 5 and 7 April 1881, p. 787.

[35] TNA, FO 27/2492, no. 34, Paris Military Attaché letter to Lord Lyons, 29 April 1881.

Writing on behalf of Ferry's government in *Le Temps*, the Paris newspaper that
devoted closer attention to official pronouncements than most of its rival publications, Théodore Roustan, consul in Tunis and the noisiest protagonist of a
takeover, insisted that the Tabarka operation was 'defensive'. It was, he said,
inspired by the need to protect foreign nationals in an increasingly anarchic political
space.[36] The anarchy in question was allegedly proven by cannon-fire from the
town's fort aimed at the French gunboats lying offshore.[37] In fact, the occupation
was systematically planned, its aim being to establish the bridgehead necessary to
resupply French forces as they marched north and eastwards towards the capital.[38]
Roustan claimed that, far from being an instance of creeping frontier imperialism,
French actions were motivated, in part by anxiety about spiralling Tunisian
violence, and in part by humanitarian concern for Europeans living in the Regency.
This was far-fetched and caused predictable harrumphing among Foreign Office
onlookers in London. If the French were really so worried about 'Mahomedan
fanaticism' that naval bombardments and troop landings were needed, then surely
Britain, too, could justifiably send warships of its own to Tunis to safeguard its
nationals. Indeed, on 1 May the Admiralty sent an ironclad to Tunis for precisely
that reason.[39] Here, again, the rhetoric of 'protection' was employed, this time as
a warning to the French government to keep its unfolding military expedition
within acceptable limits; in other words, to respect British treaty rights within the
Tunis Regency.[40]

These naval deployments were significant in another respect. They confirmed
that the rhetorical arguments advanced by French ministers in Paris and by
Roustan in Tunis in defence of what most observers recognized was an impending
unilateral French occupation threatened to make international involvement more,
not less probable. They also account for French governmental eagerness to push
ahead with land-based operations rather than depending on sea-borne landings.
Despite French ministerial reservations about adverse foreign reaction, one more
amphibious assault took place on 2 May. This time the port of Bizerta was secured,
completing the encirclement of Tunis some forty-five miles away.[41] Meanwhile,
over the preceding week the land-based expeditionary force of over 20,000 troops,
cavalry, and supporting artillery converged in two separate columns on the Tunisian capital.[42] The offensive was not without incident. Desertions—even the killing
of French officers—were reported among some battalions of Algerian infantry after
they were ordered to cross into Tunisia. And the extent of the advancing forces'
exactions from local Arab smallholders triggered attacks on French authorities in

---

[36] Copy of Roustan letters to Bey of Tunis, 20 and 23 April 1881, reproduced in *Le Temps*, 24 April
1881.

[37] 'Bulletin du jour', 21 April 1881, printed in *Le Temps*, 22 April 1881; 'L'incident de Tabarca',
La Liberté, 22 April 1881.

[38] 'Nos forces en Algérie', *L'Armée française*, 22 April 1881.

[39] TNA, FO 27/2492, Lord Lyons to Earl Granville, 1 May 1881.

[40] TNA, FO 27/2492, letter 320, Lord Lyons to Earl Granville, 28 April 1881.

[41] TNA, FO 27/2492, letter 35, Paris Military Attaché to Lord Lyons, 3 May 1881.

[42] TNA, FO 27/2492, letter no. 31, Lord Lyons to Earl Granville, 22 April 1881.

Constantine, Algeria's easternmost province.[43] These problems notwithstanding, the use of a combined force of *Armée d'Afrique* (the colonial garrison in Algeria), specialist cavalry, and local paramilitary auxiliaries retained three obvious political advantages. It obviated the need for any large-scale troop movements from metropolitan France. This, in turn, made army mobilization unnecessary. Third, and most importantly, with neither mobilization nor a declaration of war planned, Ferry's government could authorize the operation without first securing National Assembly agreement.[44]

RHETORIC AND FRENCH INTERVENTION

The notional requirement for National Assembly approval is significant from a rhetorical point of view because official justifications for the action before Parliament, press, and public were thus made *after* the expedition was in train, not before. Indeed, by the start of May the more southerly column under General Logerot had advanced rapidly, occupying Kef and Béja as it moved northwards on Tunis.[45] It was almost a fortnight before Ferry appeared before the National Assembly to justify an invasion that was by then proceeding, in his words, 'with order, method and success' towards its conclusion.[46] Even then, the French premier stuck to the official script that the impending occupation was not annexationist but merely the means by which France would compel the Bey to govern responsibly, to take frontier protection seriously, and to make financial probity an urgent priority. 'We want neither his territory, nor his throne', the prime minister claimed, although almost in the same breath he conceded that the army's 'sacrifices' would be 'poorly rewarded' by anything less than Tunisian submission.[47] What makes such double-speak comprehensible to us was the French governmental interest in imposing a Tunisian settlement as quickly as possible before either domestic or international opposition could coalesce against it. And here the delay before a full parliamentary debate occurred proved critical. What the left-republican spokesman Antonin Proust later dubbed 'well-intentioned firmness' was substantially a question of timing.[48] Ferry's attempt to appear reasonable yet unyielding was made easier because by mid-May the outcome was already certain. Indeed, by the time he outlined the government's minimum requirements to the Senate on 13 May, the Treaty of Bardo was a done deal, the Bey having signed it the night before.[49]

In a sense, then, the more significant early rhetorical skirmishing took place within the parameters of intergovernmental diplomacy, where French Foreign Minister Jules Barthélemy St-Hilaire was compelled to offer excuses for a fast-expanding

---

[43] TNA, FO 27/2492, no. 33, Paris Military Attaché letter to Lord Lyons, 26 April 1881.

[44] TNA, FO 27/2492, 'Record of a Conversation Held with M. Gambetta on Saturday, 23 April 1881'.

[45] TNA, FO 27/2492, no. 34, Paris Military Attaché letter to Lord Lyons, 29 April 1881.

[46] *Journal Officiel*, débats parlementaires. Chambre des Députés, 13 May 1881, p. 882.

[47] Ibid.

[48] *Journal Officiel*, débats parlementaires. Chambre des Députés, 24 May 1881, p. 980.

[49] *Journal Officiel*, débats parlementaires. Chambre des Députés, government declaration of 14 May 1881, p. 887.

military intervention to an increasingly disbelieving British government. Defying the accumulating evidence to the contrary, he offered repeated assurances that no occupation was planned. A former professor of Greek philosophy at the Collège de France and a relative ingénue in foreign affairs, Barthélemy St-Hilaire was strongly influenced by his director of political affairs, Baron Alphonse Chodron de Courcel, an advisor who shared Roustan's predilection for decisive action in Tunis.[50]

In this instance, the keenest empire rhetoric emanated from an unelected official who worked the backrooms of the Quai d'Orsay to raise the imperial horizons of France's new republican political elite beyond the machinations of coalition politics. In August 1880, de Courcel, the moving force of the political affairs directorate—the Foreign Ministry's diplomatic engine-room—had brow-beaten Barthélemy St-Hilaire's predecessor, Charles de Freycinet, into approving a punitive army expedition combined with a demonstration of French naval power in the waters off Tunis.[51] The chance to crush Algerian dissidents in exile in Tunis, the need to deter Italy from comparable intervention, and above all the prospect of decisive influence over Tunisia's royal administration—these were opportunities de Courcel insisted be seized, regardless of any wavering by his political masters. Consul Roustan in Tunis and Admiral Bernard Jauréguiberry, responsible for colonial affairs as minister of marine, endorsed de Courcel's analysis. Together they formed a powerful triumvirate from the summer of 1880 onwards. Roustan supplied persuasive political intelligence as required. Sometimes this indicated that the vocal Italian settler community in Tunis wanted the Rome government to steal a march on France by intervening first. At other times, it suggested that the Bey would prefer to yield to French pressure. Meanwhile, Jauréguiberry, a distinguished veteran of the Crimean campaign and the Franco-Prussian war, warned his civilian ministerial colleagues against fatal indecision. Finally, de Courcel offered the grand imperial perspective of geopolitical interest, as well as the diplomatic and legal pretexts in which to clothe an otherwise naked colonial takeover.[52]

This returns us to the assault on Bizerta, something that Jauréguiberry strongly supported. Reports that over 3,000 troops had disembarked from three ironclads—a force in excess of the total number of French warships officially patrolling off Tunisia—occasioned the one and only British protest over French actions on 5 May 1881. Incredibly, the Quai d'Orsay position remained unaltered: even major landings on Tunisia's eastern seaboard were allegedly part of a limited punitive operation against the Khmir, a highland-dwelling community on Tunisia's western fringe.[53] At the same time, neither Barthélemy St-Hilaire nor his *éminence grise*, de Courcel, made much effort to conceal actual French intentions. The foreign minister speculated that private contractors might soon be invited to bid

[50] J. P. T. Bury, 'Gambetta and Overseas Problems', *English Historical Review*, 82:323 (1967), 285–9.

[51] MAE, 77PAAP2/Dossier C, Charles de Freycinet papers, Tunisie 1880–6, de Courcel letter to Charles de Freycinet, 18 August 1880.

[52] As examples, see: MAE, 77PAAP2/Dossier C, Charles de Freycinet papers, Tunisie 1880–6, tel. 18 de Courcel to Freycinet, 18 August 1880; tel. 89 Roustan, Tunis, to Direction politique, 20 August 1880.

[53] TNA, FO 27/2492, letter 432, Lord Lyons to Earl Granville, 5 May 1881.

for contracts to build a naval base at Bizerta, and looked forward to a future where French bankers would restore probity to Regency finances.[54]

What was initially depicted as a limited punitive action against the Khmir became something more: a pre-emptive dash to Tunis to preclude all conceivable external threats to the French presence in Algeria, whether from dissentient Tunisians or from any 'foreign power' directing their activities. In plainer language, the French government was now telling its British partner that the *de facto* annexation of Tunisia was primarily to create a buffer state to protect the colony of Algeria against any attempted Ottoman subversion. What were the implications of allowing such blatant expansionism to pass unremarked? Here was the nub of the developing argument between France and Britain over Tunisia. Alongside the matter of empire-building lay a juridical question crucial to both imperial rivals. Did the Ottoman Empire have any meaningful power of oversight over Tunisian affairs? For Britain's Liberal government and its diplomats anxious at this stage to avoid a rupture with Constantinople, the answer was yes. Meanwhile, rejecting Ottoman claims of suzerainty was pivotal to the entire French justification for installing a protectorate of its own. The resultant rhetorical strategy rested on three dubious foundations: first, that Ottoman claims were illegitimate; second, that there was a real danger of Turkish intervention; and, third, that France, by pre-empting it, was serving the interests of the wider international community, or, as it was more properly termed, the Concert of Powers. The issue for the British government was less whether it would challenge these propositions and more whether it could tolerate such a crass manipulation of the facts without damaging its own interests in Tunis, in North Africa more generally, and in the Ottoman Empire above all. How far, in other words, could the disingenuous rhetoric of French imperial aggrandizement go unremarked without undermining Britain's regional influence?

On 24 May 1881, the Chamber of Deputies, lower house of the National Assembly, debated the Treaty of Bardo establishing France's protectorate over Tunisia. With French forces parading outside his palace, the Bey had had little choice other than to sign the treaty twelve days earlier. The sense of bowing to the inevitable also pervaded the parliamentary discussion in Paris. George Clemenceau, a leading republican sceptic, editor of *La Justice*, and head of the commission appointed to scrutinize the treaty, caught the mood. He conceded that the settlement made Algeria more secure and offered financial reassurance for French investors in Tunisia's public debt. But, he suggested, the rhetoric used to justify the original expedition should leave any genuine republican profoundly alarmed. It was obvious that talk of limited objectives, improved frontier security, and 'protection' had been a smokescreen to conceal full annexation. And parliamentary assent was either carefully bypassed or simply taken for granted throughout the process. Perhaps worst of all, this cavalier attitude antagonized Ottoman Turkey and sapped British goodwill towards the Third Republic.[55]

---

[54] TNA, FO 27/2492, letter 463, Lord Lyons to Earl Granville, 10 May 1881.
[55] *Journal Officiel*, débats parlementaires. Chambre des Députés, 24 May 1881, pp. 980–5.

Taking to the floor after Clemenceau's relatively restrained performance, two right-wing deputies, the Bonapartist Jules Delafosse and the Italian-born Gustave Cuneo d'Ornano, went much further. The government had prosecuted a small war without parliamentary authorization. This violated Article 9 of the very constitution that so many republicans had supported to prevent precisely such authoritarian behaviour. Government members had lied about their intentions, even denying that annexation was intended after it had taken place. Only when cornered by sceptical deputies and senators did the government shift to more familiar rhetorical ground, claiming other, altruistic motivations: security along a dangerous frontier, an end to financial mismanagement in Tunis, and the opportunity to spread French cultural norms and spiritual values. Translated into political vernacular, Ferry had behaved worse than Napoleon III, acting with the devious imperiousness he professed to despise.[56] Ferry's ministers had got away with their adventurism on this occasion but, as the impending Egyptian crisis and, even more so, the resumption of annexationist policies in Indochina would prove in 1884–5, the indulgence of foreign powers and the tolerance of the National Assembly had limits. By 1885, reeling from attacks by monarchist conservatives on government misconduct of an attempted French push into the northern Vietnamese Tonkin region, Ferry's reputation for inflated rhetoric and crass colonial incompetence was sealed.[57]

BRITAIN AND EGYPT

The literature on the British invasion of Egypt focuses mainly on its causes, but does include some discussion of the way in which it was publicly rationalized. John Newsinger has commented on the hypocrisies surrounding British claims to have overthrown a 'military despotism'.[58] Dan Halvorson has noted the stress on 'prestige' in public statements by government figures, although he seems to take these at face value.[59] P. J. Cain has demonstrated the importance of the language of 'character', as used by the British officials who controlled Egypt's finances, and has shown how this helped them argue that the Egyptians were unfit to govern, thus shoring up Britain's own interests.[60] M. E. Chamberlain, in a valuable article on public and press opinion, discusses the surprising shortage of opposition to an act that appeared contrary to the principles on which the Liberal Party had been elected.[61] We lack, however, a systematic account of how the arguments for (and

---

[56] *Journal Officiel*, débats parlementaires. Chambre des Députés, 24 May 1881, pp. 983–5.

[57] Kevin Passmore, *The Right in France from the Third Republic to Vichy* (Cambridge: Cambridge University Press, 2013), 49–50.

[58] John Newsinger, 'Liberal Imperialism and the Occupation of Egypt in 1882', *Race & Class*, 49:3 (2007), 54–75.

[59] Halvorson, 'Prestige', 436–7.

[60] P. J. Cain, 'Character and Imperialism: The British Financial Administration of Egypt, 1878–1914', *Journal of Imperial and Commonwealth History*, 34:2 (2006), 177–200.

[61] M. E. Chamberlain, 'British Public Opinion and the Invasion of Egypt, 1882', *Trivium*, 16 (1981), 5–28.

against) intervention worked, and of what they tell us about how imperial issues were discussed in the public sphere. In the absence of such an explanation, it is all too easy to latch on to particular tropes such as prestige, character, and attacks on despotism, and to place excessive weight upon them. What needs to be considered, in addition, is the impact of interparty rivalry on the terms of the discourse, and how hostility towards France played a significant part in the responses to the British government's approach to Egypt.

The arguments of 1882 cannot be understood without reference to the tumultuous events of the previous ten years, which had seen Gladstone fall from power at the hands of Disraeli's Conservatives, only for the Liberal leader to reclaim office in spectacular fashion, after a period of nominal retirement. Disraeli's charge against the Liberals, when in opposition at the beginning of the 1870s, was that they had long been engaged in a subtle and continuous effort to bring about the empire's disintegration. His ability to present himself and his party successfully as the champions of 'national principles' as against Liberal 'cosmopolitan principles' was likely a significant factor in his 1874 election victory, at a time when—as he at least believed—popular sympathy for the empire was growing.[62] Fairly soon, however, Gladstone turned the tables. First, there was his 'Bulgarian agitation', in protest at the government's allegedly callous and cynical approach to massacres of Christians within the Ottoman Empire, in view of its desire to prop up the 'sick man of Europe' as a bulwark against Russia. Then—arguably more successfully—came the 'Midlothian campaign' of 1879–80, during which Gladstone gave a series of thrilling speeches denouncing the immorality of the government's foreign policy, which he labelled 'Beaconsfieldism'.[63] (Disraeli had been elevated to the Lords as Earl of Beaconsfield.) The Gladstonian attack on Beaconsfieldian 'Imperialism' was part of a broader attack on the allegedly sinister and autocratic 'system of government' with which it was intimately entwined.[64] Thus expensive military adventurism (marked by notable failures in Zululand and Afghanistan) was linked with the government's neglect of domestic issues and its supposedly secretive and despotic tendencies. Indeed, the word 'imperialism'—that 'newfangled term over which there is much unprofitable controversy'—had gained its negative connotations from its association with the French Second Empire of Napoleon III.[65]

As may be seen, it was governing style that was at stake in this critique as much as territorial expansion. So, while Gladstone was undoubtedly influenced by the radical views of John Bright and Richard Cobden, his opposition to 'imperialism' did not mean he was opposed to empire as such.[66] In this context, there were

---

[62] 'Mr. Disraeli At Sydenham', *The Times*, 25 June 1872.

[63] See P. J. Durran, 'A Two-Edged Sword: The Liberal Attack on Disraelian Imperialism', *Journal of Imperial and Commonwealth History*, 10:3 (1982), 262–84.

[64] 'Mr. Gladstone', *The Times*, 31 March 1880.

[65] 'Lord Carnarvon on Imperial Administration', *Saturday Review*, 9 November 1878; Richard Koebner and Helmut Dan Schmidt, *Imperialism: The Story and Significance of a Political Word, 1840–1960* (Cambridge: Cambridge University Press, 1964), 1–26.

[66] For the influence of the Radicals, see Andrekos Varnava, 'British and Greek Liberalism and Imperialism in the Long Nineteenth Century', in Matthew P. Fitzpatrick (ed.), *Liberal Imperialism in Europe* (Basingstoke: Palgrave, 2012), 219–39, at 226–7.

striking parallels with leading republican figures such as Léon Gambetta and Georges Clemenceau in France, politicians who managed to combine rhetorical disdain for colonial expansionism with indulgence towards the continued growth of the French Empire overseas.[67] In their case, Gambetta's limited engagement with colonial affairs during the 1870s, much like Clemenceau's enduring Anglophilia put them outside the expansionist currents of mainstream elite opinion. At no point did Gambetta, Clemenceau, or Gladstone become avid supporters of colonial expansion. Yet all three, at times, faced accusations of disingenuity. Gladstone's argument against further British expansion—although he did not rule out annexations in all circumstances—was that it would in fact weaken the empire through military and financial overstretch. Whereas the origins of the empire might not have been very creditable, he argued, it was the duty of the generations which had inherited it to redeem it and 'elevate [it] into honour'. The British were bound, not to do away with the empire, but to administer it in line with 'the principles of justice and goodwill, of benevolence and mercy'.[68]

Examination of Gladstone's views on Egypt illuminates this point further. In 1877 he published an article in *The Nineteenth Century*, in response to two previous contributions by Edward Dicey, journalist and brother of the jurist A. V. Dicey, advocating the immediate occupation of the Nile Delta. Gladstone opposed this, observing—in a much-quoted passage—that 'our first site in Egypt, be it by larceny or be it by emption [purchase], will be the almost certain egg of a North African Empire, that will grow and grow'.[69] The irony of this is obvious in the light of later events, but it is easy to miss another point: Gladstone, as well as Dicey, at this stage viewed the Egyptian question, not merely as a foreign policy question, but primarily as an imperial matter. Going beyond the famous quotation, moreover, casts Gladstone's thinking in a more complex light. Noteworthy, from the Anglo-French perspective, was his

> belief that the day, which witnesses our occupation of Egypt, will bid a long farewell to all cordiality of political relations between France and England. There might be no immediate quarrel, no exterior manifestation; but a silent rankling grudge there would be [. . .] Nations have good memories.[70]

Even more significant was his treatment of India. Contrary to those like Dicey, who saw the retention of India as essential to Britain's power—and who therefore demanded that the canal be secured in order to guarantee this—Gladstone denied Britain's 'dependence' on its own imperial possession. Nevertheless, the maintenance

[67] MAE, 79PAAP50 Léon Gambetta papers: questions coloniales, 1871–82; Bury, 'Gambetta and Overseas Problems', 277–84; Robert K. Hanks, 'Georges Clemenceau and the English', *Historical Journal*, 45:1 (2002), 53–77.
[68] W. E. Gladstone, *Political Speeches in Scotland, November and December 1879*, W. Ridgway (ed.), (London, 1879), 203.
[69] W. E. Gladstone, 'Aggression on Egypt and Freedom in the East', *Nineteenth Century*, August 1877, 149–66, at 158.
[70] Ibid., 161–2. This was a rejection of Dicey's claim that French interests 'are pretty well circumscribed within the area of France': 'Our Route to India', *Nineteenth Century*, June 1877, 665–85, at 670.

of British power in India remained 'a capital demand upon the national honour'.[71] In response, Dicey pointed out that, even though Gladstone played down the strategic importance of the canal, it might in practice turn out to be crucial for Indian defence. Therefore Gladstone's own argument implied 'that, under certain conceivable circumstances, it might be our duty to occupy Egypt for the protection of India'.[72] In fact, the occupation eventually came about for different reasons, but Gladstone's willingness to endorse it in spite of his previous concerns suggests he did indeed subscribe to a cross-party conception of national and imperial interest.[73]

Yet this apparent near-consensus did not prevent bitter public/rhetorical disagreement between the parties: a struggle as it were between different ways of justifying empire. 'Between the two parties in this controversy there is a perfect agreement that England has a mighty mission in the world,' Gladstone claimed, 'but there is a discord as fundamental upon the question of what that mission is.'[74] It was the relationship between morality and national self-interest that marked the faultline between Gladstonian and Conservative imperial views, as expressed rhetorically. For high-minded Liberals, improvements in native welfare, to be worked for as part of a sacred trust that had been bequeathed them, were the ultimate and only justification for an empire, which Britain, in the last analysis, did not actually need for her survival.

For the Conservatives, improvements in the well-being of the population were the by-product of empire, not the essential reason for it, but by the same token they were the inevitable result of the irrepressible struggle between nations. Although they did not use the term, they in effect posited a kind of 'invisible hand' whereby the pursuit of national (or at least British) self-interest would have positive general consequences. As far as they were concerned, the Liberal idea that international relations were subject to 'moral laws' in the same way that relations between individuals were, was absurd. Good would come of the empire, but not through conscious efforts to do good. Conservatives did have their own concept of imperial 'duty', albeit a duty to develop British character much more than one to improve native welfare, which helped counter Liberal claims that their empire policy was merely atavistic by lending it a lofty moral tone.[75] Cain writes that 'some Conservative imperialists like Lord Carnarvon distinguished between "true" and "false" imperialisms', rather as Gladstone did. However, he fails to note that Carnarvon—formerly colonial secretary, and the only example Cain cites—had resigned from the government over its Turkish

[71] Gladstone, 'Aggression on Egypt and Freedom in the East', 153.

[72] Edward Dicey, 'Mr. Gladstone and Our Empire', *Nineteenth Century*, September 1877, 292–308, at 305.

[73] See John Darwin, 'Imperialism and the Victorians: The Dynamics of Territorial Expansion', *English Historical Review*, 112:447 (1997), 614–42, at 622.

[74] W. E. Gladstone, 'England's Mission', *Nineteenth Century*, September 1878, 560–84, at 570.

[75] P. J. Cain, 'Empire and the Languages of Character and Virtue in Late Victorian and Edwardian Britain', *Modern Intellectual History*, 4:2 (2007), 249–73, at 270; 'Lord Carnarvon on Imperial Administration', *Saturday Review*, 9 November 1878; Peter Gordon, 'Herbert, Henry Howard Molyneux, Fourth Earl of Carnarvon (1831–1890)', *Oxford Dictionary of National Biography* (Oxford: Oxford University Press, 2004; online edition, January 2008) <http://www.oxforddnb.com/view/article/13035>, accessed 23 October 2012.

policy and aspired to hold office under Gladstone. At the time, Carnarvon's remarks were understood as an attack on Disraeli.[76]

INTERVENTION DEBATED

Such conflicting Conservative and Liberal interpretations were reflected in the debates of 1882. The crisis was the culmination of longstanding European involvement in Egyptian political and economic affairs, in the face of an indigenous proto-nationalist movement resentful of both foreign meddling and the maladministration of the country's traditional rulers. The Khedive Tewfik owed nominal allegiance to the Ottoman sultan—a point frequently invoked by those British (and French) politicians who hoped to find some sort of Turkish-backed solution to Egypt's problems.[77] In reality, Tewfik's true masters were the British and French, whose involvement with Ottoman finances dated back to their guarantee of the Ottoman Crimean War loan of 1854.[78] In 1876, the two countries had imposed their own 'dual control' over Egypt's revenues and expenditure, in order to secure repayment of the large foreign debts run up by Tewfik's father, the Khedive Ismail. After Ismail proved insufficiently pliable, in 1879 he was deposed by the sultan on Britain's and France's instructions. Yet the problems he had faced remained, and the nationalists, led by Colonel Ahmed 'Urabi and angered by the power and privileges of the foreign community in Cairo, were a continuing challenge to Tewfik's authority. In January 1882, an Anglo-French Joint Note reasserted the two countries' backing for the Khedive, but this backfired. Tewfik now looked like a cats-paw of the foreigners, and there was an upsurge of support for 'Urabi, whom he was forced to appoint as minister of war.[79]

Meanwhile the effervescence characteristic of French parliamentary politics in the early years of the Third Republic threatened to boil over. This was due, in part, to mounting internal disorder in Tunisia. Widespread political violence over the autumn called French annexation into question once more and helped bring down Ferry's government in October 1881.[80] In part, the National Assembly's increasingly febrile atmosphere mirrored the disintegration of the republican bloc into opposing factions. Most remained nominally loyal to Gambetta, but each was exasperated by their patron's reluctance to return to office without a solid electoral mandate for the constitutional reforms he considered necessary to entrench the progressive 'republicanization' of France. Reflecting on the situation before he eventually tried and failed to form his *Grand Ministère* in November 1881, Gambetta told his confidante Léonie Léon, 'You can hardly decorate the incoherent tumult of the various factions of the left [with the name politics]; it's more a

[76] Cain, 'Empire and the Languages of Character', 269–70. 'Lord Carnarvon on Imperial Administration', *Saturday Review*, 9 November 1878; Peter Gordon, 'Herbert, Henry Howard Molyneux, Fourth Earl of Carnarvon (1831–1890)'.

[77] *Journal Officiel*, débats parlementaires. Chambre des Députés, 1 June 1882, p. 755.

[78] Varnava, 'British and Greek Liberalism and Imperialism', 222.

[79] Michael J. Reimer, *Colonial Bridgehead: Government and Society in Alexandria, 1807–1882* (Oxford: Westview Press, 1997), 175.

[80] Ashley, 'The Failure of Gambetta's *Grand Ministère*', 109–13.

delirium tremens, something like Saint Vitus' dance.'[81] In the event, Gambetta, terminally ill with intestinal cancer, limped from office never to return in January 1882. The greatest republican rhetorical voice of the early Third Republic was gone. A fraught, unstable coalition under Gambetta's erstwhile colleague, the Protestant Senator Charles de Freycinet, was left to step into the breach just as the Egyptian crisis exploded.

The new French government's priorities were largely domestic—and highly contentious. Reforms to the electoral system, restructuring the judiciary, and reducing the military service term consumed most attention. But there was also an economic stimulus package centred on new commercial tariffs that was bound to antagonize Gladstonian free traders. For his part, de Freycinet was determined to complete a thoroughgoing overhaul of the Foreign Ministry's internal organization, making entry and advancement in the French diplomatic corps more transparent, more meritocratic, and more republican.[82] Immensely busy, and conscious of his isolation among a still reactionary Foreign Ministry staff resentful of the new premier's reforms, de Freycinet had no appetite for confrontation with Britain over another contested region of north-east Africa.[83]

It perhaps did not seem this way at the time, but as this snapshot of the French political situation indicates, Gladstone had little to concern him in Paris. Not so in Cairo. Under the influence of the radical poet and adventurer, Wilfrid Scawen Blunt, he was prepared to concede, somewhat to his own surprise, the possibility that the Egyptians might be capable of generating a genuine national movement.[84] The prime minister wrote to his foreign secretary, Lord Granville: ' "Egypt for the Egyptians" is the sentiment to which I should wish to give scope: and could it prevail it would I think be the best, the only good solution of the "Egyptian question" '.[85] This was in contrast to the powerful strand of opinion which pointed to the country's ethnic diversity and social divisions and argued that such slogans were specious. The Oxford Egypt specialist Alfred J. Butler claimed: 'There is no body of men large and united enough to be called a National party, and there is no such people as the Egyptians.'[86]

Gladstone's sympathy for the national movement was conditional, weak, and short-lived. Distracted by the problems of Ireland, he was reliant on the slanted information provided to him by British officials in Cairo and in the end proved susceptible to pressure from ministers, notably Charles Dilke, Joseph Chamberlain, and Lord Hartington, who took an aggressive line. Undoubtedly, though, his fundamental assumption was the same as theirs: that the Khedive had to be

---

[81] Ashley, 'The Failure of Gambetta's *Grand Ministère*', 108.

[82] *Journal Officiel*, débats parlementaires, De Freycinet inaugural speech, 31 January 1882, 69.

[83] 77PAAP1/D1, Charles de Freycinet papers: Égypte 1882–6, 'Œuvre administrative de M. de Freycinet au Ministère des Affaires Étrangères en 1880–1882'.

[84] For Blunt's influence, see H. C. G. Matthew, *Gladstone 1809–1898* (Oxford: Clarendon Press, 1997), 383, and Luisa Villa, 'A "Political Education": Wilfrid Scawen Blunt, the Arabs and the Egyptian Revolution (1881–82)', *Journal of Victorian Culture*, 17:1 (2012), 46–63, at 59.

[85] Gladstone to Granville, 4 January 1882, in Agatha Ramm (ed.), *Political Correspondence of Mr. Gladstone and Lord Granville, Vol. I: 1876–1882* (Oxford: Clarendon Press, 1962), 326.

[86] Alfred J. Butler to the editor of *The Times*, 2 May 1882.

maintained in power as the tool of European control.[87] The need for firmness was also reinforced by the great majority of the press.[88] As the *Times* correspondent in Alexandria put it, foreigners would 'laugh at a failure of the two great nations of the West to govern the most easily governed people in the world'.[89]

However, Conservative charges against the government over its handling of the crisis during the first part of the year were wrapped up with suspicions of the French. This was part of a broader critique of its alleged weakness and ineffectuality in foreign policy. During the Midlothian campaign Gladstone had denounced Beaconsfield's policies 'in the most unmeasured terms', and yet, after two years in office, had the Liberal Party done any better? The state of affairs in Egypt, and the failure of trade talks with the French, hardly seemed to suggest that Britain was now better respected abroad.[90] (After the election of 1880 Gladstone publically distanced himself from his previous 'polemical language', but this was not much of an advertisement for his consistency.)[91] There was concern that the French were trying to inveigle the British into a joint expedition against Egypt. The objection was not to intervention per se, but rather to undertaking it in tandem with an untrustworthy nation whose interest in Egypt was said to be much less significant than that of Britain. The *Morning Post* argued that the British could be relied upon to defend the international right of free passage through the canal, because such freedom was vital to the defence of her Indian Empire. But, supposedly, Arabi and his party were fearful of the French, given their occupation of Tunisia the previous year: 'the advance of France is feared as implying the violent dispossession of native government'. It would therefore be disastrously provocative for Britain to be thought to be cooperating with the French, and the only reason that such a sinister rumour could gain credence was because of Gladstone's reputation for not caring for 'the ancient traditions of the country'.[92]

Ministers could at least point out that, although cooperation with France was potentially problematic, it was necessary on account of the Dual Control initiated under Disraeli and which the new government was bound to continue.[93] Conservatives did acknowledge that French interests in Egypt were legitimate, but they argued that these were purely financial rather than strategic. There was certainly no British recognition of France's 'preponderance' in Egypt, still less of the unique historic attachments dating from Napoleon's Nile campaign of which French parliamentarians made more and more as the 1882 crisis unfolded.[94] Rather, as the former Indian Viceroy Lord Lytton put it, there was a point beyond which

---

[87] Newsinger, 'Liberal Imperialism', 64.

[88] M. E. Chamberlain, 'British Public Opinion'.

[89] 'Egypt', *The Times*, 26 January 1882.

[90] 'Mr. Gibson', *The Times*, 20 January 1882. Edward Gibson, the speaker reported here, was Conservative MP for Trinity College Dublin and later served as Lord Chancellor for Ireland.

[91] 'Mr. Gladstone on the Foreign Policy of Austria', *Birmingham Daily Post*, 11 May 1880; ' "Polemical Language" and its Results', *Blackwood's Edinburgh Magazine*, July 1882.

[92] Untitled editorial, *Morning Post*, 5 January 1882.

[93] Dilke's speech, reported in the *Daily News*, 1 February 1882.

[94] TNA, FO 146/2420, Earl Granville letter 458 to Viscount Lyons, Paris, 28 April 1882; *Journal Officiel*, débats parlementaires, Chambre des Députés, 1 June 1882, pp. 754–5.

'the influence of France cannot be admitted, or the initiative of French policy followed', without the British placing themselves in 'a false and dangerous position'. This was because any combination with the French that changed the status quo would be regarded by other countries as a threat to the European balance of power. In other words, keeping the French out of Egypt was necessary in order to ensure that Britain's interests there were still recognized by rival powers.[95]

Gambetta's short-lived ministry, as we have seen, fell at the end of January. One Tory MP quipped: 'M. Gambetta had just been removed from office by the French Legislature because he was despotic, and had attempted to overawe it. There was some little encouragement to English Conservatives in this, since Mr. Gladstone was as despotic as he was crotchety.'[96] Consistent with de Freycinet's pledge to revitalize cooperation, the British and French appeared to continue to work in harmony, although the French prime minister caused a stir with a speech in May which seemed to imply that France might intervene even if England did not.[97] Speaking in the Lords a few days later, Granville was able to cite de Freycinet's assurance that he had not intended 'to separate the preponderance of France in Egypt from that of England'. Granville also reiterated—with no mention of empire, or the safety of the canal—that the government's policy was based on the 'maintenance of the Sovereign rights of the sultan, of the position of the Khedive, and of the liberties of the Egyptian people under the Firmans of the Porte [i.e. Ottoman decrees], the prudent development of their institutions, and the fulfilment of all international engagements'.[98] Granville's position, then, was based on the need to maintain existing rights and interests; this type of quasi-contractual language would also be adopted by Gladstone and other ministers. And it suited the French government, too, as de Freycinet grew increasingly anxious that the sultan might yet intervene in defiance of French and British wishes.[99]

The emphasis on equilibrium incorporated balance-of-power concerns, yet at the same time appeared to transcend them, given that the interests of the Egyptians was one of the items to be weighed. The way in which the government couched its actions in terms of the fulfilment of obligations—some of which, conveniently, had been contracted by the previous Conservative government—helped it avoid the type of explicitly imperial language that radical critics would have seized upon. However, it also led them to be accused of secrecy and obscurity. In his reply to Granville, Lord Salisbury, the Conservative leader in the Lords, claimed to offer patriotic, bipartisan support at a time of crisis. However, with characteristic wiliness he suggested that the 'Palmerstonian' Granville did not share 'Gladstonian' principles and started to apply subtle pressure for the use of force. Furthermore, 'if the

[95] 'The Earl Of Lytton On India', *The Times*, 2 February 1882.
[96] 'Sir H. Selwin-Ibbetson At Chelmsford', The Times, 1 February 1882.
[97] 'The Crisis in Egypt', *The Standard*, 12 May 1882.
[98] HL Deb, 15 May 1882, vol. 269, cols 647–50.
[99] TNA, FO 146/2425, tels. 67, 71, and 182, Lord Lyons to Earl Granville, 28, 29, and 30 May 1881.

sword must be used, it should be the sword of Turkey [...] The worst arrangement that could be adopted would be to use the sword of France.'[100]

Within the House of Commons, the most overt anti-imperialism was voiced by
Irish nationalists. Tim Healy warned of a potential crisis in the British Empire,
because Irish MPs 'might consider that the interference of England in the affairs of
Egypt was simply a question of cash, and that a similar interference might be
brought about in Ireland if they had a few foreign bondholders investing money in
that country'. Criticizing the government's statements as uninformative, Frank
O'Donnell noted that it 'might be singularly embarrassing' for the Liberals 'to
confess that their policy now was the very policy they had so pitilessly denounced
when Lord Beaconsfield was in Office'. He asked: 'Were Her Majesty's Government engaged in suppressing the nationalities of North Africa, like France, and
wounding the feelings of the Mahomedan population? Were they aware of the
interpretation put by the Mahomedan world upon their warm cooperation with
and apparent dependence on France?' He warned that 'It was believed among the
Mahomedan nations that Europe was once more embarking upon a sort of modern
copy of the Crusades.'[101] Michael De Nie has pointed out the tendency of many
scholars of empire to ignore Irish opinion (which was not, of course, homogen-
ous).[102] The significance of the nationalist comments lay less in their influence on
events, which was probably non-existent, than in the mere fact of the challenge they
presented to the dominant assumptions of the government and opposition. Notwithstanding their marginality, they were a sign of the diversity of opinion on
empire, as expressed in the metropole.

That diversity was also evident among Liberals, although the party's divisions
were not so severe that they threatened the government's position. At one end of
the spectrum was Sir Wilfred Lawson MP, who was incredulous that a Liberal
ministry should avow support for the maintenance of the integrity of the Ottoman
Empire. At the other was Joseph Cowen MP, a strong imperialist, who had
managed to persuade himself that 'England, unlike France, was not seeking
conquest. All that she required was to maintain her road to the East. He was
prepared to go any length for the maintenance of that highway. He would fight for
it if it was essential.'[103] Having listened to MPs debate, Gladstone wrote to
Granville of his irritation with French ministers, who he felt were insufficiently
sensitive to British public opinion. This, he said, was 'very jealous of France on
account of the transactions in Tunis, and very jealous of any subservience on our
parts towards France, of which we are already more or less suspected. This was

[100] HL Deb, 15 May 1882, vol. 269, cols 651–2. If Salisbury was positioning himself to support
eventual British intervention, not all in his party agreed, on account of even greater hostility to
the French. See the speech of the newspaper proprietor Thomas Gibson Bowles (later a
Conservative MP, and subsequently a Liberal one), reported in 'The Conservative Association for
Lowestoft & District", *The Ipswich Journal*, 27 May 1882.
[101] HC Deb, 26 May 1882, vol. 269, cols 1726–32.
[102] Michael de Nie, '"Speed the Mahdi!" The Irish Press and Empire during the Sudan Conflict of
1883–1885', *Journal of British Studies*, 51:4 (October 2012), 883–909.
[103] HC Deb, 26 May 1882, vol. 269, cols 1711–14, 1721–3.

sufficiently evident in the House of Commons yesterday, although the House behaved extremely well.'[104]

Egypt was widely thought to be in a state of chaos; justifications for intervention rested to a great extent on the idea that it would bring back 'order'. At the end of May, Britain and France both sent ships to Alexandria to back up their demand that the Egyptian ministry should resign and that Arabi should go into temporary exile.[105] They claimed that their sole interest in Egypt was to maintain the status quo through the restoration of the Khedive's authority.[106] The British also agreed to a French request for an international conference at Constantinople.[107] The Conservatives could not attack conferences as such—Disraeli had had a great triumph at the 1878 Congress of Berlin—but they could warn that an excessive desire to cooperate with other countries could lead to a neglect of British interests. The Liberals, it was hinted, were too much interested in placating foreigners.[108] At the start of June, Gladstone upped the ante by suggesting in the Commons that Arabi had 'completely thrown off the mask' and was planning to depose the Khedive.[109] We should perhaps try to ascertain the sources and relative quality/quantity of the Cairo political intelligence on which the British and French were relying. Did they commit themselves rhetorically/irreversibly on the basis of flimsy evidence? Afterwards, although he thought the phrase accurate, he wondered if it had been expedient to use it.[110] The government had now committed itself so far that it would be difficult for it *not* to intervene; and yet it still lacked a definitive excuse to do so. In these circumstances it was hardly wise to raise the temperature in this way.

Fortunately for the government—or at least for the interventionists—events in Egypt came to their aid. On 11 June, there were riots in Alexandria leading to a massacre of Europeans. 'Urabi was soon blamed for the violence, even though it brought him no advantage and though he moved quickly to restore order; in fact, it is possible that the Khedive had instigated it in the hope of provoking European intervention.[111] Retaliation was not immediate, however. In the Commons three days later Gladstone did not treat the riots as an Arabist conspiracy and repeated that the government stood for the 'general maintenance of all established rights in Egypt'. The latter was predictable enough. But he included along with the rights of the sultan, the Khedive, and the people of Egypt 'those of the foreign bondholders'.[112] In Paris, French shareholders represented on the Suez Canal Company's Judicial Council had been lobbying for intervention in Egypt for

[104] Gladstone to Granville, 27 May 1882, in Ramm, *Political Correspondence Vol. I*, 374.
[105] TNA, FO 146/2420, tel. 87, Sir E. Malet (Cairo) to Earl Granville, April 22 1882; FO 146/2425, French Embassy dispatches to FO, May 1882.
[106] 'The Egyptian Crisis', *The Standard*, 26 May 1882.
[107] Matthew, *Gladstone*, 385.
[108] 'Sir Stafford Northcote on Public Affairs', *Birmingham Daily Post*, 3 June 1882.
[109] HC Deb, 1 June 1882, vol. 269, cols 1780–1.
[110] Gladstone to Granville, 2 June 1882, in Ramm, *Political Correspondence Vol. I*, 378.
[111] M. E. Chamberlain, 'The Alexandria Massacre of 11 June 1882 and the British Occupation of Egypt', *Middle Eastern Studies*, 13:1 (1977), 14–39.
[112] HC Deb, 14 June 1882, vol. 270, cols 1143–50.

months.[113] But, in London, Gladstone's statement caused a sensation (likely to have been stronger still, had the extent of Gladstone's own holdings been known).[114] Even Dicey, in making the case for occupation five years earlier, had been careful to state that he did not have much sympathy 'for the wrongs of the foreign bondholders'.[115] Now, Gladstone's comments sent the markets rising and also gave some Liberals cause for serious disquiet.[116] He had set the idea of a 'bondholders' war' running before the war itself was even launched. But the dissenters were in a minority. Dilke, the Foreign Office under-secretary, wrote in his diary: 'Our side in the Commons are very Jingo about Egypt. They badly want to kill somebody. They don't know who. Mr. G., who does not like the Stock Exchange, sent "Egypts" up 3½ per cent, by a word in his speech.'[117]

While Dilke and Hartington upped the pressure within the Cabinet for intervention, Conservatives did so from outside. French involvement looked less likely by mid-June. De Freycinet's government only conceded a full National Assembly debate on the Egyptian crisis at the start of the month, almost a fortnight after the Anglo-French naval force arrived off Alexandria. And this despite wave after wave of petitions from Alexandria's French residents pleading for salvation from the city's growing intercommunal violence.[118] Ensuing criticism of French actions, once again spearheaded by the fervent Bonapartist Jules Delafosse, focused, not on the need for muscular French intervention, but rather on the dangers inherent in antagonizing Ottoman Turkey and the specious assumption that French and British interests in Egypt were compatible. In an echo of Gladstone's June 1877 article in *Nineteenth Century*, Delafosse did not mince words:

> there is no intimate accord [between France and Britain], there never was one, nor will there ever be one, and that for an excellent reason, namely, that there is no identity of interest. We do not have common interests in Egypt; we only have rival interests.[119]

De Freycinet had assured the National Assembly three weeks earlier that his government 'would not be party to any demarche, to any negotiation or to any other arrangement which left Egypt less independent than it presently was'. This, surely, was meant to be interpreted as a warning against Turkish intervention or excessive British claims. Taking up Delafosse's refrain, his colleague le Comte de Colbert Laplace lambasted the French premier for ignoring the essential point that Franco-British interests in Egypt were fundamentally at odds. The British, he said, were, as ever, 'sensibly unemotional and rational in their calculation of the worth of

---

[113] TNA, FO 146/2420, Edward J. Standon (Paris) to Earl Granville, 18 April 1882.

[114] Richard Shannon, *Gladstone: Heroic Minister 1865–1898* (London: Allen Lane, 1999), 303.

[115] Dicey, 'Our Route to India', 678. See also the comments of Salisbury and Northcote: HL Deb, 25 July 1882, vol. 272, col. 1678; 'Sir S. Northcote At Glasgow', *The Times*, 5 October 1882.

[116] 'Commercial and Markets', *Liverpool Mercury*, 15 June 1882; 'Our London Correspondence', *Liverpool Mercury*, 17 June 1882.

[117] Stephen Gwynn and Gertrude M. Tuckwell, *The Life of the Rt. Hon. Sir Charles W. Dilke, Bart., MP*, Vol. I (London: John Murray, 1917), p. 460.

[118] MAE, 23ADP7, Affaires diverses politiques 1814–97: Egypte, 1882, Dossier: pétitions.

[119] *Journal Officiel*, débats parlementaires, Chambre des Députés, 1 June 1882, p. 755.

French friendship', knowing that hegemonic control over Suez was an essential pivot of their global power and thus more important.[120]

Meanwhile, in London, the criticism of the risks inherent in a potential joint Anglo-French expedition was replaced by allegations of pusillanimity against Gladstone's government, which had so far failed to make good on its promises to the Khedive. The matter was, the *Daily Telegraph* urged, no mere 'technical question of legality and interlocking rights'; Britain's high road to India was at stake.[121] On 29 June, Salisbury addressed a ticketed meeting in Willis's Rooms, the London club that had been the site of the foundation of the Liberal Party in 1859. It is striking that existing accounts, including that of Robinson and Gallagher, fail to mention this occasion or to consider what its impact on government thinking might have been. The propriety of such a meeting, which its organizers disingenuously described as non-partisan, was called into question by its critics, among whom was the Conservative MP Lord Randolph Churchill.[122] According to the London correspondent of the *Liverpool Mercury*, who alleged that it was 'a "Jingo" meeting' from start to finish, 'Lord Salisbury was mild (for him) and Sir Stafford Northcote was vigorous (for him), and the meeting was wild enough for both of them'.[123] Salisbury began his speech by denying allegations that it was a bondholders' meeting. He poured scorn on the conference at Constantinople, and cast the Egyptian issue in explicitly imperial terms, using the language of prestige, although he did not use that precise word. Having sent a fleet to Alexandria to demand the removal of 'Urabi, the government must back up its words with actions, he said, or the credibility of the imperial power would be undermined elsewhere. He explained to his audience that although the 'half civilised peoples' of the empire benefitted from British rule, they did not on the whole feel well-disposed to Britain, and they were only kept in line by the reserve threat of force. He said: 'I believe that the most enlightened of the Indian population would deeply deplore that you should ever be driven from their land; but that does not interfere with the fact that for those vast millions of population your title to rule is the sharpness and readiness of your sword.'[124] Here was an overt example of 'dominant-imperialist' language of the kind that Bernard Porter has suggested was in relatively short supply; and Salisbury was by no means atypical of his party.[125]

The current of opinion that opposed intervention was represented by a meeting of the recently founded Anti-Aggression League, held a few days before the Willis's Rooms affair. Frederick Harrison, its chairman, sought to remind the government

---

[120] *Journal Officiel*, débats parlementaires, Chambre des Députés, 1 June 1882, pp. 756, 758.

[121] Quoted in 'Epitome of Opinion', *Pall Mall Gazette*, 22 June 1882.

[122] For a round-up of views, see 'Epitome of Opinion', *Pall Mall Gazette*, 29 June 1882. For debates surrounding the culture of public meetings, see Jon Lawrence, *Electing Our Masters: The Hustings in British Politics From Hogarth to Blair* (Oxford: Oxford University Press, 2009).

[123] 'Our London Correspondence', *Liverpool Mercury*, 30 June 1882. Northcote was the Conservative leader in the Commons.

[124] 'The Crisis In Egypt', *The Times*, 30 June 1882.

[125] Bernard Porter, *The Absent-Minded Imperialists: Empire, Society, and Culture in Britain* (Oxford: Oxford University Press, 2004), especially 312–14.

of the principles of Midlothian and denied that the canal was in danger.[126] Quite soon, however, the League collapsed, when many of its members proved reluctant to oppose Gladstone.[127] This is not to say that mainstream Liberals felt no disquiet. Dilke argued that:

> There is a belief among the great majority of Liberals that intervention in Egypt is only contemplated on account of financial interests. If we are to intervene to protect the Canal, or if we confine ourselves to exacting the reparation due to us for the Alexandria outrages, this feeling need not be taken into account. If, however, we are going to Cairo we ought to make our position clear. I do not wish for any compromise with Arabi. He in no sense represents the national life of Egypt, but, on the contrary, he holds the Egyptian nationality by the throat. His use of the phrase 'national party' is a mere prostitution of the term. But there is in Egypt a desire to see Egyptians in office, and a certain amount of real national sentiment. That sentiment we might conciliate and for our own sakes here we should at least explain how we stand towards it.[128]

John S. Galbraith and Afaf Lutfi al-Sayyid-Marsot have used the first two sentences of this passage to argue that 'The "security of the canal" argument as justification for the occupation of Egypt was put forward not because the gravity of the menace justified such weighty action in the view of the well informed, but because it provided the most palatable explanation to the Liberal party and the general public.'[129] The general point may not be unfair, but it overlooks the import of the passage as a whole. Dilke was arguing that the government should make clear that it was not opposed to Egyptian nationalism as such, only to the Arabist version of it. This was probably a better way to appeal to Liberals than simply to emphasize the canal, which was a line better calculated to appeal to Conservatives and the public as a whole. In practice, the government integrated claims about the security of the canal into its existing arguments, creating justifications for intervention that were distinct from the Salisburyite rationale, albeit they had some elements in common with it.

At the beginning of July, Admiral Seymour, the British commander at Alexandria, requested permission to launch a bombardment if the Egyptians did not stop work on improvements to their forts on the shore. The French government, its parliamentary support ebbing inexorably ever since the 1 June Egyptian debate in the Chamber of Deputies, declined to subscribe to the planned ultimatum.[130] Dilke wrote in his diary: 'When the French ships steam out from Alexandria our sailors ought to pursue them with ironical cheers such as those with which in the

---

[126] 'The Crisis In Egypt', *The Times*, 27 June 1882.

[127] Chamberlain, 'Public Opinion', 18; Martin Ceadel, *Semi-Detached Idealists: The British Peace Movement and International Relations, 1854–1945* (Oxford: Oxford University Press, 2000), 119–20.

[128] Note by Dilke, 4 July 1882, PRO 30/29/132, TNA; M. E. Chamberlain, 'Sir Charles Dilke and the British Intervention in Egypt, 1882: Decision-Making in a Nineteenth Century Cabinet', *British Journal of International Studies*, 2:3 (1976), 231–45, at 236.

[129] Galbraith and al-Sayyid-Marsot, 'The British Occupation', 473. See also Hopkins, 'The Victorians', 374.

[130] Robinson and Gallagher, *Africa and the Victorians*, 110.

House of Commons we assail members who walk out to avoid a division.'[131] Yet the French decision made things politically much easier for the British government at home, because, if they intervened, they could no longer be accused of being in thrall to Gallic wiles. Seymour increased his demands, and when the Egyptians refused to surrender the forts, the bombardment took place, on 11 July, causing the loss of hundreds of lives.[132] Far from cowing the population into submission, there were new outbreaks of anti-European violence. 'Urabi issued a proclamation declaring that 'the defence of our country and our religion is obligatory, according to the Mahommedan law and faith. War irreconcilable between us and the English exists.'[133] It now appeared that the canal really could be under threat, and with the French only confirming ten days later that they might send troops to help secure it, the British Cabinet agreed to send an expeditionary force to Cyprus and Malta where it would be held ready for operations in Egypt.[134] The veteran radical John Bright resigned from the government in protest at the bombardment, prompting a notorious letter from Gladstone in which he described himself as 'a labourer in the cause of peace'.

The prime minister's reasoning may have been twisted and self-deceiving, but it is worth noting the broader argument of the letter, which stressed the supposed *legality* of the Alexandrian action. By exercising 'the right & duty of self defence' the government was helping build a rule-bound system of international relations, and thus were standing up for 'peace as against war, & law as against violence & arbitrary will'.[135] The parallel with Ferry's earlier justification for Tunisia's annexation was obvious: Europe's imperial powers were obligated to use force to enforce better standards of governance on 'lesser' nations.

Therefore, when the Commons debated a vote of credit for the expedition, Gladstone again placed much emphasis on law, contractual duty, sovereign rights, and the approval given to British proceedings by the great powers at the Constantinople conference. He acknowledged that 'the fact that you have great interests in a foreign country, and that those interests are seriously suffering in consequence of its civil war or its anarchy, does not of itself suffice to establish the theory of the right of a stranger to enter into that country by force and undertake to find a solution for its political difficulties'. But Britain had incurred obligations on account of the creation of the Dual Control under the Conservative government: 'it is not free to you with honour, after once entering into such relations, to say that

---

[131] Dilke diary, 10 July 1882, Dilke Papers, British Library, Add MS 43925.

[132] Newsinger, 'Liberal Imperialism', 66.

[133] Undated proclamation, in 'Egypt. No. 17 (1882): Correspondence Respecting the Affairs of Egypt', C.3391 (London, 1882), 184–5.

[134] Robinson and Gallagher, *Africa and the Victorians*, 115; TNA, FO 146/2433, letter 778, Viscount Lyons to Earl Granville, 21 July 1882, enclosure 1; no. 790, enclosure 5, Captain Rice to Viscount Lyons, 23 July 1882. The Ministry of Marine advised the British naval attaché that up to 24,000 French troops might be made available to defend the Suez Canal, but only if the Chamber of Deputies, which debated the issue on 19–20 July, supported intervention.

[135] Gladstone to John Bright, 14 July 1882, in H. C. G. Matthew (ed.), *The Gladstone Diaries With Cabinet Minutes and Prime Ministerial Correspondence Vol. X: January 1881–June 1883* (Oxford: Clarendon Press, 1990), 298–9.

you will regard those engagements as if they had never been contracted'. His emphasis on the canal was minimal. Indeed, securing it would not in itself be sufficient to put things right: 'The insecurity of the Canal is a symptom only, and the seat of the disease is in the interior of Egypt, in its disturbed and its anarchical condition'. The British, moreover, would treat it as a sacred duty 'within the limits of reason, to favour popular liberty' once the rule of law was substituted for 'Urabi's reign of 'military violence'.[136]

Gladstone's speech, according to the *Bristol Mercury*'s correspondent, was 'one prolonged effort of eloquent argument' which 'held the whole House spell-bound'.[137] According to the *Glasgow Herald*, by contrast: 'His admission that the earnest efforts that the Government had made to preserve the concert of Europe had resulted in nothing more than "moral support and sympathy," except in the case of France, who, however, had carefully limited her work to securing the safety of the Suez Canal, was received somewhat contemptuously by the Opposition.'[138] Gladstone had in fact made clear that France, in spite of her stated commitment to help guarantee the canal's security, was unlikely to send troops; and indeed de Freycinet's government was heavily defeated a few days later when it sought a vote of credit for the expedition.[139] Speaking, as usual, on behalf of the left republicans in the Chamber of Deputies debate on possible intervention, Clemenceau congratulated de Freycinet for his restraint thus far. Just as it made no sense for French warships to join in the Alexandria bombardment, so landing soldiers along the Suez Canal would only dissipate precious military resources to no lasting benefit. France in North Africa, he warned, risked following in the footsteps of the Habsburg Monarchy in the Balkans, getting sucked ever deeper into local conflicts that it had little prospect of suppressing.[140]

Clemenceau's caution was not enough to allay abiding British fears that the French might yet be tempted to act. Gladstone's critics feared at the time that French proponents of intervention might inveigle a way into the canal zone while the British were tied up elsewhere in Egypt. Liberal opinion did for the most part accept Gladstone's claims to be upholding international law, fulfilling Britain's obligations, and acting in the interests of the Egyptian people's liberties. Intervention could even be presented as consistent with Gladstone's policy of 1876. Then he had urged intervention to prevent massacres in Bulgaria; now he was acting to prevent massacres in Egypt.[141] Although much of the Tory press now rallied behind the government's actions, for the *Standard*, Gladstone's claim that Britain was not acting out of selfish interests showed that he had a false conception of statecraft:

[136] HC Deb, 24 July 1882, vol. 272, cols 1574–91.

[137] 'Parliamentary Notes', *Bristol Mercury and Daily Post*, 25 July 1882.

[138] 'Our London Correspondence', *Glasgow Herald*, 25 July 1882.

[139] Robinson and Gallagher, *Africa and the Victorians*, 119; TNA, FO 146/2433, no. 753, Viscount Lyons to Earl Granville, 20 July 1882.

[140] TNA, FO 146/2433, no. 763, Viscount Lyons to Earl Granville, 20 July 1882.

[141] Editorial, *Leeds Mercury*, 25 July 1882; 'Our London Correspondence', *Liverpool Mercury*, 25 July 1882; 'Our London Letter', *Northern Echo*, 25 July 1882.

England is to take special and exceptional military action in Egypt, but England is to have no special or exceptional interests and privileges there. [. . .] It may accord with Mr. Gladstone's conceptions of the 'moral law' to take that self-denying course. But it is not statesmanship, and we doubt if the English people will be altogether gratified by it.[142]

Dilke's speech the following day placed rather more emphasis on the canal, which, he noted, was a road to Britain's empire in Australia and New Zealand as well as to India. Thus, as befitted the author of *Greater Britain* (1868), he made quite explicit use of imperial language. There were other elements to his argument too. 'Our position seems to arise from necessity, from Treaty right, and from duty', he suggested. The demands of imperial necessity were thus supplemented by both a legal framework and by Britain's responsibilities towards the Egyptians.[143] Chamberlain, who shared Dilke's reputation as a radical, avoided the use of the word 'empire', but he too presented the British action as a defence of legality. He could not understand, he said, how the idea of dispute resolution through international arbitration, urged by many pacifically minded Liberals, could 'ever become a practical policy, unless it is coupled with the idea of an international police'. The present circumstances, he suggested, were 'a case for the intervention of an international police', but since none existed, 'the duty and burden' of action had been thrown upon Britain.[144] Granville, in the Lords, did not explicitly mention empire either, and stressed that Britain's interest in the canal was based on the principle of 'absence of monopoly, absence of special privilege; and whatever interest we have in the Canal, military or commercial, consists in its passage being perfectly secure and perfectly free'.[145] The only Liberal parliamentarian who can really be said to have foregrounded empire was Henry Labouchère MP, publisher of *Truth* and himself a bondholder, albeit one who later turned against intervention.[146] He said he 'really believed this intervention was absolutely necessary if England was to remain the great empire she was', although even he agreed that it was important to develop Egyptian 'national feeling'.[147] In general, any suggestion that Britain would extend her rule in Egypt permanently, on a similar basis to that which obtained in India, was highly problematic for Liberals. The *Pall Mall Gazette*, Gladstone's favourite paper, was pleased to find 'no trace of this sinister policy' in the government's statements.[148]

The government's action had now taken much of the wind out of the Conservatives' sails. The party's spokesmen had to be careful not to be seen to undermine

[142] Editorial, *The Standard*, 25 July 1882. For other examples of Conservative opinion, see 'The Press on Mr. Gladstone's speech', *Pall Mall Gazette*, 25 July 1882.
[143] HC Deb, 25 July 1882, vol. 272, cols 1710–25.
[144] HC Deb, 25 July 1882, vol. 272, cols 1799–1805.
[145] HL Deb, 24 July 1882, vol. 272, cols 1484–94.
[146] Chamberlain, 'British Public Opinion', 20; Herbert Sidebotham, 'Labouchere, Henry Du Pré (1831–1912)', rev. H. C. G. Matthew, *Oxford Dictionary of National Biography* (Oxford University Press, 2004; online edn, Oct. 2009) <http://www.oxforddnb.com/view/article/34367>, accessed 31 October 2012.
[147] HC Deb, 27 July 1882, vol. 272, cols 2044–53.
[148] 'The Radical Ministers on Egypt', *Pall Mall Gazette*, 26 July 1882.

national unity at a time of crisis. Northcote wrangled over Gladstone's efforts 'to throw the responsibility for the present state of things in Egypt' on to the Disraeli government, and protested at ministers' recent incompetence.[149] Salisbury accused the government of mishandling relations with the sultan, with the consequence that its use of the term 'European concert', in the absence of effective cooperation with Turkey, appeared to set up a confrontation between Christianity and Islam, 'very like a crusade'. He argued:

> the parading of this European concert as the principle of your action—the bringing forward on every opportunity of this combination of six Christian Powers to effect some particular thing in Mussulman territory—inevitably has the effect of impressing on the minds of Mussulmans, and especially of fanatical Mussulmans, that these enterprises are undertaken by Christians against the interests of Islam.[150]

Later in his career, Salisbury described Islam as a 'false religion', but at this point, in suggesting that the government's actions threatened to trigger a Christian–Muslim struggle, he revived the spectre of the 1857 Indian mutiny.[151] The government, for its part, agreed on the importance of not alienating Muslims, but claimed that the Khedive had the support of the 'most reasonable and sensible part of the Mahomedan population' and stressed that they themselves had 'no quarrel with the Mahomedan world'.[152] Whereas it is probably fair to say that the majority of politicians at this time held a rather stereotyped view of a fanatically disposed *homo islamicus*, it is also worth noting that here was also considerable variation in how this notion was deployed and the uses to which it could be put.[153] The danger posed by appearing to engage in crusade was, ironically enough, something that gave Salisbury some common ground with the Irish critic of intervention Frank O'Donnell.

In the lobbies, the government triumphed overwhelmingly. On the August bank holiday, Salisbury spoke at a Conservative demonstration at his country seat, Hatfield House. He noted, with satisfied amusement, that Bright and Gladstone, in their public exchanges over the former's resignation, had been disputing over the 'moral law': 'I hope that spectacle may have opened their eyes to the fact that the question of the duty of a nation is not to be settled by a summary phrase like that.' He pointed out too how the Disraeli government had been lambasted for its actions in Zululand four years earlier: 'in what we did we were not departing from the moral law, but were exercising the duty of self-defence, as our successors in the Government have done also'.[154] This, of course, accepted that Gladstone and

---

[149] HC Deb, 24 July 1882, vol. 272, cols 1591–7.

[150] HL Deb, 24 July 1882, vol. 272, cols 1497–1508.

[151] E. D. Steele, 'Lord Salisbury, the "False Religion" of Islam, and the Reconquest of the Sudan', in Edward M. Spiers (ed.), *Sudan: The Reconquest Reappraised* (London: Frank Cass, 1998), 11–33. Salisbury made the comment in a speech in June 1898.

[152] Dilke's speech, HC Deb, 25 July 1882, vol. 272, cols 1711–12. Note also Gladstone's interjection in response to Conservative speech at col. 1698.

[153] For a succinct discussion of the *homo islamicus* concept, see Zachary Lockman, *Contending Visions of the Middle East: The History and Politics of Orientalism*, 2nd edition (Cambridge: Cambridge University Press, 2010), 74–8.

[154] 'Lord Salisbury At Hatfield', *The Times*, 8 August 1882.

his ministers were now doing the right thing in Egypt. As Northcote put it, 'when Mr. Gladstone dissected and abused the policy of Lord Beaconsfield he never thought he should live to adopt it'. Conservatives could comfort themselves, he said, that 'we have contributed somewhat towards the vigorous prosecution of the campaign in Egypt'.[155] British forces landed on 16 August and within a month had scored a complete victory at the battle of Tel el-Kébir.[156] This did not mark the end of the debate about Egypt. The following year, Lord Randolph Churchill took up Blunt's charge that the Khedive had deliberately inspired the original Alexandria riots and the British had been complicit; he never received a satisfactory answer.[157] However, military triumph was the best reply to the government's more conventional critics. Meanwhile, the insistence that the occupation was only temporary formed a part of the government's rhetorical armoury that would in due course be maintained by its Conservative successors.

A few days before the expeditionary force landed, Gladstone had given a speech at London's Mansion House in which he said that Britain was acting in Egypt 'in prosecution of great interests of empire, which it is our duty to cherish and defend'.[158] The flourish was uncharacteristic; and, as ever, the prime minister faced accusations that he was not speaking up for British interests overtly enough. His pose of 'saintly disinterestedness' was said to be a sham by the *Saturday Review*. 'Nobody will believe that England undertakes the settlement of Egypt for nothing, and declarations which appear to bind her to do so are useless, and may be dangerous.'[159] The speech throws into relief how little, in general, Liberals chose to defend the intervention in explicitly imperial terms, even though that rhetoric was available to them. It also illuminates how, although there was a fundamental two-party consensus on the key question of invading Egypt, the language of selfless moral duty that Gladstone used to justify it was very different from Salisbury's 'dominant-imperialist' mode, even when Gladstone did choose to invoke empire explicitly.

Jonathan Parry has argued that during the 1880s debates over African and Asian issues came to be conducted mainly 'in terms of simple national interest and prestige', and that the progressive Liberal patriotic discourse of the previous decades was marginalized.[160] Yet in the case of Egypt, as we have seen, the position was more complex. Although the language of prestige and British interests certainly did come into play, these themes were integrated into recognizably Liberal languages of contractual duty, international cooperation, hostility to despotism, the aspiration to national freedom, and the rule of (moral and actual) law. If Conservative rhetoric helped drive the actual policy agenda to a greater extent than has been previously

---

[155] 'Sir Stafford Northcote At Weymouth', *The Times*, 25 August 1882.

[156] For some trenchant criticisms of the government's claims that the conflict was not a war, see 'The Trouble in Egypt', *The Herald of Peace*, 1 September 1882, copy in Gladstone Papers, British Library, Add MS 56450, ff. 51–2.

[157] Chamberlain, 'The Alexandria Massacre', 27–32.

[158] 'Banquet To Her Majesty's Ministers', *The Times*, 10 August 1882.

[159] 'Official Oratory at the Mansion House', *Saturday Review*, 12 August 1882.

[160] Parry (cited in De Nie).

recognized, then the Liberals nonetheless found distinctive ways of justifying their actions that were—if only at the linguistic level—far from completely incompatible with the principles of Midlothian. It was, of course, far easier for them to do this at a time of victory than it would be during their subsequent flailing over the Sudan. Nonetheless, the tendency to justify empire in apparently non-imperial and liberal terms was one that would also be in evidence in subsequent crises, and not only during ones that took place under Liberal governments. The tendency to define the virtues of the British Empire by reference to the flaws of the French 'other' would also be recognizable in later years.

Ironically, remarkably similar rhetorical justifications were being invoked to justify the adoption of a more strident French imperialism in Africa and elsewhere. On 10 September 1882, Gabriel Charmes, a Gambettiste and longstanding advocate of external intervention in Egypt, justified imperial expansion in the same way as his political mentor had done, combining social Darwinist thinking with an evocation of French global primacy in the Napoleonic age.[161] Writing in the pro-empire *Journal des Débats*, Charmes summarized his thoughts thus:

> The time is past when it was enough to be a great nation in Europe to be assured a future and to hold a preponderant place in history. The struggle of races and of peoples has from now on the whole globe as its theatre: each advances towards the conquest of unoccupied territories. Soon all the places will be taken . . . in the middle of this general expansionist movement, of this universal push, it would be the case that a France which stubbornly chose to take abdication for introspection [*recueillement*], on the pretext of having lost provinces in Europe, would lose again her prestige and her possessions on the Mediterranean.[162]

The mention of 'lost provinces' was, of course, a reference to Germany's annexation of Alsace-Lorraine in 1870—a loss so painful to Charmes, it appears, that he could not bring himself to name it. His comment highlights how, both in Britain and France, the obverse of the quest for 'prestige' was an equally desperate need to avoid its opposite, 'national humiliation'. As the rhetoric surrounding the 1898 Fashoda crisis was to show, emotional factors were intrinsic to the ways in which the two countries' interests were conceived. Their rivalry was not just about the pursuit of power and material interests, but also about the need to stave off the psychic threat of lost honour, respect, and esteem, perceived as a form of national abasement.

---

[161] Gabriel Charmes, Cairo letter reproduced in *Journal des débats*, 20 April 1882; also reproduced in TNA, FO 146/2420, enclosure 6 to Lord Lyons letter to Earl Granville, 20 April 1882.

[162] John Chipman, *French Power in Africa* (Oxford: Blackwell, 1988), 50.

2

Fashoda, 1898

'At the present moment it is impossible to open a newspaper without finding an account of WAR, DISTURBANCE, THE FEAR OF WAR, DIPLOMATIC CHANGES ACHIEVED OR IN PROSPECT, in every quarter of the world', noted an advert in *The Times* in May 1898. 'Under these circumstances it is ABSOLUTELY ESSENTIAL for anyone who desires to follow the course of events to possess a thoroughly good ATLAS.' One of the selling points of the atlas in question—published by *The Times* itself—was that it would allow its owner to follow the 'most minute details of the campaign on the Atbara, Fashoda, Uganda, the Italian-Abyssinian conflict &c.' The name Atbara would already have been quite familiar to readers, as the British had recently had a battle triumph there as part of the ongoing reconquest of the Sudan. Fashoda, much further up the Nile, remained for the time being more obscure. Newspaper readers might have been dimly aware that an expedition led by the French explorer Jean-Baptiste Marchand was attempting to reach the place via the Congo, but his fate remained a mystery. Within a few months, however, Captain Marchand and his successful effort to establish himself at Fashoda would be the hottest political topic, and the subject of multitudes of speeches and articles on both sides of the English Channel as the British and French empires collided, or at least scraped each other's hulls. It never did come to 'WAR', but there was certainly sufficient 'DISTURBANCE, FEAR OF WAR and DIPLOMATIC CHANGES ACHIEVED OR IN PROSPECT' to justify a *Times* reader purchasing an atlas, perhaps even the half-morocco version, 'very handsome, gilt edges', that retailed at 26 shillings.[1]

The clash in the Sudanese province of Bahr el-Ghaza, indicated in Map 2.1, was both a seminal moment in Anglo-French relations and a revealing one with respect to imperial language.[2] The existing literature, insofar as it discusses the rhetoric of the crisis, focuses on the diplomatic aspect, which is indeed significant. Robinson and Gallagher commented briefly on what they referred to as 'the new diplomacy' of the 1890s onwards, 'with its addiction to public warnings', which was very much

---

[1] *The Times*, 20 May 1898. The most detailed account of the Mission are Marc Michel, *La Mission Marchand* (Paris: Mouton/EPHE, 1972) and Pierre Pellissier, *Fachoda et la Mission Marchand, 1896–1899* (Paris: Perrin, 2011). Marchand's impact in France is expertly analysed in Edward Berenson, *Heroes of Empire: Five Charismatic Men and the Conquest of Empire* (Berkeley, CA: University of California Press, 2012), 166–96; and Berny Sèbe, *Heroic Imperialists in Africa: The promotion of British and French colonial heroes, 1879–1939* (Manchester: Manchester University Press, 2013), 105–6, 125–6, 163, 187, 198–200, 225–58.

[2] The crisis, of course, had wider repercussions as well, see: Jamie Cockfield, 'Germany and the Fashoda Crisis, 1898–99', *Central European History*, 16:3 (1983), 256–75.

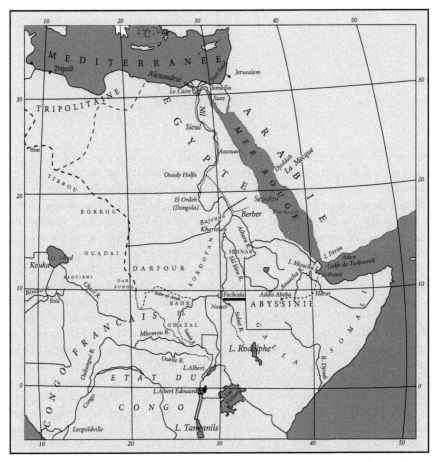

Map 2.1. The French geographical survey of the route to Fashoda. Fashoda lay on the eastern margins of the Sudanese province of Bahr el-Ghazal. As this 1897 map indicates, the French Foreign Ministry, too, needed help in identifying Marchand's location.

MAE, 123CPCOM15: Commandant Marchand, 1895–8

in evidence during the crisis.[3] Bernard I. Finel and Kristin M. Lord have used Fashoda as an example of how, in relatively 'transparent' political systems such as the British and the French, bellicose 'noise' created by domestic politics may drown out the more nuanced messages that diplomatic actors try to send each other. They observe that—at a time when the press verged on the hysterical and when politicians from both political parties made inflammatory public comments—there

---

[3] Ronald Robinson and John Gallagher, *Africa and the Victorians: The Official Mind of Imperialism*, Macmillan, London, 1961, p. 335. They may have exaggerated the novelty of this phenomenon.

'seems to have been a systematic bias in the nature of international communication which overstated aggressive, belligerent statements, and downplayed conciliatory statements'.[4]

DOMESTIC CONTEXTS

In addition to rhetoric's role in stoking up tensions, there are further angles to be considered. The debate over Fashoda lays bare both the similarities and the differences between Anglo-French assumptions about 'civilization', the rights that attended conquest, and how the process of 'co-imperialism' was to be regulated. Falling at the height of the Dreyfus affair in which a Jewish army officer, Captain Alfred Dreyfus, endured a protracted retrial after being wrongly convicted of spying for Germany, British official readings of the Fashoda crisis were also conditioned by the growing conviction that the worst aspects of French political culture—an overweening state, an irresponsible military leadership, and an intrusive Catholic Church—were too apparent for comfort.[5] Viewed from the British perspective, *dignity*, above all, was at stake. The French were obsessed with the prospect of their own impending humiliation; whereas the British, from a position of strength, showed verbal concern for French *amour propre*, even though their own actions seemed guaranteed to dent it severely.

What the rhetoricians of both countries had in common was their willingness to discuss the fate of the disputed area exclusively as a problem in their own relations, without the slightest reference to the possible wishes of the indigenous population. This is unsurprising, but there was more to the diplomatic grandstanding than appeared at first sight. The British were superficially united, but the episode revealed domestic political tensions with respect to empire that were to boil over once the Boer War started a year later. This was something that French ministers were only too happy to point out. The hypocrisy underlying British claims to be serving wider European interests by buttressing a venal Egyptian regime were, the French claimed, of a piece with a Conservative rhetoric of fairness belied by British actions in Ireland and, most recently, South Africa.[6]

Certainly, the British political environment had changed radically in the sixteen years since Gladstone's government had occupied Egypt. In 1885, General Charles Gordon was killed in Khartoum before the arrival of a relief column belatedly sent to rescue him and his Egyptian troops from their siege by rebels led by the Mahdi, or 'Expected One'. Britain and Egypt withdrew from the Sudan, which had been under Egyptian/Ottoman control since the 1820s; at home, Gladstone was vilified

[4] Bernard M. Finel and Kristin M. Lord, 'The Surprising Logic of Transparency', *International Studies Quarterly* (1999) 43, 315–39, at 327.

[5] Robert Tombs, '"Lesser Breeds without the Law": The British Establishment and the Dreyfus Affair, 1894-1899', *Historical Journal*, 41:2 (1998), 495–510; Ruth Harris, *The Man on Devil's Island: Alfred Dreyfus and the Affair that Divided France* (London: Penguin, 2010), 223, 247.

[6] MAE, 189PAAP11 Gabriel Hanotaux papers, 'Relations franco-britanniques, note à consulter', n.d. June 1898.

as the 'Murderer of Gordon'. During the political convulsions of 1885–6 he became a convert to the policy of Irish Home Rule, splitting the Liberals and bringing to an end their long period of hegemony. The departure of the Liberal Unionists—prominent among them Joseph Chamberlain—severely weakened the Liberal Party, but this was not its only significance. In the longer run, the Liberal Unionist alliance with Lord Salisbury's Conservatives would significantly affect the dynamic of British imperial politics. The chaos of the 1892–5 Liberal government (which saw Gladstone's final retirement and his replacement by the vain and ineffectual Lord Rosebery) was followed by Chamberlain's appointment as colonial secretary in Salisbury's new administration. 'Radical Joe', as he had once been known, was by no means wholly trusted by the Tory establishment, but he now espoused an assertive variety of constructive imperialism that sat uneasily with Salisbury's more cautious balance-of-power approach. It might even be said that the adherence of the Chamberlainites to the Conservative Party was as serious for the fate of that body as the departure of the free trade Peelites (including Gladstone) had been in the 1840s. Already, at the time of Fashoda, Chamberlain was a potentially destabilizing factor, increasing the pressure on Salisbury to avoid any sign of willingness to negotiate with the French.

The complexion of French politics had also changed markedly since the early 1880s, with profound implications at home and overseas. The looser republican alignments of the Third Republic's early years were, by the late 1890s, calcifying into more ideologically polarized positions identifiable with a liberal republican centre-left and a fervently anti-Socialist, nationalist right.[7] The latter was epitomized by the rabble-rousing *anti-Dreyfusard* ideologue, Paul Déroulède, and his political instrument, the *Ligue des Patriotes* (LDP). This was a fiercely anti-establishment movement likely to provide the plebiscitary vanguard for any concerted efforts to overthrow the republican regime.[8] As the Fashoda crisis neared its climax, on 25 October 1898, Déroulède, speaking to his supporters in Paris, lambasted the weakness of republican combinations. 'We want neither anarchy, nor monarchy,' he insisted, 'we want [hier]*archy*. France has a thirst to be governed!'[9]

In the event, Déroulède nosedived into treasonous self-destruction after a failed coup attempt in February 1899.[10] But the radical nationalism and street protest of Déroulède's Parisian LDP proved something of a model for *Action Française*, a movement that coalesced in the spring of 1898 and one that signified the consolidation of a more lasting far rightist threat to republican democracy.[11] Meanwhile, an emergent Socialist Party and class-based trade union militancy were changing the very nature of French republican identity, of what it meant to be an engaged

---

[7] Bertrand Taithe, *The Killer Trail: A Colonial Scandal in the Heart of Africa* (Oxford: Oxford University Press, 2009), 185–7.

[8] Peter M. Rutkoff, 'The *Ligue des Patriotes*: The Nature of the Radical Right and the Dreyfus Affair', *French Historical Studies*, 8:4 (1974), 587–8, 594–601; Harris, *The Man on Devil's Island*, 229–36; Passmore, *The Right in France*, 101–15.

[9] 'M. Paul Déroulède', *Le Figaro*, 25 October 1898, p. 1.

[10] Maurice Larkin, '"La République en danger"? The Pretenders, the Army and Déroulède, 1898–1899', *English Historical Review*, 100:394 (1985), 101–2; Rutkoff, 'The *Ligue des Patriotes*', 587–8.

[11] Passmore, *The Right in France*, 113–14, 122–3.

citizen in a polity still overwhelmingly run by an *haut bourgeois*, professionally trained, male elite.[12] As the Fashoda crisis entered its final weeks in September 1898, the French capital's *grands boulevards* were repeatedly paralysed by striking building workers who reviled the well-to-do *entrepreneurs* and *fonctionnaires* they saw as their nemesis.[13] By mid-October thousands of troops were deployed to police the marches amid official fears of a syndicalist-inspired general strike.[14]

It was, however, the Dreyfus case that best illustrated how embittered the country's politics had become. Dreyfus's cause divided French society along several fault lines: institutional, ideological, religious, and juridical. By 1898 the issue was less about the officer's innocence and more about the discredit and sheer humiliation likely to befall the army and, to a lesser degree, the Catholic Church (each of them decidedly imperialist institutions), were the original conspiracy against him revealed.[15] So much so that the writer Emile Zola—whose fiery open letters in the new print voice of radical socialism, *L'Aurore*, in early 1898 compelled the Dreyfus case to be reopened— was twice convicted of libel over the course of the year. Twelve months before Dreyfus was shipped back from Devil's Island to be retried a safe distance from Paris at Rennes, Zola's convictions confirmed that justice ran a poor second to elite self-interest.[16]

High Command cover-ups, the ingrained anti-Semitism of the Catholic bishopric, and the grisly prison suicide on 31 August of Colonel Hubert Joseph Henry, the real traitor behind the original spying offence, brought French political culture to a new low. From the ashes would spring a new human rights lobby, the League of the Rights of Man (*Ligue des droits de l'homme*). The crying need for it in a Republic supposedly founded on principles of equality before the law was striking.[17] The *Dreyfusard* press, led since 1897 by the indomitable, if obsessive, *L'Aurore*, wrote feverishly meanwhile of alleged coup plots to which Marchand, once he returned from Africa, might or might not be enlisted.[18]

During the weeks after Captain Marchand, his eight fellow officers, and their escort of 120 or so *tirailleurs sénégalais* settled into the long-vacated Egyptian government buildings in Fashoda on 10 July 1898, France's domestic politics were particularly venomous.[19] In these circumstances, colonial expansion, which,

---

[12] Christophe Charle, 'Les parlementaires: avant-garde ou arrière-garde d'une société en mouvement', in Jean-Marie Mayeur, Jean-Pierre Chaline and Alain Corbin (eds), *Les Parlementaires de la Troisième République* (Paris: Publications de la Sorbonne, 2003), 49–60.

[13] 'Les terrassiers—18,000 grévistes', *L'Aurore*, 16 September 1898; 'La grève—résistance des entrepreneurs', *L'Aurore*, 30 September 1898.

[14] 'La Grève générale du bâtiment', *L'Aurore*, 4 October 1898; 'Paris en état de siège', *L'Aurore*, 8 October 1898; 'L'extension de la grève', *L'Aurore*, 11 October 1898. For the dangers intrinsic to the army's policing of strikes, see Anja Johansen, *Soldiers as Police: The French and Prussian Armies and the Policing of Popular Protest, 1889–1914* (Aldershot: Ashgate, 2005), especially chapters 3 and 6.

[15] For the Affair's colonial echoes, see: James P. Daughton, 'A Colonial Affair? Dreyfus and the French Empire', *Historical Reflections/Réflexions Historiques*, 31:3 (2005), 469–74.

[16] 'Déroulède jugé par Rochefort', *L'Aurore*, 22 October 1898; 'La triomphe de la liberté. Dreyfus Innocent', *L'Aurore*, 28 October 1898.

[17] William Irvine, *Between Justice and Politics: The Ligue des Droits de l'Homme* (Stanford, CA; Stanford University Press, 2006), 5–52 *passim*.

[18] 'On cherche un homme pour faire un coup d'état', *L'Aurore*, 15 September 1898, p. 1.

[19] For a succinct depiction of France's many internal political fault-lines at the turn of the century, see Passmore, *The Right in France*, 101–42 *passim*.

in the previous decade, had divided as much as it had united the French people, offered an antidote. Unabashed imperial heroism, uncomplicated and easier to digest than the endless polemics of the Dreyfus case, offered a welcome tonic to a France whose institutional fabric seemed to be tearing apart.[20] Whatever the international crisis it provoked, Marchand's underdog obstinacy at Fashoda became a rare source of consensus in France. To ardent republicans on the *Dreyfusard* left, Marchand, thanks to his martial valour, his charismatic leadership, and, of course, his British adversary, personified all that was best in Napoleonic legend: a loyal servant of the Republic untainted by the army's reactionary politics at home. In the rhetoric of the anti-republican right, he represented something more, a selfless patriot betrayed by a venal political class and a saviour who might yet return, if not from exile, then from the African interior to rescue his beloved homeland from sclerotic government by coalition.[21]

By contrast, historical explanations for the British expansion towards the Upper Nile tend to focus, not on the machinations of domestic politics, but on Great Power rivalry.[22] In Robinson and Gallagher's analysis, the 'official mind' did not regard the area as having any inherent worth; it only became necessary to secure it when the prospect that the French might intrude threatened British security in the Mediterranean and hence the safety of the route to India. Terje Tvedt has countered convincingly that British officials in Egypt appreciated the value of controlling the Nile waters, and yearned to improve their regulation because of the centrality of irrigation to the Egyptian economy, irrespective of any threat posed by France's activities. These officials—notably Lord Cromer, consul-general in Cairo—assumed that the reconquest was a matter of when, not if.[23]

French officials in Cairo and their Foreign Ministry patrons in Paris discerned the thrust of British expansionism. Anticipating that a deal over Sudan would have to be done, their principal concern was to construct a strong negotiating platform. This would, in turn, be built on watertight arguments about Khedival autonomy, respect for residual Ottoman interests in Egypt, and France's legitimate right to delimit the eastern boundaries of its three nascent colonies that abutted Sudan: the French Congo, Ubanghi-Chari, and Chad.[24] It was, for instance, indicative that

---

[20] Edward Berenson, 'Fashoda, Dreyfus, and the Myth of Jean-Baptiste Marchand', *Yale French Studies*, 111:1 (2007), 136–7.
[21] Berenson, 'Fashoda, Dreyfus, and the Myth', 140–2; Sèbe, *Heroic Imperialists*, 225–6. For longer-term context, see: Venita Datta, *"L'appel au soldat"*: Visions of the Napoleonic Legend in Popular Culture of the *Belle Epoque*', *French Historical Studies*, 28 (Winter 2005), 1–30.
[22] T. W. Riker, 'A Survey of British Policy in the Fashoda Crisis', *Political Science Quarterly*, 44:1 (Mar., 1929), 54–78; A. J. P. Taylor, 'Prelude to Fashoda: The Question of the Upper Nile, 1894-5', *English Historical Review*, 65:254 (1950), 52–80; Keith Eubank, 'The Fashoda Crisis Re-examined', *The Historian*, 22, 2 (1960), 145–62; Patricia Wright, *Conflict on the Nile: The Fashoda Incident of 1898* (London: Heinemann, 1972); Darrell Bates, *The Fashoda Incident of 1898: Encounter on the Nile* (Oxford: Oxford University Press, 1984).
[23] Terje Tvedt, 'The Race to Fashoda: Robinson and Gallagher Revisited', *Forum for Development Studies*, 19:2 (1992), 195–210; on Egypt's economic position after the British arrival, see Roger Owen, *The Middle East in the World Economy, 1800–1914* new edn (London: I.B. Tauris, 1993), 216–43.
[24] MAE, 123CPCOM15, Foreign Ministry Direction Afrique, 'Projet de règlement des questions pendantes dans le nord-est Africain', 10 February 1897.

Théophile Delcassé, foreign minister as the Fashoda crisis came to a head, prided himself on the internal logic and rhetorical cohesion of the arguments put forward in refutation of Britain's claim to southern Sudan.[25] If anything, greater French assertiveness accelerated the advancement of Britain's imperial claims, and the *public* dimension of this was in some sense more important than the finer points of strategic calculation. As G. N. Sanderson has put it: 'Ultimately, the quarrel was not about Fashoda, or about the fate of the Sudan, or even about the security of the Nile waters and of Egypt; it was about the relative status of Britain and France as powers.'[26] And that status rested on the manipulation of political symbols.

Triumph and defeat, it seemed, would not be determined solely by boots on the ground. They would also be defined rhetorically: victory was something to be *claimed*, although the ability to do this persuasively was of course strongly determined by diplomatic and military realities. The political economy of the European presence in Africa was also changing more rapidly than ever. In Africa especially, the French and British colonial annexations of the 1880s and early 1890s were, by the latter half of the decade, matched by the proliferation of trading company ventures, exploratory mining, and agro-business, transport, and infrastructure projects.[27] The stakes in this rhetorical contest were thus increasingly high, even if the basic strategic equation of British military predominance in the Upper Nile Valley suggested only one outcome.

In light of this, French leaders faced the harder task, turning unedifying defeat into noble self-sacrifice. This meant focusing on three things. One was quasi-juridical: the significance of the earlier Anglo-Egyptian evacuation of Sudan and the supposed *terra nullius*, or unclaimed space, which resulted. Another was politically calculating: the affirmation of stoical French restraint in the face of jingoistic British bullying. Last, and most important, was the figure of Marchand himself. His principled refusal to withdraw without firm instructions became the embodiment of the contrast between French respect for diplomatic form and legal process next to Britain's roughshod land-grabbing.[28] Recalling the outcome of the crisis in hindsight in the penny press newspaper, *Le Journal*, one former French minister captured the rhetorical flavour of this French claim to the moral high ground: Marchand, he claimed, 'represented a France so morally superior, so

[25] MAE, 123CPCOM17, Delcassé to French Ambassador, St Petersburg, 2 October 1898.

[26] G. N. Sanderson, 'The Origins and Significance of the Anglo-French Confrontation at Fashoda, 1898', in Prosser Gifford and Wm. Roger Louis (eds), *France and Britain in Africa: Imperial Rivalry and Colonial Rule* (New Haven, CT: Yale University Press, 1971), 285–331, at 289.

[27] See MAE, 123CPCOM15 for details of African commercial contracts awarded between 1895 and 1898.

[28] Typical of contemporary work that cast Marchand as a heroic redeemer of French national pride were: Louis Guétant, *Marchand-Fachoda. La Mission Congo-Nil, Sa préparation. Ses pratiques. Son but. Ses résultats* (Paris: Bureaux des Temps Nouveaux, 1899); Gabriel Galland, *Une poignée d'héros: La Mission Marchand à travers l'Afrique* (Limoges: Eugène Ardant, 1900); Michel Morphy, *Le Commandant Marchand et ses compagnons d'armes à travers l'Afrique. Histoire complète et anecdotique de la mission* (Paris: Geffroy, 1899–1900). Morphy was the most prolific producer of literary 'Marchandise'. His serialization of Marchand's African journeys ran to twenty-eight volumes, see: Sèbe, *Heroic Imperialists*, 74.

indifferent to economic gain, that its "only honorarium is honor itself"'.[29] Simi-larly, the preface to one of the many hagiographical accounts of Marchand's adventures crowding French bookstands at the turn of the century began thus: 'Here, written with sincerity and emotion, is a brief history of the Marchand Mission. Its purpose is to confirm our young people's love of their flag by offering them an example of one of the purest glories of our young army.'[30]

The British government naturally wanted to prove the opposite. Hence the importance of public opinion—in the sense of opinions expressed in public, via speeches and the press, rather than that of 'what the public really thought', which in this instance is largely unknowable. It was not that public opinion drove the British government to adopt expansionist policies against its inclination. Rather, the brou-haha foreclosed options for resolving the crisis in a way consistent with French dignity by forcing Salisbury—who might have preferred to be emollient, even as he insisted on Marchand's withdrawal—to adopt a more overtly hard-line public stance than he probably cared for. Only by so doing could he ensure that a British strategic advance—which was always on the cards, in the particular circumstances of the Anglo-French collision at Fashoda—was converted into a domestic political and rhetorical success.

REGIONAL RIVALRIES

If Fashoda itself was not much of a name to conjure with before the late summer of 1898, it can hardly be said that the crisis came out of a clear blue sky. The possibility of some sort of clash between Britain and France in the region had been widely canvassed for years. Many French politicians resented the marginal-ization of France's interests in Egypt under the British occupation which, in spite of repeated protestations, was turning out not to be temporary at all. Most influential was Gabriel Hanotaux, respected republican senator, youthful foreign minister (he arrived at the Quai d'Orsay aged forty-one), and a firm protagonist of France's recently minted alliance with Imperial Russia.[31] A skilled rhetorician, Hanotaux brought three operating assumptions to imperial affairs.[32] First was that French empire-building was ultimately contingent on the prior necessity to sustain liberal republican rule in France. Second was that the competitive edge to European overseas expansion, while intrinsic to the process, should not become the pretext for armed conflict within Europe itself. Third was that this diplomatic containment of imperial rivalry depended on mutual recognition between France and Britain, still the two leading colonial actors, that the legal devices used to justify either territorial acquisition or exclusive privileges should be consistent.[33]

[29] Cited in Berenson, 'Fashoda, Dreyfus, and the Myth', 140.
[30] M. Perrenet, *Fachoda: L'épopée de Marchand* (Limoges: M. Barbou, 1901), preface by François Coppet.
[31] Jerome Greenfield, 'Gabriel Hanotaux and French Grand Strategy, 1894–8', *International History Review*, 38:3 (2016), 462–8.
[32] As Jerome Greenfield has recently suggested, colonial matters were generally secondary to Hanotaux's overriding desire to consolidate France's alliance with Russia: see Greenfield, 'Gabriel Hanotaux', 468–72.
[33] MAE, 189PAAP11, Hanotaux papers, Hanotaux letter to Cairo Consul, 21 June 1898.

All three were linked, and each demanded rhetorical ingenuity. Republicans, meaning those who considered the prevailing system of government in France preferable to monarchist, presidential, conservative, or more theocratic alternatives, were never united in their attitude to empire.[34] But republican defenders of the regime generally rallied to imperial causes when failure to do so threatened to concede political advantage to their anti-republican opponents.[35] Hanotaux's steadfast opposition to Britain's accretion of power over Egypt and, increasingly, Sudan, should be seen in this light. He was equally well aware that French colonial governments, some reliant on colonial army officer-administrators, were pursuing their own aggressive frontier imperialism in Indochina, sub-Saharan Africa, and on Algeria's border margins.[36] Often they acted with powerful encouragement from the colonialist lobby, the *Parti Colonial* at home. France's 1894 expedition to Madagascar was but the latest example of this expansionism in action.[37]

Hanotaux, for his part, seemed ambivalent about such expansion. He knew some of its military protagonists, Marchand included, and—surreptitiously—endorsed their schemes.[38] He also recognized that it made more sense to conciliate the *Parti Colonial* than to antagonize it. But if the latest burst of French annexations—and their British equivalents in Sudan and elsewhere—were hard to prevent, and harder still to control, their consequences for European politics had to be restricted nonetheless.[39] War, certainly, was to be averted. But the French Empire must hold even so. Without it, Hanotaux feared, France risked sinking to the rank of Spain, a once great imperial nation whose remaining overseas possessions from Cuba to the Philippines were breaking away.[40] Racially conditioned and instrumentally self-serving, this crisis management of one empire clash after another was substantially a game of rhetorical prowess. The stronger the case made before the eyes of domestic and international opinion, the greater the likelihood that the particular crisis would not escalate.

Britain's advance into Sudan was anomalous from this French official perspective because the justifications advanced for it seemed unconvincing and crudely manipulative.[41] The resulting escalation of the crisis in southern Sudan was thus of

[34] As Jonathan Derrick notes, anti-colonial opinion among the republican left remained something of an anti-militarist, *Dreyfusard* reflex: see his 'The Dissenters: Anti-Colonialism in France, 1900-40', in Tony Chafer and Amanda Sackur (eds), *Promoting the Colonial Idea: Propaganda and Visions of Empire in France* (Basingstoke: Palgrave-Macmillan, 2002), 54–5.

[35] Berenson, 'Fashoda, Dreyfus, and the Myth', 141–2.

[36] Pascal Venier, 'A Campaign of Colonial Propaganda: Gallieni, Lyautey and the Defence of the Military regime in Madagascar', in Chafer and Sackur, *Promoting the Colonial Idea*, 32–4.

[37] MAE, 189PAAP4, Hanotaux papers, mémoires et documents, tome IV, 1894–1896, lettre de M. Lemyre de Villers, Tamatave, 3 novembre 1894, 'Début de l'affaire de Madagascar'.

[38] Sèbe, *Heroic Imperialists*, 227, 232.   [39] Greenfield, 'Gabriel Hanotaux', 473–4.

[40] MAE, 189PAAP11 Hanotaux papers, 'Relations franco-britanniques, note à consulter', n.d. June 1898. It is worth noting that the news that France had sunk to fourth place as a global exporter of manufactured goods provoked adverse press comment and political soul-searching in early summer 1898: see, *Le Petit Journal*, 18 May 1898.

[41] MAE, 189PAAP4 Hanotaux mémoires et documents, IV, 'A.S. de l'expédition du Soudan', 25 September 1896.

Britain's doing: the diplomatists and their legal advisers had not built an incontro-vertible case and, knowing this, the politicians worked up public opinion instead. Alphonse de Courcel, the long-serving French ambassador to London, put it nicely: taking refuge in 'the effervescence of popular passion' was the last resort of a British political leadership unable to win the argument through cordial negotiation.[42] There was, for instance, abiding resentment in Paris at Britain's 1894 treaty with Belgium, which had attempted to block the French route to the Sudan by leasing the Bahr al-Ghazal area in the south of the country to the Congo Free State.[43] (This failed: under French pressure, Emperor Leopold II re-leased half of it to them.)[44]

In Paris, with Anglophobia raging but with ministers divided on the merits of challenging the British, a mission to the Upper Nile was announced and then abruptly recalled.[45] This provided the context for a Commons statement made by Sir Edward Grey, under-secretary of state for foreign affairs in the Rosebery govern-ment, in March 1895. He poured cold water on rumours of a new French mission:

> I cannot think it is possible that these rumours deserve credence, because the advance
> of a French Expedition under secret instructions right from the other side of Africa,
> into a territory over which our claims have been known for so long, would be not
> merely an inconsistent and unexpected act, but it must be perfectly well known to the
> French government that it would be an unfriendly act, and would be so viewed by
> England.[46]

This was to be a touchstone pronouncement that was repeatedly referred to in Britain during the 1898 crisis. It was convenient for Conservatives to quote it as it gave evidence of bipartisan support for their policy; it was equally convenient for Liberals do so, as it allowed them to claim that the British policy of firmness originated with them, rather than with their opponents.

French ministers and press commentators were equally willing to cite Grey's remarks, but to make a very different case. Foremost among them was Grey's opposite number, the former *Grande École* academic, Hanotaux. True to his historian's training, Hanotaux set out to dismantle Grey's arguments with a devastating narrative of contrary evidence. This he did with a set-piece Senate speech on 5 April 1895. Hanotaux dwelt first on Sudan's sheer immensity, which, when combined with the ferocity of Mahdist resistance, made titular colonial control meaningless. Egypt's Khedival government had the sense to recognize this. Their British patrons, on the other hand, concocted various diplomatic devices to carve out a notional sphere of influence that was, at best, theoretical; at worst, a

---

[42] MAE, 123CPCOM17, Ambassador de Courcel, London, to Delcassé, 10 October 1898.

[43] F. H. Hinsley, 'International Rivalry, 1885-1895', in E. A. Benians, James Butler and C. E. Carrington (eds), *The Cambridge History of the British Empire Vol. III: The Empire-Commonwealth 1870–1919* (Cambridge: Cambridge University Press, 1959), 255–91, at 283–4.

[44] Guy Vanthemsche, *Belgium and the Congo, 1885–1980* (Cambridge: Cambridge University Press, 2012), 105.

[45] Thomas Pakenham, *The Scramble for Africa 1876–1912* (London: Weidenfeld and Nicolson, 1991), 456–7.

[46] HC Deb, 28 March 1895, vol. 32, cols 405–6.

subterfuge. The 1890 Anglo-German agreement partitioning the domains of the sultan of Zanzibar was typical in this regard: a unilateral claim to territory stretching as far as the Upper Nile Valley was as vague as it was expansive. More to the point it had nothing to do with Zanzibar; nor did France ever recognize its validity. Much the same was true of Britain's May 1894 accords with the Congo Free State. This, too, the French refuted, something that the Belgian Royal House and the Foreign Office recognized under an amended, and more limited convention produced three months later in August. It recognized French rights in the Upper Ubanghi Basin, which bordered Sudan's Bahr el-Ghazal province. This was significant because, if anything, it situated the outer margins of French colonial control closer to the Upper Nile than the southern limits of Anglo-Egyptian administration to the north.[47]

Faced with this reversal, the Liberal government had decided to reactivate their claims under the 1890 accord with Germany. Although these claims were already moot, as a good European and a responsible imperial neighbour, France, Hanotaux declared, was willing to talk. This reasoned French approach, he implied, stood in marked contrast to Britain's blundering. Asserting a 'sphere of influence' where none existed and, still worse, without defining its precise extent, was not just premature, it was diplomatically amateur. 'Tell us,' he said, 'where Egypt ends, and where this sphere which you claim commences.' It was Britain's refusal to do so that constituted the 'unfriendly proceeding'. Having thus thrown Grey's words back at him, Hanotaux finished in more emollient mood. Fruitful negotiations, as the recent Anglo-French agreement delimiting the Sierra Leone frontier confirmed, were based on compromise and precise cartography. Here was the sting in the tail. For good maps demanded great explorers. And their enterprises should be encouraged, not hampered.[48]

Why did Hanotaux say this? He was, after all, more concert diplomat than African imperialist, meaning that he understood the international complications intrinsic to the *Parti Colonial*'s penchant for using exploratory missions as the vanguard of French frontier imperialism.[49] This did not alter the fact of mounting *Parti Colonial* pressure, orchestrated by the *Comité de l'Afrique française*, to sanction more exploratory missions through eastern Congo towards the Upper Nile. Furthermore, this was pressure to which the recently established Ministry of Colonies seemed likely to bend. It was no secret that senior ministry personnel were receptive to *Parti Colonial* support for greater ambition in empire affairs. In the following year, 1896, their ministerial head—a relatively junior figure, André Lebon, who, like Hanotaux, came into politics by way of Paris academia—won the colonial lobbyists' plaudits for his vigorous response to a major uprising in France's newest dependency: Madagascar. Hanotaux, who kept a firm grip on Egyptian affairs to

---

[47] MAE, 123CPCOM17: Blue Book, Egypt, no. 2 1898, annex item no. 5: Hanotaux speech, 5 April 1895.
[48] MAE, 123CPCOM17: Blue Book, Egypt, no. 2 1898, annex item no. 5: Hanotaux speech, 5 April 1895.
[49] C. M. Andrew and A. S. Kanya-Forstner, 'Gabriel Hanotaux, the Colonial Party and the Fashoda Strategy', in Ernest Penrose (ed.), *European Imperialism and the Partition of Africa* (London: Frank Cass, 1975), 61–4.

the exclusion to Lebon's ministry, risked being outflanked by his more conservative ministerial colleagues.[50] So the foreign minister's apparent support for the likes of Victor Liotard (whose foraging through the Ubanghi Basin had alarmed Whitehall observers) and, later, Jean-Baptiste Marchand, served two rhetorical functions. It was a sop to the troublesome imperialists at home. And it warned the British that, unless they negotiated, the *Parti Colonial* would only make things worse.[51]

For all his rhetorical skill, Hanotaux's remarks did not have the lasting impact of Grey's. Perhaps this was unsurprising. The deputy foreign secretary's comments had lent a 'somewhat sensational tone' to parliamentary proceedings, 'which had promised to be dull enough'.[52] When French Ambassador de Courcel called at the Foreign Office on 1 April to deliver a formal protest at the junior minister's intemperate remarks, Grey twisted the screw even more. He began by conceding that bilateral talks over the Upper Nile territories would have to take place. But he justified his strong language on the grounds that Britain would have grounds for complaint if, once such discussions began, France were to send a military mission into the disputed territory.[53]

Heavy-handed and eerily prescient as it was, perhaps more to the point was that Grey's 'masculine statement of English claims' was no spontaneous *ex cathedra* pronouncement.[54] The government was under attack for its alleged weakness in the face of French expansionism in Siam and in foreign policy generally. 'It is the contempt excited by the habitual demeanour of our Foreign Office under Glad-stonian Administrations which makes the Anglophobe Party among our Parisian contemporaries,' argued the right-wing *Morning Post*, 'and we may hope that the language of Sir Edward Grey last night is a pledge of a permanent change in our demeanour.'[55] By braving the wrath of the radicals—Henry Labouchère attacked Grey's 'speech of menace addressed to France'—the government was able to compel the support of the Unionist opposition.[56] This was delivered in Chamberlain's typical double-edged fashion. He said that Grey's assurance was 'perfectly satisfactory if, as we most earnestly hope, the position is understood and accepted with equal clearness by the Representatives of the French Government'. However, he immediately called that into question: 'If we have ever entertained any doubt on that point I must say it is due to those Debates in the French Assembly which are not always characterised by the reserve which we endeavour to maintain here.' He

---

[50] MAE, 123CPCOM15, André Lebon to Hanotaux, 'A.S. de Bahr el-Ghazal', 16 March 1897. In the event Lebon was ousted from the Ministry of Colonies in 1898 after it emerged that he had sanctioned the especially harsh conditions under which Dreyfus was detained on Devil's Island. His dismissal from office gave him the time to write one of the earliest insider's accounts of the crisis: André Lebon, *La Politique de la France en Afrique, 1896–1898: Mission Marchand—Niger—Madagascar* (Paris: Plon, 1901).
[51] MAE, 123CPCOM17: Blue Book, Egypt, no. 2 1898, annex item no. 5: Hanotaux speech, 5 April 1895.
[52] 'Our London Letter', *Aberdeen Weekly Journal*, 29 March 1895.
[53] MAE, 123CPCOM17, De Courcel, London, to Delcassé, 10 October 1898.
[54] 'E Nilo Quid Fit', *Pall Mall Gazette*, 29 March 1895.
[55] Untitled editorial, *The Morning Post*, 29 March 1895.
[56] HC Deb, 28 March 1895, vol. 32, col 417.

demanded that the French government repudiate the *Parti Colonial* extremists.[57] Stopping short of accusing him of deliberate mischief-making, the *Daily News* observed that 'It can do no good to quote in the House of Commons the reckless observations [of] irresponsible Deputies in the French Chamber.'[58]

Grey's statement fulfilled its function of dealing with domestic criticism rather more effectively than it succeeded in warning off the French. Obviously, the government must have hoped that it would serve to deter them; but what could be sold in London as a calm and deliberate statement 'with nothing in it that could give umbrage' was regarded in Paris as impudent and highly provocative.[59] As far as the French were concerned, the British did not possess any genuine claims in their own right. The *Journal des Débats* stated: 'The Khedive in our eyes is the sole legitimate head of the whole valley of the Nile under the suzerainty of the sultan. France will respect under all circumstances the rights of the Porte and of Egypt on the Upper Nile. She recognizes no others.'[60] These views were widely disseminated to newspaper readers in Britain via Reuters telegram, confirming the beliefs of those who thought that the French used the Egyptian issue as a 'stock grievance' to be brought out whenever their colonial policies were called into question.[61] (French diplomats and press commentators later insisted, albeit disingenuously, that their Tunisian protectorate respected the Ottoman sultan's treaty rights whereas Britain ignored them in its domineering control of the Khedive.)[62] There was, however, a degree of nuance in British conceptions of how French imperial politics operated. 'It is necessary, of course, to distinguish between responsible official opinion on the Seine, and the ill-regulated pretensions of the "Colonial Party" outside', observed the *Standard*. 'The exponents of the aspirations of this school are comparatively few, and find very little solid response in the temper of the masses throughout France.'[63] Attempted subtlety thereby acted as the servant of British complacency.

And the French, of course, were not in the end dissuaded. The background to their final decision was complex. Rosebery's government collapsed in June, and the Liberals were heavily defeated in the general election that followed. Salisbury was now foreign secretary as well as prime minister. Gabriel Hanotaux, still the French foreign minister, was eager to secure a rapprochement with the British, although he remained reluctant to accept their supremacy in Egypt.[64] He found that the new government was responsive; the British Foreign Office downplayed Grey's statement, by which so much store would be set three years later. But in November, the French government fell in its turn. Hanotaux's replacement, the accomplished

---

[57] HC Deb, 28 March 1895, vol. 32, col. 408.

[58] 'England and France in Africa', *Daily News*, 29 March 1895.

[59] Untitled editorial, *The Standard*, 29 March 1895.

[60] Quoted in 'Britain and France', *Glasgow Herald*, 30 March 1895.

[61] 'England, France and Africa', *The Morning Post*, 30 March 1895.

[62] MAE, 189PAAP11, Hanotaux papers, Hanotaux letter to Cairo Consul, 21 June 1898; *La Croix supplément*, Monday 31 October 1898: 'Le Protectorat de l'Egypte', p. 1; for context, see: Mary Lewis, *Divided Rule*, 22–3, 59–64.

[63] Untitled editorial, *The Standard*, 29 March 1895.

[64] Andrew and Kanya-Forstner, 'Gabriel Hanotaux', 65–8.

scientist but relative political novice Marcellin Berthelot, was persuaded by colonial enthusiasts in officialdom to support a mission headed by Marchand; something of a *fait accompli* as Hanotaux had already acceded to it.[65] Even so, the more experienced foreign minister remained nervous about the mission's potential impact on rivalries among Europe's imperial powers. But by the time Hanotaux returned as foreign minister in late April 1896, the expedition's wheels were rolling. Marchand's journey, with barely a company of colonial troops (and many more African porters) was to be an epic; he would not arrive at Fashoda until July 1898.[66] By that point, the situation in the Sudan had changed radically.

That, of course, was on account of the British-led reconquest. After the crisis, W. T. Stead's *Review of Reviews* observed: 'If the Unionists who carried [the] last General Election had been charged by their opponents with the intention of adding 1,500,000 square miles of African territory to the burden of the British Empire, they would have repudiated the charge as a calumny.'[67] Robinson and Gallagher appeared to accept this assessment as accurate, but it was by no means the whole truth.[68] Certainly, the Conservatives made no specific pledge to reconquer the Sudan. And true, only 11 per cent of Unionist election addresses made explicit mention of the empire. (The top issue, Irish Home Rule, was referred to in 80 per cent of them.)[69] But they did not disguise their general desire to 'preserve and *increase* the greatness and *the magnitude* of the Empire'.[70] Moreover, if the Liberals did not charge the Tories with favouring reckless expansionism, it was not because it had occurred to no one that the African Empire might be enlarged. In fact, as Grey's statement indicated, they themselves did not shy away from the logic of growth driven by Great Power rivalry. 'We must race France to avoid the possibility of having to fight her', commented the *Pall Mall Gazette*, a Liberal paper, in the wake of his speech.[71]

Furthermore, although the Liberal Party was unquestionably divided on empire matters at this time, its official leader, Rosebery, was strongly imperialistic. A few days before the government fell, Chamberlain made a speech in which he mocked Liberal divisions, and yet in the process drew attention to the relative ineffectualness of the empire-sceptic viewpoint when it came to influencing policy. He dwelt on the uncomfortable position of Sir William Harcourt, chancellor of the exchequer and Rosebery's nemesis, who now supported a railway-building project he had earlier denounced to consolidate the recently declared Uganda protectorate, and of John Morley, chief secretary for Ireland and keeper of the Gladstonian flame. Chamberlain said that Morley had come into office holding that the empire

---

[65] Pakenham, *Scramble for Africa*, 466–7; Sèbe, *Heroic Imperialists*, 232.

[66] MAE, 123CPCOM17: Afrique—Missions d'exploration, no. 342, Delcassé to London Embassy, 2 October 1898.

[67] 'The Progress of the World', *Review of Reviews*, April 1899.

[68] Robinson and Gallagher, *Africa and the Victorians*, 378.

[69] Paul A. Readman, 'The 1895 General Election and Political Change in Late Victorian Britain', *Historical Journal*, 42:2 (1999), 467–93, at 492.

[70] 'Mr. [Arthur] Balfour In Manchester', *The Times*, 13 July 1895. Emphasis added.

[71] 'E Nilo Quid Fit', *Pall Mall Gazette*, 29 March 1895.

ought under no circumstances to be extended, but now hung on in the Cabinet, looking on 'while the Government, under the irresistible pressure of public opinion, strengthens our hold upon Egypt (loud cheers), extends the confines of our dominions in Asia and Africa, and adds millions a year to our naval and military expenditure. (Cheers.)'.[72] As the election started, Rosebery, for his part, suggested that there was nothing distinctive about Conservative imperial policies: 'I am told, vaguely indeed, that the policy of the new Government is to be the maintenance of the Empire and social legislation. In that case, why did they turn us out? (Cheers.) We maintained the Empire; we *increased* the Empire.'[73] (Waziristan was incorporated into British India in 1893; Uganda became a British protectorate in 1894.) Expansionism in Africa did not become an election issue in 1895 precisely because it was—at the broadest level—uncontroversial. Those who disliked it in principle were powerless to challenge it in practice.

Chamberlain may have been right to suggest that the public favoured expansion, but politicians may also have had a sense that popular imperialism was rather tepid, and that it could easily be cooled by some military setback in a far-off land. The reaction against the disastrous Second Afghan War, which had contributed to Gladstone's 1880 election victory, was still within living memory. One way to minimize such reverses was to place them within a wider context of an unstoppable historical process of empire development; hence Salisbury's 1888 description of small imperial wars, mentioned in the Introduction to this book, as 'merely the surf that marks the edge of the advancing wave of civilisation'.[74] However much their own actions might be responsible for provoking such wars, imperial statesmen liked to present themselves as powerless to do other than push forward into new territories, because they were obliged to follow the logic of events. This 'rhetoric of inevitability' was both a means of protecting those in charge against a backlash if something went wrong—'we had no choice but to go on'—and also served to vindicate their supposedly realistic and pragmatic statecraft—'we are on the side of history'. Arguably, the need to be able to present expansion as a form of bowing to necessity was another factor militating against political programmes that pledged the acquisition of particular territories. At the same time, it should be stressed that the authorities in London were often genuinely not in control of events, and were frequently pulled along in the wake of enthusiastic soldiers and officials 'on the spot'. This required post hoc rationalization, to which the rhetoric of inevitability was well suited.

The rhetoric of inevitability was especially in evidence in debates over the so-called 'forward policy' with respect to the North-West Frontier of India.[75]

---

[72] 'The Unionist Alliance', *The Times*, 15 June 1895.

[73] 'Lord Rosebery At The Albert Hall', *The Times*, 6 July 1895. Emphasis added.

[74] 'Banquet At The Guildhall', *The Times*, 10 November 1888.

[75] A rather brilliant contemporary analysis of how the logic worked was made by the Liberal MP Sir Lewis McIver: 'No one in authority in the Punjab—in the Government of India—in the India Office will face the facts. They all protest—quite sincerely protest—that nothing is further from their thoughts—that they are reluctant to take this step-that they regret the necessity for that, and so forth. But the process goes on steadily all along the Frontier like the action of the tides—constant, persistent, not sleeping at nights, not knocking off for dinner'. HC Deb, 8 February 1898, vol. 53, col. 109. Note the similarity to Salisbury's surf/wave metaphor.

Expansion in this area was highly controversial, not least because of the Afghan experience.[76] The Liberals were in fact, through the Rosebery government's own interventions, heavily implicated in the forward policy. But Morley and Harcourt (the latter of whom succeeded Rosebery as Liberal leader in 1896) were prominent voices denouncing the Salisbury government's actions in the borderlands as a folly which put the Indian Empire at risk.[77] Such scepticism was not the preserve of the 'usual suspects' alone. Even the arch-imperialist *Daily Mail* described the idea of turning the region's tribesmen into British subjects as a fallacy.[78] Simultaneous with these debates, and informed by them, were those over the reconquest of the Sudan. Following the Italian army's humiliating defeat by Abyssinia at the Battle of Adowa, the British Cabinet agreed to assist Italy by relieving Mahdist pressure on their garrison at Kassala in eastern Sudan. The British-Egyptian advance that followed led eventually to the defining British victory at Omdurman that was the prelude to the Fashoda crisis. After that victory was achieved, no one dared suggest that it had not been worthwhile. But during the long period leading up to it, there were prominent Liberal voices arguing that the reconquest had not been properly thought through and warning that Britain risked overtaxing her strength.[79] In Morley's case, at least, the doubts were reinforced by negative attitudes towards the newly recruited black Sudanese troops on whom the progress of the reconquest was to depend.[80]

There was another dimension to Liberal criticisms. Salisbury was realistic about the limitations of British power. A dispute with the USA over the boundary between Venezuela and British Guiana ended with the British agreeing to submit to arbitration, in effect admitting the right of the Americans to an exclusive sphere of influence in the southern hemisphere.[81] In March 1898, furthermore, the British acquiesced in the Russian acquisition of Port Arthur, on the southern tip of China's Liaodong Peninsula, now a zone of intense European rivalries.[82] Such episodes helped the opposition to build a narrative of weakness. (Gladstone died in May, finally removing the threat posed to both parties by his disruptive interventions.) With Conservative backbenchers restive, and with Chamberlain sometimes failing to disguise in public his antipathy to Salisbury's moderate approach, there was plenty of room to exploit divisions on the government side.[83] It is true that the Liberals themselves appeared equally (if not more) disunited and incoherent. But

[76] Richard Toye, 'The Riddle of the Frontier: Winston Churchill, the Malakand Field Force, and the rhetoric of imperial expansion', *Historical Research*, 84 (2011), 493–512.

[77] 'Mr. Morley At Arbroath', *The Times*, 29 September 1897; 'Sir William Harcourt At Kirkcaldy', *The Times*, 27 November 1897.

[78] 'Outlook: The Frontier Fallacy', *Daily Mail*, 30 March 1898.

[79] 'Lord Kimberley On Foreign Affairs', *The Times*, 28 Feb. 1898; 'Lord Herschell At Brighton', *The Times*, 1 March 1898.

[80] 'Mr. Morley At Stirling', *The Times*, 28 January 1898. For an overt statement of Morley's belief that the Sudanese were at 'lower stages of moral and intellectual progress than [. . .] we are ourselves', see HC Deb, 24 February 1899, vol. 67, col. 459.

[81] Kathleen Burk, *Old World, New World: The Story of Britain and America* (London: Little, Brown, 2007), 396–410.

[82] Robert Bickers, *The Scramble for China: Foreign Devils in the Qing Empire, 1832–1914* (London: Allen Lane, 2011), 327.

[83] Peter T. Marsh, *Joseph Chamberlain: Entrepreneur in Politics* (New Haven, CT: Yale University Press, 1994), 437–8; David Steele, *Lord Salisbury: A Political Biography* (London: UCL Press, 1999), 333–4.

the Fashoda crisis was to show that there was mileage in criticizing what Sir Charles Dilke referred to as the government's 'policy of concession'.[84]

This suggestion may seem surprising. After all, the standard picture is that Liberals and Conservatives were caught up together in a jingoistic, anti-French spasm: how, in this scenario, was it possible to jostle for party advantage? But political consensus over Fashoda has been too often taken for granted as an uncomplicated fact.[85] At one level, it did exist: practically everyone was, ostensibly, urging the same hard-line policy. At another level, though, it was an artefact of politics. Sniffing a chance to steal the Conservatives' clothes if Salisbury failed to stand sufficiently firm against France, they pulled themselves together surprisingly effectively—for the duration. If they presented themselves as standing four-square behind the government, it was only in order to be in a position to knife the prime minister between the shoulders if he should have the misfortune to trip up. At the same time, the leading Liberal figures were all too willing to upstage not only ministers, but each other. The rhetoric of 'unity' during the crisis should thus be seen in the light of political manoeuvre, and not simply as an expression of imperialist atavism, although that no doubt played its part as well.

THE CRISIS PEAKS

To appreciate how this rhetoric was operationalized, we need to understand not only what occurred on the ground at Fashoda but also how information about events there was conveyed to the public in Britain and France. On 18 June 1898, the French Consul in Cairo sent word to Paris of local reports indicating the reinforcement of an Anglo-Egyptian expeditionary force, which would venture into Sudan as soon as Nile floodwaters would permit. Cairo railway companies were making additional rolling stock ready, and British army officers were being recalled early from summer leave.[86] The Quai d'Orsay's political directorate was in no doubt: the first British objective would be Khartoum, after which Anglo-Egyptian predominance in Sudan would be unilaterally proclaimed. Hanotaux's countermove was simple. On the one hand, a list of arguments were readied in case the British either contested French interests in Egypt or raised compensation claims of their own—in Tunisia, Niger, or Madagascar, for instance—as a means to extract French concessions. On the other hand, the arrival of Marchand's mission in southern Sudan before the fall of Khartoum would, it was hoped, compel the British to take French claims into account.[87]

Sir Herbert Kitchener, the British head (or *Sirdar*) of the Egyptian army, secured his victory over the Mahdists at Omdurman on 2 September 1898. To French chagrin, the victory's one-sided totality enabled Kitchener to contemplate a rapid advance southwards.[88] A few days later he received word that a group of 'Turks' had

[84] HC Deb, 10 June 1898, vol. 58, cols 1324–5.

[85] Robinson and Gallagher, *Africa and the Victorians*, 377–8; Pakenham, *Scramble*, 552; Sanderson, 'Anglo-French Confrontation', 326.

[86] MAE, 189PAAP11 Hanotaux papers, no. 141, Consul Général de France en Egypte, to Direction politique, 'Affaires du Soudan', 17 June 1898.

[87] MAE, 189PAAP11, Hanotaux papers, Hanotaux letter to Cairo Consul, 21 June 1898.

[88] John V. F. Keiger, 'Omdurman, Fashoda and Franco-British Relations', in Edward M. Spiers (ed.), *Sudan: The Conquest Reappraised* (London: Frank Cass, 1998), 163–9.

established themselves at Fashoda. He deduced that this must be Marchand's party, which he was already under orders to locate and see off. He and a substantial number of troops steamed south on 10 September, and arrived at Fashoda nine days later. On meeting one another, Kitchener and Marchand had a tense but polite exchange, which resulted in a compromise. The British hoisted the Egyptian flag but the French mission remained in situ for the time being. Shots were avoided; the standoff would now have to be resolved in London and Paris. Before they sailed off, leaving a Sudanese battalion and a gunboat to keep a watchful eye, the British carried out a nice piece of psychological warfare by leaving Marchand and his men some French newspapers. These revealed the depths of societal division caused by the Dreyfus affair, lending weight to Kitchener's parting comment: 'your government won't back you'.[89]

It was a dubious assertion. The French press was indeed polarized by the Dreyfus case. Revelations of army plotting, Colonel Henry's recent suicide, and the growing probability of a retrial after Dreyfus's wife, Lucie, formally requested it on 3 September hardened divisions within the media, as in the wider French political sphere, between supporters and opponents of Dreyfus.[90] (In Britain, by contrast, *The Times* took the unusual step on 13 October of publishing a detailed repudiation of the case against Dreyfus written by former Home Office legal expert, Sir Godfrey Lushington.)[91] Conflicting French newspaper accounts, just like wider public opinion, were not entirely reducible to pro- and anti-republican sentiments, however. For some, the prospect of yet more legal proceedings and consequent discredit to once revered French institutions was just too much.[92] As for Marchand, the republican coalitions in office in late 1898 never contemplated abandoning him outright even before rising public interest in the crisis precluded such an alternative. Nor was Marchand willing to become the figurehead of an anti-republican right, a fact proven by his studied political silence when he eventually returned to France.[93]

Meanwhile, in Britain the news that the Fashoda trading post had been occupied by unspecified 'white men' had led to 'instant panic' and vilification of the French (as seen in the cartoon from *Punch* in Fig. 2.1)—although some voices urged calm, suggesting that hysteria would undermine an inherently strong British case.[94] Kitchener conveyed the information that he had established a force at Fashoda in typically laconic style, in reply to the Lord Mayor of London's congratulations on

---

[89] John Pollock, *Kitchener* (London: Robinson, 2002), 144–7.

[90] The vitriol of the Dreyfus case in autumn 1898 is captured in the headline leads of pro- and anti-Dreyfusard newspapers alike. See, for instance, 'Ponce Pilote: Le Général Zurlindin temporise', *L'Intransigeant*, 10 September 1898, p. 1; 'L'affaire Dreyfus—nouveau dissentiment ministériel', *La Lanterne*, 14 September 1898; 'Démission—defection', *La Croix*, 17 September 1898, p. 1; 'La journée historique au Conseil des Ministres', *Le Gaulois*, 18 September 1898, p. 1.

[91] Harris, *The Man on Devil's Island*, 237–8, 254, 262–70; Tombs, '"Lesser Breeds without the Law"', 501.

[92] Divisions among the Republic's monarchist, Bonapartist, and High Command opponents are nicely summarized by Maurice Larkin, '"La République en danger"?' 85–105.

[93] Berenson, 'Fashoda, Dreyfus, and the Myth', 137, 141–2; Sèbe, *Heroic Imperialists*, 238–9, 248–51.

[94] 'The French at Fashoda', *Saturday Review*, 17 September 1898.

Fig. 2.1. 'How Some People Invade the Soudan', satirical, crudely racist cartoon, printed in *Punch*, 24 September 1898.

Mary Evans Picture Library, image 1090643

the Omdurman victory. He disliked war correspondents but successfully cultivated his own image and mystique: with everyone crying out for authentic news he 'just lifts the corner of the curtain and lets it be understood that very interesting events may have been happening behind it'.[95]

In his official reports, Kitchener exaggerated the desperateness of Marchand's position, falsely suggesting that the French were running short of supplies. It was of

[95] Untitled editorial, *The Times*, 26 September 1898.

course true that, had it come to a fight, the French would have been no match for the British forces. But Kitchener's inference that Marchand's mission had somehow been neglected by the French government caused consternation in Paris. Using the pages of *Le Temps*, the Foreign Ministry printed a lengthy denial in October, explaining that Marchand had, in fact, twice requested additional supplies in July and November 1897. Both demands were met. (Indeed, although it was not something that could be publicly admitted, 29,000 francs spent on the Marchand mission in 1898 comprised the largest item drawn from the government's secret funds.[96] The sum eclipsed the 26,000 spent on the disastrous Voulet-Chanoine mission in West Africa, an expedition whose scandalous outcome and dystopian violence have been vividly documented by Bertrand Taithe.)[97] Enough provisions to last the mission a year were sent by steamer to Brazzaville from where the steamer captain, Lieutenant Fouques, oversaw their overland journey via the French Congo and Ubanghi-Chari to the Sudan. The Herculean challenges of long-distance travel, it was suggested, were no obstacle when Frenchmen were called upon to help their compatriots.[98]

Another reason for the Paris government's eagerness to set the record straight was that Kitchener was able to prevent Marchand from sending his own version of events back home via the Nile route. In a dispatch of 21 September, Kitchener made the dubious claim that had the destruction of the Mahdists at Omdurman 'been delayed a fortnight, in all probability he [Marchand] and his companions would have been massacred'. The government in London edited this message (removing some insulting comments on 'the pretensions of M. Marchand') and published it along with their diplomatic discussions with the French government over the Upper Nile.[99] This type of 'Blue Book' publication had a strong influence on the public debate; later in October, the French responded with their own 'Yellow Book', as part of the ongoing information war.[100]

The first Yellow Book was particularly long. A sequence of thirty-one diplomatic dispatches, most of which recorded conversations between the two foreign ministers, Delcassé and Salisbury, as well as their respective ambassadors in London and Paris—Baron Alphonse de Courcel and Sir Edmund Monson—it helped compensate for the lack of parliamentary discussion as the crisis deepened. The idiosyncrasies of the French parliamentary calendar only partially explain this. In Paris, the Chamber of Deputies returned for its autumn session on Tuesday 25 October having been in recess since 13 July. The crisis was certainly in its final stages by then, but it was by no means over. Indeed, it was in response to demands from two

---

[96] MAE, 189PAAP11 Hanotaux papers, Allocations exceptionnelles pour 1898 prises à la charge des fonds spéciaux.

[97] Taithe, *The Killer Trail*, chapters 1–6.

[98] 'Affaires Coloniales: Sur le Nil', *Le Temps*, 19 October 1898, p. 1.

[99] Kitchener's message was published in the second of two Blue Books published in October: 'Egypt. No. 2 (1898): Correspondence with the French Government Respecting the Valley of the Upper Nile', C. 9054, October 1898; Egypt. No. 2 (1898) 'Further Correspondence Respecting the Valley of the Upper Nile', C. 9055, October 1898; Bates, *Fashoda Incident*, 135–41.

[100] 'Le Livre jaune sur Fachoda', *Le Figaro*, 24 October 1898, pp. 1–2.

deputies, Louis Brunet and Albert de Mun, for a debate on Fashoda that Delcassé distributed three Yellow Books of French diplomatic correspondence to National Assembly members.[101] But no sooner was the door to parliamentary dissection of French government actions wrenched open than the foreign minister slammed it shut. Insisting that the Yellow Book materials made the motivations behind the coalition's policy transparently clear, by 8 November Delcassé persuaded the two deputies to withdraw their interpellations. Remarkably, the decision not to hold a full Chamber of Deputies debate on the crisis was greeted with loud applause from all sides. In part, this registered the breadth of political trust in the experienced Delcassé; in part, it signalled the comparative lack of trust between parliamentary blocs whose splits had widened in the wake of the Dreyfus retrial.[102]

The absence of any sustained discussion of the Fashoda crisis in the National Assembly lent added weight to French press commentaries on the Yellow Books' contents. Such was surely the Foreign Ministry's intention. Delcassé was unwilling to risk being pressured to adopt a dangerously intransigent position by clamouring from the nationalist right in parliament. He was much happier to exploit press anger over Britain's refusal to give ground as a means of wresting concessions from London. Self-justificatory in their careful selection of diplomatic dispatches, the British Blue Book and, even more so, its French Yellow Book equivalent represented an interesting twist in the rhetorical battle between the diplomatists of both countries. For both sides, the selective—and carefully timed—publication of official correspondence became a means to mobilize their national press and, through them, public opinion, to strengthen their hand in negotiation. This tit-for-tat release of documents soon acquired a momentum of its own. One Yellow Book followed another Blue Book, and so on, until the Foreign Office decided to halt the process having not only published records from 1898 but rereleased those dating from the siege of Khartoum in 1884 as well.[103]

It was the Yellow Book release on Monday, 24 October 1898 that garnered most extensive coverage in the French press. *Le Figaro* caught the mood. Diplomatic communiqués, it began, are sometimes considered dull; not anymore—they attract a passionate readership. Perhaps, though, that passion was misdirected. Delcassé and Lord Salisbury, it appeared, had behaved with statesmanlike restraint. The problem was that their common sense was drowned out by the bombast of British politicians' speeches, the rancour in the British press, and the jingoistic clamour of British public opinion, which demanded a humiliating French climb-down. The result, according to *Le Figaro*, was that France, its perspective undistorted by any such crude xenophobia, would have 'to concede to British obstinacy' to avert any risk of a war. And all this over an issue which, the communiqués proved, could have

[101] Louis Renault (ed.), *Archives Diplomatiques*, 2e série, tome LXVIII, Octobre-Décembre 1898, Chambre des Députés, séance du 4 Novembre 1898, p. 2134.

[102] *Archives Diplomatiques*, 2e série, tome LXVIII, Octobre–Décembre 1898, Chambre des Députés, séance du 8 Novembre 1898, p. 2156.

[103] See, for instance, Blue Book, Egypt, no. 3 1898, 'Further Correspondence Respecting the Valley of the Upper Nile [in Continuation of Egypt no. 2 (1898)]'; and Blue Book, Egypt, 1884, no. 12 (also rereleased in October 1898).

been settled amicably.[104] Echoing Hanotaux's earlier disdain for Britain's undiplomatic and ill-judged bullying, conceding defeat, in this reading, signified the triumph of reason and adherence to higher ethical standards next to the brutish fervour of the British public. The French people were to be congratulated for refusing to sink to this level of playground politics.[105]

The editorialists of *L'Aurore* summarized the Yellow Book's contents more pithily: the British refused to take France's claims under international law seriously because they knew that, after Omdurman, the local 'facts' favoured Britain's cause. France, by contrast, was quite willing to talk, even to give ground, but only if Lord Salisbury's government offered it a way to do so 'with its honour intact'.[106] Here, the echo was with Delcassé's elegant statement to Ambassador Monson on 27 September—which, ironically, was published in the second Foreign Office Blue Book. Responding to the latest British demand to order Marchand's immediate withdrawal, Delcassé, in Monson's words, replied 'that he himself was ready to discuss the question in the most conciliatory spirit, *but that I must not ask him for the impossible*'.[107]

Marchand, according to other republican press accounts, personified this more reasonable approach. He was well aware of his relatively weak position but refused to see France's legitimate claims swept aside. Strength was on Britain's side, but honour was on France's.[108] Remarkably, this was a view shared by the arch anti-republicans, the *anti-Dreyfusard* Catholic reactionaries at *La Croix*.[109] A paper originally founded by the Assumptionist order in 1880, its editorial writers saw no reason for Marchand—or France—to turn the other cheek and were especially blunt in their rhetorical condemnation of British realpolitik. The Omdurman victory may have transformed Britain's prospects, but that did not alter the fact that Anglo-Egyptian legal claims over the Sudan were 'of recent vintage'. Britain's reassertion of these supposed rights owed everything to Kitchener's *force majeure* and nothing to natural justice. Sudanese preferences were, not surprisingly, ignored entirely.[110]

Consistent with this 'might versus right' interpretation of the prelude to Marchand's withdrawal, French newspapers dwelt on the stark imbalance between the resources available to the two military protagonists at the centre of the drama. The odds stacked against him, Marchand remained to his core a loyal, well-trained army officer. He would not move until his superiors, in this case the government of the

---

[104] 'Le Livre jaune sur Fachoda', *Le Figaro*, 24 October 1898, pp. 1–2.   [105] Ibid.

[106] 'La Question de Fashoda: *le livre jaune*', *L'Aurore*, 24 October 1898.

[107] Egypt No. 2 1898, item 19: Sir E. Monson to the Marquis of Salisbury, Paris, 27 September 1898. Our italics.

[108] 'La question de Fachoda', *Le Petit Parisien*, 27 October 1898; 'Bulletin de l'étranger', *Le Temps*, 30 October 1898. *Le Petit Parisien*, along with its competitor, *Le Petit Journal*, led the way in producing picture *Suppléments* whose visual imagery and storybook captions reinforced Marchand's saintly image, see: Sèbe, *Heroic Imperialists*, 103, 106.

[109] Other hard-right, anti-Dreyfusard newspapers, including *Le Gaulois* and *L'Intransigeant*, were as vituperative, but less sanctimonious, Sèbe, *Heroic Imperialists*, 235, 243.

[110] 'Affaire de Fachoda: Le *livre jaune*', *La Croix*, 25 October 1898.

day, told him to do so. This was something that Kitchener understood, it being admitted that he, too, was a man of honour (unlike the British politicians he served). Hence, the importance attached to the long-distance communication that Delcassé, in that same 27 September meeting with Monson, had asked the British to relay to Marchand, via Cairo and Khartoum. Again, French adherence to higher standards was in evidence, the foreign minister having offered to submit his message *en clair* to prevent any British misreading of French intentions.[111]

This particular subplot soon focused on another French military hero: Marchand's third-in-command and chosen envoy, the cavalry officer Captain Albert Baratier. Baratier's letters home to his family were already in the public domain, helping to cement the mission's reputation for superhuman endeavour and last-stand bravery in the face of a Mahdist assault on their Fashoda redoubt. Indeed, Baratier would later become the mission's quasi-official biographer, his obsessive promotion of Marchand fed by the French public's appetite for *Marchandise* in the form of mission narratives and serialized accounts, maps and postcards, illustrated newspaper covers, and other, assorted memorabilia.[112]

For his part, Baratier's reputation soared after he was dispatched to Paris carrying Marchand's preliminary account of his mission (Marchand wanted to deliver his full report in person). Days later, Baratier found himself aboard the same steamer, *Sénégal*, that was transporting Kitchener and Cairo Consul Lord Cromer homeward via Marseille. Here again, the image of gentility and mutual understanding between the colonial 'men on the spot' radiated through the French press accounts of this voyage.[113] Far from sullen quietude or disputatious confrontation, all three reportedly got on well, a prelude to the polite reception that Kitchener would be accorded on arrival in France.[114] Readers were invited to draw the conclusion that only the British public did not know how to behave in a time of crisis.

It fell to *Le Temps*, which, it's worth recalling, spoke with the Quai d'Orsay's voice, to provide the long-term juridical background to the arguments at stake.[115] Marchand was merely asserting French claims to natural outlets (*débouchés naturels*) on the Nile for its Congolese trade. This he was entitled to do since the Anglo-Egyptian renunciation of claims over southern Sudan in 1885. Three days later, on 22 October, *Le Temps* went further. Without formally attributing its true source, over a full page the newspaper replicated the Foreign Ministry's Political Directorate 5 October brief for Delcassé, which repudiated Britain's legal claims over Sudan.[116] As that brief concluded, the British High Commission in Cairo, the Foreign Office, and even Queen Victoria herself were certain by late 1883 that

[111] Egypt No. 2 1898, item 19: Sir E. Monson to the Marquis of Salisbury, Paris, 27 September 1898.
[112] Sèbe, *Heroic Imperialists*, 74–82, 243–5.
[113] 'La Mission Marchand', *La Croix*, 26 October 1898, p. 2; 'Arrivée du Capitaine Baratier à Marseille', *Le Petit Parisien*, 27 October 1898, p. 1.
[114] 'La Journée, Paris', *La Croix*, 27 October 1898.
[115] 'Affaires Coloniales: Sur le Nil', *Le Temps*, 19 October 1898, p. 1.
[116] 'Les antécédents de Fashoda l'affaire de Fachoda', *Le Temps*, 22 October 1898.

Egypt's political grip over southern Sudan was untenable. Gordon of Khartoum might have thought otherwise, but his death only proved the point. In 1885, Egypt's Khedival government accepted British advice, and abandoned the former Egyptian territories situated south of Wadi Halfa 'without intending to return'.[117] The *Le Temps* piece provided even more context: admittedly, Egyptian Khedive Ismail established Cairo's rule over the Southern Sudanese provinces of Sennaar, Darfur, Bahr el-Ghazal, and Equatoria—and at terrible human cost. But his ill-fated son, Tewfik, had surrendered those claims after his remaining garrisons, and the British troops sent to assist them, were defeated by Mahdist forces. Equatoria and Bahr el-Ghazal, in particular, were completely evacuated by the end of 1884. The British, in their colonial dealings with Italy and with Belgian King Leopold's Congo Free State since then, had treated these territories as *terra nullius*. An inconvenient truth for London, this was a fact nonetheless. So, too, was France's steadfast refusal to accede to the other arrangements—with Germany over Zanzibar for instance—by which the British had sought to re-establish some notional claim over Sudan.[118] In colonial terms at least, Fashoda was in no man's land.

This version of events was also publicized nationally and repeated regionally by members of the *Comité de l'Afrique Française*, the Africa wing of the Parti Colonial lobby group. The committee not only backed the original Marchand mission, but remained its most influential supporters in business, finance, politics, and the civil service. Its October *Bulletin* provided a detailed description of the overland routes traced by Marchand and an earlier Liotard mission, making plain that these eastward marches were overwhelmingly conducted through French-ruled territory towards a Nile outlet that, in turn, lay in *unclaimed* territory.[119]

In a special supplement, published on 31 October, *La Croix* brought matters back down to earth. French rights in Egypt had been trampled over yet again, just as they had been in 1882, thanks to the petty factionalism of republican politicians. For De Freycinet's feeble response to the Alexandria bombardment back then, read Delcassé's inability now to speak without the authority of a government behind him. French newspaper journalists, by commenting on these Yellow Books, were doing the politicians' job for them! As for the British, they had simply reverted to type. Their 'constant practice' was to exploit French weakness to advance their own interests.[120] The scene was set for a winter of bitter political invective in France, the prelude to Déroulède's abortive February coup.

There was no street protest in Britain to match the French experience, but a different similarity did exist, one that affected the way Fashoda was talked about in both countries. This was the fact that neither the Westminster Parliament nor the French National Assembly was sitting as the Fashoda crisis intensified. This highlights a significant aspect of the rhetorical cultures evident on each side of

---

[117] MAE, 123CPCOM17: Missions d'exploration Commandant Marchand, Direction Politique 'Note pour le Ministre—L'abandon du Soudan par l'Egypte en 1884–85', 5 October 1898.
[118] 'Les antécédents de l'affaire de Fachoda', *Le Temps*, 22 October 1898, p. 1.
[119] *Bulletin du Comité de l'Afrique française*, October 1898.
[120] *La Croix Supplément*, 'Le Protectorat de l'Egypte', 31 October 1898, p. 1.

the Channel. In Britain, despite the growing pressure of legislative business, it was quite common at this time for there not to be an autumn session, and so it was in 1898: parliament was prorogued in mid-August and did not meet again until the following February. Here again, the cross-Channel resonances are obvious. The French legislature only began its autumn session in late October after a recess of over four months. Even then, deputies' attempts to debate the Fashoda crisis were, as we have seen, stymied by Delcassé. The National Assembly was anyway pre-occupied by ferocious argument over the planned reopening of the Dreyfus case, which provoked a string of ministerial resignations.[121] These culminated on 25 October in the departure of the coalition's final appointee as war minister, General Jules Chanoine. The third minister of war to resign from the government in seven weeks, Chanoine's departure was the last straw for a government still reeling from the September resignation from the same office of Jacques Godefroy Cavaignac. Hitherto the most influential *anti-Dreyfusard* voice within government, Cavaignac, a 'Progressist' republican moderate, resolved to go once the full extent of the High Command's complicity in securing Dreyfus's original conviction became public knowledge.[122] With him collapsed a vital bridge between a republican and predominantly *Dreyfusard* government and an army executive mired in crisis. Within twenty-four hours Henri Brisson's coalition, his second in three years, was gone. The risk of a right-wing coup was also significantly increased.[123]

The collapse of Henri Brisson's second coalition ministry on 26 October left France without a government during a critical week in which final clearance for Marchand's withdrawal was left in abeyance. Indeed, it took another seven days' ministerial horse trading until Charles Dupuy assembled a broadly equivalent republican coalition. Its most urgent task was, arguably, not to confirm the end of the French presence at Fashoda, which was by then a matter of bowing to the inevitable. It was, rather, to seek some means of reconciliation with the French army command as preparations for Dreyfus's retrial in early 1899 continued.[124] The return of ministerial veteran Charles de Freycinet as war minister was cause for guarded optimism; but not much. Paul Déroulède's failed coup attempt on 23 February 1899, during the funeral of President Félix Faure (a head of state who famously expired in the company of his lover after taking a powerful quinine-based aphrodisiac) reminds us of the extent to which the Fashoda crisis, and even Marchand's feted return to Paris, had to jostle for French public attention with other sensational events.[125]

Meanwhile, in the relative calm of London, the lack of a sitting parliament did not mean that political discussion stopped. Rather, there was an autumn

---

[121] *Le Temps*, extended review of Dreyfus proceedings, 31 October 1898.

[122] 'La chute du Cabinet', *Le Petit Parisien*, 26 October 1898, p. 1; 'La Crise Ministérielle', *L'Aurore*, 27 October 1898; Passmore, *The Right in France*, 101. Unwisely as it turned out, Cavaignac affirmed his belief in Dreyfus's guilt in a widely acclaimed speech to the Chamber of Deputies in July 1898, see Tombs, '"Lesser Breeds without the Law"', 500.

[123] 'Le coup de l'État-Major. Démission du Ministère Brisson', *L'Aurore*, 26 October 1898.

[124] 'La crise ministérielle: Dupuy accepte', *La Croix*, 29 October 1898, p. 1.

[125] Sèbe, *Heroic Imperialists*, 246–51.

speech-making season dominated by addresses by leading statesmen outside Parliament, and the techniques of the platform were generally thought to lend themselves to populism, rabble-rousing, and grandstanding, in contrast to the supposedly more thoughtful and discursive atmosphere of Parliament.[126] A Cabinet minister speaking in a major city on 'political affairs in general' was thought to mark the beginning of 'the serious business of the recess'.

On this occasion, Rosebery got in first with a speech at Epsom, although, because his focus was mainly on domestic affairs, this was said not to count.[127] This was in spite of the acknowledged fact that he also made an important pronouncement on Fashoda. That he did so—in advance of any statement by the official Liberal leadership—was typical of him. Formally in retirement, he now started a pattern by which he would emerge periodically to make a speech, giving hope to his supporters among the nascent Liberal Imperialist grouping that he would soon return to head the party. These hopes were always to be dashed, but usually not before he had caused disruption. His premiership had been paralysed by his totally dysfunctional relationship with Harcourt, who was sure to be angered by a move that would open the leadership question again. Rosebery's decision to breach his long silence was taken as a clear sign 'that he does not repudiate the efforts of those who intend to place him once more at the head of the Radical Party'.[128]

Still, Salisbury also had grounds for worry. As an advocate of bipartisanship and continuity in foreign policy, Rosebery was ostensibly wholly behind the government, but his words were double-edged. He emphasized that its current policy of firmness towards France was founded on Grey's 1895 declaration, made during his own administration. He also stated: 'I am perfectly certain that no idea or intention of any weakening on this point or this question have entered the heads of Her Majesty's present advisers. Were it otherwise, I say their existence would be short.'[129] In other words, he was putting the government on notice that any suggestion of compromise would seal its political doom.

Much of the press simply took Rosebery's words at face value: he could bask in the approbation due to the statesman who put country before party. Some Liberals, such as former home secretary H. H. Asquith, interpreted his cue straightforwardly, and gave unequivocal backing to the government.[130] Harcourt in due course followed suit, albeit in a rather low-key way and—unsurprisingly—without mentioning Rosebery.[131] Some observers, though, took Rosebery to mean something deeper. Alfred Emmott, later MP for Oldham, observed that if one read 'between

[126] Valuable discussion of the politics of the platform can be found in H. C. G. Matthew, 'Rhetoric and Politics in Britain, 1860–1950', in P. J. Waller (ed.), *Politics and Social Change in Modern Britain* (Brighton: Harvester, 1987), 34–58, and Jon Lawrence, *Electing Our Masters: The Hustings in British Politics from Hogarth to Blair* (Oxford: Oxford University Press, 2009).

[127] Untitled editorial, *The Times*, 19 October 1898.

[128] 'Our London Letter', *Dundee Courier & Argus*, 14 October 1898.

[129] 'France and Fashoda', *Manchester Guardian*, 13 October 1898.

[130] 'Mr. Asquith On Fashoda', *The Times*, 14 October 1898.

[131] 'Sir W. Harcourt At Aberystwyth', *The Times*, 27 October 1898.

the lines of Lord Rosebery's speech, it was difficult to avoid the conclusion that his Lordship was of the opinion that the present Government, with its enormous majority, had [. . .] allowed matters to drift into such a condition that the country might almost be spoken of abroad as a negligible quantity'.[132] According to the London correspondent of the *Leicester Mercury*, people had been anxiously asking each other whether Salisbury would 'unflinchingly back up the policy of Lord Rosebery' or would merely prepare 'more graceful concessions'.[133] The former Cabinet minister Lord Tweedmouth argued that Salisbury's decision to release the detail of Britain's diplomatic exchanges in the form of a Blue Book suggested that he had finally woken up to the nation's distrust of his policy, and felt obliged to show that Britain's affairs were being handled with firmness. 'The second proof of [the] reality of the disquietude felt in the country was a chorus of praise in every section of the Press of the speech of Lord Rosebery.'[134] Lord Crewe, who had served as Lord Lieutenant of Ireland under Gladstone and Rosebery, similarly alleged weakness on Salisbury's part. Only the instinct of political self-preservation prevented Salisbury 'meekly retiring' before the French, he said. Rosebery's speech, moreover, 'showed that British opinion was united on this question'.[135] In this account, the public were not united *behind* Salisbury; rather they were united in the more difficult job of trying to get him to show some backbone. Months later, when a settlement over Fashoda had been reached, one Liberal MP explained that the successful resolution was all down to Rosebery's intervention.[136] The 'weakness' line was one that could be adapted for own purposes by the pacific, nonconformist wing of the party too.[137]

This is not to say that all Liberals welcomed Rosebery's approach. The existing literature is right to stress the very limited overt opposition to the government's line on Fashoda. The *Manchester Guardian* was unique among the press in suggesting that France's claims should be in any way taken seriously.[138] 'We know now that a policy which may call itself humanitarian but is in essence one of sheer aggression would have been followed as unhesitatingly had Lord Rosebery been in office as it has been under the present Government', the paper commented sardonically.[139] There was also dissent from future prime minister David Lloyd George, who had already achieved some prominence as a backbencher. His contribution was significant (and amusing) enough to merit consideration in detail.

Towards the end of October, Lloyd George made a speech at Haworth, in Yorkshire, which was reported at length in the *Bradford Observer*, but received only the briefest coverage elsewhere. 'We had a quarrel with France over what seemed to

---

[132] 'Liberal Meeting at Oldham', *Manchester Guardian*, 14 October 1898.
[133] 'Our London Letter', *Leicester Chronicle and the Leicestershire Mercury*, 15 October 1898.
[134] 'Lord Tweedmouth on the Fashoda Crisis', *The Standard*, 15 October 1898.
[135] 'The Earl Of Crewe On Fashoda', *The Times*, 18 October 1898.
[136] 'Stretford Division Liberal Association: Mr. W. H. Holland MP on Lord Rosebery's Speech', *Manchester Guardian*, 18 May 1899.
[137] See 'Congregational Union and Fashoda', *Dundee Courier & Argus*, 14 October 1898.
[138] Riker, 'Survey', 69; Robinson and Gallagher, *Africa and the Victorians*, 377.
[139] Untitled editorial, *Manchester Guardian*, 24 October 1898.

men of ordinary vision to be a very trifling mater indeed', he said. Fashoda was insignificant 'and there two great Empires, with millions of human beings, were snarling at each other, barking and threatening to bite and destroy each other, over that miserable little place in the middle of the Egyptian Soudan'. The only thing preventing an amicable settlement, Lloyd George claimed, was the bullying and hectoring tone adopted by British ministers. He was confident that if war came, Britain would win. However, 'If we defeated France, we should be defeating the only Power on the Continent with a democratic constitution.' The French did not really want Fashoda anyway, he claimed: they only wanted an outlet to the Nile, which was not unreasonable, he said. But Lloyd George then changed tack, arguing that the weakness of Salisbury's diplomacy had encouraged France to think that the prime minister was 'squeezable', like 'a kind of india-rubber dummy'. According to the report:

> Mr. Lloyd George went on to refer to Lord Salisbury's policy with regard to Venezuela, Crete, Madagascar, Tunis, and Siam, and in satirical language which caused great amusement showed why that 'strong' Foreign Minister had hesitated and 'gracefully' receded from his position time after time. It was, he observed, rather a good thing for his hearers that the French Foreign Minister had not asked for Yorkshire (laughter). Or they would have been French-men now (laughter and cheers).

There was no 'anti-imperialism' in Lloyd George's speech, merely a critique of imperial mismanagement and bad faith. It concluded with a sharp attack on the government's failure to defend Ottoman Christian subjects from the Turks in Armenia, thus evoking recent memories of Gladstone's final political intervention before his death.[140] Lloyd George's comments demonstrate the continuing viability of a distinctively Liberal language of empire, albeit one may question how substantive his differences with Conservative imperialism really were. It is easy to see how the sceptic of 1898 evolved into the war minister of 1914–18, who stressed the moral importance of treaty commitments to justify British involvement in an epic European conflict.

After the crisis was over, Chamberlain at first praised 'the ungrudging support' that the government had been afforded by the Liberal leadership.[141] But it was not long before he began to exploit the fact that the reality had been more complex. He identified two extremes within the party: on the one hand, Rosebery, Grey, and 'one or two more' (whose support he accepted as sincere); and on the other Morley and Harcourt (whom he considered outright opponents, although the former had said nothing and the latter had been supportive). Between these poles of opinion, he identified another school: 'a section who profess to agree with our objects, with the objects which Lord Rosebery has in common with us, but who are captious and take critical objection to the methods, and the only methods, by which these objects could be secured'.[142] It was certainly true that few Liberals were prepared

---

[140] 'Mr. Lloyd George at Haworth', *Bradford Observer*, 25 October 1898, typescript copy in Lloyd George Papers, LG/A/8/4/27.
[141] 'Mr. Chamberlain in Manchester', *The Times*, 16 November 1898.
[142] 'Mr. Chamberlain at Wakefield', *The Times*, 9 December 1898.

to give the government a free pass: naturally enough, they wanted to exploit the crisis for party purposes if they could. It was also true that the fundamental tensions within Liberalism had not been resolved. Perhaps the most striking thing about the Liberal divisions is not that they existed but rather that they did not, at least for the duration of the Anglo-French confrontation, lead to open acrimony or internal party warfare.

In Chamberlain's view the 'captious' group consisted of those who admitted that the French had no right to be at Fashoda but who accused the government of using excessively provocative language in the attempt to warn them off.[143] Without a doubt, some ministers made strongly worded statements. Sir Michael Hicks Beach, the chancellor of the exchequer, asserted that although war would be a calamity, 'there are greater evils than war'.[144] It is possible that the chancellor was hoping to increase the pressure on Salisbury to stand firm. In a Cabinet meeting soon after, the prime minister resisted the demand of Chamberlain and George Goschen (First Lord of the Admiralty) that France be presented with a formal ultimatum.[145] Because Salisbury revealed so little about his thinking to others, it is unclear what effect the public debate may have had on his diplomatic strategy.[146] The intensity of feeling, however, did make it vital that the ongoing discussions with the French were not seen to have the status of a 'negotiation'; and he might well have been more inclined to negotiate, and thus to help France find a way of saving face, had the rhetorical temperature been cooler. It was notable that, for whatever reason, it suited him to leave the fire-eating to others.

At the start of November, Henri Brisson's fledgling government finally decided to back down. A furious Marchand, who had arrived in Paris to report in person, was ordered to return and evacuate the mission.[147] The right-wing press, fixated over the previous week on the likely composition of the new government and its consequent approach to the Dreyfus case, resumed its veneration of Marchand. *La Croix* went furthest, offering a pen portrait of Marchand's entire family as an exemplar of nationalist rectitude. Rising from humble provincial beginnings in the eastern town of Thoissey (Ain), Jean-Baptiste was inspired to join the military by accounts of the French conquest of Tonkin. His brother, Petrus, followed him, joining a marine artillery unit and serving in the conquest of Western Soudan (Mali), where he gave his life—dying of sunstroke somewhere on the road between Tombouctou and Bafoulabé. Undaunted, their youngest brother, Constant, still a schoolboy, was studying hard to win a place at the *École Navale*.[148] This inspiring, if sugary, narrative was, of course, a none-too-oblique way of criticizing the alleged

---

[143] Chamberlain cited Lord Tweedmouth, Lord Ripon, and Sir Henry Campbell-Bannerman as members of this school of thought. 'Mr. Chamberlain at Wakefield', *The Times*, 9 December 1898.

[144] 'Sir M. Hicks Beach on the Situation', *The Times*, 20 October 1898.

[145] Andrew Roberts, *Lord Salisbury: Victorian Titan* (London: Weidenfeld & Nicolson, 1999), 707.

[146] Sanderson, 'Origins and Significance', 327.

[147] David Levering Lewis, *The Race to Fashoda: European Colonialism and African Resistance in the Scramble for Africa* (London: Bloomsbury, 1988), 226–7.

[148] 'La Question de Fachoda', *La Croix*, 1 November 1898, p. 2; 'La famille Marchand', *La Croix*, 2 November 1898, p. 3. Petrus's illustrious brother, Jean-Baptiste, was also twice wounded in the western Sudan during campaigning in 1889 and 1891: Sèbe, *Heroic Imperialists*, 316.

patriotic deficiencies of the republican establishment and siding with the army as the institutional embodiment of an eternal (and by no means republican) France.

Next to this, the more analytical tone struck by the leader writers at *Le Temps*, as usual drip-fed information by Delcassé's Foreign Ministry, at first glance seemed rather pedestrian. But a closer reading revealed a final twist of the rhetorical knife. Marchand's behaviour, it began, was, like that of France itself, impeccably correct. It was also measured. For, when all was said and done, Fashoda was of no real strategic value—and certainly not an occasion for war. (Four days earlier *Le Temps* had approvingly quoted Kitchener's comments to a P&O shipping agent on arrival in Marseille to the effect that Fashoda was nothing more than 'an infected swamp'. To fight over it, the general reportedly said, would have been ludicrous.)[149] That such a possibility had even been contemplated, the whole world knew, was due to Britain's intransigence. The British government had become trapped by a ferocious popular jingoism that it chose to whip up. Rather than disabusing the British people of their misperceptions about France, Salisbury and others allowed these sentiments to fester. (By implication, and as the Foreign Ministry had earlier protested, Hicks Beach, the Duke of Devonshire, and their hard-line supporters stirred the pot to the very last.)[150] It was left to France's leaders to act responsibly, attaching proper value of the decades of peace between the two countries. Marchand in situ and Delcassé in Paris might not have won 'victory' at Fashoda, but they had defused the crisis.[151] Behind the diplomatic façade, the sense that a duplicitous, rapacious Britain, personified in this case by Kitchener, had tricked France into submission was captured in a cartoon printed in *Le Petit Journal* on 20 November 1898 (Fig. 2.2).

Back in London, Salisbury was able to announce the French climb-down during a banquet in honour of Kitchener at London's Mansion House; Rosebery and Harcourt were also present.[152] Now that the war scare had passed, new infighting broke out within the Liberal Party, and Harcourt resigned as leader. Annoyed at having been overshadowed by Rosebery at the Mansion House, and at his intervention over the Fashoda question in general, Morley also stood down from the front bench.[153] Harcourt was succeeded by Sir Henry Campbell-Bannerman, widely seen as a stop-gap candidate, who, soon after the crisis was resolved, had given an uncharacteristically jingoistic speech praising Rosebery and denouncing 'this great abortive intrigue' by the French.[154] Early in 1899, Morley made a series of speeches denouncing the reactionary spirit which, he said, had found its way into the Liberal Party. He did not attack imperialism as such, but argued that true

---

[149] 'Arrivée de Capitaine Baratier, Marseille, 26 Octobre 1898', *Le Temps*, 27 October 1898.

[150] MAE, 123CPCOM17, no. 517, Geoffray, French Embassy, London, to Delcassé, 'Discours du duc de Devonshire et Sir Michael Hicks Beach: question de Fachoda', 20 October 1898.

[151] 'Bulletin de l'étranger', *Le Temps*, 31 October 1898.

[152] 'The Sirdar in London', *The Manchester Guardian*, 5 November 1898.

[153] Leo McKinstry, *Rosebery: Statesman in Turmoil* (London: John Murray, 2005), 413.

[154] Speech of 24 November 1898, quoted in John Wilson, *CB: A Life of Sir Henry Campbell-Bannerman* (London: Constable, 1973), 281–2.

Fig. 2.2. Kitchener as big bad wolf to Marianne's Goldilocks, *Le Petit Journal*, front cover illustration, 20 November 1898.

Mary Evans Picture Library, image 10119413

imperialism needed to be limited by common sense.[155] As Asquith then pointed out, this definition was a commonplace with which everyone could agree; but agreement in theory was not the same as agreement in practice, as the split caused by the Boer War was soon to show.[156]

CONCLUSION

Something of a contrived crisis—or, at least, an avoidable one—Fashoda was also a Franco-British battle of words in which competing claims of imperial destiny, legal rights, ethical superiority, and gentility preserved in the face of provocation belied the local reality of yet more African territory seized by force. If the Sudanese were the forgotten victims in all this, the Fashoda crisis was patently unequal in Franco-British aspects as well. On the imperial periphery, Marchand's mission was outnumbered and overextended next to Kitchener's Anglo-Egyptian expeditionary force. In the metropolitan capitals a self-confident Conservative government was able to exploit the internal fissures within French coalition administrations wrestling with the unending scandal of the Dreyfus case. Hence the imperative need for ministers to be seen to be standing up in Marchand's defence.

The two foreign ministers, Gabriel Hanotaux and Théophile Delcassé, at the heart of Fashoda diplomacy from 1895 onwards were too shrewd to risk escalating colonial competition in southern Sudan into violent confrontation. Moderate republicans, each sought to rise above the violent political storms lashing their coalition ministries. Between 1895 and 1897, Hanotaux enjoyed more room to manoeuvre than his successor, safe in the knowledge that the British had yet to defeat their Sudanese opponents. He was in his rhetorical element, relentlessly playing on the hollowness of supposed British treaty rights. Hanotaux made three things clear by doing so. One was that France was more scrupulous (and more sophisticated) in its imperial application of international law. Another was that Britain's actions were, by contrast, as aggressive as they were irresponsible. But perhaps more significant was Hanotaux's wider didactic purpose in using incipient confrontation in Sudan to illustrate that uncompromising imperial expansionism was a menace to European peace.

Delcassé was just as determined that France should be seen to have followed higher standards of behaviour and correct procedure. But his room for manoeuvre was minimal. The primordial requirement to save Marchand in order to accomplish a wider political purpose was most apparent in the final weeks of unusually public negotiation during which the terms, first of French withdrawal, then of the mission's homeward passage from Sudan, were arranged. By this point both sides were conducting their diplomacy in the public eye. This was unusual—and

---

[155] 'Mr Morley at Brechin', *Manchester Guardian*, 18 January 1899.
[156] 'Mr. Asquith, MP, at Louth', *Manchester Guardian*, 20 January 1899. On the rhetoric of the Boer War split, see Simon Mackley, 'British Liberal Politics, the South African Question, and the Rhetoric of Empire, 1895–1907', unpublished PhD thesis, University of Exeter, 2016.

potentially dangerous. The Foreign Ministries in London and Paris claimed to be releasing information to dispel popular misapprehensions—and so ease tensions—in both countries. This was, at best, disingenuous. For Delcassé's Quai d'Orsay especially, French diplomatic strategy acquired a sharper rhetorical edge thanks to the sequential publication of Blue Books and Yellow Books, which became a focal point for political discussion and extended press coverage as the crisis developed.

This explains the French insistence in October 1898 that effective communication (and thus a proper chain of command) between the government in Paris and Marchand in situ be re-established, so that the mission could be formally instructed to withdraw. Viewed in Britain as a last desperate bid to avoid conceding defeat, the French preoccupation with procedural correctness served bigger objectives. It helped extricate Marchand from Fashoda with his mission more or less intact, and with French national honour visibly upheld. Ultimately, the challenge was to turn a clear strategic reverse into a moral victory. And this meant focusing on Marchand the individual: praising his grace under pressure, bringing him home safely, and, finally, claiming him as a republican patriot rather than a cheerleader for an insurrectionist anti-republican nationalism. In terms of political rhetoric, then, the French side of the Fashoda crisis was conditioned by official efforts to narrow the country's deep internal divisions in the same way that the Republic's opponents in politics, in the press, and on the streets sought to widen them.

As for the British experience, the standard picture of near unanimity needs to be substituted with a more complex account that recognizes how 'unity' was to some extent the product of party political competition and individual manoeuvre. Clearly, Liberal criticisms of the *tone* of government speeches should not distract from the considerable areas of substantive cross-party agreement that genuinely did exist. Although he disapproved of the government's handling of the crisis, even Morley could agree that the French occupation of Fashoda had been 'ridiculous'.[157] There was broad agreement that national honour was at stake, yet also general agreement that France should not be 'humiliated'. The way round this was for Marchand to be praised in his capacity as an 'emissary of civilization' and allowed to go home with all due honour; but he could not be recognized as an official carrier of the French flag.[158] Questions of honour and civilization were wrapped up together, as Grey suggested when he tried to explain why withdrawal would be compatible with French dignity: 'If with his [Marchand's] departure civilization were to disappear [. . .] then I would agree that the honour of France was involved, because the honour of civilization was involved also.' But this was not the case, because although Marchand's mission had been heroic, the presence of civilization did not depend on him because the British were there to uphold it.[159]

A final, negotiated settlement was reached in 1899, when the British and French agreed on the demarcation of their respective spheres of influence. Given that it

[157] 'Mr. Morley on the Political Situation', *The Times*, 18 January 1899.
[158] This helps explain why British governmental and press announcements stressed the cordiality of Kitchener and Marchand's face-to-face exchanges: Sèbe, *Heroic Imperialists*, 198–9.
[159] 'The Fashoda Question', *The Times*, 28 October 1898.

was, in fact, possible to solve the problem 'rationally', it is worth considering whether Fashoda had in fact been built into a crisis by the deliberate actions of Westminster's political grandees. Jingoistic sentiment beyond the confines of London might suggest otherwise, but it is worth pausing none the less. In this reading of events, Bernard Porter's concept of 'absent-minded imperialism' might be reconfigured, less as evidence of significant variation in levels of interest in empire, and more as a rhetorical pose that allowed the officials and politicians to portray themselves as simply as falling in with the inexorable logic of events. They could not be blamed for submitting to the inevitable. It is also worth noting that the rhetoric of 'the nation' was selective and exclusionary. As one commentator noted afterwards, 'through the dispute the Metropolitan press and M.P.'s kept harping on how the "English" people were determined upon a definite line of action. It was rarely indeed that the word "British" was used, and taking this as a token of the times, the Irish and Scottish regiments would not have been called upon to assist their English brethren.'[160]

Support for Marchand, if not for war with Britain, was certainly a national phenomenon in France, with several provincial towns eager to bestow civic awards on the returning hero.[161] By contrast, French consular staff in Liverpool reported the anger among the city's industrialists at the irresponsibility of remote Westminster politicians who seemed willing to stoke up tensions with France without a thought for the adverse impact on Anglo-French trade. Still worse, according to Liverpool's city fathers, was the danger of a general European conflagration arising from some relatively marginal colonial dispute.[162] Arguably, though, the successful management of the Fashoda crisis to a non-violent conclusion—in spite of the heat of the rhetoric that it generated—was a harbinger of twentieth-century Anglo-French co-imperialist cooperation, and, thus, a fitting point of departure as our analysis moves forward.

[160] 'Through London Spectacles', *The Wasp*, November 1898.
[161] Sèbe, *Heroic Imperialists*, 226.
[162] MAE, 123CPCOM17, no. 1, E. Rocher, French Consulate Liverpool, to Delcassé, 13 October 1898.

3

The Rhetoric of the Moroccan Crises, 1905 and 1911

Within half a dozen years of the Fashoda crisis, Anglo-French relations had improved dramatically. In 1904, the Entente Cordiale was sealed.[1] The following year, a crisis broke out over Morocco, which was resolved after Britain and other powers backed France against Germany. In 1911, the Moroccan issue recurred in more dramatic form, when the Germans sent the gunboat *Panther* to Agadir in an attempt to safeguard their interests. Again, the British supported the French.[2] A powerful speech by Chancellor of the Exchequer David Lloyd George at the Mansion House, in which he warned Germany that the British would not stand aside where her vital interests were affected, was followed by a Franco-German compromise. The rapprochement between France and Britain was not reached without difficulty, nor was the compact between the two countries without its problems; it did not follow that the alliance of World War I was a foregone conclusion. Nevertheless, there was a genuine reduction in imperial tension.

Conflict eased partly because the British were no longer pursuing major colonial expansion, and the continued French efforts in that direction did not occur in areas that were likely to bring the former antagonists into collision—at least not until Ottoman rule in the Middle East finally collapsed. Britain, moreover, did not have a colonial lobby in the same sense that France did. Major disagreements over empire policy did exist in the UK, but these were connected with the questions of imperial tariff protection and Home Rule for Ireland, and were not the result of pressures either to acquire new territory or to avoid its surrender. Therefore, although the Moroccan issue was of considerable importance to Britain it did not (save at moments of crisis) generate a substantial volume of public rhetoric. For the French, by contrast, it provoked considerably more agony—and hence the production of more words—especially when the outcome of the Agadir episode resulted in the cession of colonial territory to the hated victor of the Franco-Prussian War.[3]

---

[1] Paul Cambon, the long-serving and immensely influential French ambassador to London, was pivotal to the Entente Cordiale's conclusion, see: M. B. Hayne, *The French Foreign Office and the Origins of the First World War, 1898–1914* (Oxford: Clarendon Press, 1993), 84–7; John Keiger, 'Sir Edward Grey, France, and the Entente: How to Catch the Perfect Angler?' *International History Review*, 38:2 (2016), 285–9.

[2] For an excellent summary, see Christopher Clark, *The Sleepwalkers: How Europe Went to War in 1914* (London: Penguin Books, 2013), 204–12. The most detailed narrative remains Jean-Claude Allain, *Agadir 1911: Une crise impérialiste en Europe pour la conquête du Maroc* (Paris: Publications de la Sorbonne, 1976), especially chapters 11–14 dealing with the culmination to the crisis.

[3] 'The Debate in the French Chamber', *The Times*, 18 December 1911.

This chapter, then, reverses the analytical lens from the imperial rhetoric emanating from political cultures in the throes of major colonial confrontation, to focus instead on the use of rhetoric as a means to cement the improving Franco-British relations signified by the entente.

BACKGROUND TO FRENCH INVOLVEMENT

Close French interest in Morocco, its politics, its trade, and its strategic potential was always likely.[4] Already the dominant imperial power in the North West African Maghreb, its colonial administrations in Algiers and St Louis (federal capital of French West Africa) had long and unstable Algerian and Saharan frontiers to police. The mixed population of Arabs, Berbers, and Jews, plus rising numbers of Southern European settlers that comprised Morocco's population struck a chord with French colonial officialdom in Algeria. So much so that a key reason for the original creation of a French consulate in the Moroccan imperial capital, Fez, in July 1894, was to gain some oversight over the large numbers of Algerian Muslim families resident in the country. As Algerians they remained French colonial subjects, but as Muslims living in Morocco they were able to claim the sultan's protection, a situation that galled French diplomats more accustomed to playing the role of protecting power.[5]

Equally familiar was the symbiotic relationship between interior agricultural markets, desert traders, and urban trading centres that governed Moroccan economic activity. Less geographically sprawling than the vast Algerian colony, Morocco was, at the same time, loosely administered from Fez, its royal capital. The Moroccan Alaouite dynasty, or sultanate, was more widely revered than the beylical rulers swept aside in Tunisia twenty years earlier. Its Islamic lineage conferred religious juridical authority as well as political power. The sultanate also retained a distinct governmental apparatus: the makhzen. Sometimes referred to as a shorthand for central royal bureaucracy, the makhzen, properly defined, comprised eight to ten senior figures at the cherifien court, some drawn from Fez's wealthy bourgeoisie, others from aristocratic military backgrounds who often occupied the roles of *grand caïds* (effectively, provincial governors) in the rural interior.[6] Whichever way the appellations were applied, by 1900 the sultanate and its makhzen were in trouble. Sultan Abdelaziz was still a teenager. His treasury was

---

[4] For the background to takeover, see: Daniel Rivet, *Lyautey et l'institution du protectorat français au Maroc, 1912–1925* (Paris: L'Harmattan, 1988), vol. I; Daniel Rivet, *Le Maghreb à l'épreuve de la colonisation* (Paris: Hachette, 2002); William A. Hoisington Jr, *Lyautey and the French Conquest of Morocco* (Basingstoke: Macmillan, 1995), chapters 2–5.

[5] MAE, 179CPCOM350, Rapport sur le Vice-Consulat de France à Fez, par M. Michaux Bellaire (head of mission), July 1897–May 1898.

[6] 'L'état politique du Maroc', *Bulletin du Comité de l'Afrique française*, 30 January 1905, p. 83; for French (and Spanish) impact on the distribution of rural power, see David M. Hart, *Tribe and Society in Rural Morocco* (Abingdon: Routledge, 2000), 16–18, 111–30; Robin Bidwell, *Morocco under Colonial Rule French Administration of Tribal Areas, 1912–1956* (London: Frank Cass, 1973), chapters 2–9.

empty. Utterly reliant on European loans and faced with a major regional revolt, royal administration was weakening fast.[7] For these and other reasons, French imperialists were especially assertive about France's claims on the place.

Supporters of the influential *Comité de l'Afrique française*, who helped install Théophile Delcassé as foreign minister, expected their voices to be heard. Foremost among them was Eugène Etienne, deputy for the western Algerian city of Oran and Chamber of Deputies president. In February 1904, Etienne established a Morocco Committee as a fund-raising instrument to advance the declared policy of 'peaceful penetration'. Supporting the Morocco Committee's work was a sociable affair. Famously known as 'the committee that dines', this new group organized high-profile salon dinners in which invited speakers lauded the work of French army officers and colonial administrators in North Africa or dwelt on the untapped investment opportunities to be had. With donations and grants assured from sympathetic investment houses, chambers of commerce, mining companies, and banks, the Morocco Committee became the Parti Colonial's most effective public relations tool.[8]

Etienne's lobbyists were pushing at an open governmental door. Just before Christmas 1900, the French Army Staff's intelligence office produced the most extensive military report to date on conditions and prospects in Morocco. It was strident in tone, uncompromising in its contempt for the sultanate, and unabashedly forthright in its support for intervention. Morocco, the intelligence analysts noted, was 'incomparably richer than Algeria'. Agriculture, the mainstay of the country's economy, offered rich pickings. Morocco's extensive mineral deposits, from iron ore and copper to silver and tungsten, were barely exploited and, with relatively short internal communications and deep-water harbours on its Atlantic and Mediterranean coasts, a welter of transoceanic trade beckoned. In this rhetorical line, the tragedy for Moroccans was the obscurantism of a sultanate, whose central administration had neither the wit nor the means to exploit the untapped wealth that surrounded it. Worse, the sultan and his cliquish makhzen advisors squandered time and resources in factionalism and feuding, steadily losing their grip on the country in the process.[9] But, the planners pointed out, even in this anarchic condition, Moroccan customs revenues in 1898 were more than half the size of Algeria's. With French guidance, that sum could be doubled in no time,

---

[7] For a summary of Morocco's internal problems, see Jonathan C. Katz, *Murder in Marrakesh: Émile Mauchamp and the French Colonial Adventure* (Bloomington, IN: Indiana University Press, 2006), 9–14.

[8] James J. Cooke, 'Lyautey and Etienne: The Soldier and the Politician in the Penetration of Morocco, 1904–1906', *Military Affairs*, 16:1 (1972), 14; Katz, *Murder in Marrakesh*, 62–3; more generally, see Stuart Michael Pursell, *The French Colonial Lobby, 1889–1938* (Stanford, CA: Hoover Institution Press, 1983). For details of leading investors in Morocco, see: MAE, 179CPCOM238, Etat-Major de l'Armée (EMA) 2eme Bureau, 'Notice sur le Maroc: Géographie, Armée, Politique intérieure, Intérêts internationaux', December 1900, 9–13.

[9] A classic study of Moroccan civil society, which brings out the extent of French misreading of it, is Edmund Burke III, *Prelude to Protectorate in Morocco: Precolonial Protest and Resistance, 1860–1912* (Chicago, IL: University of Chicago Press, 1976).

not least because Morocco's foremost trading partners—Britain and France—were ready to invest in its mining sector.[10]

What stood in the way of such bountiful progress? Not much, according to the French army analysts. On the one hand, the sultan's military forces, a combination of loyalist levies, or *mokhaznia*, poorly paid volunteers, and tribal auxiliaries, were shambolic. The European military advisors brought in to lead them were out of their depth, and hopelessly compromised. Largely organized for punitive operations against internal dissenters, the sultan's 'army' collected taxes by force, preying on the population rather than protecting them. Its military value was, in the *deuxième bureau*'s words, 'nugatory', and a single brigade of French colonial troops would suffice to rout it.[11] If organized military opposition could be discounted, wider international objections might, on the other hand, count for more. But here again, confidence bubbled over. Spain had legitimate strategic interests, which France was best placed to uphold. Britain's respect for non-interference in the sultan's affairs was contingent. If Moroccan internal breakdown jeopardized Britain's investments, its commerce, or its maritime security, it would accept the logic of French suzerainty. As for the commercial stakes of other foreign powers, Germany included, these were best served, the analysts argued, by the imposition of European control over a country whose endemic civil strife was approaching civil war.

As in the case of Tunisia twenty years earlier, for the French general staff the icing on this appetizing cake was the opportunity to resolve persistent disorder along a colonial land frontier to French strategic and economic advantage. Blaming the naïvety of French Algeria's early rulers for failing in an 1845 treaty with the sultanate to delimit the Algeria-Moroccan frontier along its 'natural' boundaries of the Moulouya River (over 100 miles west of the existing frontier) and the western pre-Sahara, the French army commands in Algiers and the western Algerian province of Oranie were determined to set things right.[12] This implied less the expansion of Algerian territory than the imposition of French political control along both sides of the disputed frontier region. Again, as with Tunisia a generation earlier, the seeds of intervention were sown by local arguments over frontier insecurity. Towns on either side of the volatile Morocco-Algeria border were meshed together by trade in livestock, wool, salt, candles, and other products. But these exchanges were uneven. Moroccans typically sold animals and goods without buying much Algerian produce in return. Equally damaging was the notorious insecurity of the interior caravan routes plied by the traders. Indeed, Morocco's north-east was becoming more rebellious, not less.

Discriminatory tariffs and worsening Moroccan disorder irked the Algerian colonial government.[13] When these matters were first raised formally, in January

[10] MAE, 179CPCOM238/Dossier EMA-2, Bureau, 'Notice sur le Maroc: géographie, armée, politique intérieure, intérêts internationaux', n.d. December 1900, pp. 1–13.
[11] MAE, 179CPCOM238/Dossier EMA-2, ibid, n.d. December 1900, 56.
[12] MAE, 179CPCOM238/Dossier EMA-2, ibid, n.d. December 1900, 19–50.
[13] A July 1867 law provided French tariff exemption to Moroccan goods traded across Algeria's land frontier. This was finally rescinded in late 1911: MAE, 179CPCOM353, no. 48/3/11, 'Relations commerciales de l'Algérie avec le Maroc par la frontière de terre', 18 November 1911.

1897, Jules Cambon headed the Algiers administration. He was the brother of Paul, ambassador to London, and, like him, was a vocal member of the *Comité de l'Afrique française*.[14] Jules received intelligence from the French Legation in Tangier indicating that the young Abdelaziz had neither the wherewithal nor the inclination to rectify the situation.[15] In response, the Governor and Foreign Minister Hanotaux in Paris set about establishing local free trade zones (so-called *marchés francs*) straddling the frontier in conjunction with the regional power-brokers of Morocco's turbulent north-east.[16] By late 1900, the Foreign Ministry joined forces with the Ministries of Finance and Commerce to investigate similar French-imposed arrangements to regulate commodities traded across the Sahara.[17] Their colleagues in the Ministry of Interior (responsible for Algeria) and the Ministry of Colonies (responsible for the nascent federation of French West Africa) were meanwhile compiling ethnographic surveys, detailed maps, and trade statistics intended to make the case for a definitive and French-designed delimitation of Saharan frontiers.[18]

Reflecting on seventy years of French rule in Algeria, Paul Révoil, one of Jules Cambon's successors as governor-general, declared in July 1901 that effective colonial exploitation of the Sahara was at last within their grasp.[19] With it came the prospect of commercial and strategic integration via the colonies of Mauritania and French Sudan (Mali) to France's West African territories. Morocco, the one large north-west African territory outside French control, was becoming an anomaly. Beyond the corridors of government, the *Comité de l'Afrique française* ramped up its claims about the sultan's inadequacies as a ruler. Internal insecurity and the absence of effective security forces were cited as proof that the makhzen required total overhaul. Much of the Paris press, its imperial fervour reanimated by the Fashoda crisis, was happy to dwell on these shortcomings. Accounts of settler families living terrified of attack, plus a spate of kidnappings, in which European and American diplomats and traders were held for ransom, lent a sensationalist air to this reportage. Heavily influenced by what could be construed as a propaganda campaign, as the Army Staff survey cited earlier indicates, initial French governmental demands for freer, safer cross-border trade became

[14] MAE, 179CPCOM350, no. 138, Jules Cambon to Delcassé, 'Au sujet des transactions commerciales entre l'Algérie et le Maroc', 18 January 1897.

[15] MAE, 179CPCOM350, Tangier Legation to Foreign Minister Hanotaux, 'Transactions entre l'Algérie et le Maroc', 26 April 1897.

[16] MAE, 179CPCOM350, Foreign Ministry, Sous-direction du Midi, Hanotaux to Governor Cambon, 'Transactions entre l'Algérie et le Maroc', 19 September 1897; no. 2953, Cambon reply to Hanotaux, 30 October 1897.

[17] MAE, 179CPCOM350, Direction Politique note, 15 December 1900.

[18] MAE, 179CPCOM350, Rapport présenté à la Commission interministérielle du Nord-Ouest Africain, n.d. 1901.

[19] MAE, 179CPCOM350, Ministère de l'Intérieur, Services Algériens, 'Commission interministérielle chargée d'élaborer et de soumettre au Gouvernement un programme de reconnaissance et d'organisation des régions dépendant de la sphère d'influence française dans l'Afrique du Nord-Ouest', procès-verbal, 20 July 1901. The heavy human price of this Saharan conquest is examined in Benjamin Claude Brower, *A Desert Named Peace: The Violence of France's Empire in the Algerian Sahara, 1844–1902* (New York: Columbia University Press, 2009).

subsumed into broader rhetorical critiques of Morocco's royal regime and Moroccan statehood itself.[20]

Aside from its local colonial dynamics, greater French assertiveness in Morocco was also explicable in light of the fundamental shift in Franco-British relations taking place in the first years of the twentieth century. So before returning to the first Moroccan 'crisis', it's worth dwelling on these wider international shifts as evinced in changing imperial rhetoric.

FROM ENMITY TO ENTENTE

Fashoda was one of the last great moments of British imperial confidence, spilling over into the hubris that marked the onset of the Boer War in 1899. The early British reverses in South Africa were humiliating, but, once the military tide had turned, Salisbury's government was able to profit from the divisions between 'Liberal Imperialists' and 'pro-Boers' in the ranks of the opposition. The so-called khaki election of 1900 saw a Unionist triumph, achieved very much on the basis of patriotic platform appeals.[21] But the Liberal disarray added lustre to a false picture of Conservative health. The South African War dragged on through a drawn-out guerrilla phase by which time Salisbury was physically ailing and his colleagues felt his grasp was slipping. Though he continued as prime minister, they obliged him to give up the Foreign Office. His replacement was Lord Lansdowne, the man who would eventually negotiate the Anglo-French entente.

Popular French Anglophobia resumed meanwhile. Shortly before his fatal over-exertions, President Félix Faure reiterated that Britain, not Germany, was France's true enemy. It was a sentiment echoed within the professional army. The officer trainees who graduated from the Saint Cyr military academy in 1900 were dubbed 'the Transvaal year', a significant number having decided to fight as volunteers alongside the Boers. Paris milliners, meanwhile, discovered a healthy profit selling customized felt hats *à la Boer* to their local clients.[22] In many ways, the British cause in South Africa was profoundly dubious. But, as the pro-Dreyfus journalist and Socialist politician Francis de Pressensé pointed out to readers of the *Manchester Guardian*—many of whom likely had pro-Boer sympathies themselves—there was a deeply unattractive element in the French opposition to it. 'A new and non-descript party—the so-called Nationalists—does not scruple to deal nearly exclusively in calumnies and full-blown lies', he wrote, citing the experience of the Dreyfus affair in support. This group's true aim, he claimed, was to destroy the Republic and return to the glories of Caesarism. It had 'pleased these people to take a violent fancy to the Boers', even though the latter, as republicans and Protestants,

[20] MAE, 179CPCOM185, EMA 2e Bureau report, 'Le Maroc en 1904', pp. 6–7, 13–16.

[21] Paul Readman, 'The Conservative Party, Patriotism, and British Politics: The Case of the General Election of 1900', *Journal of British Studies*, 40:1 (2001), 107–45.

[22] John Keiger, 'How the Entente Began', in Richard Mayne, Douglas Johnson and Robert Tombs (eds), *Cross-Channel Currents: 100 Years of the Entente Cordiale* (London: Routledge, 2004), 4–5.

were unlikely allies for Catholic French nationalists. It was enough for them that the Boers were opposed to the British, de Pressensé suggested; and he argued that it was England's liberalism, not its imperialism, to which they objected.[23]

French governmental moderation was far removed from the embittered Anglo-phobia of the ultra-nationalist right. In an important revisionist work published in 1968, Christopher Andrew challenged the orthodoxy that France's long-serving foreign minister, Théophile Delcassé, had realized the necessity for an Anglo-French alliance as early as 1899: indeed, he is said to have wanted to intervene in the Boer War as a means of reopening the issue of Egypt.[24] However, Pascal Venier has in turn mounted a persuasive challenge to Andrew, arguing that the evidence for a desire to intervene is weak, and that the pragmatic Delcassé's key concern was to avoid the nightmare scenario of an Anglo-German alliance. Certainly, the foreign minister gave impetus to a cross-Channel *détente* with a speech to the Senate in April 1900.[25] Calling for the two countries to respect each other's rights and dignity, Delcassé noted that France was 'a great European Power, that has become a colonial Power'. But, he pointedly observed, the new colonies had to be defended with the resources that were at the mother country's disposal.[26] Britain, by implication, had every right to do the same.

This may have helped diminish tensions at a time when the threat of French invasion was being discussed, somewhat hysterically, in the British public prints.[27] In the House of Lords, Rosebery had offered his own dark warnings about Britain's vulnerability to its European neighbours.[28] Not everyone in Britain succumbed to these fears, though. The liberal *Speaker* advised the public not to interpret continuing French military expansion in North Africa as proof of hostility towards Britain.[29]

Although talk of a planned French invasion continued,[30] Germany, its naval strength increasing, supplanted France as the paramount continental threat, both in the public mind and within British strategic planning.[31] Tellingly, William Le Queux's sensational 1894 novel *The Great War in England in 1897* dealt with a French invasion; his 1906 follow-up *The Invasion of 1910* described a German one.[32] The route to the entente may not have been easy but powerful factors pushed

[23] Francis de Pressensé, 'The French Government and the Boer Republics', *Manchester Guardian*, 19 March 1900.
[24] Christopher M. Andrew, *Théophile Delcassé and the Making of the Entente Cordiale* (London: Macmillan, 1968), 158–79.
[25] Pascal Venier, 'French Foreign Policy and the Boer War', in Keith Wilson (ed.), *The International Impact of the Boer War* (Chesham: Acumen, 2001), 65–78.
[26] 'France's Foreign Policy', *Manchester Guardian*, 4 April 1900.
[27] See, for example, 'Britain's Danger and How to Meet it', *Review of Reviews*, April 1900.
[28] HL Deb, 15 February 1900, vol. 79, cols 28–34.
[29] 'The Morocco Scare', *The Speaker*, 9 June 1900.
[30] See, for example, 'Invasion', *National Review*, June 1900. For a sceptical view, see 'The Nightmare of a French Invasion', *The Speaker*, 25 August 1900.
[31] David Morgan-Owen, 'The Invasion Question: Admiralty Plans to Defend the British Isles, 1888–1918', PhD thesis, University of Exeter, 2013, 64–7.
[32] Roger T. Stearn, 'Le Queux, William Tufnell (1864–1927)', *Oxford Dictionary of National Biography* (Oxford University Press, 2004; online edition, October 2007) <http://www.oxforddnb.com/view/article/37666>, accessed 1 August 2013.

Britain and France together. Fears of Germany were actually secondary. Talks started in 1903 when tensions between Russia and Japan were growing. Britain had signed an alliance with Japan the previous year.[33] A looming Russo-Japanese war therefore threatened to embroil the British in conflict with Russia's ally, France, unless a cross-Channel rapprochement could be reached. There was an important colonial dimension to the final agreement. Crucially, the French recognized the British occupation of Egypt, gaining a free hand in Morocco in return.[34] Equally significant, the two governments agreed 'to afford to one another their diplomatic support, in order to obtain the execution of the clauses of the present Declaration regarding Egypt and Morocco.'[35] This pledge would have consequences once Germany challenged French primacy in the latter country.

By the time the agreement was signed, the Conservative government was in deep trouble. Following the conclusion of the Boer War, Salisbury had finally resigned, to be replaced in Downing Street by his nephew Arthur Balfour. In 1903, Chamberlain launched his campaign for imperial protection under the label Tariff Reform. This threat to Britain's long-established free trade system not only split the Unionists. It was further guaranteed to unite the factious Liberals, who also benefitted from concerns, catalysed by the war, about national decline, military inefficiency, debilitating poverty, and general societal weakness.[36] 'Striking proof of the hopelessness of the position of a water-logged Ministry is found in the fact that conclusion of the Anglo-French Agreement has done nothing in the way of re-establishing its position', commented the veteran parliamentary sketch-writer Henry Lucy in April 1904, about a week after the entente was signed.[37]

The lack of controversy in Britain surrounding the agreement was equally striking. The *Saturday Review* took this as a sign of the childishness of a public that had embraced the French as enthusiastically as it had suddenly decided to start hating the Russians, and had instantly dismissed memories of 'the pin-pricks of the Fashoda era and the "vile caricatures" of the [Boer] war'.[38] But the political class too was almost wholly accepting of an accord which—like the Japanese alliance—signified an abandonment of the longstanding policy of 'splendid isolation'.

[33] Admittedly, Anglo-Japanese co-operation was facilitated by shared worries about deepening Russo-German interventionism in China. See: MAE, 161CPCOM9, no. 276, London Ambassador Geoffray to Direction politique, 8 October 1901, 'Rapports de l'Angleterre avec le Japon.'

[34] Pierre Guillen, 'The Entente of 1904 as a Colonial Settlement', in Prosser Gifford and Wm. Roger Louis (eds), *France and Britain in Africa: Imperial Rivalry and Colonial Rule* (New Haven, CT: Yale University Press, 1971), 333–68.

[35] Agreement of 8 April 1904, Article 9, reproduced in 'Declaration between the United Kingdom and France Respecting Egypt and Morocco, Together with the Secret Articles Signed at the Same Time', Cd. 5969, 1911.

[36] On Free Trade politics and culture in this era, see Frank Trentmann, *Free Trade Nation: Commerce, Consumption and Civil Society in Modern Britain* (Oxford: Oxford University Press, 2008), and also David Thackeray, *Conservatism for the Democratic Age: Conservative Cultures and the Challenge of Mass Politics in Early Twentieth Century England* (Manchester: Manchester University Press, 2013), chapter 1.

[37] Henry W. Lucy, *The Balfourian Parliament 1900–1905* (London: Hodder and Stoughton, 1906), 314.

[38] 'The Childish Public', *Saturday Review*, 13 August 1904.

Rosebery denounced it as the latest in a series of disadvantageously 'one-sided' agreements that the government had concluded with other powers over the previous several years.[39] But his complaints merely served to emphasize his estrangement from mainstream politics and to confirm his irrelevance to a rejuvenated Liberal Party that now seemed to carry all before it. In 1898, Rosebery's rhetoric of firmness against France had appeared an act of statesmanship. Now *The Times* twitted him for an extraordinary lapse of judgment, while expressing relief that no impartial person would take his mischievous pronouncement seriously.[40]

It was Grey who had eclipsed Rosebery as the doyen of respectable Liberalism in the field of foreign affairs, and he presented the entente as a step by which Britain would generously allow France to develop her empire as part of a joint civilizing mission. 'Of course the coolness of our relations with France some years ago arose out of the fact that we had an expanding colonial empire and France wanted a colonial empire', he explained to the House of Commons. 'But now France has such an empire—no doubt to a great extent undeveloped, but full of possibilities— and France has come to realise that the concessions we have made in Africa of rights indisputably ours are willingly made with the object of enabling her to develop the power she has there.' Moreover, 'in the future we shall see these two Empires side by side in West Africa, for to a considerable extent they will be conterminous, with an increasing development of their resources and an increase of the friendly relations between the two Powers'.[41]

At the broadest level, then, it is true to say that the entente was warmly received across the political spectrum. Nevertheless, there were some background complexities. Howard S. Weinroth has emphasized Radical warmth towards the agreement.[42] Thus the *Manchester Guardian* commented that 'the idea of friendship with France is curiously antagonistic to the Imperialist movement which in the heyday of its favour flouted the Latin races and courted Germany'.[43] Yet the entente was not without potential problems for those of a Radical bent. On the one hand, it seemed to herald a new spirit of pacific internationalism, whereby nations settled their differences through rational discussion rather than by the threat of war. On the other, the colonial aspect of the settlement looked like an old-style carve-up, in which the fate of the colonized was settled without reference to their wishes. Thomas Gibson Bowles, a rogue Conservative MP who later became a Liberal, described the entente as 'a compact of plunder' as regarded from the imperial perspective. Yet, 'from a European point of view', he simultaneously argued, the agreement was of 'the highest import and may be of the greatest advantage'.[44]

Trade was also an issue. The Liberal MP Joseph Walton did not deprecate the agreement as such, but complained that the government had not done enough to

---

[39] 'Lord Rosebery on the Situation', *The Times*, 11 June 1904.
[40] Untitled editorial, *The Times*, 11 June 1904.
[41] HC Deb, 1 June 1904, vol. 135, col. 523.
[42] Howard S. Weinroth, 'The British Radicals and the Balance of Power, 1902–1914', *Historical Journal*, 13 (1970), 653–82, at 657–8.
[43] Untitled editorial, *Manchester Guardian*, 9 April 1904.
[44] HC Deb, 1 June 1904, vol. 135, col. 534.

make ensure the French kept an open door to British trade in their colonies.[45] The British tended to valourize their own empire over the French one on account of its greater commercial openness: the exclusion of much British trade from French-occupied Madagascar was a particular sore point. But the Balfour government, caught up in the throes of the tariff controversy, was hardly a credible champion of free trade. Referencing the Tory swing to protectionism, Liberal MP William Robson quipped: 'Perhaps it is scarcely fair to expect such enthusiasm on the part of this Government for open ports when we know that they are so extremely anxious to close our ports at home.'[46]

For his part, Delcassé was exceptionally well served by a strongly pro-British team at the French embassy in London. Ambassador Paul Cambon, who, incidentally, accumulated direct North African experience during two terms as French resident-general in Tunisia, shared Delcassé's conviction that Franco-British colonial rivalries were trifling next to gathering German power.[47] His senior embassy counsellor, Léon Geoffray, went further still, arguing that Westminster politicians and the City of London, which he identified as Britain's 'governing elite', were true successors to Napoleon's 'nation of shopkeepers'. Their concern, he insisted, was to make money without fuss or interruption, so their appetite for colonial confrontation with France was drained by the twin shocks of the South African War and the Russo-Japanese conflict. The entente, in this interpretation, was less a strategic instrument than a better way of doing imperial business, albeit one whose military benefits to France would become clearer as the first Moroccan crisis developed.[48]

MOROCCO TAKES CENTRE STAGE

In April 1903, an uprising centred on the city of Taza in eastern Morocco entered a new phase. It was led by Jilali ben Driss Zirhouni al-Youssefi, or Bou Hamara, a pretender (or *rogui*) to the sultan's throne. Revolt spread further eastwards and throughout the Rif Highlands along Morocco's northern rim. Sultan Abdelaziz's authority was shrinking fast. So were the makhzen's all-important tax-raising powers. In May, the sultan dismissed the foreign (and mainly British) military instructors brought in to reorganize the sultan's levies (or *tabors*). The instructors' refusal to leave Fez brought the splits within the makhzen administration into the open. Abdelaziz's decision to revoke these dismissals only made matters worse. Much was made in French military and press analyses of Moroccan governmental 'disarray' as the country descended into 'complete anarchy'.[49]

[45] HC Deb, 1 June 1904, vol. 135, cols 556–61.

[46] HC Deb, 1 June 1904, vol. 135, col. 555.

[47] John F. V. Keiger, *France and the First Origins of the World War* (Basingstoke: Macmillan, 1983), 18–19, 31–3.

[48] MAE, 161CPCOM9, no. 344, Geoffray to Direction politique, 22 December 1904, 'La question fiscale et la situation générale'.

[49] MAE, 179CPCOM185, no. 1540, EMA 2e Bureau report, 'La situation au Maroc au commencement de Juillet 1903'.

The makhzen's inability to organize its forces to confront the eastern rebellion naturally spiked local and international interest in the possibility of French intervention. Indeed, French military commanders and colonial officials in western Algeria were already taking matters into their own hands. Local *caïds* and clan chiefs were enlisted as allies, and a military occupation of the Moroccan border town of Oujda was planned. The sultan's troops were eventually dispatched on punitive operations against the dissident Beni Zeroual tribal confederation in the Rif. But any salutary effect this might have had was undermined when the colonnade of Algeria's colonial governor, Charles Jonnart, was ambushed while returning from talks about the border problem with the municipal authorities in the Moroccan frontier town of Figuig on 31 May. In a highly symbolic move widely commented on in the British press, French artillery began a retaliatory bombardment a week later, compelling the heads of seven Moroccan *djemaas* (village assemblies) to submit to French authority. Little by little, France was taking over.[50]

The attack on Jonnart was so politically useful to the colonial lobby that some suspected the episode had been staged. Whatever the case, the Figuig ambush gave carte blanche to those colonial army officers spoiling for confrontation.[51] They were vocally led by Brigadier-General Louis-Hubert Lyautey, the man destined to become French Morocco's first resident-general. He was appointed in September 1903 to command the French Army's Algerian sub-division at Aïn Sefra, a strategic node from which he launched a series of probing attacks.[52] Disguised as frontier security operations, they pushed France's military control steadily westward, persuading even sceptics in Paris officialdom that untrammelled intervention might be worth the risks.[53] Foreign Minister Delcassé was still determined to achieve French pre-eminence in Morocco by suborning the makhzen rather than humiliating it. But he faced accusations of timidity from Lyautey's supporters among the Parti Colonial, Jonnart's colonial administration in Algiers, and their settler backers in politics, industry, and the press.[54]

Lyautey's sub-imperialist policy of creating advantageous 'facts on the ground' by incremental military advances westwards continued to wrong-foot governments in Paris and Fez. The sultan's declining fortunes lent further nourishment to French expansionism and the rhetoric supporting it. In marked contrast with Lyautey's string of victories, assaults by Moroccan royal troops on the main rebel-held towns of Taza and Oujda, as indicated in Map 3.1, came to nothing. The sultanate's inability to restore meaningful control became plainer still. It served French interests to depict Morocco's internal situation in conventional military terms of territory lost or won, and thus to strengthen the case for France's intervention. The absence of any comparable arguments in Fez pointed to a subtler local understanding of internecine disputes customarily settled through alliances

---

[50] Ibid.   [51] Hoisington Jnr., *Lyautey*, 21.   [52] Ibid., 22–4.
[53] J. Kim Munholland, 'Rival Approaches to Morocco: Lyautey and the Algerian-Moroccan Border, 1903–1905', *French Historical Studies*, 5:3 (1968), 328–43.
[54] Hoisington Jnr., *Lyautey*, 25–6.

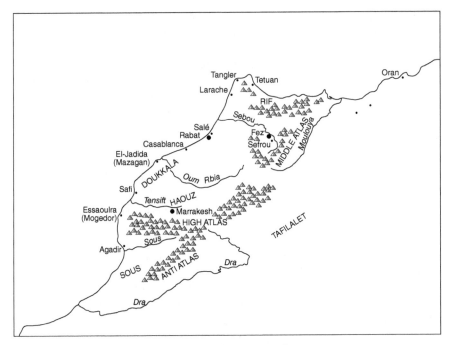

Map 3.1. The French conquest of Morocco

formed or broken with clan confederations, tribal chiefs, *pachas*, and *caïds*. Bou Hamara's challenge for the throne was threatening, but containable.[55]

In this sense, the makhzen's failure was as much rhetorical as real. The country's traditional leaders were hamstrung because they relied so heavily on the community of European consular officials in Fez and Tangier to disseminate information about local events. These consular diplomats were in post to advance national commercial and strategic interests increasingly at odds with Morocco's continued independence. Makhzen officials failed to persuade them that the country could and should govern itself. Even the German representatives that would assume the mantle of defenders of the sultan's rights were, in truth, animated by European rivalries and imperial clashes, not by Moroccan concerns.[56]

Sensing they had the upper hand, traditionalists within the makhzen administration pushed the sultan to reassign ministerial roles and expel all European advisors from the imperial capital. But by January 1904, significant numbers of

---

[55] One of the few French observers to concede that violent internal dissent did not signify a departure from the normative standards of Moroccan politics was A. Pimienta, the *Comité de l'Afrique française* correspondent in Fez. But he concluded from this that Moroccans would respect forceful French intervention. 'L'état politique du Maroc–de notre correspondant (A. Pimienta)', *Bulletin du Comité de l'Afrique française*, 30 January 1905, pp. 82–3.

[56] MAE, 179CPCOM185, no. 2209 EMA 2e Bureau report, 'La situation au Maroc à la fin d'Octobre 1903', pp. 1–24.

European diplomats and members of military missions returned to Fez.[57] Antagonized by the politicking in government, their interest quickly focused on Morocco's deepening economic and social crisis. Continuing rebellion fuelled spiralling inflation and rising food prices, in turn provoked urban rioting. It was against this backdrop that the April 1904 entente was signed. More than anything else, the Moroccan government's chronic financial weakness explained its inability to resist the entente's provisions for French encroachment in the crucial matters of fiscal reform, internal policing, and trade.[58] An interim state loan secured from the *Banque de Paris et des Pays-Bas* in July 1904 relieved the financial pressure, if only briefly.[59] But the anchoring of two French warships, *Kléber* and *Galilée*, off Tangier at the end of the month, confirmed the French government's intention to press ahead with a takeover: in its words, 'discretely but energetically'.[60]

Days later, the contradiction inherent in this phrase became obvious. Makhzen resentment at French financial leverage was matched by local hostility to the French military pressure on the eastern frontier. Lyautey's decision in June to send a column of 800 troops to seize Ras-el-Aïn, a Moroccan frontier oasis due south of Oujda, was conducted surreptitiously, and without government authorization. It fell to Delcassé, the former advocate of a forward imperial policy in Africa, to call for a pullback from the Moroccan territory occupied by French forces. Whereas Delcassé was preoccupied by the perilous diplomatic consequences of this frontier imperialism, his colleague, Prime Minister Émile Combes, as well as the French general staff in Paris, were more concerned about the breach of civil-military authority involved. Frustrated, the young general implored his allies in Paris, Etienne, and the economist and writer, Joseph Chailley-Bert, to warn against retreat. Their favoured rhetorical device was to summon up a 'second Fashoda', a humiliation to France's imperial pride bound to play to Britain's advantage.[61] The gambit worked. In venomous exchanges during Chamber of Deputies' debates on Morocco in late 1904, Etienne and his fellow French Algerian Deputy, Gaston Thomson, outflanked Socialist leader Jean Jaurès and other anti-imperial critics. They deliberately blurred the line between 'defence' of the Algerian-Moroccan frontier—in other words, the legitimate restoration of order to a disorderly pocket of an existing French colony—and a less defensible policy of advance into Morocco. Knowing that Lyautey enjoyed Governor Jonnart's unwavering support and Parti Colonial patronage, Prime Minister Combes went along with the ruse.

---

[57] MAE, 179CPCOM185, EMA 2e Bureau report, 'Le Maroc en 1904', pp. 1–3.
[58] *Le Maroc*, 14 April 1904.
[59] The *Banque de Paris et des Pays Bas* took the lead in 1902 in underwriting a French holding company, the *Compagnie Générale du Maroc*, intended to support French investors in the country. Most of France's leading banks signed up. Among them were *Crédit Lyonnais, Société Générale, Comptoir National d'Escompte de Paris, Banque de l'Union Parisienne, Société Marseillaise de Crédit Industriel et Commercial et de Dépôts, Banque Française pour le Commerce et l'Industrie, Banque de l'Indochine*, and *Crédit Algérien*, see: MAE, 179CPCOM353, *Banque de Paris et des Pays-Bas*, Président du conseil d'administration to Foreign Minister, 19 February 1912.
[60] MAE, 179CPCOM185, EMA 2e Bureau report, 'Le Maroc en 1904', pp. 8–9.
[61] Hoisington Jnr., *Lyautey*, 24–5; Cooke, 'Lyautey and Etienne', 15–16.

Fig. 3.1. Front cover from popular daily *Le Petit Journal* in April 1905 depicting the shifting power relations signified by the arrival of Saint-René Taillandier's Fez mission.

Mary Evans Picture Library, image 10078897

He ordered Lyautey's column to evacuate, but only as and when Jonnart and Lyautey thought best.[62]

Painfully aware of the more aggressive turn in French diplomacy, the sultan again announced the expulsion of foreign advisors (ostensibly to reduce budget costs) in what looked like a final act of defiance. The impression that the embattled sultan was increasingly powerless was strengthened when Abdelaziz relented definitively as the year came to a close. On 11 January 1905, Georges Saint-René Taillandier, head of the French diplomatic mission assigned to restructure the mahkzen administration and restore its finances, left Tangier for Fez, appropriately enough aboard the cruiser *Du Chayla*—a gunboat (Fig. 3.1).[63]

THE 1905 CRISIS

The crisis of 1905 showed the strength of the entente in the face of German efforts to disrupt it. Alarmed and antagonized by the thaw in Franco-British relations, Imperial Germany also held limited commercial interests in Morocco, its ports above all. But Morocco was less a significant German interest than an opportunity to test the changing diplomatic waters of inter-imperial competition. On one side of the world, Russia, France's principal ally, was laid low by its Far Eastern defeat by Japan. Closer to home, German industrial and naval competition with Britain was intensifying.[64] Chancellor Bismarck had, decades earlier, reined in German appetites during what Christopher Clark describes as Europe's colonial 'feeding frenzy' during the scramble for African territories in the 1880s. That restraint, it seemed, had elicited precious little gratitude in London or Paris.[65] Small wonder that in the more fluid international order of the early 1900s, the temptations felt within the Berlin Chancellery, the Foreign Ministry, and the Imperial Palace to divide Britain from France proved hard to resist.[66]

In the spring of 1905 it became known that the kaiser was to visit Tangier. Shortly before he arrived, Lansdowne received an official report which noted: 'Ever since the signing of the Anglo-French Agreement, the dislike and suspicion of the native population towards the French has greatly increased, and the belief is universal amongst them that it is their intention to take possession of the country.' It was natural, then, 'that the visit of the Emperor, coming at such a time, should cause the greatest satisfaction amongst all classes of the native population, who

[62] Hoisington Jnr., *Lyautey*, 26; Cooke, 'Lyautey and Etienne', 16.

[63] MAE, 179CPCOM185, EMA 2e Bureau report, 'Le Maroc en 1904', pp. 17–19; *Bulletin du Comité de l'Afrique française*, 'Pays indépendants—Maroc', p. 79, January 1905.

[64] MAE, 179CPCOM238/Dossier: Etat-Major de l'Armée 2eme Bureau, 'Notice sur le Maroc: Géographie, Armée, Politique intérieure, Intérêts internationaux', December 1900, p. 13; MAE, 179CPCOM350, no. 3966, Préfet du département d'Oran to Governor General Jonnart, 'Au sujet de la création d'un nouveau service maritime entre de port d'Oran et les ports de la côte Ouest du Maroc', 18 May 1904.

[65] Clark, *The Sleepwalkers*, 140–50, quote at 141.

[66] John C. G. Röhl, *Wilhelm II: Into the Abyss of War and Exile, 1900–1941* (Cambridge: Cambridge University Press, 2014), 329–53.

Fig. 3.2. 'The Stealer', 1905. A French satirical take on the Kaiser's intervention in the cat and mouse game over Morocco, which demonstrates that some, at least, recognized foreign interference in Morocco for what it was. Edward VII and Delcassé, with characteristic pince-nez, are shown in the foreground.

Getty Images, image 2666397

regard it as conforming their belief that the German Government is willing to assist the Sultan [Abdelaziz] to withstand the French.'[67]

In the Reichstag, Chancellor von Bülow denied that the upcoming visit signalled any aggressive intention: the kaiser had already made clear that he sought no territorial advantages in Morocco, he said. With significant commercial interests at stake, Germany simply demanded 'the maintenance of the open door, i.e., the equal treatment of all nations doing business there'.[68] When the kaiser arrived in Tangier at the end of March, he spent only two hours in the city, but was received rapturously.[69] In a speech at the German legation he reiterated Bülow's sentiments and also emphasized that he was 'one perfectly independent Sovereign visiting another'—a clear move to bolster the sultan against French efforts to control him. In another dig at Paris, the kaiser also counselled caution in introducing reforms, 'as the religious sentiments of the population must be duly taken in to consideration' (Fig. 3.2).[70]

---

[67] TNA, FO 881/86665, Herbert E. White to Lord Lansdowne, 25 March 1905.

[68] TNA, FO 881/86665, 'Extract from Count Bülow's Speech in the Reichstag on March 29, 1905'; regarding German involvement, see Pierre Guillen, *L'Allemagne et le Maroc de 1870 à 1905* (Paris: P.U.F., 1967).

[69] 'La visite de l'empereur d'Allemagne à Tanger, réponse à la *Gazette de Cologne*', *Le Temps*, 30 March 1905; 'Les Affaires du Maroc—La visite de l'empereur d'Allemagne à Tanger', *Le Temps*, 1 April 1905.

[70] 'The German Emperor at Tangier', *The Times*, 1 April 1905; TNA, FO 881/86665, White to Lansdowne, 3 April 1905.

Maurice Rouvier's government reacted to German machinations in Morocco with a measured indignation. Rouvier's ministry replaced Emile Combes' relatively long-lived and strongly reformist republican administration on 24 January 1905. The new government, in some ways, marked a relaunch of its predecessor. As premier, Rouvier, a prominent banker, retained his former position as finance minister. Delcassé, now identifiable as much with the entente as with African expansionism and France's Russian alliance, remained at the Foreign Ministry. He could count on a wide circle of sympathetic commentators in the press. Numerous journalists, among them *Le Temps*' foreign affairs editor and future premier André Tardieu and his colonial affairs expert, Paul Anthelme Bourde, had been instrumental in explaining Delcassé's imperial diplomacy to the public for years. As Frederick Thorpe explains:

> Because diplomatic protocol precluded ministers from discussing their views in public, Delcassé relied on influential journalists, several of whom were also leading political figures, to argue the subject in the press. Supporters floated trial balloons on his behalf, independent newspapermen proffered their perspectives, and adversaries severely criticized his policies.[71]

If Delcassé could assure the government a sympathetic hearing in the newspapers, other, younger ministerial faces, such as the Radical-Socialist war minister and army reformer, Maurice Bertéaux, and Minister of Justice Joseph Chaumié, a campaigning *Dreyfusard*, confirmed the new government's vigour.[72] Etienne Clémentel, later to become a notable labour reformer, was at this stage intent on improving colonial workplace conditions as minister of colonies. To the right of the political spectrum, Eugène Etienne, cheerleader for the Parti Colonial, took up the Interior Ministry with which came responsibility for Algeria. Aside from Etienne's presidency of the Morocco Committee, his working partnerships with Algiers Governor Jonnart and Brigadier-General Lyautey afforded him exceptional influence over the direction of French North African expansion.[73] To underline this, his first appointee was Roger Trousselle, the *Comité du Maroc* secretary, who became Etienne's *Chef de Cabinet* at the Interior Ministry.[74] Another North Africa specialist and fellow *pied noir*, Gaston Thomson, began a three-year stint as minister of marine.[75] Thomson had stood alongside Etienne in the Chamber of Deputies in depicting French domination of Morocco as an issue of vital national interest. He used his responsibility for France's navy to advance the same imperial cause. The new government, then, was more identifiable with empire defence than the old (Fig. 3.3).

The new French administration endorsed Saint-René Taillandier's work, the prospects for which looked promising at first. In early February 1905, Abdelaziz

[71] Frederick J. Thorpe, 'The French Press and the Franco-Spanish Convention of 1904 on Morocco', *French Colonial History*, 3 (2003), 159.

[72] 'La séparation des églises et de l'état', *Le Temps*, 30 March 1905.

[73] Cooke, 'Lyautey and Etienne', 15.

[74] *Bulletin du Comité de l'Afrique française*, Comité du Maroc, séance du 21 janvier 1905.

[75] 'Colonies françaises et pays de protectorat: généralités', *Bulletin du Comité de l'Afrique française*, January 1905.

Arguing about Empire

Fig. 3.3. *Le Petit Journal's* pictorial guide to Maurice Rouvier's new government, 5 February 1905.

Mary Evans Picture Library, image 10139077

told the *Le Temps* correspondent in Fez that Moroccans anticipated great results from closer relations with France. Necessary reforms would be welcomed so long as they remained compatible with Islamic belief and practice.[76] Locally, the French authorities reacted to the kaiser's unwelcome visit with some gunboat diplomacy of their own. Again, the French cruiser *Du Chayla* featured prominently, ferrying the French and British *Chargé d'Affaires* from Tangier to Gibraltar to rendezvous with Edward VII aboard his royal yacht on 29 March. To drive the message home in Tangier, Fez, and Berlin, Saint-René Taillandier reaffirmed that France, Britain, and Spain were completely united on Moroccan matters.[77]

Gunboats were all very well, but as the kaiser's earlier intervention made plain, the problem facing Delcassé's Foreign Ministry lay less in imposing the French mission's reforms than with the exclusion of German interests that this implied. Robert de Caix got to the crux of things. Chief editor of the *Comité de l'Afrique française* monthly bulletin, an acolyte of Philippe Berthelot, and Delcassé's secretary-general at the Quai d'Orsay, de Caix vented the frustration felt by Parti Colonial lobbyists over the foreign minister's lack of foresight. German commercial interests in Morocco were real enough, but they counted for less than the *Kaiserreich*'s prestige. Although Berlin was a party to earlier multilateral agreements on Moroccan trade and security, Delcassé had not pursued bilateral accords with Germany as he had done with Britain and Spain.[78] Indeed, quite the reverse: Delcassé had escalated tension by feeding details of British military preparations to the press in an effort to browbeat the Berlin government.[79] Ignoring German *amour propre* jeopardized the otherwise inexorable progress of French influence. De Caix's argument was simple: commercial concessions were easy enough but the real challenge was political. Delcassé might have to be sacrificed to get the French takeover back on track. De Caix remained sanguine about this because of an inadvertent benefit of Germany's actions. As he put it, 'One of the curious effects of the German incident in Morocco has been to nurture interest in our imperial policy there among political groups hitherto uninterested in the question.' The kaiser's aggressiveness had accomplished what Parti Colonial propaganda could not: Morocco had been made to seem a French national interest.[80]

De Caix returned to this theme in April. Ironically, for all the harrumphing of its nationalist press, German public opinion, he claimed, was minimally affected by the dispute over Morocco, unlike its French equivalent.[81] De Caix thus credited the populations on either side of the Rhine with enough political sophistication to see what was really at issue. The German government, in this first stage of the Moroccan crisis, was seeking a diplomatic victory and in May rejected suggestions

---

[76] 'Une interview du sultan', *Bulletin du Comité de l'Afrique française*, 9 February 1905, p. 81.

[77] 'La France et la politique marocaine', *Le Temps*, 30 March 1905, p. 1.

[78] Thorpe, 'The French Press', 161–9.   [79] Clark, *The Sleepwalkers*, 231.

[80] Robert de Caix, 'L'incident Allemand-Marocain', *Bulletin du Comité de l'Afrique française*, no. 4, April 1905, pp. 153–5, quote at p. 135.

[81] *Le Temps*, expressing the Foreign Ministry line, agreed; pan-Germanist celebration of the Kaiser's actions did not represent broader opinion: 'Les Affaires du Maroc—La visite de l'empereur d'Allemagne à Tanger', *Le Temps*, 1 April 1905.

from general staff chief, Count Alfred von Schlieffen, of a preventive strike against France.[82] Rouvier's administration also ruled out any war preparations, anxious to avoid escalating tension.[83] The French premier, deeply pessimistic about France's strategic position, then went further still, initiating private exchanges with Berlin in which he intimated his willingness to force Delcassé from office to placate the German government.[84] De Caix was right to conclude that the authorities in Berlin were seizing the moment, exploiting Russia's prostration after its crushing defeat by Japan to impose a kind of 'diplomatic vassalage' on France. The success of this gambit was never vital for the Germans; ensuring its failure, by contrast, was absolutely critical to the French.[85]

The German intervention meanwhile provoked surprisingly little political debate in Britain, given that it had the potential to unleash a war into which the country might have been dragged. Germany demanded a conference of European powers to discuss the Moroccan question, and the Berlin government clearly hoped that this would both increase its influence in the country and disrupt the Anglo-French entente. In June, in an apparent boost to the Germans, Delcassé resigned as foreign minister.[86] His departure, prefigured by Rouvier's underhand dealings with Berlin, was acrimonious—and highly symbolic. It signified the French government's readiness to make the political sacrifice necessary to defuse the Moroccan crisis without relinquishing French interests in the process.[87] But it also confirmed the widespread political frustration with Delcassé's methods. Sniped at in parliament and the press by Lyautey's supporters in Paris and Algiers, Delcassé also faced more widespread criticism for his inconsistency. Having staked his reputation on more cautious methods of advancing French claims on Morocco, the hapless foreign minister seemed slow-footed and obdurate at precisely the point that diplomatic dexterity was most required.[88]

Having toed the official line throughout the spring, the editorialists at *Le Temps* let rip once Delcassé's resignation was announced. The paper's views mirrored those of Delcassé's ministerial colleagues who lined up against him in a decisive Cabinet meeting on the morning of 6 June.[89] As Rouvier would later admit, they

---

[82] Stevenson, *Armaments and the Coming of War*, 64–76.

[83] David Stevenson, 'Militarization and Diplomacy in Europe before 1914', *International Security*, 22:1 (1997), 129–31.

[84] Keiger, *France and the First Origins of the World War*, 22.

[85] Robert de Caix, 'La Crise franco-allemande', *Bulletin du Comité de l'Afrique française*, May 1905, pp. 235–9.

[86] 'Les affaires du Maroc: M. Delcassé démissione', *L'Ouest-Éclair*, 7 June 1905.

[87] Christopher M. Andrew and A. S. Kanya-Forstner, *France Overseas: The Great War and the Climax of French Imperial Expansion* (London: Thames & Hudson, 1981), 28, 57; Andrew, *Théophile Delcassé*, 285–301. Delcassé's departure also confirmed that the Entente Cordiale would not be converted into a more formal Franco-British alliance, see: Keiger, 'Sir Edward Grey', 287–9.

[88] In fact, things were not as they seemed. As Christopher Andrew and John Keiger point out, Delcassé, who had been reading decoded correspondence between Rouvier and the German authorities, chose not to challenge his dismissal for fear of letting slip the fact that the French Foreign Ministry was decrypting Berlin's telegram traffic, see: Andrew, *Théophile Delcassé*, 273–89; Keiger, *France and the First Origins of the World War*, 22.

[89] 'La démission de M. Delcassé', *Le Petit Parisien*, 7 June 1905.

were exasperated by Delcassé's reluctance to conciliate the sultan, the makhzen, or their new-found German protector. In *Le Temps'* words:

> It has seemed to us that *la pénétration pacifique*, pursued in a style at once hesitant and brittle and with a sluggishness (*mollese*) worsened by acts of pointless brutality, lacked the necessary care and financial resources. It was presented to the makhzen in an abstract, dogmatic form so unappealing to Muslim thinking that it was liable to result in fruitless discussions.

The newspaper had a point. Little wonder that Germany's intervention was seized upon in Fez to thwart Saint-René Taillandier's work.[90]

A day later the paper tacked back. In light of Delcassé's abiding popularity, this, too, was probably at the government's prompting. Rouvier's parliamentary associates moved quickly to stifle the Chamber of Deputies' calls for discussion of the matter. Reluctantly, Socialist leader Jean Jaurès withdrew his interpellation but kept up the pressure for a full debate on Morocco.[91] In practice, although the government meanwhile placed the army on alert and even conducted a trial mobilization, it was only in mid-December that Jaurès got his parliamentary debate, and then only because Rouvier chose that moment to release a Foreign Ministry 'Yellow Book' intended set the record straight ahead of the Algeciras conference.[92] The government's pre-emptive silencing of Parliament in June was matched by the stream of information it fed to the press. Readers of *Le Temps* were reminded that neither the foreign minister's departure, nor the Fez mission's failure, signified a fundamental reverse. Rouvier, a fixture in republican governments since the 1870s, took up the reins at the Quai d'Orsay, and his government was determined that France should remain the Maghreb's power broker. French support for progressive reform could only benefit Morocco. Its implementation would rescue the sultanate from bankruptcy and set the administration on the footing necessary to cure the prevailing 'anarchy'.[93] Germany could hardly object to this, or so it was argued.[94]

The combination of steely resolve and altruistic imperial intent that Rouvier's ministers sought to convey was nicely captured by Interior Minister Eugène Etienne, who, now Delcassé was gone, was the Cabinet member most personally invested in Moroccan affairs. Etienne secured national press coverage of what, at first glance, seemed a run-of-the-mill ceremonial visit to a local council—the Charente Conseil Général in Angoulême—on 11 June. Charente's Prefect Adophe

---

[90] 'Bulletin de l'étranger: la démission de M. Delcassé', *Le Temps*, 7 June 1905.

[91] 'La démission de M. Delcassé', *Le Petit Parisien*, 7 June 1905.

[92] 'La Chambre—Déclaration de M. Rouvier', *Le Figaro*, 17 December 1905, p. 3; 'La question marocaine: Une déclaration de M. Rouvier', *Le Matin*, 17 December 1905, p. 1; Stevenson, 'Militarization and Diplomacy', 131.

[93] Using the term 'anarchy' as rhetorical shorthand for Morocco's internal politics borrowed from *Comité de l'Afrique française* propaganda. Typical in this vein was a widely publicized 'expert' survey of the Moroccan situation by Commandant Edmond Ferry: 'La réorganisation marocaine', *Renseignements coloniaux et documents publiés par le Comité de l'Afrique française et le Comité du Maroc*, no. 12 *bis*, 1905, pp. 517–27.

[94] 'La situation extérieure de la France', *Le Temps*, 8 June 1905.

Carnot enjoyed an unusually high profile, however. He was joint founder of the centre-right party, the Alliance Démocratique, and was the brother of a former president of the Republic. In a carefully orchestrated sequence of speeches, Etienne seized on the prefect's assurances that the people of Charente were peace-loving patriots committed to good order at home and overseas. The government, Etienne insisted, sought exactly the same. He reiterated the point during a visit to the local troop garrison later that day. Patriots, by implication, were bound to endorse the pursuit of peace and order in France's North African backyard.[95] Etienne's appeal to provincial patriotism and common sense resonated, even in those regions identifiable with more radical republicanism. The influential *Dépêche de Toulouse*, for instance, became more uncompromising in tone, even if its so-called 'orchestra stalls policy' still followed a middle line between the two extremes of Socialist internationalism and outright Germanophobia.[96]

At the level of high diplomacy, French official statements were also couched in the rhetoric of normal service resumed.[97] After discussions with German Ambassador Prince Hugo von Radolin, on 28 June, Rouvier announced that Paris and Berlin agreed a remit for a future conference. Disingenuously, the premier conceded that Moroccan sovereignty should be conserved; the German government accepted in return that France, as the dominant regional power, was entitled to lead the reform process in Fez.[98]

None of this generated controversy in London; it seems to have been taken as axiomatic that France would be supported.[99] Lansdowne merely issued a brief statement about the forthcoming conference, made in response to a parliamentary question.[100] This is not to say that there was no popular interest in Morocco, which was the subject, at around this time, of a series of classically Orientalist representations in the *London Illustrated News*.[101] But in that same journal, one writer claimed to have once been told by an experienced diplomat 'that only journalists speak freely about Morocco. "It's one of the subjects we don't care to discuss," he said, "it bristles with difficulties of which everybody can see the beginning and none can foretell the end."'[102] Was there really a conspiracy of silence on the issue

[95] 'M. Etienne à Angoulême', *Le Temps*, 12 June 1905.

[96] Jean-Marie Mayeur and Madeleine Rebérioux, *The Third Republic from its Origins to the Great War, 1871–1914* (Cambridge: Cambridge University Press, 1984), 293.

[97] 'Bulletin de l'étranger: La négociation marocaine', *Le Temps*, 10 June 1905.

[98] The German government still insisted that previous French demands were incompatible with the Madrid conference accords, which established that no single power could establish unilateral control in Morocco without the prior assent of the other signatories. 'Les relations franco-allemandes', *Le Temps*, 29 June 1905.

[99] *The Spectator*, 8 April 1905; 'The Morocco Crisis', *Western Times*, 19 June 1905.

[100] HL Deb, 11 July 1905, vol. 149, cols 240–1.

[101] See, for example, 'The Lepers' Portion: A Wayside Scene in Disturbed Morocco', *Illustrated London News*, 14 January 1905, and 'The Inter-Tribal Friction in Morocco: The End of a Blood-Feud', *Illustrated London News*, 16 September 1905.

[102] 'Europe and Morocco', *Illustrated London News*, 15 July 1905. Interestingly, Grey used the same phrase in conversation with German ambassador Count Metternich: TNA, CAB 37/107, no. 71, Grey note, 21 July 1911.

perpetrated by the foreign policy elite? If that seems doubtful, it was nonetheless true that the press had more to say on Morocco than the statesmen did.

Thus, while there was no Fashoda-style hysteria, there was much agreement that the Germans were in the wrong. According to the Conservative *Spectator*, 'all history shows that the French are liable to sudden fits of uncontrollable anger'. Although it was unlikely that the French would want to go to war at this moment— their Russian allies being in the final throes of the war with the Japanese—it was conceivable that the kaiser's action would produce an explosion of French rage leading to military conflict. If so, he would only have himself to blame for his terrible diplomatic blunder.[103] At the other end of the spectrum, *The Speaker* acknowledged that the kaiser's advocacy of resistance to European reform at first sight had 'something attractive in it, as a kind of cry of "Morocco for the Moors." But the advice comes from a sovereign whose only interest in native obstinacy is the use to which he can put it.' The journal argued that one always had to be suspicious when stronger powers justified their interference in the affairs of the weaker in terms of claims to paramountcy or the need to restore order, but in this case the French were justified:

> France's right, relatively to other nations, to interfere in Morocco may be challenged *pro forma* by the Kaiser, but it cannot be morally challenged by anyone who knows the history of French action in North-West Africa. Her positive right is defended on the ground that ever since she interfered on behalf of Europe to rid the Mediterranean of a nest of pirates at Algiers seventy-four years ago, she has honestly been carrying out a great scheme of peaceful and orderly civilisation.[104]

Similarly, *The Economist* was certain that the French were very suitable people to undertake 'the immense and most complicated' job of 'civilising Morocco'.[105]

Weinroth rightly notes the different position of the *Manchester Guardian*, although he fails to do full justice to its complexities. Whereas he suggests that the paper shifted from initial acknowledgement of France's grievances to sympathy for the German case, in fact it was fairly consistent.[106] From the beginning it suggested that although the French were justifiably annoyed by Wilhelm's methods, his actual policy had something to commend it: 'The main object of the Kaiser's visit is to emphasise the fact—quite worth emphasising—that no two countries have a right to settle the affairs of a third country as pleases them without consulting the interests of other Powers.' Support for free trade was the key to the *Guardian*'s attitude: the commercial 'open door' advocated by Germany was something that Manchester opinion would instinctively support. The entente had recognized the principle in Morocco, but only on a time-limited basis. That, as far as the paper was concerned, was regrettable: the British government in its view could have applied more pressure and made the arrangement permanent, but

---

[103] 'Germany, France and Morocco', *The Spectator*, 1 April 1905.
[104] 'The Isolation of Germany', *The Speaker*, 8 April 1905.
[105] 'The Moroccan Question', *The Economist*, 1 April 1905.
[106] Weinroth, 'British Radicals and the Balance of Power', 659.

had not done so because of its lack of enthusiasm for free trade: 'In attempting to enforce it [the open door] in Morocco in the interests of Germany the Kaiser is, therefore, acting in the spirit of the Agreement, not against it.'[107] Certainly, as Weinroth observes, the *Guardian* at first spoke up strongly in favour Delcassé's policy of 'pacific penetration' of the country. This, however, needs to be understood in the context of what it saw as the alternative—direct conquest, Algerian style. Delcassé was portrayed as following a peaceful and restrained path in the face of the 'fire-eating colonels' of the military party in Paris and the excessive zeal of French agents on the ground. Crucially, formal conquest of Morocco—it was assumed—would put an end to British commercial rights there.[108]

The paper became critical of Delcassé, after his resignation, only when it concluded that he had 'thought less of Anglo-French friendship as an instrument of human progress' than as a means of isolating Germany and securing 'the consolidation of the Mediterranean Empire of France'.[109] To a considerable extent, the *Guardian* took its cue from Delcassé's French Socialist critics. Its overall position can be summarized as opposition to aggressive imperialism combined with faith in the pacific and civilizing power of free trade and a conviction that the Moroccans could benefit from the guidance of the Concert of Europe, especially if interference focused on the commercial interests that the Powers had in common. This did not preclude an exclusive place for France as the power that would actually execute reforms.[110] According to this vision, benign imperialism was both possible and acceptable but would benefit from some form of international accountability.

The implicit question here was whether Germany would accept this outcome. As we have seen, at first it seemed not. As Heather Jones points out, the German government's strategy to sabotage French policy had three parts: angry insistence on prior consultation; gunboat diplomacy to underline that Germany could not be ignored; and feigning the role of protector of sultanate interests. All three had a strong rhetorical dimension. But the unspoken aim was quite different: to humiliate France and supplant it in Morocco, which would become a German sphere of influence. Initially, the strategy seemed to work. The makhzen cleaved to Germany's Tangier mission to the exclusion of Saint-René Taillandier. And Rouvier's Cabinet offered up Delcassé's resignation in June to clear the path to a bilateral accord with Germany akin to those concluded in preceding years with Britain, Spain, and Italy.[111]

These German methods proved too much for other powers to stomach, however.[112] Having at first defied the Concert system by coercing France directly, the German government's subsequent reversion to that system by accepting the

[107] Untitled editorial, *Manchester Guardian*, 8 April 1905. See also the editorial of 29 June 1905.
[108] Untitled editorial, *Manchester Guardian*, 29 June 1905.
[109] Untitled editorial, *Manchester Guardian*, 9 August 1905.
[110] Untitled editorial, *Manchester Guardian*, 29 June 1905.
[111] Heather Jones, 'Algeciras Revisited: European Crisis and Conference Diplomacy, 16 January–7 April 1906', EUI Working Paper, 2009.
[112] 'A Fez', *Le Petit Journal*, 16 April 1905, p. 1.

multilateral conference at Algeciras to resolve the crisis saw Berlin isolated once more. (By the end of the year the British and French general staffs were talking to each other about possible joint action, the prelude to eventual, more formal exchanges from 1910 onwards.)[113] The sultanate suffered as well. Algeciras undermined Moroccan sovereignty decisively, imposing a European-run state bank and formalizing foreign control of internal security, thanks to Franco-Spanish organization of policing in Morocco's eight major commercial ports. The creeping French imperial control, which the German government derisively labelled 'Tunisification', accelerated apace.[114]

At the end of 1905, Balfour resigned and the Liberals came to office under Campbell-Bannerman as prime minister. The general election that followed turned substantially on free trade, but the seemingly obscure question of Chinese indentured labour in South Africa also became an important issue. The hot controversy over allegations that the Conservatives had introduced 'Chinese slavery' masked important continuities in imperial policy, however. The grant of self-government to the former Boer republics marked an awareness of the limits on London's capacity to direct the empire centrally, but the changes introduced were evolutionary rather than revolutionary.[115] So too in foreign policy there was no dramatic shift of direction, although there were some changes of emphasis. Grey, as foreign secretary, was, if anything, more pro-French than Lansdowne had been.[116] Referring to the programme of a forthcoming conference on Morocco, very shortly after taking up his post, he wrote: 'We shall of course do what they [France] want about it, as there is nothing we want to put forward.'[117] The twelve-nation conference met at Algeciras early in 1906. The Germans overreached themselves and, through a series of diplomatic blunders, were unable to prevent the financial and policing reforms mentioned earlier from being agreed in a way that essentially confirmed France's Moroccan position, albeit with a significant role for the Spanish.[118]

---

[113] This Franco-British military cooperation, although tentative, marked a significant advance on the previous year when the newly appointed French military attaché to London, Colonel Victor Huguet, complained of French Army disdain for its British equivalent—a dismissiveness also evident in French political rhetoric of the time. On Huguet, see Elizabeth Greenhalgh, *Victory through Coalition: Britain and France during the First World War* (Cambridge: Cambridge University Press, 2005), 6–7.

[114] Ibid.

[115] See Ronald Hyam, *Elgin and Churchill at the Colonial Office 1905–1908: The Watershed of the Empire-Commonwealth* (London: Macmillan, 1968).

[116] Lyle A. McGeoch, 'On the Road to War: British Foreign Policy in Transition, 1905–1906', *The Review of Politics*, 35 (1973), 204–18.

[117] TNA, FO 800/49, Grey papers, Grey to Bertie, 13 December 1905; McGeoch, 'On the Road to War', 205. It should be noted that Grey's comment was about procedure, and did not amount to a diplomatic blank cheque. See also Keith Wilson, 'The Agadir Crisis, the Mansion House Speech, and the Double-Edgedness of Agreements', *Historical Journal*, 15:3 (1972), 513–32, at 528.

[118] Jones, 'Algeciras Revisited' <http://hdl.handle.net/1814/10527>. Matthias Schultz's work is useful in gauging the extent to which Algeciras marked a reversion to nineteenth-century Concert-style settlement of colonial disputes: 'Did Norms Matter in Nineteenth-Century International Relations? Progress and Decline in the "Culture of Peace" before World War I', in Holger Afflerbach and David Stevenson (eds), *An Improbable War? The Outbreak of World War I and European Political Culture before 1914* (Oxford: Berghahn, 2007), 43–63.

The Speaker read the result not merely as a deserved French triumph, but as a broader victory for the 'Latin' peoples, as Italy and Spain appeared supportive of her aspirations. It argued:

> By her occupation of practically the whole of the north-west of Africa, by her steady progress and opening up of the country, and by the genius she has displayed for organising, pacifying, and developing the annexed territories France has placed herself naturally and by right, at the head of those aspirations which the Latin peoples have long cherished in regard to North African expansion. Her position is now recognised.[119]

This was just one example of a pervasive Liberal rhetoric in which colonization was best advanced not by international rivalry and military struggle, but by pacific cooperation between powers with legitimate and recognized interests.

Such sentiment accorded with the line spun in the French Foreign Ministry's Yellow Book, published on 14 December, three days before Rouvier made his long-awaited speech on Moroccan affairs. Retracing France's Moroccan diplomacy over the preceding year, the Yellow Book achieved several objectives at once. First of all, it scotched persistent complaints in the German media that Delcassé had tried to use the Moroccan dispute to forge a coalition of powers against Germany, a scheme only undone by the Berlin government's timely intervention.[120] Indeed, Yellow Book dispatches suggested the exact reverse: French moderation in the face of the kaiser's provocation. This immediately drew favourable commentary within the *Dreyfusard* press at home and within the Liberal press in Britain.[121] Far from warmongering or wilfully ignoring German interests, Delcassé emerged from the selection of Foreign Ministry documents as judicious, even scrupulous in his attention to German rights.

Why, then, did the foreign minister resign? In the interpretation suggested by the Yellow Book, it was Delcassé's recognition of the greater good (and not his disgruntled ministerial colleagues) that persuaded him to go. Rouvier's platonic statesmanship was meanwhile proven by his skill in defusing what remained a dangerous situation. For other Yellow Book dispatches confirmed that German governmental belligerence persisted even after Delcassé was sacrificed. So much so that Prince de Radolin ultimately confronted Rouvier with a brutal choice—a conference or war. Unruffled, the French prime minister instead discerned a middle path: he acceded to the conference in principle, but only after its composition and scope was properly defined. In this way, the spoiling tactics of Count Tattenbach's German mission to the sultan were revealed for what they were.[122] And this was sweet, if belated, revenge for the earlier damage done to Saint-Taillandier's mission.

---

[119] 'The Latin Alliance', *The Speaker*, 21 April 1906.

[120] 'Les "révélations" diplomatiques: L'opinion allemande', from Berlin special correspondent, *Le Temps*, 18 October 1905. This was first officially denied in a French diplomatic statement published in the *Dépêche de Toulouse* in October 1905.

[121] 'Le Livre Jaune', *La Justice*, 16 December 1905, p. 2, also citing reports in the *Daily Chronicle* and the *Daily News*.

[122] 'Le livre jaune sur le Maroc: Ou la conférence ou la guerre', by Stéphane Lauzanne, *Le Matin*, 15 December 1905.

To amplify the point, the former head of the French mission was awarded the *Légion d'honneur* on 17 December.[123]

Obviously one-sided, as a rhetorical exercise the December 1905 Yellow Book could be read differently as a means to soften up French parliamentary opinion in readiness for Rouvier's decisive statement of French intentions in Morocco on 17 December. Its overwhelmingly favourable portrayal of French diplomacy not only exonerated Delcassé, but accorded the prime minister the decisive role of peacemaker.[124]

Before a packed Chamber and a row of ambassadors crammed into the spectators' gallery, the prime minister was thus able to claim that his government's actions were guided by moderation and legitimate interest in Moroccan stability. The moderation was apparent in his willingness to resolve matters through an international conference; the legitimacy derived from three things: France's pre-eminence in north-west Africa, its consequent determination to end the 'contagious anarchy' afflicting Morocco, and its service to wider European interests in doing so. Algeciras, then, was a conference for jurists, not politicians. Its core purpose was to agree the legal basis for the restoration of Moroccan internal security, its policing above all.[125] In defending French actions, Rouvier thereby accomplished his core objective. He reconciled the internationalization of the Moroccan crisis (as evident in the upcoming Algeciras conference) with continued French primacy in the outcome (as indicated by France's presumptive control over Moroccan finances and policing).

TOWARDS THE SECOND MOROCCAN CRISIS

The outcome of the Algeciras Conference, capped in May 1906 by Sultan Abdelaziz's reluctant accession to it, confirmed Rouvier's confident reassertion of French dominance in Morocco. A French-run Moroccan state bank directed the country's budgetary affairs. Joint Franco-Spanish municipal police authorities regulated security and commerce in eight coastal cities.[126] And Lyautey's military forces, still nominally part of the Algerian colonial garrison, probed further west, extending French strategic control to the Moulouya River and, ultimately, onwards towards Fez. Viewed differently, little was definitively resolved. Crucially, neither the sultanate, nor Morocco's leading clan confederations, nor the German government were reconciled to *de facto* French supremacy in Morocco. And all three became more stridently hostile after 1906, not less.[127]

During late 1906, merchants and tribal leaders in and around Tafilalet, the oasis hub for south-east Moroccan trade, coalesced into an anti-French insurrectionist

---

[123] 'M. Saint-René Taillandier', *Le Matin*, 17 December 1905.

[124] 'La question marocaine: Une déclaration de M. Rouvier', *Le Matin*, 17 December 1905, p. 1; 'La Chambre—Déclaration de M. Rouvier', *Le Figaro*, 17 December 1905, p. 3.

[125] 'Les affaires du Maroc: déclaration du Président du Conseil', *Le Petit Parisien*, 17 December 1905.

[126] Jones, 'Algeciras Revisited'.   [127] Hoisington, *Lyautey*, 28–9.

movement. Their grievances about French commercial interference and the divide and rule tactics pursued by General Lyautey's military staff resonated throughout the country, adding to popular resentment about Abdelaziz's ineffectual leadership. French residents in the larger towns of the north became targets of mob violence. On 19 March 1907, Émile Mauchamp, a prominent French physician, was murdered outside his house in Marrakesh. Ostensibly a lynching, the killing, it appeared, was organized by district headmen and sanctioned by the makhzen.[128]

Georges Clemenceau, republican radical and one-time anti-colonialist, was six months into his first prime ministerial term when news of Mauchamp's death reached Paris. Responsible for Moroccan affairs, Clemenceau's foreign minister, Stephen Pichon, a fiercely anti-clerical Freemason, shared his Radical-Socialist beliefs. So did Albert Sarraut, Clemenceau's deputy and an eloquent spokesman for the Parti Colonial. More unusual was War Minister General Georges Picquart. His public defence of Alfred Dreyfus had cost him his army career until Clemenceau, the staunch *Dreyfusard*, rescued him. This quartet set France on the path to military occupation in Morocco. First, Clemenceau ordered Lyautey's colonial troops into the eastern border town of Oujda until the makhzen made restitution for Mauchamp's murder.[129] Dissent only spread more widely, so much so that in late July 1907 French attention shifted from Oujda to the port of Casablanca.[130] The killing of eight French construction workers occasioned a spate of retributive violence by crewmen of the warship *Galilée*. In moves redolent of the events in Tunis and Alexandria in 1881 and 1882, the ship's captain ordered the shelling of Casablanca's oldest districts causing hundreds of fatalities. Desperate to restore order, Clemenceau ordered a 2,000-strong expeditionary force to occupy the port.[131] With strict instructions to remain in Casablanca, its commander, General Antoine Drude looked on as the population of the Chaouïa, the Casablanca hinterland (sometimes rendered in English as the *Shawia*), rose up against this French 'invasion'.[132]

By late August 1907, the dissidents had a champion: Moulay Abd el-Hafid, brother of Abdelaziz and challenger for the throne. Backed by a broad coalition of Arab and Berber tribal confederations determined to oust the French, Moulay Abd el-Hafid confronted his brother with the stark choice of abdication or civil war. It would be another twelve months—a year punctuated by worsening internecine violence and devastating French use of artillery against warring tribal levies—before Abdelaziz abdicated. Bitterly anti-French, the new sultan nonetheless reached a compromise agreement in March 1910, which gave freer rein to Lyautey and his

---

[128] Katz, *Murder in Marrakesh*, 138–43; Jonathan C. Katz, 'The 1907 Mauchamp Affair and the French Civilizing Mission in Morocco', *Journal of North African Studies*, 6:1 (2001), 143–66.

[129] Hoisington, *Lyautey*, 30–1.

[130] French suspicions that the German government secretly funded Moroccan print propaganda against the French were by then intense: see MAE, 179CPCOM4, no. 99, French Ambassador, Berlin, to Pichon, 30 May 1907; *Gazette de Cologne*, 29 May 1907.

[131] The extent of violence and destruction became apparent in the resulting claims for compensation, see: MAE, 179CPCOM417/Dossier 1, événements de Casablanca—indemnités, 1907–10.

[132] Ibid, 31–2; Burke III, *Prelude to Protectorate*, 93–117 *passim*.

lieutenants to crush the remaining pockets of organized resistance.[133] The inevitable climax was the dispatch of another, larger expeditionary force, this one sent to 'relieve' the capital, Fez, in May 1911.[134] It was this move, tantamount to a unilateral military occupation, which internationalized Morocco's long-running internal disorder once more.[135] A second 'crisis' resulted.

THE 1911 CRISIS

On 13 March 1912, nine months after the second Moroccan crisis kicked into life, a note crossed French Prime Minister Raymond Poincaré's desk advising him to contact the official publishing house, the *Imprimerie Nationale*. Responsible for printing government documentation, the *Imprimerie* was struggling to cope with a backlog of Finance Ministry budget reports. This was holding up publication of the latest Foreign Ministry Yellow Book containing the French version of the preceding year's Moroccan events.[136] Unusually, this latest Yellow Book included War Ministry memoranda and military reports alongside the usual diplomatic dispatches. The intention was to explain the strategic and humanitarian imperatives that made the occupation of Fez and Lyautey's long-cherished westward march to the Moulouya River essential.[137]

As in 1907, so in 1911, the violent death of Frenchmen became prelude and pretext for a wider military occupation. On 14 January 1911, an Army intelligence officer based at Boucheron Camp outside Casablanca ventured eastwards to arbitrate in an intertribal dispute over rival claims to pasturage along the Chaouïa margins near Kasba Merchouch.[138] Zaer tribesmen massacred his four-man escort on arrival. The assault took place close to the point where a French lieutenant had died in similar circumstances eleven months earlier.[139] These attacks persuaded two key figures, General Charles Moinier, commander of French forces at Casablanca, and Louis Leriche, Rabat consul and former Algeciras conference delegate, to lobby for a fundamental policy shift.

The irony was that, while confrontation between French troops and their Moroccan opponents escalated, tensions with Germany over France's gradual Moroccan takeover had significantly diminished. Deftly negotiated by the Berlin

---

[133] For details, see: MAE, 179CPCOM16 and 179CPCOM352.

[134] Hoisington, *Lyautey*, 32–6.

[135] Archives départementales de la Sarthe, Fonds Caillaux, 39J15/DMA16, Expédition de Fès, 'Note sur l'attitude de l'Allemagine en mars, avril, mai 1911'.

[136] MAE, 179CPCOM425, Foreign Ministry, 'Note pour le Président du Conseil', 13 March 1912.

[137] MAE, 179CPCOM425, no. 496–9/II, EMA-Section d'Afrique, to Direction des affaires politiques et commerciales, 'A.S. du livre jaune sur les affaires du Maroc', 31 January 1912.

[138] TNA, FO 881/9920, no. 15, Reginald Lister, Tangier, to Grey, 'Summary of events in Morocco', 16 January 1911.

[139] MAE, 179CPCOM210, Corps de Débarquement de Casablanca, Etat-Major, Service de Renseignements, 'Journal politique du mois de Janvier 1911', compiled by Colonel Branlière, deputy to GOC, 19 February 1911.

ambassador, Jules Cambon (whose brother meanwhile remained in post at France's London embassy), on 9 February 1909 the French and German governments signed a compromise agreement on Morocco. France's political primacy was acknowledged, in return for which German commercial interests were to be respected. French press reactions were generally favourable. The republican radicals of *L'Aurore* commended '*une belle victoire*', while, at the far right of the political spectrum, the ultra-nationalist *Action Française* managed a passing reference to the benefits of cooling international friction over Morocco.[140] There was even some optimism that Franco-Moroccan cooperation might blossom thanks to joint ventures in railway construction and other, more speculative investments in Moroccan development.[141] It was not to be. The continuing breakdown of Moroccan internal order, and, more importantly, the determination of the arch imperialists of the French colonial lobby to exploit it, ensured the opposite outcome. Successive French governments had refused to authorize armed intervention beyond the Chaouïa region inland from Casablanca, reluctant to finance an expedition likely to prefigure lasting military occupation. Moreover, Sultan Moulay Abd el-Hafid also pressed his French advisors not to take this step, promising that his forces would bring the Zaer and other rebellious tribal confederations to heel. Leaving lands beyond the Chaouïa unoccupied was thus the acid test of whether Morocco would or would not become a *de facto* French protectorate.

Signs of change came quickly in the early weeks of 1911. A week after the four soldiers' deaths, the parliamentary budget commission approved eight-and-a-half million francs in supplementary military spending on the Moroccan expeditionary force.[142] Equally revealing, the comments made by commission reporter, Charles Dumont received prominent coverage in *Le Temps*. Frontier garrisons, Dumont alleged, were left needlessly exposed, jeopardizing the very future of French colonization of Morocco: 'The security of our empire, the development of our race and of our North African interests demand that defence of France's local rights be considered essential to the very existence of France itself.'[143] With expansion into Morocco and French national interest thus conflated, it is little wonder that the money was voted through. But no authorization was forthcoming for an army offensive against the offending 'rebels'. During February and early March, Moinier and Leriche insisted that change was overdue. Zaer fighters meanwhile extended the scope of their assaults to include areas already under occupation. Loyalist tribes complained of worsening harassment, and Moinier predicted in garish terms that French garrisons strung along the Chaouïa margins would be wiped out. The general reminded Paris that he was pledged reinforcements from Algeria if his men faced imminent danger. It was time to keep the promise (Fig. 3.4).[144]

[140] 'L'accord Franco-Allemand: une interprétation cordiale et logique', *L'Aurore*, 10 February 1909; 'L'accord Franco-Allemand', *L'Action Française*, 10 February 1909.

[141] Allain, *Agadir*, chapter 7; E. W. Edwards, 'The Franco–German Agreement on Morocco, 1909', *English Historical Review*, 78:308 (1963), 483–9; Clark, *The Sleepwalkers*, 167, 194–5.

[142] 'Bulletin de l'étranger: le rapport du M. Charles Dumont sur les crédits marocains', *Le Temps*, 19 January 1911.

[143] Ibid.   [144] MAE, 179CPCOM210, 'Résumé de la question des Zaër', 10 March 1911.

Fig. 3.4. General Moinier (left) observing Berber positions at the battle of El Arroussi, 1911. Moinier's rhetorical jibes played a decisive role in escalating the 1911 crisis.
Getty Images, 542903127

Initially, the Foreign Ministry took fright at Moinier's lobbying. Pursuing tribal insurgents further inland would alienate the sultan, his Grand Vizir, and Foreign Minister Si Tayeb El Mokri, making cooperation with the makhzen impossible.[145] Just as important, it would violate both the Act of Algeciras and the Franco-German agreement of 1909, which affirmed Morocco's independent neutrality.[146] To avoid this, it was therefore critical to persuade the sultan to request assistance. As yet, he showed no inclination to oblige.[147] The political stalemate in Fez shifted attention back to Paris. There, the civil-military arguments over the appropriate response to the killing of the Camp Boucheron patrol acquired a sharper rhetorical edge once the national press took up the issue. After the *Echo de Paris* reported rumours that the new government of Ernest Monis, only in office since 2 March, planned to follow the same cautious line as Aristide Briand's previous ministry,

[145] MAE, 179CPCOM210, Direction des affaires politiques, 'Note pour le Ministre', 12 March 1911.

[146] TNA, CAB 37/107, no. 164, Grey to Berlin, 21 July 1911. German ambassador Count Metternich later complained to Foreign Secretary Grey about France's 'free-and-easy manner' in Morocco. Their tendency, he said, was to assume that neither the Algeciras Treaty nor Germany existed: TNA, CAB 37/107, no. 168, Grey to Goschen, 25 July 1911.

[147] TNA, CAB 37/107, Foreign Office memo. for Cabinet, 2 August 1911. The 1909 agreement underwrote Germany's continued entitlement to commercial concessions in Morocco and led to the creation of several Franco-German commercial syndicates, notably in the mining sector.

journalists' demands for 'justice' for France's dead soldiers left the new coalition cornered. Most exposed was Jean Cruppi, a former magistrate newly appointed as foreign minister. Unfamiliar with his new job and with little sway in government, Cruppi was particularly prone to the influence of the Quai d'Orsay's professional staff, the men of the so-called 'Centrale'. Encouraged by the Foreign Ministry's communications chief, Maurice Herbette, who used his press connections to spread his own bitter anti-Germanism, the Foreign Ministry took a dangerously adventurist turn.[148] Moinier could now bank on powerful backing at the heart of France's foreign policy machine.

A few days earlier, with public anger at Briand's apparent inaction rising, the Havas News Agency issued an official denial of any climb-down, confirming instead that 'the government will obtain the necessary reparations'. The Havas report further claimed that Briand's ministers were discussing suitably punitive measures with Moinier, making a substantial military operation appear a foregone conclusion.[149] *L'Aurore*, the paper closest to Briand's outgoing government, underlined the point: the extent of Moroccan instability rendered the guarantees of neutrality within the Algeciras provisions outmoded. On 11 March the *Echo de Paris, Le Journal, La Liberté, Le Gaulois, La République Française*, and *Le Figaro* all praised a statement from Monis's prime ministerial office affirming its commitment to curb the dissidence of the Zaer. This was taken as confirmation that General Moinier would get his reinforcements.[150] Rightly so: an official announcement in the evening edition of *Le Temps* the next day confirmed the Council of Ministers' decision that afternoon to dispatch two infantry battalions and accompanying artillery to enforce order throughout the Chaouïa.[151] The rhetorical message was simple: this was not imperial expansion; it was justifiable retribution designed to assist an embattled local ally—the sultan.[152]

Moulay Abd el-Hafid was becoming amenable to stronger French military backing meanwhile. Anxious to suppress worsening dissent in the Sous region south of Marrakesh, the sultan also felt compelled to deploy additional troops to keep order in Fez.[153] In early March, numerous tribal confederations joined a working alliance to overthrow the sultanate. Their rebellion threatened either to isolate or to engulf the imperial capital.[154] By the end of March, a mixed force of

---

[148] Clark, *The Sleepwalkers*, 195–6; Hayne, *The French Foreign Office*, 200–9.

[149] MAE, 179CPCOM210, Direction des affaires politiques, 'Note pour le Ministre', 12 March 1911.

[150] Ministère des Affaires Etrangères, Direction des Affaires politiques, 'Analyse générale de la presse française', 11 March 1911.

[151] TNA, FO 881/9920, no. 65, Sir Francis Bertie, Paris, to Grey, 14 March 1911.

[152] Even France's larger-circulation provincial newspapers, such as *L'Ouest-Éclair*, published in Rennes, offered their readers a detailed analysis of German party political reactions to the unfolding events in Morocco. Coverage of this type confirmed the deepening French public interest in the ways in which French actions were depicted—and interpreted. See: 'La politique extérieure de l'Allemagne', *L'Ouest-Éclair*, 31 March 1911.

[153] TNA, FO 881/9920, no. 9, Reginald Lister to Grey, 'Summary of Events for Week Ending January 16, 1911'.

[154] TNA, FO 881/9920, nos 44, 48, 49, 54: Lister telegrams to Grey, 4, 5, 6, and 7 March 1911.

tribal levies led by fighters of the Beni M'tir confederation were camped eight miles outside Fez, preparing, it seemed, for a definitive assault on the capital.[155]

A failed attempt by a makhzen force to rout this encampment at Ras el-ma compelled the sultan's government to acquiesce in a French relief mission. Its ostensible purpose was to protect the French military advisors, other European consular staff, and their families from massacre.[156] Events moved quickly thereafter. French governmental instructions issued during the final fortnight in April 1911 cleared a path for military occupation of Morocco. But these decisions were taken reactively—and reluctantly. Ernest Monis's coalition was already deeply unpopular. Its fiscal reforms attracted even harsher press coverage than its alleged dithering over the killing of French servicemen in the Chaouïa. André Tardieu's foreign affairs editorials in *Le Temps*, so often the mouthpiece for centre-rightist ministries, led the charge against what the paper derided as a mealy-mouthed collection of Radical-Socialist ministers. It accused the government of sectarianism, of being more concerned with advancing its radical agenda at home than with upholding French interests overseas.[157] This was unfair, but it placed Monis's Cabinet on the defensive.

In a decisive ministerial meeting held on 23 April, War Minister Maurice Bertéaux and two generals, Chief of Army Staff Auguste Dubail and Alfred d'Amade, Moinier's predecessor as commander of the Morocco expeditionary force, persuaded the other ministers present that the government could not risk half measures.[158] The resultant official announcement the following day mixed the robust language of decisive action with claims of altruistic intent.[159] Two 'flying columns' of French colonial troops were to leave for Fez. The reinforcements previously announced for limited punitive operations around Casablanca were now merely the vanguard for a much larger force capable of 'pacifying' northwest Morocco as a whole.[160] Mindful of likely European reaction, Foreign Minister Cruppi stressed that these measures represented an act of urgent humanitarian assistance, not the prelude to a protectorate that they became.[161]

An expeditionary force marching on Fez both to save European lives and to rescue the sultanate from the sad consequences of its own misrule might have been expected to play well with French public opinion after the outrage over the earlier killings of French soldiers in the Chaouïa. This was not to reckon either with the anti-militarism of the Socialist left or with the press campaign, led by *Le Temps*, in support of even firmer action. Socialist leader Jean Jaurès saw through the official rhetoric of humanitarian rescue, wondering aloud in the Chamber of Deputies how

[155] TNA, FO 881/9920, no. 124, Lister to Grey, 4 April 1911.

[156] TNA, FO 881/9920, no. 119, enclosures 1 and 2: Macleod to Lister, 26 and 27 March 1911.

[157] 'Bulletin de l'étranger', and 'Les affaires du Maroc', *Le Temps*, 22 April 1911.

[158] TNA, FO 881/9920, no. 166, Bertie, Paris, to Grey, 24 April 1911.

[159] 'La marche en avant est décidée', *Le Matin*, 24 April 1911, p. 1.

[160] TNA, FO 881/9920, no. 237, enclosure 2, Casablanca consular report, 26 April 1911, no. 282, enclosure, 'Note by Colonel Fairholme on the Situation in Morocco and Progress of the French Expedition'.

[161] TNA, FO 881/9920, no. 281, Bertie to Grey, 14 May 1911; the phrase 'prelude to Protectorate' is borrowed from Edmund Burke III's book of the same title.

much it suited the government and the general staff to exaggerate the threats faced
by Europeans in Fez. His scepticism was vindicated by the actions of Lyautey and
his fellow colonial army commanders.[162] They encouraged Parti Colonial lobbyists
and *Le Temps* editorialists to demand that an additional occupation force drawn
from Algeria's colonial army garrison should march westwards from their *de facto*
frontier at the Moulouya River.[163] These demands became louder still after French
soldiers were killed in skirmishing near the Moulouya on 10 May.[164] The prelude
to a fuller occupation certainly, this was also dangerously provocative. The standing
instructions for French troops not to cross the Moulouya River were pivotal to the
government's self-image as a force for moderation. In this reading of events,
the units sent to Fez literally comprised a rescue mission. To the government's
opponents, the flying columns represented something else entirely: the beginning
of Morocco's transition to orderly military government.[165] Denying the Fez
expedition the support of well-equipped French forces to the east was not only
irresponsible, it was an implicit rejection of Morocco's inexorable progress towards
protectorate status.

These arguments were, in turn, overtaken by two events. One was predictable,
the other not. On 12 June, the French government announced the final 'relief' of
Fez by Moinier's expeditionary force. Still depicted as a temporary measure driven
by humanitarian impulse, the pronouncement served another purpose, stealing the
thunder from the advocates of more full-blooded military occupation.[166] Less
predictably, completion of the Fez expedition became the epitaph for the Monis
coalition. On 22 May, both the prime minister and his war minister were seriously
injured when their aircraft crashed on departure for Madrid where they were to
hold talks over Morocco. In late June, Finance Minister Joseph Caillaux, the
government's ardent tax reformer, would take office at the head of a new, more
widely supported coalition.[167]

These were the circumstances in which reports spread from consular offices in
Morocco to European chanceries of the arrival of a German gunboat, *Panther*, in
the port of Agadir on 1 July.[168] With Fez already occupied and the German
government using bluster and bluff to cajole its entente rivals, the ship's arrival
heralded the second, and more British-oriented, phase of the crisis.[169] On 4 July
1911, Grey told the German ambassador that Britain insisted on being consulted in

---

[162] 'La question du Maroc', *Le Figaro*, 12 May 1911.

[163] 'Bulletin de l'étranger—les mesures militaires au Maroc', *Le Temps*, 12 May 1911.

[164] 'Sur les rives de la Moulouïa', *Le Temps*, 18 May 1911, p. 2; 'Les affaires du Maroc', *Le Temps*,
19 May 1911, pp. 1–2.

[165] TNA, FO 881/9920, no. 301, Bertie to Grey, 20 May 1911.

[166] TNA, FO 881/9920, no. 378, French government *communiqué*, 12 June 1911, no. 379, Grey
to Bertie, 12 June 1911.

[167] For evidence of Caillaux's long-standing commitment to tax reform, including the 1914
introduction of an income tax, see Fonds Caillaux, 39J11 and 12.

[168] There was less disquiet when a larger warship, *Eber*, docked in Casablanca in mid-March to
protect German nationals and commercial interests: TNA, FO 881/9920, nos 53 and 73, Lister to
Grey, 5 and 11 March 1911. The *Panther* was later relieved by a much larger vessel, the German
cruiser, SMS *Berlin*.

[169] Stevenson, 'Militarization and Diplomacy', 136–8.

the drawing up of any new arrangements with respect to Morocco.[170] Asquith—who had become prime minister in 1908—echoed this, in a somewhat muted way, in the Commons.[171] But no official German response was forthcoming, and Grey managed to overcome the Cabinet's instinct for caution.[172] On 21 July, Lloyd George, now chancellor of the exchequer, made his annual speech to a City audience at the Mansion House. He stated that he would go to great lengths to preserve peace,

> But if a situation were to be forced upon us in which peace could only be preserved by the surrender of the great and beneficent position which Britain has won by centuries of heroism and achievement, by allowing Britain to be treated where her interests were vitally affected as if she were of no account in the Cabinet of nations, then I say emphatically that peace at that price would be a humiliation intolerable for a great country like ours to endure.[173]

In a dramatic memoir account, Lloyd George's colleague Winston Churchill recalled that this statement was 'a thunder-clap to the German Government'. And until only a few hours before, Churchill noted, even Lloyd George's colleagues had not known what the chancellor was planning to say. 'Working with him in close association, I did not know. No one knew. Until his mind was definitely made up, he did not know himself.'[174]

Several points about the speech are worthy of comment. In *The Struggle for Mastery in Europe*, A. J. P. Taylor argued, with typically brilliant perversity, that Lloyd George's message was actually directed at the French: 'this was not a pledge to support France against Germany; it was a warning that Great Britain could not be left out of any new partition of Morocco'.[175] Yet there is no evidence that the speech was either intended or received in this way.[176] Keith Wilson is correct to note that the demand to be consulted was inherently double-edged; in a situation that might involve Britain in war, or otherwise redound to her disadvantage, the French could not be simply left a completely free hand.[177] But it is clear that Lloyd George, on this occasion, was not attempting to browbeat France. The next day, *Manchester Guardian* editor C. P. Scott recorded a conversation in which the chancellor repeatedly 'spoke of France's weakness and terror in the face of Germany. [. . .] The impression I got is that he is not immune from the microbe of Germanophobia.'[178]

---

[170] Wilson, 'Agadir Crisis', 521.   [171] HC Deb, 6 July 1911, vol. 27, col. 1341.
[172] Clark, *The Sleepwalkers*, 209.
[173] 'Mr. Lloyd George On British Prestige', *The Times*, 22 July 1911. Lloyd George's notes for the speech can be found in the Parliamentary Archives, HL/PO/LB/1/15. See also Timothy Boyle, 'New Light on Lloyd George's Mansion House Speech', *Historical Journal*, 23:2 (1980), 431–3.
[174] Winston S. Churchill, *The World Crisis 1911–1918, Vol. I* (New York: Barnes and Noble, 1993), 33–4.
[175] A. J. P. Taylor, *The Struggle for Mastery in Europe 1848–1918* (Oxford: Oxford University Press, 1954), 471.
[176] Richard A. Cosgrove, 'A Note on Lloyd George's Speech at the Mansion House, 21 July 1911', *Historical Journal*, 12:4 (1969), 698–701.
[177] Wilson, 'Agadir Crisis', 513–32.
[178] Trevor Wilson (ed.), *The Political Diaries of C. P. Scott, 1911–1928* (London: Collins, 1970), 48 (entry for 22 July 1911).

Furthermore, the content of what Lloyd George said accorded with the views of Asquith and Grey, both of whom he consulted. Asquith made essentially the same point in the House of Commons a few days later, but in much more guarded and restrained language.[179] The difference was in the tone. Although Lloyd George also talked about Britain's contribution to 'the cause of human liberty'—a standard Radical theme—his use of the language of 'prestige' was striking. So too was his reference to centuries of British 'heroism and achievement'.[180] Even though the empire itself was not explicitly mentioned, this was a sentiment that might more usually have come from the mouths of Liberal Imperialists or even Conservatives. And herein lay the significance of the speech: not so much in what Lloyd George said, but the fact that it was he personally who said it.

As Churchill recalled, throughout the life of the government thus far, the Liberal Imperialist ministers who were in charge of foreign policy 'were narrowly watched and kept in equipoise by the Radical element' within the Cabinet, which included Lords Morley and Loreburn. 'In these circumstances the attitude of the Chancellor of the Exchequer became of peculiar importance.'[181] In spite of his opposition to the Boer War, Lloyd George had never been an anti-imperialist—but his reputation (and personal persuasiveness) was such that he was ideally placed to win over waverers of the pacific, nonconformist wing of the party.[182] (This would be seen clearly in August 1914.) That is not to say that he did persuade all of them; his speech caused considerable disquiet to many.[183] Morley and Loreburn protested in Cabinet.[184] Another minister, Walter Runciman, feared that the French government was 'sorely tempted to keep themselves politically alive by a plunge' towards war, and that British support and assurances would only encourage her.[185] Ramsay MacDonald, chairman of the still-nascent Labour Party, argued in public that:

> Mr. Lloyd George's statement at the Mansion House was a profound blunder, because the effect of it was to discourage the peace organizations and peace forces in Germany. Mr. Asquith was associated with the Liberal Imperialist wing, and if he had made that statement it would undoubtedly have warned the Prussian bureaucracy that there was danger ahead, without paralysing the peace forces, because they did not expect anything else.[186]

The chancellor's words may also have had a deadening effect on the British 'peace forces'; at the least, they helped ensure that there would be no major split in Liberal ranks. It should be emphasized that they did not bring about an immediate end to the crisis, however.[187] That was not finally settled until November, when

---

[179] HC Deb, 27 July 1911, vol. 28, cols 1827–8.
[180] 'Mr. Lloyd George On British Prestige', *The Times*, 22 July 1911.
[181] Churchill, *The World Crisis*, 31.
[182] Bentley Brinkerhoff Gilbert, *David Lloyd George: A Political Life. The Architect of Change, 1863–1912* (Columbus, OH: Ohio State University Press, 1987), 178.
[183] Howard S. Weinroth, 'British Radicals and the Agadir Crisis', *European History Quarterly*, 3:1 (1973), 39–61.
[184] MS. Eng. C. 8266, Harcourt papers, Lewis Harcourt Cabinet diary, 31 July 1911.
[185] MS. Eng. C. 8266, Harcourt papers, Walter Runciman to Lewis Harcourt, 24 August 1911.
[186] 'The Labour Party's Attitude', *The Times*, 7 August 1911.
[187] Gilbert, *Architect of Change*, 454.

Franco-German negotiations led to Germany's acceptance of France's position in Morocco, in exchange for French territory in the Congo. France established a formal protectorate over Morocco the following year.

Lloyd George's speech helped create an impression of British national unity in the face of German expansionism. As we have suggested, this may have been somewhat illusory, given Radical unease; although many of those who voiced open criticism after the crisis was over did not do so at the time.[188] But the impression was also fostered by the consensual approach of Balfour as leader of the opposition. After standing down as prime minister, he had continued to serve on the government's Committee of Imperial Defence (CID), helping provide an element of policy continuity. But in late 1911, he was pushed out as leader of the Conservative Party, to be replaced by Andrew Bonar Law, who was determined to be more aggressive. In a speech early in the New Year, Law gave a partisan spin to the previous summer's events:

> The Morocco, incident has ended, thank Heaven, without war (cheers); but it has also ended in this, that our French friends have got all the advantages, while we have got all the ill-will. That is a strange result. What is the explanation? [. . .] We drifted towards war because not only Radical members of parliament, but the most influential men in the government, had made speeches which cause foreign nations to believe—and I think they had some cause to believe—that this Government would never assert our rights by force. Of all offenders the Chancellor of the Exchequer was, I think, the worst. (Booing, and cries of 'Traitor!') I did not blame him for his speech at the Mansion House last summer. It was probably the only means left open to him to repair the evil which he had himself done.[189]

If in practice there was little difference between Conservative and Liberal policy on the Moroccan issue, then, it was nonetheless possible for Tories to locate their opponents' efforts at rhetorical 'firmness' within an overall narrative that dwelt on their weakness and tendency to drift.

In November 1911, Grey faced a reaction from colleagues who had been alarmed to discover the degree to which he had committed Britain in support of France. He had allowed the continuation of supposedly non-binding Franco-British 'military conversations', with the prime minister's agreement but without the Cabinet's knowledge. The Cabinet now resolved that he should not engage in military talks with the French without its approval.[190] Some Radicals—annoyed both by France's protectionism and her methods of expansion—also expressed their disapproval at recent events. But their priority remained European peace rather than the avoidance of colonial exploitation. If peace could only be maintained by dividing the imperial spoils, so be it: the point was to do this calmly and rationally, avoiding emotional war scares. Hence the demand for the democratic control of foreign policy, which would take these affairs out of the hands of statesmen who

---

[188] Weinroth, 'British Radicals and the Agadir Crisis'.
[189] 'Mr. Bonar Law's Appeal', *The Times*, 27 January 1912.
[190] Clark, *The Sleepwalkers*, 212.

held false conceptions of how to maintain the balance of power. Of course, like the backlash against Grey, these aspirations proved to be a dead letter.[191]

CONCLUSION

The two Entente Powers viewed the two Moroccan crises very differently. Although they remained more or less united through both, that unity—and the rhetoric that underpinned it—was forged in a fast-changing strategic environment. In 1905 the Entente Cordiale was substantially untested. Its scope and its implications remained poorly understood domestically and internationally. For Maurice Rouvier's government the entente's attractions became clearer over time. Acutely conscious of France's international vulnerability after Japan's defeat of its Russian ally, Rouvier's administration became bitterly divided over how best to pursue—and to portray—its actions in Morocco. Théophile Delcassé was the principal political victim of this infighting. This was ironic. Rouvier, after dismissing and personally replacing his foreign minister, later justified the reinsertion of René Saint-Taillandier's mission and the consolidation of France's financial and military influence in Fez in terms that vindicated Delcassé's longstanding pursuit of French supremacy in Morocco. That being said, Delcassé's departure and the extensive French military preparations taken in 1905 indicate that this first international clash over Morocco was the greater of the two crises for France. Significantly, not until December did the French premier feel sufficiently confident of success to make a fulsome declaration of French intent.

The second Moroccan crisis escalated, not because of misunderstandings between its protagonists, but because each correctly perceived the other to be seeking decisive advantage at their expense. Viewed from the Berlin government's perspective, the oddity was that France, which had for years flouted the spirit if not the letter of the Algeciras treaty, and its entente partner Britain, which connived in the process, each claimed to be affronted by Germany's forceful objections. Judged from the French perspective, it was Germany that violated the bilateral 1909 deal between them by sending the *Panther* to Agadir and claiming a right of veto over legitimate French security measures taken to contain Morocco's undeclared civil war. Worse, Germany's methods and its territorial demands were guaranteed to galvanize French parliamentary and public opinion. Berlin, in other words, manufactured a crisis to test French resolve, making longer term compromise harder to reach.[192] Long prefigured and always likely, a squalid Franco-German deal compensating Germany with tropical African territory in return for its acquiescence over Morocco was thus rendered more problematic, largely because it was played out in the public sphere. Seen from the British perspective, Germany's actions were unacceptable on at least three grounds. For one thing, the Berlin government was hypocritical, crying foul over Algeciras while offering, behind the scenes, to

---

[191] Weinroth, 'British Radicals and the Agadir Crisis'.
[192] *Journal Officiel de la République Française*, Senat, séance du jeudi 6 Avril 1911.

dispense with the treaty and Morocco more generally in exchange for French colonial territory elsewhere.[193] For another thing, swapping colonial territory in Central or West Africa—the ethical objections to which the British government conspicuously ignored—was better done with Britain's assent than without it.[194] Finally, the conviction remained that Germany was really playing alliance politics, using Morocco to drive a wedge between France, Britain, and Russia.

Rhetoric was central to each of these perspectives and the resulting interpretations of events. On the second Friday in August 1911, Britain's ambassador to Berlin, Sir Edward Goschen, dined with Kaiser Wilhelm following the unveiling of a memorial to Edward VII at Homburg von der Hoebe. The kaiser seized the opportunity to defend Germany's recent actions in Morocco. The French, he said, had been offering swaps of colonial territory, including the French Congo and Madagascar, since at least 1910 in return for a German recognition that France could do whatever it wanted in Fez.[195] A deal on this basis, the kaiser implied, might have succeeded but for Lloyd George's inflammatory speech. Not only did this rouse hostile public sentiment in Britain, but, worse, it made the pursuit of backstairs diplomacy harder. As Goschen retorted, this was rich. Germany's decision to send the gunboat *Panther* to the port of Agadir was just as public, and far more inflammatory. At minimum, it suggested an intention to coerce concessions from France; at maximum, a readiness to establish a bridge-head, land troops, and go to war. Dismissed by Wilhelm II as 'a little ship with two or three little pop guns', the *Panther*'s arrival signalled a new phase in Great Power rivalry over Morocco; one in which rhetorical posturing supplanted inter-governmental negotiation.[196]

[193] TNA, CAB 37/107, no. 329, Grey to Sir Francis Bertie, Paris, 1 August 1911.
[194] TNA, CAB 37/107, no. 181, Grey to Goschen, 1 August 1911.
[195] The Foreign Office could find no record of any such large-scale offers of territory having been made: TNA, CAB 37/107, Grey memo: 'Sir E. Goschen's Dispatch no. 230 of 16 August 1911'.
[196] TNA, CAB 37/107, Sir E. Goschen to Grey, 16 August 1911.

4
The Chanak Crisis, 1922

In the autumn of 1922 a dispute over the presence of Allied troops in a neutral zone on the banks of the Dardanelles Straits near Constantinople threatened to pitch France and, even more so, Britain into war with a resurgent, nationalist Turkey. Played out against the backdrop of impending Turkish victory in a devastating war with Greece, the Chanak crisis was the sternest test of co-imperialism in the years between the 1904 signature of the Entente Cordiale and the Suez crisis of 1956. Britain's coalition government and, above all, its premier, David Lloyd George, were widely seen as pro-Greek; their French partners, largely for reasons of strategic interest, as pro-Turk. But Chanak, for each of them, was primarily an imperial crisis—an argument about empires. Such were the mutual recriminations between London and Paris in the final months of 1922 that it is arguable that Chanak, rather than other, better-known imperial flashpoints in Western Asia-in Syria, Palestine, and Iraq, did more to shape the bitter rhetorical invective that would characterize French and British relations in the Middle East during the interwar years and beyond.

The Chanak crisis also provoked powerful criticism closer to home. In October 1922, the novelist E. M. Forster published an article in the Independent Labour Party's weekly paper, *The New Leader*. It was headlined 'Our Graves in Gallipoli', and satirized the British government's efforts to whip up support for a new military conflict with resurgent, nationalist Turkey. By the time Forster's piece appeared, the Chanak crisis, as the episode became known, was already over. It had not resulted in war, albeit not for the want of trying by the prime minister, David Lloyd George, and some of his key Cabinet colleagues, notably Winston Churchill. Churchill was just one of the politicians who had publicly deplored the prospect of Turkish forces seizing control of areas where British and empire servicemen killed at Gallipoli were buried. Forster portrayed the Anglo-Turkish confrontation at Chanak, on the eastern side of the straits, as part of Lloyd George and Churchill's quest for new land for further graves:

> There is still room over in Chanak. Also, it is well for a nation that would be great to scatter its graves all over the world. Graves in Ireland, graves in Irak, Russia, Persia, India, each with its inscription from the Bible or Rupert Brooke. When England thinks fit, she can launch an expedition to protect the sanctity of her graves, and can follow that by another expedition to protect the sanctity of the additional graves.[1]

---

[1] *New Leader*, 20 October 1920, quoted in David Roessel, 'Live Orientals and Dead Greeks: Forster's Response to the Chanak Crisis', *Twentieth Century Literature*, 36:1 (1990), 43–60, at 58.

WESTERN EMPIRE IN WESTERN ASIA

Forster's litany of gravesites is indicative of the extent of Britain's post-war global imperial crisis. As his non-exhaustive list suggested—he might well have added Egypt—these years saw conflict within the British Isles, within the established formal empire, within newly conquered territories, and within the informal empire where British influence was longstanding.[2]

Yet Britain at the same time attempted to project its power even further, on behalf of the Whites in the Russian civil war, and within Turkey itself, having already divided up former Ottoman territories with the French. Chanak of course now looks grossly hubristic. Indeed, it looked so at the time not merely to Forster—who was soon to publish *A Passage to India*, the classic novel of liberal imperial angst—but also to a powerful strand of Conservative opinion, represented by the party's former leader, Andrew Bonar Law. Britain's military leaders were equally alarmed by the government's apparent readiness to add new overseas commitments while also cutting back on military spending. One who shared Bonar Law's logic was Field Marshal Sir Henry Wilson, the gruff Irishman whose plain-speaking and pro-Unionist sentiments as chief of imperial general staff endeared him to Conservative opinion but, fatally as it turned out, earned him the opprobrium of the IRA.[3] Acutely aware of the numerous challenges to power within Britain's empire, Wilson's instinctive response to imperial insecurity was 'to govern or get out'. As Map 4.1 shows, Britain's interwar empire was, at the time, geographically larger and more geopolitically volatile than ever. Governing so large an empire required the concentration of military means, so, in those locations where vital British interests were not at stake, as in Turkey, Wilson favoured withdrawal.[4]

The prospect of slipping into an avoidable war with the Turkish nationalists was certainly too much for Bonar Law. When he signalled his disquiet in public, it led to a chain of events that triggered Lloyd George's political downfall. But if the 1918–22 period appears in many ways as a classic example of imperial overstretch, it must be remembered that excess confidence and anxiety were two sides of the same coin. Turning away from external threats to meet internal ones did not seem like an option to those politicians who believed that Bolsheviks, Indian nationalists, and domestic revolutionaries were part of a worldwide conspiracy against the British Empire.[5] A global problem, it seemed, demanded a global response. If Lloyd George's post-war coalition engaged in some crucial pragmatic retreats—notably in Ireland—then Chanak marked the persistence until the end of a visionary element, liberal most obviously in its anti-Turk philo-Hellenism, in

---

[2] Keith Jeffery, *The British Army and the Crisis of Empire, 1918–1922* (Manchester: Manchester University Press, 1984).

[3] Keith Jeffery, *Field Marshal Sir Henry Wilson: A Political Soldier* (Oxford: Oxford University Press, 2006), 281–4.

[4] Jeffery, *Field Marshal Sir Henry Wilson*, 239, 244.

[5] Foreign Secretary Lord Curzon is most readily identified with this tendency, see: John Fisher, 'The Interdepartmental Committee on Eastern Unrest and British Responses to Bolshevik and Other Intrigues Against the Empire during the 1920s', *Journal of Asian History*, 34:1 (2000), 1–34.

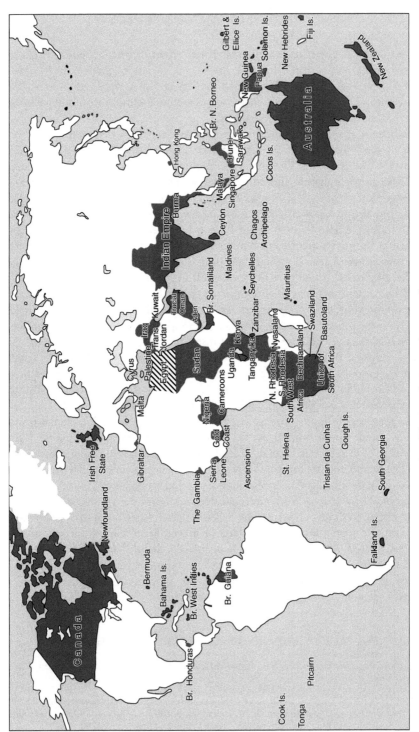

Map 4.1. The British Empire between the wars

other ways seemingly conservative. Yet the invocation of the empire's war dead proved to be no trump card in the face of the critics of adventurism. The outcome was also influenced by the wartime split in the Liberal Party into factions led by Lloyd George and Asquith respectively. The former displaced the latter as prime minister at the end of 1916; Lloyd George's new coalition was heavily dominated by Conservatives, who existed in a state of uneasy tension with their Liberal partners. Meanwhile, the Asquithian faction was heavily defeated at the 1918 general election, but played a continuing role in shaping the rhetorical environment, presenting itself as the upholder of traditional Liberal purity in the face of the coalition's corruption and irresponsibility.

British governmental interference in the conflict between Turks and Greeks was based on a combination of geopolitical miscalculation and sentimental attachment. Free passage through the straits of the Bosphorus and Dardanelles had long been an article of faith in British foreign policy. The thousands of Australian and British lives lost at nearby Gallipoli underscored the poignancy but also, some might say, the dubiousness of the commitment. That being said, the symbolic power in British eyes of settlements such as Chanak, shown in Map 4.2, which overlooked the Turkish Straits was assured. The sacrifices of Gallipoli originated in fatal underestimation of Turkish resistance, something that, by 1922, was haunting the British once more. Indeed, British assessments could be faulted on all counts. The presumption that a Turkish nationalist takeover in Istanbul would result in closure of the straits was dubious at best. Support for Greek irredentism in Thrace and Anatolia owed as much to the impressive advances of Greek military forces in the initial engagements of their war with nationalist Turkey as it did either to Greece's earlier contributions to the Allied cause or the longer history of British backing for Hellenic independence in the Aegean. But the Greek Army's early victories were soon reversed, the revitalization of Mustapha Kemal's forces as dramatic as the collapse in Greek resistance.[6] Finally, the popular mobilization that underpinned nationalist success exposed the fallacy of extending the practices of imperial partition to Turkey's Anatolian heartland.

These points are worth highlighting because they explain the profound Franco-British disagreements over the future of this crucial region of western Asia. French calculations were not just fundamentally different from the British: they were diametrically opposed to them.[7] Politically then, the Chanak crisis resolved itself into a zero-sum game for the entente partners. French bargaining with Kemal undermined Lloyd George's pro-Greek position, injecting real venom to the inter-Allied exchanges over the Near East. For all that, neither partner wanted to break entirely with the other. The sourness between them was, in consequence, expressed

---

[6] The India Office and the government of India were highly critical of British backing of Greeks against Turks, which Indian Army Chief Henry Rawlinson termed 'suicidal': see John Ferris, 'The British Empire vs. the Hidden Hand: British Intelligence and Strategy and "The CUP-Jew-German-Bolshevik Combination", 1918–1924', in Keith Neilson and Greg Kennedy (eds), *The British Way in Warfare: Power and the International System, 1856–1956* (Farnham: Ashgate, 2010), 341.

[7] For background, see Yücel Güçlü, 'The Struggle for Mastery in Cilicia: Turkey, France and the Ankara Agreement of 1921', *International History Review*, 23:3 (2001), 580–603.

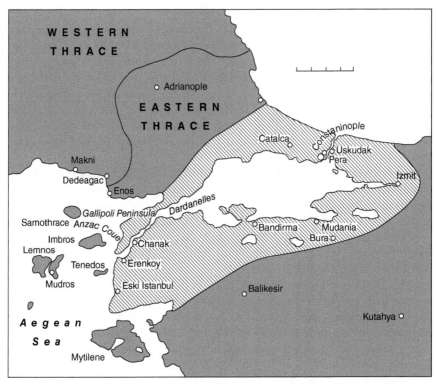

Map 4.2. The Chanak Crisis, 1922

otherwise: at times rhetorically, at times through fiercely acrimonious, but secret, negotiations and a tight-lipped silence in public. The outrage provoked in London by alleged French double-dealing only added to the satisfaction expressed by French ministers in averting an unwinnable confrontation over the straits.

The diplomatic and intelligence aspects of Chanak are well covered in the literature, as are the repercussions within the Dominions and the political crisis that led to the fall of the Lloyd George coalition.[8] By contrast, the public arguments within Britain and France—and what they tell us about attitudes to empire—have

---

[8] David Walder, *The Chanak Affair* (London: Hutchinson & Co., 1969); J. G. Darwin, 'The Chanak Crisis and the British Cabinet', *History*, 65 (1980), 32–48; J. Douglas Goold, 'Lord Hardinge as Ambassador to France, and the Anglo-French Dilemma over Germany and the Near East, 1920–1922', *Historical Journal*, 21 (1978), 913–37; John R. Ferris, '"Far too Dangerous a Gamble"? British Intelligence and Policy during the Chanak Crisis, September–October 1922', *Diplomacy & Statecraft*, 14:1 (2003), 139–84; Mark Arnold-Forster, 'Chanak Rocks the Empire: The Anger of Billy Hughes', *Round Table*, 58 (1968), 169–77; Peter M. Sales, 'W. M. Hughes and the Chanak Crisis of 1922', *Australian Journal of Politics & History*, 17 (1971), 392–405; Terry Reardon, *Winston Churchill and Mackenzie King: So Similar, So Different* (Toronto: Dundurn, 2012), 45–9. Kenneth O. Morgan, *Consensus and Disunity: The Lloyd George Coalition Government 1918–22* (Oxford: Clarendon Press, 1979) remains a valuable entry point into the extensive literature on the politics of the coalition and its collapse.

received little attention. By the time the crisis broke, the entente was already in trouble, and Lloyd George's open recriminations at France's alleged desertion of the British were a factor in the breakdown of his relationship with his foreign secretary, Lord Curzon. For his part, Curzon's vituperative negotiations with French Prime Minister Raymond Poincaré at the height of the crisis in late September 1922 marked the most acrimonious high-level talks between British and French politicians of the entire interwar period.[9] Curzon knew from intelligence decrypts of French diplomatic traffic that his negotiating partners were not only deal-making with the Turkish nationalists but were secretly arming them as well.[10] Yet it was Poincaré who confronted the British foreign secretary with the more uncomfortable truths about Britain's unpopularity, its precarious isolation in the Near East, and French resolve to make their peace with Turkish nationalism. This verbal lashing, combined with Poincaré's mulish stubbornness, was enough to reduce Curzon to tearful, but impotent fury.[11]

Colourfully undiplomatic, these exchanges took place behind closed doors at the Quai d'Orsay.[12] Ultimately, the tensions they exposed proved surmountable because, for all its endemic friction, Anglo-French co-imperialism in the Middle East was precisely that: a joint venture that, while rhetorically depicted by each partner as nationally distinct, was actually part of a larger, joint enterprise of Anglo-French dominion in the Arab world. Much as they may have wanted to do so, before 1940 at least, neither imperial power could pursue this venture alone.[13]

MÉSENTENTE IN THE NEAR EAST

World War I had been a major test of the two countries' relationship. The story of the Western Front is well known, but it is also worth remembering that thousands of French troops, including colonial army units, served alongside the British and the ANZACs (Australian and New Zealand Army Corps) at Gallipoli, and many of them ended up buried there too.[14] (The disastrous campaign came to be viewed in France as a classic piece of British bungling.)[15] The (initially secret) Sykes–Picot

[9] Drawing heavily on John Ferris's pioneering research in ' "Far too Dangerous a Gamble" ', an excellent account of the background to these talks is Zara Steiner, *The Lights that Failed: European International History, 1919–1933* (Oxford: Oxford University Press, 2005), 113–19.

[10] Keith Jeffery and Alan Sharp, 'Lord Curzon and Secret Intelligence', in Christopher Andrew and Jeremy Noakes (eds), *Intelligence and International Relations* (Exeter: Exeter University Press, 1987), 113–14; Ferris, ' "Far too Dangerous a Gamble" ', 159–60; Steiner, *The Lights that Failed*, 115–16.

[11] John F. V. Keiger, *Raymond Poincaré* (Cambridge: Cambridge University Press, 2002), 294.

[12] The full sequence of Paris meetings from 20 September to 7 October 1922 is documented in MAE, série Levant 1918–29, 51CPCOM166, Chanak (microfilm P1399).

[13] Martin Thomas, 'Anglo-French Imperial Relations in the Arab World: Intelligence Liaison and Nationalist Disorder', *Diplomacy & Statecraft*, 17:1 (2006), 1–28.

[14] Matthew Hughes, 'The French Army at Gallipoli', *RUSI Journal*, 150:3 (2005), 64–7.

[15] Eleanor van Heyningen, 'Helles: The French in Gallipoli', Imperial War Museums, 2000, <http://archive.iwm.org.uk/upload/package/2/gallipoli/pdf_files/French.pdf> accessed 11 September 2013.

agreement of 1916 proposed a future carve-up of Ottoman provinces between France and Britain. Whether or not Sykes–Picot was in strict contradiction with other wartime pledges, such as the McMahon–Hussein correspondence of 1915–16 and the Balfour Declaration of 1917, it is certainly true that the multiple, ambiguous promises created a very confused situation.[16] It appears that, at any rate, Lloyd George and French Prime Minister Georges Clemenceau made an unwritten agreement at the war's end that altered the details of the deal.[17]

The effect of these various arrangements was that Britain acquired Palestine and Mesopotamia (later Iraq) and France acquired Syria and Lebanon, albeit there was some measure of accountability to the League of Nations for the running of the territories under the newly devised mandates system.[18] As indicated in Map 4.3, the acquisition of Syrian and Lebanese territory, in addition to the greater part of former German Cameroon and Togoland in West Africa, meant that the French Empire, like the British, was larger, more diverse, and more unmanageable than ever. As Susan Pedersen notes pithily, 'League oversight could not force the mandatory powers to govern mandated territories differently; instead, it obliged them to *say* that they were governing them differently'. During the 1920s especially, transparent scrutiny by a supranational authority internationalized the process of imperial oversight to an unprecedented degree.[19] At the heart of this process was the League's Permanent Mandates Commission (PMC). Its cycles of regular reporting on internal mandate conditions and the sophisticated petitioning by aggrieved parties compelled imperial powers to fight one rhetorical battle after another with their anti-colonial opponents, domestic and foreign alike.[20] As the leading mandatory powers, particularly as holders of formerly Ottoman-ruled territories in the Middle East, Britain and France found themselves thrown into uncomfortable alignment before the PMC. If the criticisms they faced sometimes coincided—ignoring the wishes of local populations being uppermost among them—their responses differed fundamentally. British ministers and delegates to the League tended to accept this process of internationalization, hoping thus to contain it, whereas their French counterparts strove to do the opposite, working to

---

[16] Timothy J. Paris, *Britain, the Hashemites and Arab Rule: The Sherifian Solution* (London: Frank Cass, 2003), 19–45; more generally: David Fromkin, *A Peace to End All Peace: The Fall of the Ottoman Empire and the Creation of the Modern Middle East* (New York: Henry Holt & Co., 1989); John Gooch, '"Building Buffers and Filling Vacuums": Great Britain and the Middle East, 1914–1922', in Williamson Murray and Jim Lacey (eds), *The Making of Peace: Rulers, States, and the Aftermath of War* (Cambridge: Cambridge University Press, 2009), 240–64.

[17] Matthew Hughes, *Allenby and General Strategy in the Middle East, 1917–1919* (London: Frank Cass, 1999), 122–3.

[18] The huge significance of the League dimension is explored by Susan Pedersen, *The Guardians: The League of Nations and the Crisis of Empire* (Oxford: Oxford University Press, 2015), part I.

[19] Pedersen, *The Guardians*, 3–4, quote at p. 3.

[20] Running into thousands, few petitions achieved their declared objectives. Increasingly focused on matters of sovereignty and human rights violations, they nonetheless transformed the rhetorical practices of the PMC and those who appeared before it. See Natasha Wheatley, 'The Mandate System as a Style of Reasoning: International Jurisdiction and the Parcelling of Imperial Sovereignty in Petitions from Palestine', in Cyrus Schayegh and Andrew Arsan (eds), *The Routledge Handbook of the History of the Middle East Mandates* (Abingdon: Routledge, 2015), 106–16; Pedersen, *The Guardians*, 78–91.

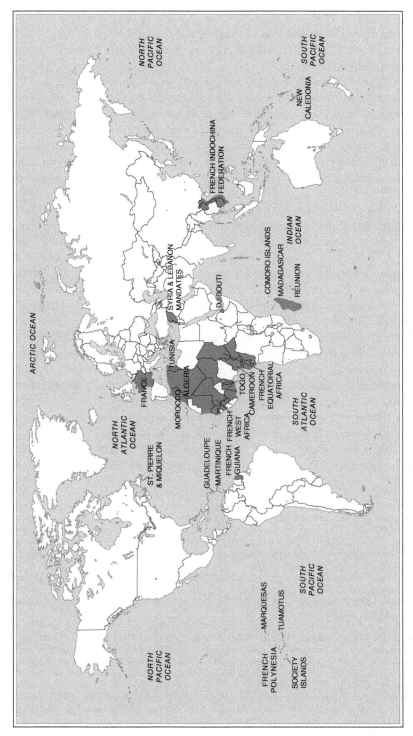

Map 4.3. The French Empire between the wars

ARCTIC OCEAN

NORTH PACIFIC OCEAN

NORTH PACIFIC OCEAN

NORTH ATLANTIC OCEAN

SOUTH PACIFIC OCEAN

FRANCE

ST. PIERRE & MIQUELON

GUADELOUPE

MARTINIQUE

FRENCH GUIANA

MOROCCO

TUNISIA

ALGERIA

SYRIA & LEBANON MANDATES

DJIBOUTI

FRENCH WEST AFRICA

TOGO

CAMEROON

FRENCH EQUATORIAL AFRICA

SOUTH ATLANTIC OCEAN

COMORO ISLANDS

MADAGASCAR

RÉUNION

INDIAN OCEAN

FRENCH INDOCHINA FEDERATION

NEW CALEDONIA

SOUTH PACIFIC OCEAN

FRENCH POLYNESIA

MARQUESAS

TUAMOTUS

SOCIETY ISLANDS

SOUTH PACIFIC OCEAN

limit the extent of PMC oversight, effective petitioning, and consequent inter-national scrutiny.[21] The point to note here is that the mandates system's regulatory agencies thus reinforced the rivalries—rhetorical and material—between Britain and France in the Arab world.

Barely three months after the Ottoman Empire's surrender was sealed by the Mudros Armistice on 30 October 1918, General Louis Franchet d'Espèrey, commander of the Allied occupation forces in Constantinople, complained to his friend Charles de Freycinet, the republican elder statesman and veteran of the 1882 Egyptian crisis, that his British colleagues were scheming for regional advantage at French expense. Always the stronger power militarily in the Near East, the British, according to Franchet d'Espèrey, were even more domineering in victory.[22]

The British and French soon provoked revolts against their interference; there were also mutual jealousies, particularly in relation to the northern Iraqi region of Mosul. Tellingly described by a German exploratory mission at the turn of the century as 'a veritable "lake of petroleum"', the Mosul hinterland was, not surprisingly, coveted by both entente partners.[23] In the event, it was the British who grabbed it in contravention of the provisional allocation of mandate terri-tories and, ultimately, riding roughshod over claims for self-determination from the region's Kurdish majority.[24] Meanwhile, not far to the west, Feisal bin Hussein bin Ali al-Hashimi, who had fought alongside the British during the wartime Arab Revolt, briefly rode a wave of populist nationalism to power in Syria, but was expelled by the French.[25] He subsequently became king of Iraq, thanks to the manipulations of the British, who wanted a nominally independent but pliable client. Again, the image of a Hashemite royal figurehead belied the depth of Arabist sentiment; much of it channelled through officers' movements and other civil society groups that fed local animus to foreign rule.[26]

These transitions of power have been labelled 'the Wilsonian moment', but nationalist movements inspired by some peacemakers' talk of self-determination

[21] Pedersen, *The Guardians*, 102–3.

[22] MAE, 77AAP1, Charles Freycinet papers, Général Franchet d'Espèrey à M. de Freycinet, 14 February 1919. Franchet d'Espèrey was not averse to shows of strength in principle: he rode into Constantinople in February 1919 on a white horse, emulating Mehmed II's triumphant entry to the city after it fell to the Ottomans in 1453.

[23] Pedersen, *The Guardians*, 272; Peter J. Beck, '"A Tedious and Perilous Controversy": Britain and the Settlement of the Mosul Dispute, 1918–1926', *Middle Eastern Studies*, 17:2 (1981), 256–76.

[24] Pedersen, *The Guardians*, 279–81; David McDowall, *A Modern History of the Kurds* (London: I.B. Tauris, 1996), chapter 8.

[25] James L. Gelvin, 'The Social Origins of Popular Nationalism in Syria: Evidence for a New Framework', *International Journal of Middle East Studies*, 26 (1994), 645–61; Elizabeth F. Thompson, 'Rashid Rida and the 190 Syrian-Arab Constitution: How the French Mandate Undermined Islamic Liberalism', in Schayegh and Arsan, *Routledge Handbook of the History of the Middle East Mandates*, 247–53; Dan Eldar, 'France in Syria: The Abolition of Sharifian Government, April–July 1920', *Middle Eastern Studies*, 29:3 (1993), 487–504.

[26] Eliezer Tauber, *The Formation of Modern Syria and Iraq* (London: Frank Cass, 1995); Efraim Karsh, 'Reactive Imperialism: Britain, the Hashemites, and the Creation of Modern Iraq', *Journal of Imperial and Commonwealth History*, 30:3 (2002), 55–70.

were not the sole threat facing the mandate powers.[27] Pan-Islam remained a preoccupation for the British, as the rhetoric surrounding Chanak demonstrates.[28] The tragedies of intercommunal violence, mass killing, and population displacement that accompanied the Ottoman Empire's implosion presented an unprecedented humanitarian challenge for the League powers.[29] They also exposed the most interventionist among them to charges of imperialist self-interest and religious prejudice in their selection of preferred victim groups, whether Armenians, Greeks, or Assyrians.[30] At the same time, Britain and France were obliged to pay lip service to the principle that common ethnicity conferred certain group rights, even while they frequently rode roughshod over it in practice.[31] The precise division of responsibility for the protection of minorities in former Ottoman territories between the Allies as occupiers and the League of Nations as arbiter of the peace triggered multiple splits: within the Supreme Allied Council, among the entente partners, and between each one and the League bureaucracy in Geneva.[32] The multiple economic dislocations and strategic dilemmas of the post-1918 era, meanwhile, unmasked tensions in Anglo-French relations that, while always implicit, were previously concealed by the exigencies of fighting the Great War.

Relative harmony attended the peace discussions at Versailles, but afterwards tensions developed over the exaction of the reparations that had been agreed, with the French less inclined than the British to show leniency towards the Germans. This was crucial. The extent of inter-Allied disagreement over the appropriate response to a German default on reparations payments was becoming clearer as the crisis over Turkey intensified during summer 1922.[33] The incipient reparations crisis, soon to escalate into a Franco-Belgian occupation of the cities, coalfields, and steel mills of the Rhineland zone, remained the dominant foreign policy concern for all French political leaders throughout the Chanak crisis.[34] Framed in this light, and before the issue of Syria was even taken into account, accommodating Turkish irredentism became strategically imperative.

[27] Erez Manela, *The Wilsonian Moment: Self-Determination and the International Origins of Anticolonial Nationalism* (Oxford: Oxford University Press, 2009).
[28] Ferris, 'The British Empire vs. the Hidden Hand', 327–36, 341–2.
[29] Bruno Cabanes, *The Great War and the Origins of Humanitarianism, 1918–1924* (Cambridge: Cambridge University Press, 2014), 6–7, 173–9.
[30] Keith David Watenpaugh, 'The League of Nations' Rescue of Armenian Genocide Survivors and the Making of Modern Humanitarianism, 1920–1927', *American Historical Review*, 115:5 (2010), 1316.
[31] Eric D. Weitz, 'From the Vienna to the Paris System: International Politics and the Entangled Histories of Human Rights, Forced Deportations, and Civilizing Missions', *American Historical Review*, 113:5 (2008), 1313–15, 1326–31.
[32] MAE, 29PAAP31, Léon Bourgeois papers, 'Note sur le rôle et les responsabilités de la Société des Nations en Turquie et en Arménie', 19 March 1920.
[33] *Documents Diplomatiques Français* (DDF), 1922, vol. 2, docs 75, 81, and 141. A temporary reparations moratorium came into force on 1 September.
[34] As examples of the intensive French coverage of the reparations issue, see the following articles in the foreign affairs-focused *Journal des Débats*: 'À la Commission des réparations', *Le Journal des Débats*, 28 August 1922; 'L'heure des décisions', *Le Journal des Débats*, 30 August 1922; 'Les événements d'Orient', by Pierre Bernus, *Le Journal des Débats*, 31 August 1922; Le Gouvernement français et les dettes interalliés', by Pierre Bernus, *Le Journal des Débats*, 2 September 1922.

Nor did this French realpolitik signify a new departure. In the aftermath of the Treaty of Sèvres the French showed greater willingness than the British to conciliate the Turks whose implacable revisionism was represented, not by the decrepit Ottoman sultanate in Istanbul but by its rival: the dynamic nationalist regime in Ankara. Negotiated with the Ottoman government, the Treaty of Sèvres was punitive. Kemal and his supporters repudiated it and were obviously never likely to recognize it. Stronger French diplomatic attachment to the juridical power of international law was significant here because, in the absence of any Turkish ratification of a peace treaty, formal devolution of sovereignty to the Middle East mandates could not take place. Thus, quite apart from the ethical implications of a quasi-colonial takeover, French and British administration of their Middle East mandates was, in juridical terms, at best provisional, at worst illegal.[35]

In the Great War's aftermath, French preoccupation with diplomatic legalism, an established feature of its approach to foreign policy matters, registered with unprecedented force in French diplomatic rhetoric as peacemaking and consequent treaty enforcement became pivotal to the long-term security of France and its empire.[36] British political leaders tended to view this French concern for a solid juridical framework to underpin foundational changes in international sovereignty in Europe and the Near East in more instrumental terms of bargains to be struck. Early in 1921, a Foreign Office memorandum noted: 'there have been some important indications of a general orientation of French policy in the direction of allowing to Great Britain a leading and predominating position in the settlement of Eastern affairs, provided France, by such a concession, can obtain the definite support of England in her relations with Germany'. However, the memorandum continued, 'It is to be feared that, failing some general settlement of the German question which will satisfy French public opinion, we may drift into a serious quarrel, if not a definite breach, with France.'[37] The basis for that quarrel soon became apparent.

During multilateral talks in London in March 1921, French premier Aristide Briand promised the Ankara government a partial withdrawal of French occupation forces from southern Anatolia pending the negotiation of a definitive border settlement with French-ruled Syria. This arrangement was the prelude to a definitive accord with the Ankara government over the disputed region of Cilicia, the so-called Franklin-Bouillon agreement of October 1921 (after the French diplomat Henry Franklin-Bouillon). Each was negotiated without notifying the British and in apparent contradiction of France's commitments under the Treaty of Sèvres.[38] Churchill judged that these arrangements were 'designed not merely to safeguard

[35] MAE, 29PAAP32, Léon Bourgeois papers, Service Français de la Société des Nations, 'Note au sujet des Mandats A', 2 February 1921.
[36] Peter Jackson, *Beyond the Balance of Power: France and Politics of National Security in the Era of the First World War* (Cambridge: Cambridge University Press, 2013), 200–4, 209–15, 317–22; Peter Jackson, 'Tradition and Adaptation: The Social Universe of the French Foreign Ministry in the Era of the First World War', *French History*, 24:2 (2010), 164–96, especially 185–9.
[37] Memorandum, possibly by Lord Curzon, dated 12 February 1921, Curzon Papers, British Library, MSS Eur F112/242.
[38] Güçlü, 'The Struggle for Mastery', 590–1; TNA, FO 141/504/6, British Military Liaison Officer, Cairo, to War Office Intelligence, 12 July 1921.

French interests in Turkey, but to secure these interests wherever necessary at the expense of Great Britain'.[39]

FRANCE: THE PATH TO WITHDRAWAL

The French decision to compromise with the nationalist regime in Ankara was never the act of unprincipled expediency that the British, and Foreign Secretary Curzon especially, painted it to be.[40] Nor was there much substance to the notion, recycled in the French press, that the accord was payback for Britain's earlier intrigues in Syria with the Hashemite King Feisal.[41] British recriminations over the accord were more serious than these jibes implied; indeed, serious enough to poison entente relations during the final months of Briand's premiership in November and December 1921. The chief objection was that France, in negotiating unilaterally with the nationalists in Ankara, had undermined the Allies' ability to uphold the treaty arrangements made since the Mudros armistice.[42] For one thing, France effectively treated Kemal's regime not just as a *de facto* authority whose writ ran throughout most of Turkey, but as the nation's *de jure* government.[43] For another thing, Briand's government was accused of consistently misleading the British about the scope and content of the negotiations. Briand, in this reading, at first denied that Franklin-Bouillon was acting in an official capacity; later, he concealed the extent of the concessions offered.[44] There was truth in each of these accusations—all of which were rehearsed with the studied indignation of a cuckolded partner. But what Curzon and his Foreign Office colleagues refused to admit was the severity of the crisis the French were facing along the northern rim of their Syrian mandate.[45]

The agreement reached on 20 October 1921 between chief French negotiator Henry Franklin-Bouillon and Youssef Kemal Bey, foreign minister and representative of the Ankara Grand National Assembly, ended a two-year war in the southern Anatolian region of Cilicia that marked the first outright defeat of French

[39] He added: 'They apparently believe that we have a similar anti-French arrangement with the Greeks. They are, of course, very angry about King Feisal, and would be delighted to see Iraq thrown into such a state of disorder that Feisal and the British policy associated with him would fall together.' Winston Churchill, 'French Negotiations with Angora', 26 October 1921, TNA, CAB 24/129, C.P. 3447. See also C.P. 3500, Lord Curzon to the Count de Saint-Aulaire, 5 November 1921.

[40] Hostile French press coverage of British objections to the agreement is discussed in TNA, FO 141/504/6, Lord Hardinge, Paris, to Lord Curzon, 7 November 1921.

[41] TNA, FO 141/504/6, E12164/1/44, Lord Curzon to Lord Hardinge, Paris, 3 November 1921.

[42] TNA, FO 141/504/6, E12944/1/44, Lord Curzon to M. de Montille, 25 November 1921.

[43] TNA, FO 141/504/6, E12528/1/44, Sir Horace Rumbold, Constantinople, to Lord Curzon, 8 November 1921.

[44] TNA, FO 141/504/6, E12164/1/44, Lord Curzon to Count de Saint-Aulaire, 5 November 1921; E12440/1/44, Lord Hardinge, Paris, to Curzon, 11 November 1921; tels. 928 and 930, Hardinge to Curzon, 3 and 6 December 1921.

[45] Robert de Caix letters to Albert Kammerer, 21 May and 17 June 1921 in Gérard D. Khoury, *Une tutelle coloniale: Le Mandat français en Syrie et au Liban. Écrits politiques de Robert de Caix* (Paris: Belin, 2006), 348–50, 360–2; Yücel Güçlü, *The Question of the Sanjak of Alexandretta: A Study in Turkish-French-Syrian Relations* (Ankara: Turkish Historical Society, 2001), 37–41.

imperial arms since the loss of Quebec in 1763.[46] For a while at least, the accords stabilized relations along the northern frontiers of France's new Syrian mandate. Commerce in the northern hinterland of the Aleppo *wilayet* was safeguarded.[47] Admittedly, the more lucrative prize of exclusive French trade and investment privileges radiating outwards from Adana through southern Anatolia was lost.[48] But the notion that Cilicia's rich agricultural and cotton resources could be harnessed to a French-ruled Greater Syria was a pipedream, whatever some diehard Parti Colonial supporters insisted to the contrary.[49] The region was predominantly, although by no means exclusively, ethnically Turkic and its economic potential was integral to the nationhood envisaged in Turkey's 'National Pact'. This statement of intent, passed by the Ottoman Chamber of Deputies on 20 January 1920, articulated nationalist claims to exclusive Turkish sovereignty over Anatolia and Thrace.[50] A rare source of consensus between politicians of the crumbling regime in Constantinople and Kemal's followers in Ankara, the National Pact sacrificed Ottoman imperial claims but made Turkish sovereignty over all areas 'inhabited by an Ottoman Muslim majority, united in religion, in race, and in aim' an unalterable objective.[51] The Pact, or Covenant as it was sometimes called, was the most powerful rhetorical instrument deployed by any of the warring parties engaged in Turkey at the time.

Within weeks of the Pact's announcement, Turkish fighters harried French occupation forces in Cilicia at every turn. These occupying units were an amalgam of North and West African colonial troops, backed by the local irregulars of the *Légion Armenienne* and the *Légion Syrienne*.[52] But there were sufficient metropolitan soldiers among them to fire up parliament and press in France when heavy losses occurred. Compelled to withdraw from the city of Maras after a lengthy siege in early 1920, the retreating French garrison was all but wiped out with the loss of almost 500 troops. Urfa and Pozanti, towns equally vital to Cilicia's internal chain of communications, were soon surrendered as well.[53] Once better armed and more organized Turkish military formations deployed to the region in strength following an initial Franco-Turkish armistice on 30 May 1920, the longer-term outcome of the struggle for control in Cilicia was never in doubt.[54]

[46] DDF, 1921, vol. 2, docs 277 and 279: text of the Ankara accord & Aristide Briand note to General Gouraud, both 20 October 1921; Güçlü, 'The Struggle for Mastery', 580: Lying directly north and west of Syria, Cilicia encompassed the Ottoman province of Adana and the sanjak of Maraş.
[47] 'Bulletin du jour: Le partage de la Haute-Silesie, l'accord franco-turc', *Le Temps*, 22 October 1921; 'L'accord Franco-Turc', *Le Figaro*, 23 October 1921.
[48] DDF, 1921, vol. 2, doc. 35, Aristide Briand to General Gouraud, 15 July 1921.
[49] Güçlü, 'The Struggle for Mastery', 583–5. Backed by the influential Chambers of Commerce in Marseilles and Lyon, the French Foreign Ministry commissioned geographical surveys of Cilicia's economic assets in 1919, which concluded that the region's agricultural output outstripped that of France's North African territories. For the long-term background to French interest in the region, see Jacques Thobie, *Intérêts et impérialisme français dans l'Empire ottoman, 1895–1914* (Paris: Documentation française, 1977).
[50] Donald Bloxham, *The Great Game of Genocide: Imperialism, Nationalism, and the Destruction of the Ottoman Armenians* (Oxford: Oxford University Press, 2005), 154.
[51] Steiner, *The Lights that Failed*, 110.   [52] Bloxham, *The Great Game of Genocide*, 141–2.
[53] Güçlü, 'The Struggle for Mastery', 586–8.
[54] Bloxham, *The Great Game of Genocide*, 151–4.

The irony for the Entente Powers was that it was precisely as France was adjusting to the Turkish nationalist resurgence that Lloyd George's coalition plunged headlong into support for Greece.[55] British military occupation of Istanbul in March 1920, accompanied by the ouster of the National Pact's supporters, had three immediate consequences, each of them inimical to the coalition's declared intention to enforce the terms of the Treaty of Sèvres. First, the expulsion of Turkish nationalist politicians from the Ottoman seat of government in Istanbul facilitated Kemal's efforts to build a rival power-base for Turkish nationalism in Ankara. Second, Britain's heavy-handed treatment of Turkish claims to self-determination drove a wedge between the Allied Powers, making it easier for the French and the Italians (the third Allied occupier) to repudiate the occupation as unfair, unworkable, and unwise. This rhetorical stance acquired stronger credibility following the British decision in June 1920 to invite Greek forces to participate in the Istanbul occupation. The Quai d'Orsay's favoured press commentators were fed a diet of communiqués depicting the Lloyd George coalition as not merely quixotic but manifestly biased. This interpretation was strengthened by Britain's accompanying support for a wider Greek occupation of the coastal hinterland surrounding the city of Smyrna (Izmir).[56]

Two points bear emphasis here. One is that Anglo-French disunity over policy towards Turkey was abundantly clear more than two years before it peaked during the Chanak crisis itself. The other is that French room for manoeuvre was severely curtailed by the overarching requirement to secure their Syrian mandate. Lacking the military resources available to the British in the Near East, French policy necessarily attached greater weight to a settlement with the Turks. This was something that Lloyd George and Foreign Secretary Curzon refused to recognize.[57] But the French logic was abundantly clear to Britain's service chiefs. Still preoccupied by the mismatch between Britain's limited military resources and its expanding overseas commitments, Wilson (then chief of the imperial general staff) warned a Cabinet committee in June 1921 that Britain's dilemmas in Turkey and Ireland 'were substantially the same & the choice of solutions the same i.e. either knock the gentleman on the head or come out'. In Ireland, he argued 'we *must* knock the gentleman on the head and so can't come out. In Turkey we *can't* knock the gentleman on the head & so we *must* come out'. He amplified this message six months later in a letter to his former deputy, General Sir Charles 'Tim' Harington, then serving as general officer commanding in Constantinople: 'We will never do any good until we clear out of Constantinople altogether, and we will certainly

[55] Steiner, *The Lights that Failed*, 107–9.

[56] Bloxham, *The Great Game of Genocide*, 154–5; Christopher M. Andrew and A. S. Kanya-Forstner, *France Overseas: The Great War and the Climax of French Imperial Expansion* (London: Thames & Hudson, 1981), 197, 222–3. Greek forces had landed at Smyrna to the delight of their local confreres in May 1919. French scepticism about the landings remained consistent throughout the Chanak crisis, see: 'Le problème orientale', by Pierre Bernus, *Le journal des débats*, 10 September 1922.

[57] MAE, série Levant 1918–29, 51CPCOM166, Chanak, October 1922 (microfilm P1399), 'Conférence de Paris entre les Ministres des affaires étrangères de Grande-Bretagne et de France, et l'Ambassadeur d'Italie', 20–3 septembre 1922.

never do any good until we make friends with the Turks.'[58] Britain's top soldier, in other words, thought that France had got it right in reaching its accommodation with Ankara.

So did Briand, who served as premier and foreign minister throughout 1921. A lawyer by training, an experienced political leader and capable coalition builder, Briand personified the juridical internationalism that was embedded among the French diplomatic corps and which characterized France's approach to treaty-making after 1919. This outlook was strongly positivist in its operating assumption that rational political actors could be brought to an acceptance that agreements, scrupulously enforced through a panoply of international treaty law, were the best means to prevent interstate conflict. This juridical approach to foreign policy is most strongly identified with the Versailles settlement.[59] But there were traces of the same republican legalism in the rounds of shuttle diplomacy that Franklin-Bouillon conducted, first on Briand's behalf, later in Poincaré's name, during 1921 and 1922. More than just a bid to safeguard French supremacy in Syria, negotiation with the Ankara regime sought to reconcile the Kemalists' territorial revisionism with longer term Turkish acceptance of a treaty-based peace in the Near East.[60] Ultimately, this French strategy of engagement flowered with the signing of the Lausanne settlement in 1923.

As chair of the French Senate foreign affairs commission, Franklin-Bouillon shared Briand's primordial interest in overseas affairs. A close working partnership, the two men detested Lloyd George, their distrust of British actions in the Middle East confirmed by the loss of Mosul at the start of the year.[61] Admittedly, Britain's Mosul takeover was prefigured—even condoned—during face-to-face meetings between Britain's prime minister and his French counterpart, Georges Clemenceau, before the Paris Peace Conference in 1919.[62] But Clemenceau's successors, including Briand and his foreign policy team, disdained the old tiger's willingness to make concessions over former Ottoman territory the better to secure French interests on the Rhine.[63] A blunt and unilateral application of *force majeure*, Britain's seizure of Iraq's northernmost region was everything that juridical internationalism was not. While French protests at the British action were confined to rhetorical laments about might not making right, they also built a diplomatic bridge to the Ankara nationalists who shared French antagonism to Britain's northerly thrust in Iraq. Briand also made common cause with the Kemalists in

[58] Jeffery, *Field Marshal Sir Henry Wilson*, 252.

[59] Jackson, *Beyond the Balance of Power*, 357–60.

[60] Güçlü, 'The Struggle for Mastery', 593–7.

[61] Chamber of Deputies, Foreign Affairs commission report, 1921.

[62] Edward P. Fitzgerald, 'France's Middle Eastern Ambitions, the Sykes-Picot Negotiations, and the Oil Fields of Mosul, 1915–1918', *Journal of Modern History*, 66:4 (1994), 697–701; for background, see: John Fisher, 'Syria and Mesopotamia in British Middle Eastern Policy in 1919', *Middle Eastern Studies*, 34:2 (1998), 129–70.

[63] Andrew and Kanya-Forstner, *France Overseas*, 174–6, 197–8, 214. It was during Briand's wartime premiership in 1915 that French forces landed at Salonika, a clear signal of his abiding interest in the Eastern Mediterranean, see: David Dutton, *The Politics of Diplomacy: Britain, France and the Balkans in the First World War* (London: I.B. Tauris, 1998), especially chapters 4–6.

rejecting the Treaty of Sèvres as unfit for purpose as a peacemaking instrument. Speaking in the National Assembly on 11 July 1921, the French prime minister combined a sharp appreciation for international law with a more basic appeal to French pockets. Sèvres, he said, was not a settlement but a source of regional tension. That tension was worsened by Greece's refusal to accept outside offers of mediation in its war against Turkey. France, in these circumstances, could not be blamed for wanting to reduce its military commitments in Cilicia, the one regional war zone where it could take effective measures both to curb levels of violence and to cut military expenditure.[64]

Characteristically, when Briand rose to the podium in the Chamber of Deputies on 21 October 1921 to defend the Franklin-Bouillon accord, he focused on four related concerns. First and foremost were the lives of French soldiers saved by ending a pointless war in predominantly Turkish territory. Those same troops could now return home to help protect France's eastern frontier, a more worthy task and a second discreet advantage. Redeployment was especially crucial at a point when unrest in Upper Silesia and shortfalls in reparations payments pointed to looming confrontation with Germany. Rhetorically, then, Briand set Near Eastern problems lower down a global order of priorities in which first place went to the risk of the Treaty of Versailles unravelling. This, his third concern, was tied to the fourth: the Franklin-Bouillon accord, the reward for pursuing difficult talks with a revisionist adversary, confirmed the wisdom of reducing regional tensions through dialogue.[65] By the time he sat down the overall message to be inferred from his statement was clear: Briand, the methodical peacemaker, was the antithesis of Lloyd George, the impetuous adventurist.[66]

A WIDENING DIVIDE

Unabashed by French contempt for his scheming, at the European conference at Cannes in January 1922, Lloyd George hoped to link economic and political issues in order to solve the reparations problem and guarantee French security. Things did not go as planned. His attempt to give Briand a golf lesson was portrayed in the French media as a humiliation for the Frenchman. His government already in trouble, Briand fell from office during the conference.[67] His replacement, the former president, Raymond Poincaré, had even less time for Lloyd George, whom he would later accuse of always seeking British advantage at French

---

[64] TNA, FO 141/504/6, Sir M. Cheetham, Paris, to Lord Curzon, 11 July 1921.

[65] 'M. Briand définit sa politique', *Le Figaro*, 22 October 1921.

[66] Unsurprisingly, Briand said nothing about French arms supplies to Kemalist forces. Britain's War Office intelligence suspected that 80,000 rifles figured as part of the Franklin-Bouillon deal, weapons which, they feared, might be used as part of a Turkish thrust against British forces in Mosul: TNA, FO 141/504/6, Satow, Beirut, memo. to War Office Intelligence, Cairo, 6 October 1921: 'Anglo-French Relations in the Near and Middle East and their Effect on Islamism'.

[67] Morgan, *Consensus and Disunity*, 268–9; Roy Hattersley, *David Lloyd George: The Great Outsider* (London: Little, Brown, 2010), chapter 34.

expense.[68] Discussions about a peacetime Anglo-French military alliance, which Poincaré thought should include British guarantees of France's growing Eastern European alliance network, ran into the sand.[69]

If golfing on the Riviera helped finish Briand, it did not do much for Lloyd George's image either. The artificial bonhomie of the golf course typified the prime minister's preference for conference diplomacy over attending the House of Commons. But this remoteness from urgent problems of domestic reconstruction seemed heartless as unemployment climbed alarmingly high.[70] His government could boast some achievements, notably the treaty that put an end to the conflict with Ireland, but that deal remained bitterly contested and it alienated many of his ministry's Conservative supporters. By the spring of 1922, the coalition was living on borrowed time, even before the failure of the Genoa conference of April–May. Intended to bring both Bolshevik Russia and Weimar Germany in from the cold, the Genoa talks were torpedoed by the revelation of a bilateral agreement between the two states. The diplomatic wreckage brought the deepening Franco-British disagreement over permissible reparations exactions into starker relief.[71] The summer's cash-for-honours scandal discredited Lloyd George further. Many Tories wanted rid of him, preferring to fight the coming election as an independent party rather than on a new coalition ticket. Austen Chamberlain, who had replaced Bonar Law as leader due to the latter's ill health, remained loyal to the prime minister, but the tensions were reaching boiling point. Lloyd George's behaviour during the Chanak crisis looked to some like the last, desperate throw of the dice, an effort to renew his popularity by drumming up a war scare.

Things came to a head at the end of the summer. As mentioned earlier, after the war, and with British encouragement, Greek forces landed at Smyrna. The city was home to large Greek and Armenian populations, whose fate now became contingent on the success of this expedition.[72] Under the Treaty of Sèvres, the Constantinople government renounced its claims to territory outside Turkey and agreed that Smyrna and its hinterland be administered by the Greeks for five years in advance of a plebiscite. With Allied forces in his capital, the sultan had little choice.

---

[68] Keiger, *Raymond Poincaré*, 288–90. Poincaré made this accusation within the relative privacy of the Council of Ministers after the collapse of the Genoa conference. But he made no secret of his loathing for Lloyd George to his political confidant, Louis Barthou, who, as chief French representative to the inter-Allied reparations commission from October 1922, was left to pick up the pieces, see: 'Conseil des Ministres', *Le Figaro*, 6 October 1922.

[69] Patrick O. Cohrs, *The Unfinished Peace after World War I: America, Britain, and the Stabilisation of Europe, 1919–1932* (Cambridge: Cambridge University Press, 2006), 72.

[70] On Lloyd George's governing style, see Kenneth O. Morgan, 'Lloyd George's Premiership: A Study in "Prime Ministerial Government"', *Historical Journal*, 13:1 (1970), 130–57.

[71] Cohrs, *The Unfinished Peace*, 73–4; Steiner, *The Lights that Failed*, 211–13. For multi-perspective analysis, see Carol Fink, Axel Frohn, and Jürgen Heideking (eds), *Genoa, Rapallo and European Reconstruction in 1922* (Cambridge: Cambridge University Press, 1991).

[72] As Donald Bloxham records, the grisly murder of Smyrna's Greek orthodox archbishop Chrystomos prefigured mass violence against the city's Christian communities: *The Great Game of Genocide*, 165. Much of the city was destroyed in a fire that began in the Armenian quarter within days of the Turkish military occupation: Bruce Clark, *Twice a Stranger: How Mass Expulsion Forged Modern Greece and Turkey* (London: Granta, 2006), 22–3.

But the Kemalists were bound to view Smyrna as a test case of Turkish claims to unencumbered national sovereignty. Lloyd George encouraged Greece's ambitions, but without giving them any practical military support. In that respect he was constrained by the concerns of his colleagues. Churchill—who would later change his tune—argued that it was dangerous for Britain to be identified as anti-Turk, given that there were so many Muslims living within the British Empire itself. Edwin Montagu, the reforming secretary of state for India, was especially worried about the impact on Indian Muslims; the issue eventually provoked a conflict with Lloyd George that forced his resignation.[73] Believing that a friendly Turkey could act as a bulwark against the USSR, Churchill told the prime minister that 'one of the main causes of the trouble throughout the Middle East is *your* quarrel with the remnants of Turkey'.[74] Political ructions in Greece, resulting in the return of the exiled King Constantine, worsened the difficulties facing a Greek Army already chronically overextended, paving the way for its eventual rout at Kemal's hands.

Lloyd George spoke on the situation in the Commons at the start of August 1922. Cecil Harmsworth, under-secretary of state for foreign affairs, recalled:

> Ll.-G. ran over with us the notes of his speech which was all anti-Turk and pro-Greek. I asked whether it was right and wise of us to encourage the Greeks in their ambitious policy in respect of Smyrna and Asia Minor generally unless we were ready to assist them with men and arms. Ll.-G. had the bit between his teeth and nothing would stop him. The speech was fatal to him and to his Government.[75]

With the distance of years, Harmsworth greatly exaggerated the effect of this one particular speech, which had no great impact at the time. He was, however, broadly accurate about its content. Lloyd George played up Turkish atrocities and down-played Greek ones, while accusing one of his chief critics, the radical Liberal J. M. Kenworthy, of doing the opposite. While denying that the issue at stake was one of Islam versus Christianity, the prime minister concluded with an appeal reminiscent of Gladstone, urging that the 'Christian populations of Asia Minor are adequately protected against a repetition of such horrible incidents as have disgraced the annals of that land'.[76] It is noteworthy that Sir Donald Maclean, a leading member of the Asquithian (i.e. non-coalition) Liberal Party, praised the speech for its reflection of the 'great tradition of the great party to which I belong', and commended its attention to 'the note of humanity and of our obligations towards the oppressed races of the Near East' under the Turkish heel.[77] Obviously,

---

[73] Ferris, 'The British Empire vs. the Hidden Hand', 328, 335.

[74] Winston Churchill to David Lloyd George, 4 December 1920, in Martin Gilbert (ed.), *Winston S. Churchill: Companion Volume IV*, part 2 (London: Heinemann, 1977), 1260–2. Emphasis in original.

[75] Cecil Harmsworth, retrospective note of October 1936, attached to diary entry of 3 August 1922, Cecil Harmsworth Papers, University of Exeter.

[76] HC Deb, 4 August 1922, vol. 157, col. 2006. A few months earlier, Lloyd George had commented: 'I begin to think I am the only Liberal left, the only upholder of the Gladstonian policy'. Trevor Wilson, *The Political Diaries of C.P. Scott 1911–1928* (London: Collins, 1970), 423 (entry for 22 May 1922).

[77] HC Deb, 4 August 1922, vol. 157, col. 2007.

not all Liberals were persuaded—the *Manchester Guardian* certainly wasn't—and Lloyd George may well have given the impression that he was living in the past.[78] The Liberal Party's wartime split still rankled the Asquithians, who attacked the prime minister in classic anti-Tory terms for having 'wasted the people's hard-earned money on armaments and foreign adventures'.[79] But Lloyd George's willingness to talk the Gladstonian tongue indicates that he may have had half an eye on the prospect of future Liberal reunion and certainly on the party's traditional voters. It also helps explain why British self-assertion in this case turned out to be so problematic for many Conservatives.

ADJUSTING TO GREEK DEFEAT

In September, Greek forces were routed and Turkish troops occupied Smyrna. The ensuing massacres eclipsed the intercommunal violence that had accompanied the Greek takeover two years earlier.[80] The French press was more dispassionate than the British in its assessments of the Greek catastrophe.[81] On 8 September, *Le Figaro* reported that the Greek Army commander, Nicolaos Trikoupis, and his general staff had been captured by Kemalist forces at the battle of Dumlupinar. This was correctly read as affirmation of the overwhelming scale of Turkish victory after their massive counter-offensive.[82] Having lost thousands of men and the bulk of its equipment, the Greek expeditionary force was reportedly in headlong retreat, its short-term aim being to evacuate some 200,000 troops from the Turkish mainland.[83] Writing in the *Journal des Débats*, the paper's foreign affairs specialist Pierre Bernus blamed the British for the way events had unfolded in western Asia. He reeled off a litany of British mistakes: 'Their conclusion of the Mudros Armistice, their greedy and imprudent policies throughout the Middle East, Lloyd George's contradictory statements, the pretence that they are sole masters of Constantinople, their encouragement of Greek adventurism'. All of this, he concluded, explained how Allied victory had turned so quickly into Anglo-Greek defeat. This was nothing to celebrate, even if Britain's humiliation might evoke some justifiable French *Schadenfreude*. But this, Bernus reminded readers pointedly, was a Germanic emotion and not a French one. It was far better to persuade the British to change course than to revel in their difficulties.[84]

---

[78] 'The Scandal of the Near East', *Manchester Guardian*, 5 August 1922; John M. McEwen (ed.), *The Riddell Diaries 1908–1923* (London: The Athlone Press, 1986), 376 (entry for 24 September 1922).

[79] *The Liberal Flashlight*, April 1922, in *Pamphlets and Leaflets for 1922* (London: Liberal Publications Department, 1923).

[80] Bloxham, *The Great Game of Genocide*, 150–1, 164–5.

[81] 'Les conséquences de la défaite greque', by Pierre Bernus, *Le Journal des Débats*, 5 September 1922.

[82] 'Les operations en Asie Mineure', *Le Figaro*, 8 September 1922.

[83] 'Les conséquences de la défaite grecque', by Henry Bidou, *Le Figaro*, 9 September 1922.

[84] 'Le problème orientale', by Pierre Bernus, *Le journal des débats*, 10 September 1922. Seriously wounded as an infantryman in 1916, Bernus became foreign correspondent for the *Journal de Genève* before joining the *Journal des Débats* after the war.

Bernus's colleague, the *Journal des Débats* editor, Auguste Gauvain, underlined the message three days later. Criticizing British policy in the former Ottoman Empire as hubristic and duplicitous, Gauvain warned French leaders against impending British attempts to drag them into the morass.[85] The journalists' advice seemed to resonate among Poincaré's ministers. On 14 September, Poincaré responded ambiguously to the British request, made two days' earlier, for the deployment of additional French troops in the neutral zone. The French premier admitted that a stronger Allied military presence in Constantinople was desirable, but left things at that. It was the French High Commission in the city that met General Harington's request to assign troops to Chanak as well as to Scutari (Üsküdar) on the Asian shore of the Bosphorus.[86]

As soon as Poincaré learned of these deployments, he set about reversing them. The French *volte-face* was hardly unexpected. It was consistent with France's efforts to conciliate the Ankara regime over the preceding eighteen months. And it served France's imperial interests as a Muslim power. The Foreign Ministry was bombarded with warnings from France's North African administrations not to back military action against Turkish Muslims.[87] Defying colonial censorship regulations, Arabic-language newspapers from Rabat to Tunis published a string of celebratory articles lauding Kemalist military success. Moroccan Resident-General Lyautey wrote personally to Poincaré advising that he would face 'serious difficulties' in the territory if French forces engaged the Turks.[88] Poincaré's inclination to pull out French forces could also be read between the lines of the communiqué issued after a special Council of Ministers meeting at Rambouillet on 15 September. Couched in generalities, the governmental statement lent its voice to British calls for a negotiated peace, but at the same time ruled out any Allied intervention to force the issue. In essence, Poincaré's administration was inclined to accept the facts on the ground as compatible with Turkish demands for self-determination under the National Pact.[89] Kemal's advance now appeared to represent a direct threat to British forces at Chanak—and one that, as was gradually becoming apparent, they might have to face alone.[90]

By the time that news of the French communiqué reached London later on the evening of 15 September, the British Cabinet had decided to defend the neutral 'zone of the straits' (as laid out in the Treaty of Sèvres), if necessary by force. Churchill, for reasons that have never been adequately explained, had now become enthusiastically anti-Turk. He was delegated to draw up a telegram to be sent to each of the Dominions telling them of the Cabinet's decision and seeking their active support. Wartime memory and symbolism were crucial here. Churchill

[85] 'La crise orientale', by Auguste Gauvain, *Le journal des débats*, 13 September 1922.

[86] See the following articles by Gauvain: 'Les conditions de la paix orientale', *Le journal des débats*, 13 September 1922; 'La crise orientale et l'Asie', 14 September 1922.

[87] DDF, 1922, vol. 2, doc. 180, Poincaré tel. to European embassies, 18 September 1922.

[88] MAE, Série Levant, 1918–29, 51CPCOM166, Chanak, Conférence de Paris entre les Ministres des affaires étrangères, first meeting, 11.00 a.m. at Quai d'Orsay, 20 September 1922.

[89] 'Les négociations orientales', *Le journal des débats*, 17 September 1922.

[90] 'La guerre d'Orient et les Alliés', by Pierre Bernus, *Le Journal des Débats*, 8 September 1922.

noted a few days later: 'We communicated with Australia and New Zealand because of the special associations they have with Gallipoli, and we felt bound to make the message common to all the Dominions.'[91] (The Gallipoli episode provoked complex reactions in Australia, arousing intense national pride and equally visceral Anglophobia, both underpinned by horror at the waste of life.)[92] With the French and Italians reluctant to endorse sterner military measures, it seems that what the British government really wanted was declarative, symbolic, or rhetorical backing, as Dominion troops could hardly have reached the scene in time to affect the military outcome, had the Turks decided to attack. The primary aim was to produce a 'great moral effect in emphasizing [the] solidarity of British Imperial interests'.[93]

Lloyd George approved Churchill's draft, and the telegrams were transmitted late the same evening. Frances Stevenson, the prime minister's secretary and mistress, was 'horrified at the unwisdom of the message', but failed to warn him as she thought that he would never agree to it being sent.[94] On 16 September, Lloyd George and Churchill worked on a press communiqué, which said it was the duty of the wartime allies to stand together against Turkish aggression. This was another misstep. Australian Prime Minister Billy Hughes offered (qualified) public backing to Britain, but as he later recalled:

> The request of the British Government that the Dominions should not only stand by Britain, but be represented by a contingent of troops, was made public before the Dominions had received the official communication notifying them that a serious crisis existed! To say that this savoured of sharp practice, and appeared to be a dodge to manoeuvre the Dominions into a position from which there was no retreat, is not to put the matter too strongly.[95]

Canadian Prime Minister W. L. Mackenzie King—who insisted that the Ottawa parliament would have to be consulted—thought that the telegram was 'drafted designedly to play the imperial game, to test out centralization vs. autonomy as regards European wars'.[96] New Zealand and Newfoundland were supportive; the South Africans simply failed to reply.[97]

---

[91] Churchill to Lord Byng, 18 September 1922, Churchill Papers, CHAR 17/28/8-10. Curzon repeated this phraseology, calling Gallipoli a 'vital and sacred interest' for the British Empire in his first summit meeting on the Chanak crisis with Poincaré on 20 September. Ironically, Gallipoli was at the time garrisoned by a battalion of French West African *tirailleurs sénégalais*: MAE, Série Levant, 1918–29, 51CPCOM166, Chanak, Conférence de Paris entre les Ministres des affaires étrangères, first meeting, 11.00 a.m. at Quai d'Orsay, 20 September 1922.

[92] John Ramsden, *Man of the Century: Winston Churchill and His Legend Since 1945* (London: HarperCollins, 2002), 437; for official, journalistic, and soldiers' responses, see: Jenny Macleod, *Reconsidering Gallipoli* (Manchester: Manchester University Press, 2004).

[93] 'Paraphrase of Telegram from the Secretary of State for the Colonies to the Governor General of New Zealand', sent 21 September 1922, Churchill Papers, CHAR 17/28/22.

[94] Frances Lloyd George, *The Years that are Past* (London: Hutchinson, 1967), 206.

[95] W. M. Hughes, *The Splendid Adventure: A Review of Empire Relations Within and Without the Commonwealth of Britannic Nations* (London: Ernest Benn Ltd, 1929), 243.

[96] W. L. Mackenzie King, diary, 17 September 1922, <http://www.collectionscanada.gc.ca/databases/king/index-e.html> accessed 2 October 2013.

[97] Walder, *The Chanak Affair*, 251–6.

Yet while the communiqué's poor reception is well known, little attention has been paid to its actual language. A stock argument against opposing the Turks was the risk of thereby provoking Muslims elsewhere in the British Empire. Whereas Poincaré's ministers used the equivalent danger in French North Africa to justify inaction, Lloyd George and Churchill turned the threat of Muslim anger on its head. A Kemalist victory would encourage Islamic rebellion because of the Western weakness it would reveal, they implied: 'That the allies should be driven out of Constantinople by the forces of Mustapha Kemal would be an event of the most disastrous character, producing no doubt far-reaching reactions throughout all Moslem countries.' Equally striking was the explanation of the request to the Dominions, which were being invited to take part 'in the defence of interests for which they have already made enormous sacrifices and of soil which is hallowed by immortal memories of the Anzacs'.[98] This was a version of the 'graves' trope that E. M. Forster was to ridicule so mercilessly.

THE CRISIS PEAKS

In the week preceding the French decision to pull their forces back from Chanak, the Paris press chose a different analogy to describe the widening Franco-British rift. This was Britain's bombardment of Alexandria in 1882. As Auguste Gauvain described it, for some commentators Poincaré's administration faced a Hobson's choice akin to that which had confronted Charles de Freycinet's ministry forty years earlier. The cost of participation in a British-led venture might be war. But standing aside risked marginalization and the intensification of Anglo-French colonial rivalries. Gauvain rejected the parallel entirely. Any similarities were superficial at best. The secularist Kemal was no 'Urabi Pacha. Nor was Poincaré's government reduced to the role of bystander as de Freycinet's had been.[99] Pulling back from Chanak instead represented an injection of French common sense—the antidote to Lloyd George's messianic determination to embark on a hopeless anti-Turkish 'crusade'.[100] An inflammatory choice of words, but there was more than a grain of truth in Gauvain's assessment as the British prime minister fulminated over the French withdrawal and nudged his ministerial colleagues closer to war.[101] John Ferris captures the febrile atmosphere around the Cabinet table:

> The Foreign Office and ministers, responsible for the debacle, were angry at Turkey and their allies, at criticism and threats, unwilling to be pushed around and attracted to tough policy; personality became fundamental to policy. Churchill, no Turkophobe, resented Turkish challenges to British prestige and believed that, to restore its credibility,

---

[98] Press communiqué, 16 September 1922, Churchill Papers CHAR 17/28/1-5.
[99] 'L'abjection de Constantin', by Auguste Gauvain, *Le journal des Débats*, 19 September 1922.
[100] 'La crise orientale. Lord Curzon à Paris', by Auguste Gauvain, *Le journal des Débats*, 21 September 1922.
[101] Cabinet minutes (52/22), 30 September 1922, CAB 23/31, TNA. The Italians also withdrew, but drew less opprobrium than the French.

Britain must act boldly in the Straits and be seen to do so. Lloyd George, hostile to Turkey, believing Kemal had won simply because Greeks had panicked, had little appetite for more crow. Even the most realistic and pacific of major ministers, Austen Chamberlain, held Britain could neither tremble before threats nor let allies profit from treachery. Curzon's foreign policy was cool but the minister steamed, enraged by the allies and his colleagues.[102]

Britain's service chiefs, for their part, remained deeply pessimistic about the outcome of armed confrontation along the coasts of the straits. Predicting how the situation might develop if fighting broke out, the general staff suggested that Harington's forces could not hold their position. Landing reinforcements would be hazardous, as Gallipoli had shown only too well. Even if the two infantry divisions and brigade of cavalry provisionally assigned for the job could get ashore, these additional troops could not safeguard the neutral one against three converging Turkish army corps.[103] Remarkably, the Cabinet set this unequivocal warning aside. Between 28 and 30 September the British government ordered Harington, commander of the Allied forces in Turkey, to issue Kemal an ultimatum: if Turkish forces did not retreat from Chanak, they would face military assault. Harington, however, wisely held back from delivering the message, and in the event, Kemal decided not to attack and instead agreed to negotiate with the British general.[104]

On 30 September, the French press ran stories of growing unease in Whitehall as reports came in of continuing Turkish assignment of troops to Chanak. Downing Street, though, was backed into a corner by the British demand for the withdrawal of Kemal's forces from the neutral zone.[105] The contrast drawn with French diplomatic activity was striking. Franklin-Bouillon, *Le Figaro* noted, had just arrived in Smyrna aboard the cruiser *Metz*. Stepping ashore, he was greeted by Kemal's aide-de-camp and members of the Turkish Cabinet, including Youssef Kemal Bey with whom Franklin-Bouillon had negotiated his eponymous October 1921 accord. His hosts immediately whisked the Frenchman to Ankara for a *tête-à-tête* with Kemal.[106]

The contrasting French and British approaches were pinpointed even more sharply the next day, 1 October. As news reached Western capitals of Kemal's acceptance of a peace conference, *Le Figaro* ran two leading articles. The first recorded an interview between American journalist Richard Eaton and the Turkish leader; the second emphasized the irreversibility of Turkish victory.[107] Riding

---

[102] Ferris, '"Far Too Dangerous a Gamble"', 154.

[103] TNA, WO 106/709, General Staff appreciation of the situation in Gallipoli and Chanak during October 1922.

[104] Ferris, '"Far Too Dangerous a Gamble"', 159–60.

[105] 'Dernière heure: La situation en orient: Anglais et Turcs face à face', *Le Figaro*, 30 September 1922. The Communist Party mouthpiece, *L'Humanité*, suggested that the crisis was a critical test, not just for British imperialism, but for the internationalism of Britain's working class, whose party and trade union representatives, it suggested, were appalled by the government's bellicosity: 'Cabinet Anglais tient conseil sur conseil', *L'Humanité*; 'L'impérialisme anglais au bord de la guerre', *L'Humanité*.

[106] Bulletin du jour: Les puissances et l'orient', *Le Temps*, 30 September 1922.

[107] 'Une interview de Mustapha Kemal', *Le Figaro*, 1 October 1922.

roughshod over the Mudros Armistice and the Treaty of Sèvres, Kemal's nation-alists had turned their country from vanquished to victor. Crucially, while Har-ington might be credited for his steadfastness, by choosing to meet Franklin-Bouillon in Ankara, Kemal underlined his greater respect for France's prior recog-nition of Turkish claims to sovereign rights.[108] A week later, *Le Figaro's* leader writer, Henry Bidou, amplified the point. Chronically overstretched, yet desperate to bolster its imperial power, the British, he claimed, were still playing by the old rules of the Great Game in Asia. The Lloyd George coalition had substituted Greeks for Arabs as Britain's cat's paw in efforts to undermine Turkish power. *Plus ça change*: other people were, as usual, expected to die on Britain's behalf. Bidou's inference was obvious: the Briand and Poincaré governments, by acknowledging legitimate Turkey's resurgence, practiced a more responsible, modernist diplomacy—one that refused to play with others' lives so casually.[109]

On 11 October, a convention was signed pending the negotiation of a new peace treaty between Turkey and the Allies. During these tense days public debate shifted as diplomatic details began to leak out. The Asquithians turned their fire on the government, much of the criticism focusing on its alleged dishonesty and amateur-ishness. This, however, was linked to broader issues. Francis Acland MP argued:

> We had lost the reputation for the straightness of our policy and this was particularly true in the Mahomedan world. [. . .] If we escaped from war the situation at the straits would still be serious, for the word would have gone out to the Mahomedan world that the only argument to which Britain bows was force.[110]

Asquith himself blasted the government's 'ineptitude' and warned that war would probably 'involve the greater part of the Asiatic Near East, with the possibility of infinite repercussions throughout the Moslem world'.[111]

Of greater account politically was the response of Bonar Law. This came in a letter published in *The Times* (and also the *Daily Express*) on 7 October.[112] The letter is well recognized as the moment that Law—whose health had temporarily recovered—signalled his re-emergence as a potential alternative Tory leader at a time when Chamberlain was failing to satisfy the grassroots.[113] Yet his statement deserves more systematic analysis than it usually receives, not least because of its comments on the Muslim issue and the light it casts on Law's view of international relations. Law's pose was that of one who did not wish to recriminate about the past but who simply wanted to provide guidance as to what should be done next.

---

[108] 'La situation en Orient: Journée d'attente à Londres', *Le Figaro*, 1 October 1922, p. 1; for details of Kemal's meeting with Franklin-Bouillon, see DDF, 1922, vol. 2, doc. 214.

[109] 'La partie qui se joue à Londres', by Henry Bidou, *Le Figaro*, 6 October 1922. A respected war correspondent who commented extensively on General Joseph Joffre's leadership of the French Army, Bidou also wrote for other newspapers with prominent foreign affairs coverage, including *Le Journal des Débats* and *Le Temps*.

[110] 'Liberal MP's Plea for Honesty', *The Times*, 3 October 1922.

[111] 'Mr. Asquith on the Crisis', *The Times*, 7 October 1922.

[112] Anne Chisholm and Michael Davie, *Beaverbrook: A Life* (London: Pimlico, 1993), 186–7.

[113] On grassroots discontent, see E. H. H. Green, *Ideologies of Conservatism: Conservative Political Ideas in the Twentieth Century* (Oxford: Oxford University Press, 2002), chapter 4.

He was nominally supportive of the government, which, he argued, had been right to try to prevent the Turks from entering Constantinople and crossing into Thrace. British withdrawal, he argued, 'would have been regarded throughout the whole Musulman world as the defeat of the British Empire'; and whereas the government's pro-Greek stance might have alienated Indian Muslims, that was nothing to the danger that would have been raised if the British had appeared impotent in the face of the Turks.[114] (The Aga Khan riposted that Law had underestimated Muslims' intelligence, and that they would have hailed a withdrawal as a sign of improved British-Islamic relations.)[115] Law continued:

> It is not, however, right that the burden of taking necessary action should fall on the British Empire alone. The prevention of war and massacre in Constantinople is not specially a British interest; it is the interest of humanity. The retention also of the freedom of the Straits is not specially a British interest; it is the interest of the world.

This was fascinating language, because it appeared to imply that acting in 'the interest of humanity'—as opposed to the interest of Britain alone—could be a legitimate and worthy foreign policy objective. That was something that previous generations of Conservatives might have been reluctant to concede. In an ideal world, Law seemed to be arguing, this humanitarian action should be carried out jointly by the Allied Powers that were signatories to the peace treaties; he did not mention the League of Nations. However, there was an important caveat. The fact that Britain did *not* have particular direct interest in the issues at stake justified her washing her hands of the problem if other countries would not collaborate with her in dealing with them. The apparently internationalist rhetoric, then, was deployed in the interests of *avoiding* humanitarian action. Law, furthermore, appeared critical of the French, citing rumours, which he claimed not to credit, that their representative with the Kemalists had encouraged the Turks to make impossible demands. He concluded:

> We cannot act alone as the policemen of the world. [. . .] our duty is to say plainly to our French Allies that the position in Constantinople and the Straits is as essential a part of the Peace settlement as the arrangement with Germany, and that if they are not prepared to support us there, we shall not be able to bear the burden alone, but shall have no alternative except to imitate the government of the United States and to restrict our attention to the safeguarding of the more immediate interests of the Empire.[116]

Law skilfully dodged the charge of undermining the government at a time of difficulty—and voiced a frustration with France that ministers actually shared—while at the same time making clear his differences with the coalition. Trying to prevent massacres, he seemed to say, was an entirely worthy object, but there was no call to do it if the French wouldn't help. Lloyd George and his friends, he implied, were much too concerned with 'the interests of humanity' at the expense

---

[114] 'The Near East: Pronouncement by Mr. Bonar Law', *The Times*, 7 October 1922.
[115] The Aga Khan to the editor of *The Times*, published 10 October 1922.
[116] 'The Near East: Pronouncement by Mr. Bonar Law', *The Times*, 7 October 1922.

of more pressing British and empire problems. This was imperial isolationism with a humanitarian garnish.

Law's intervention gave discontented Conservative MPs the encouragement they needed to start plotting the coalition's downfall. Their frustrations can only have been increased by Chamberlain's speech to the Midland Conservative Club on 13 October, in which he urged a continuation of the alliance with Lloyd George. Chamberlain hit out at Asquith and Lord Grey (as Sir Edward Grey now was) who had urged unity with France as the best route to peace. Their language had, he said, encouraged the Kemalists, and they had presented 'Great Britain and the British Empire to France, not as an ally and an equal, but as a humble satellite in the orbit of French policy'. He also used the 'graves of Gallipoli' argument.[117]

The next day, Lloyd George mounted his own defence in a speech in Manchester. Far from being a warmonger, he said, it was only the firm action of his government that had preserved peace; it was the backing given to Harington that had 'impressed the Oriental mind'. He did not respond to Bonar Law, but reserved his scorn for those Asquithians who argued, as he put it, 'that it was none of our business to interfere between the Turks and their victims'. Noting that 'That was not the old Liberal policy', he explicitly invoked Gladstone. The Grand Old Man would have been shocked, he said, to 'witness the spectacle of Liberal leaders and Liberal newspapers attacking a Government because they are doing their best to prevent the Turks from crossing into Europe and committing atrocities upon the Christian population'. He twitted the French for their 'humiliating' retreat. He also spoke of how Australia and New Zealand had indicated their willingness to send troops 'so as to prevent the graves of Gallipoli from being desecrated'—this, he claimed, was another factor that had helped avoid war.[118] Liberal Cabinet minister H. A. L. Fisher wrote in his diary that the speech was 'Clearly a great success & very skilful—calculated to frighten recalcitrant Tories.'[119] It does seem to have gone down well with the immediate audience, but beyond the confines the Manchester Reform Club the speech was widely criticized.

Lloyd George's Orientalist prejudices and religious language did not go unnoticed. Saiyid Ameer Ali, a prominent Indian judge and Islamic scholar who had retired to England, pointedly commented that the 'Oriental mind' was not 'so simple as ministers imagine'. The prime minister should have remembered that he was 'the head of a wide-flung Empire composed of many millions of people professing the same faith as the Turks' and should have restrained his language.[120] *The Times* said that Lloyd George's approach 'would have been justified only were Christendom waging a holy war against the Turks'.[121] *The Observer* was more

[117] 'Mr. Chamberlain's Appeal', *The Times*, 14 October 1922.
[118] 'The Premier's Defence', *The Times*, 16 October 1922.
[119] F. Russell Bryant (ed.), *The Coalition Diaries of H.A.L. Fisher, 1916–1922: The Historian in Lloyd George's Cabinet Volume III 1921–1922* (Lampeter: Edwin Mellen Press, 2006), 1024 (entry for 15 October 1922). Lloyd George had said that he would relish 'freedom' if he were to cease being prime minister. He may have been trying to hold out the prospect that he would rally Liberal forces against the Tories, which may have been what Fisher considered potentially alarming to Conservatives.
[120] Saiyid Ameer Ali to the editor of *The Times*, published 17 October 1922.
[121] 'The Prime Minister's Speech', *The Times*, 16 October 1922.

sympathetic to the prime minister. However: 'We wish the Premier yesterday had frankly recognized [...] that we cannot hope to maintain our Eastern Empire without definite reconciliation of its Moslem races. We must cease to speak of the Turks as moral outlaws.'[122] Although a degree of support was to be found from the *Manchester Guardian*, it seemed to be widely recognized that the speech heralded the end of the coalition: the only question was whether the break-up would come in days or in weeks.[123]

The speech also angered one of Lloyd George's most important colleagues. Curzon had been in Paris, where his negotiations with Poincaré had led to violent recriminations; but between them the two men had in the end patched up a semblance of Allied unity towards the Turks.[124] Now, the foreign secretary read Lloyd George's speech 'with dismay'. Curzon was the person who was to be 'charged with the task of making peace with a victorious Turkish army and exultant Turkish nation', but his prime minister had 'flouted and insulted the Turkish people'. Not only that but the prime minister had rounded on the French, who were of course extremely angry.[125] *Le Temps* rejected Lloyd George's criticisms of French actions, declaring that he had become a public danger—a new Bismarck whose electorally motivated actions were throwing Europe into turmoil.[126] A few days after the speech, Curzon offered his resignation, but was able to continue as foreign secretary after the famous meeting of Conservative MPs at the Carlton Club, which voted to end the coalition. That meeting merely delivered the *coup de grace* to an already dying beast. There were few tears across the Channel. The *Gaulois* seemed to express the common view when it said that Lloyd George had 'gradually become an adversary of France'.[127] By the same token, Bonar Law's new Tory government received a warm welcome, even though his letter to *The Times* had not been notably friendly towards France.[128] In the victorious Conservative election campaign that followed, Law duly emphasized the need for cooperation with France and Italy in order to avoid chaos in Europe.[129]

FRENCH SILENCE

The Chanak crisis poisoned Franco-British relations to a greater extent than any other international crisis in the twenty years of uneasy peace between the two world wars. That being said, French governmental criticisms of British policy,

[122] 'Political Notes', *The Observer*, 15 October 1922.
[123] 'Mr. Lloyd George and the Future of Parties' and 'Our London Correspondence', *Manchester Guardian*, 16 October 1922.
[124] David Gilmour, *Curzon* (London: Papermac, 1995), 543–8.
[125] Curzon's note on the political crisis of October 1922, *c.*October 1922, Curzon Papers, MSS Eur F112/319.
[126] Cited in 'French Press Retort on Mr. Lloyd George', *Manchester Guardian*, 16 October 1922. See also 'French Criticism of the Premier', *The Times*, Monday, 16 October 1922.
[127] Quoted in 'As Others See It', *Glasgow Herald*, 21 October 1922.
[128] 'French Welcome to Mr. Bonar Law', *The Times*, 25 October 1922.
[129] 'Mr. Bonar Law on his Policy', *Manchester Guardian*, 5 November 1922.

unrestrained in the privacy of ministerial meeting rooms and Foreign Ministry salons, were not aired in public. Because 'Chanak' did not register as a shorthand for entente breakdown in the French public sphere, it might appear that French rhetoric surrounding the crisis was conspicuous by its absence. As we have seen, nervousness in the French press about the danger of conflict escalation in the neutral zone was tempered by relief that the confrontation was essentially Anglo-Turkish in character, the Paris government having ordered French forces to withdraw in the third week of September.[130] Indeed, the certainty that Poincaré's efforts focused on de-escalation combined with limited reliable evidence from the Chanak frontline to produce a remarkably docile press.[131] The same could be said of France's politicians. Whereas Briand defended the Cilicia evacuation before parliament and in newspaper editorials during October 1921, twelve months later his successor, Poincaré, remained silent. The National Assembly, which had not sat at all since 1 April, finally began an extraordinary session on 12 October 1922. This session lasted almost unbroken until the year's end. It was thus only on 12 October that the French prime minister was compelled to explain—let alone defend—the government's actions before a critical domestic audience.

If their easy ride before politicians and public at home lowered the rhetorical stakes for French leaders when compared to a British coalition torn apart by the threat of war in Turkey, one cannot simply conclude that rhetoric played no part in French governmental calculations. Throughout the three weeks of negotiation with Curzon's team at the height of the crisis, Poincaré deployed one rhetorical ploy after another to stymie his British guests.[132] And when finally called upon to justify French actions in the Chamber of Deputies on 12 October, the French premier interspersed a deliberately low-key, matter-of-fact account of strategic decision-making with appeals to peace in the Near East as both a moral duty and an essential prerequisite to the coming confrontation with Germany.

Poincaré made his parliamentary statement in reply to several questions—technically 'interpellations'—from the floor. As was normal, all of these came from the opposition benches. Less normal was that, with the exception of a single query about the future of reparations from Paul Reynaud of the centre-right Alliance Démocratique, all came from the republican left.[133] The Socialists Léon Blum and Vincent Auriol foreshadowed Paul Reynaud by focusing on the impasse over reparations. Communist leader and *L'Humanité* editor Marcel Cachin went further, insisting that bourgeois politicians were putting workers' lives at risk by seeking confrontation in the Ruhr. This was a stance that would see Cachin jailed

---

[130] MAE, Série Levant, 1918–29, 51CPCOM166, Chanak, 'Conférence de Paris entre les Ministres des affaires étrangères', second meeting, 3.00 p.m. at Quai d'Orsay, 20 September 1922.

[131] For pro-government reportage depicting the crisis as a bilateral Anglo-Turkish confrontation, see: 'Angora garde un silence inquiétant', *Le Figaro*, 27 September 1922; 'Bulletin du jour: Les puissances et l'Orient', *Le Temps*, 30 September 1922; 'Dernière heure: La situation en orient: Anglais et Turcs face à face', *Le Figaro*, 30 September 1922.

[132] MAE, Série Levant, 1918–29, 51CPCOM166, Chanak—for a full record of the Paris meetings.

[133] 'Au Palais Bourbon: premières interpellations', *L'Action Française*, 13 October 1922.

after the Rhineland occupation began in 1923.[134] The fiery Cachin was a hard act to follow, and it was left to Alfred Margaine, a Radical Party specialist on international affairs, to raise the issue of Chanak.

Margaine, a member of the Chamber's Foreign Affairs Commission since 1914, did his best to raise the temperature, accusing Poincaré's government of needlessly alienating their entente partner. This was a luxury that France could not afford, having so recently lost its American ally. It was also a betrayal, Margaine claimed, because Britain's unstinting wartime support of France's claims to Alsace-Lorraine deserved equivalent French backing for Britain's defence of the neutral zone: in Margaine's words, '*un véritable cri de guerre britannique*'.[135] Their call to arms ignored, the British had been compelled to come cap in hand to Paris, hoping that Poincaré's government might yet lend its support. Treating a steadfast ally like this did France no credit. Poincaré was typically curt, dismissing Margaine's criticisms as wrong on all counts. The fact that the entente endured was proof that no betrayal had occurred. While deputies wrestled with this tautology, Poincaré slipped in an untruth, claiming that he alerted the British immediately to his government's decision to evacuate French troops from the neutral zone. This, he said, was a decision of which he was justifiably proud because it went a long way to defusing the crisis (*j'estime qu'elle a beaucoup contribué à assurer la paix*). Rhetorically, Poincaré thereby picked up where Briand had left off a year earlier. Both men played the role of unflappable peacemaker next to the irresponsible warmongers of Lloyd George's Cabinet and General Harington's military staff in Constantinople.

Keeping to this statesmanlike tone, Poincaré went on to explain that, as soon as Harington requested French and Italian military support at Chanak, he had consulted France's senior soldiers: Marshal Ferdinand Foch, his close associate Maxime Weygand (soon to be dispatched as generalissimo to Syria), and Chief of Army Staff Edmond Buat. All three advised against the move, warning that Chanak was indefensible.[136] Unfortunately, communications delays meant that the Allied commanders in Constantinople, French General Charpy and his Italian colleague, General Mombelli, had already acceded to Harington's reinforcement request by the time Poincaré learned of it. It was to the credit of republican democracy that the government overturned that assent as soon as it was fully apprised of the dangers involved. Having dealt with the strategic calculations, Poincaré turned to the diplomatic ones. As someone who had previously led his country into war he recalled only too well that the experiences of 1912 and, more famously, 1914, proved that a few well-aimed shots could transform Balkan disputes into

---

[134] *Journal officiel de la République Française*, débats parlementaires, Séance 12 October 1922, 2584–5.

[135] *Journal officiel de la République Française*, débats parlementaires, Séance 12 October 1922, 2589. An engineer by training with a longstanding interest in public works, Margaine was one of the eighty deputies who voted against conceding full powers to Marshal Pétain's regime in July 1940.

[136] Poincaré later reiterated that the French generals' advice had swayed him when he sent the French Embassy in London a summary of his reasons for ordering the withdrawal: DDF, 1922, vol. 2, doc. 252, Poincaré to M. de Saint-Aulaire, 19 October 1922.

continental conflicts.[137] Far better, he concluded, to remove redoubtable French soldiers from the fray than to leave them hostages to fortune—or, more precisely, targets for the bullets of Turkish irregulars.[138]

Incredible as it might seem in hindsight (and in light of the decrypts confirming French backchannels to the Kemalists), this remarkable transformation of the hard-line *Poincaré-la-guerre* into an angelic *Poincaré-la-paix* disarmed his parliamentary critics.[139] With cries of *Très bien! Très bien!* ringing around the Chamber, Margaine was forced to change tack. He thanked Poincaré for his precise clarification but regretted that at no stage during the crisis had the government seen fit to make its position crystal clear in public. Nor had Poincaré made any effort to explain the French viewpoint in the British press.[140] The result was twofold: French parliamentarians were kept poorly informed about the government's decision-making and the British people were convinced of French treachery.[141]

These were piercing criticisms but they were also naïve. It was impossible for the French government to publicize its real motivations because, in terms of crisis management, there was nothing to be gained from doing so. Backing Harington to the hilt, it was thought, might induce Kemal to attack Constantinople with overwhelming force, possibly with Soviet assistance. The straits would be closed and Syria would once again be left exposed, undoing the peace achieved in 1921.[142] This was something that numerous French political commentators understood. Anxious about the a wider conflagration if shots were fired at Chanak, the French press, both pro- and anti-government, fixated on the dialogue between General Harington and Kemal in the final days of September 1922. Several published the telegrams exchanged between the two.[143] So, while misinformation and communications difficulties were central to the Chanak crisis itself, French readers mulling over their morning paper were made aware in under twenty-four hours of the decisive breakthrough signalled by Kemal's 1 October instructions to cease troop movements in the neutral zone pending negotiations at Mudania.[144]

---

[137] Whether consciously or not, Poincaré echoed the argument made in Clemenceau's newspaper *La Justice*. Its editorial leader on 1 October 1922 warned that the standoff at Chanak placed peace 'at the mercy of a gunshot': 'Les consequences du conflit gréco-turc', *La Justice*, 1 October 1922.

[138] Journal official de la République Française, débats parlementaires, 2589.

[139] For the contrasting images of Poincaré as warmonger and peacemaker, see Keiger, *Raymond Poincaré*, chapters 7–8.

[140] This, although Poincaré sent a communiqué to French Embassies across Europe repudiating accusations in the British press that the French were secretly abetting the Kemalist advance: DDF, 1922, vol. 2, doc. 180, Poincaré tel. to European embassies, 18 September 1922.

[141] *Journal officiel de la République Française*, débats parlementaires, 2589. Ironically, among French press commentators it was Paul Louis, writing in Marxian language of class in the Communist newspaper *L'Humanité*, who understood British outrage most clearly. Britain's middle classes, he noted, considered that their country had fought and won the war over Ottoman Turkey, chasing Turks out of Arab lands, ensuring the eviction of the Russians from the Straits, and cementing British imperial domination in western Asia. France had placed all of this in jeopardy: 'La menace de guerre', *L'Humanité*, 1 October 1922, p. 1.

[142] Ferris, '"Far Too Dangerous a Gamble"', 162.

[143] As examples: 'La situation s'aggrave en orient', *L'Humanité*, p. 3; 'Les affaires d'orient', *Le Temps*, 30 September 1922.

[144] 'Détente en orient', *Le Figaro*, 2 October 1922.

CONCLUSION

The British election campaign of October 1922, conducted in the toxic political fallout from the Chanak crisis, saw the different parties rehearse many of the arguments about Near Eastern events that had already been aired, but no striking new themes emerged. The Conservatives secured a weighty majority. The Liberals, still divided between Asquithians and Lloyd George-ites, were together outnumbered by the Labour Party, which became for the first time the official opposition. As the *English Review* noted, the Chanak affair had provoked 'remarkable paradoxes'. The Asquithians rejected Gladstonianism; the French 'espoused Islam' rather than follow their 'traditional "Christian" policy'; the 'Jingo Press' turned pacifist at the thought of battle; and 'our League of Nations Press preached the fiery cross'.[145] It certainly seemed that one of Liberalism's most powerful inheritances had had its last gasp. 'The country will hear with irritation and impatience the futile appeal to the Gladstonian tradition', remarked Labour's J. R. Clynes after Lloyd George's Manchester speech. 'The world has moved on.'[146] As we have seen, there were many references to Britain's status as a Muslim power, and these could be put to different uses. But this was the last time for many years that the perceived challenge of pan-Islam was a major issue in British politics. There was, it seemed, real political significance to the fact that Mehmed VI, deposed as the last sultan of the Ottoman dynasty, left Constantinople on 17 November 1922 aboard a Royal Navy warship.[147] The British thus afforded safe passage to a Muslim Caliph humiliated by the power of secular Turkish nationalism (Fig. 4.1).

Eight months later, the July 1923 Treaty of Lausanne affirmed Turkey's untrammelled sovereignty throughout Anatolia, Eastern Thrace, and the formerly neutral zone of the straits. Also underlined was the Franco-British hold over their Arab mandates in the former Ottoman Empire. The demise of the Caliphate in practice led to a fragmentation of political mobilization within Islam, with Muslim political thinkers and activists around the world working within local or nationalist movements rather than rallying to a global religious figurehead. These factors helped put an end to the (at any rate deeply misleading) Western vision of a worldwide Islamic movement commanded from a single spiritual centre. It is equally interesting that the Christian-tinged language of the 'war party' was treated with considerable suspicion, often being directly linked, of course, with the danger of alienating Muslims. Furthermore, while the 'graves of Gallipoli' motif was certainly used, it was not quite as ubiquitous as the criticism of Forster and others tended to suggest. The attempt to deploy 'sacred' memories of empire in defence of current goals was more notable for the ridicule that it attracted than for any positive impact it had on British domestic opinion.

Across the English Channel, the reality of war with Turkey from 1919 to 1921, and the threat of its resumption in September–October 1922, did not end any

[145] 'Oranges and Lemons: By the Editor', *English Review*, November 1922.
[146] '"The Plaint of a Defeated Man"', *Manchester Guardian*, 16 October 1922.
[147] Steiner, *The Lights that Failed*, 119.

Fig. 4.1. This Christmas 1922 postcard plays on the theme of Turkey's secular turn, a refugee Turkish Santa Claus passing a British soldier standing guard at Chanak.
Mary Evans Picture Library, image 10409854

French ministerial careers or bring down ruling coalitions. Quite the reverse: the Briand government persuaded even its opponents on the French right that ending the war in Cilicia through direct talks with Ankara was strategically imperative and ethically irreproachable. That it amounted to a unilateral repudiation of the Treaty of Sèvres, and with it a breach of Allied solidarity towards the rival Turkish regimes, mattered little. For the fact was that French calculations of ultimate Turkish victory in the war with Greece were made, not in 1922, but in early 1921; and they proved accurate. This French conclusion derived, on the one hand, from recent experience of defeat at Kemalist hands and, on the other, from insider knowledge about the huge increases in Turkish military resources.[148] As a result, the irreversibility of the Kemalist military advance was never seriously questioned inside government or outside it. Poincaré's coalition ministry, uncompromising in German policy, followed Briand's lead in dealings with Turkey. Backchannels to Ankara were extended as Franklin-Bouillon reprised his role as go-between to the Kemalist regime.

French dealings with Turkey were more than pragmatic, building as they did on juridical thinking about enforceable peacemaking. But neither the urgent need for a

---

[148] Poincaré did, however, overrule Colonel Louis Mougin, French military representative in Ankara, refusing to allow the shipment of armaments to the Turkish nationalists via the Syrian port of Alexandretta, see TNA, WO 106/1440: War Office Military Intelligence files, Lord Hardinge, Paris, to Foreign Office, 31 August 1922; DDF, 1922, vol. 2, doc. 18.

settlement over Cilicia, nor the legal recognition of the double standard involved in denying Turkish nationalist demands for self-determination, lent themselves to public scrutiny. France, after all, had only recently joined Britain in rejecting equivalent statehood for the Arabs of Syria and Iraq. Nor was it at ease with the widespread abuses against ethnic minority populations living under Turkish administration. Even at the height of the infamous Franco-British crisis talks in Paris, government commentary was restricted to a bare minimum.[149] By contrast, after the early-year failures of the conferences at Cannes and Genoa, Poincaré's government, a reincarnation of a more traditionalist, right-wing Bloc National coalition, took issue with Britain's more conciliatory stance on reparations. The irony was that Poincaré's administration ultimately registered more success in a Near Eastern policy into which it invested less rhetorical capital than it did in a policy of reparations enforcement into which it invested far more. Safe in the knowledge that the Chanak crisis was over, when the National Assembly finally reconvened on 12 October, Poincaré at last allowed himself some rhetorical flourish, building himself up as master strategist and guarantor of peace. The weight of historical evidence might reveal cracks in this statesmanlike façade, but that, in a way, is irrelevant. Whether through obfuscation and studied silence or realist calculation and ultimate diplomatic success, France's leaders avoided the humiliation that attended Britain's failed attempt to impose its will on a resurgent Turkish nation.

A final round of Franco-British talks at the Quai d'Orsay over the Mudania peace agreement continued long into the night of 20 October, before resuming the following morning. These conversations were devoid of the acrimony that marked the earlier exchanges at the height of the Chanak crisis. At the conclusion of his discussions with Curzon, Poincaré walked to an adjacent salon in the Foreign Ministry. There he led an impromptu Cabinet meeting that endorsed the timetable for a Greek evacuation from Eastern Thrace and the ludicrously hasty arrangements made for population transfers. The image of entente diplomacy restored to its former cordiality jarred with the horrific scenes of ethnic cleansing that attended the implementation of the Mudania peace. But it was what Poincaré's ministers and the French press chose to celebrate even so.[150]

---

[149] 'Les Ministres alliés ont délibéré hier sur la Question d'orient', *La Justice*, 24 September 1922.
[150] 'Les entretiens du Quai d'Orsay ont abouti à un accord', *La Justice*, 8 October 1922. For indications of the scale of the refugee crisis, see the sequence of dispatches from Athens, and Admiralty telegrams from the Mediterranean cruiser squadron in TNA, WO 106/1440, August–October 1922.

5

World War as Imperial Crisis, I

Changing Partners, 1939–41

The year 1923 was pivotal in the rhetorical battles between imperial Britain and imperial France. The Treaty of Lausanne, by endorsing nationalist Turkey's restorative conquests, substantially resolved the centuries-old Eastern Question. In so doing, it removed and, in so doing, it removed some of the major causes of Anglo-French imperial tension while clearing a path for others to emerge. Relations between Britain and France during the remainder of the interwar years were hardly smooth, a fact epitomized by their mutual recriminations over the infamous Hoare–Laval Pact of December 1935 in which each sought to evade their international obligations to assist Haile Selassie's Ethiopia, an early victim of fascist empire-building in Africa.[1] But abiding Franco-British colonial suspicions were increasingly eclipsed first by the impact of the global depression and, more generally, by the looming menace of German revisionism. Both empires were now severely overstretched. Each faced growing nationalist pressures from within and increasingly hostile transnational scrutiny from without.[2] Although neither of Europe's old imperial giants sought to expand, the political frictions and cultural clashes between them remained explosive as they rubbed together along disputed new imperial frontiers throughout the former Ottoman Middle East.[3] But World War II—or, to be precise, the fall of France in 1940—created a crisis in Anglo-French relations on a scale that surpasses the previous moments of friction described in this book thus far.

The cataclysm that befell the French state—and its division into rival Vichy and Free French centres of authority—propelled Britain's relationship with those who claimed to represent France to unprecedented levels of complexity. On the one

---

[1] J. C. Robertson, 'The Hoare-Laval Plan', *Journal of Contemporary History* 10 (1975), 433–64; Michael L. Roi, '"A Completely Immoral and Cowardly Attitude": The British Foreign Office, American Neutrality and the Hoare-Laval Plan', *Canadian Journal of History*, 29 (August 1994), 333–5; for multiple perspectives, see Bruce Strang (ed.), *Collision of Empires: Italy's Invasion of Ethiopia and its International Impact* (Farnham: Ashgate, 2014).

[2] See, for instance, Erez Manela, *The Wilsonian Moment: Self-Determination and the International Origins of Anticolonial Nationalism* (Oxford: Oxford University Press, 2009); Susan Pedersen, *The Guardians: The League of Nations and the Crisis of Empire* (Oxford: Oxford University Press, 2015); Natasha Wheatley, 'Mandatory Interpretation: Legal Hermeneutics and the New International Order in Arab and Jewish Petitions to the League of Nations', *Past & Present*, 227 (May 2015), 206–35; Andrew Arsan, '"This is the Age of Assocations": Committees, Petitions, and the Roots of Interwar Middle Eastern Internationalism', *Journal of Global History*, 7 (2012), 166–88.

[3] Martin Thomas, 'Anglo-French Imperial Relations in the Arab World: Intelligence Liaison and Nationalist Disorder', *Diplomacy & Statecraft*, 17:1 (2006), 1–28.

hand, there was open, if sporadic conflict with Vichy. Physical clashes occurred in two theatres. One was at sea, where the Churchill government's determination to cripple a potentially hostile fleet was matched by Royal Naval enforcement of the Allied blockade of occupied Europe and its dependencies. The other was in the colonies, whether at the margins of Vichy-controlled territory or as a result of their invasion by Allied forces. On the other hand, there were the dizzying oscillations in Winston Churchill's relations with Charles de Gaulle, leader of the London-based Free French movement. This was far more than a clash of personalities, reflecting, as it did, Churchill's singular pursuit of British national—and imperial—interest through the vicissitudes of war and de Gaulle's equally steadfast, if sometimes apparently quixotic identification of Free France with French national restoration.

Both leaders proved canny manipulators of the asymmetries between an un-defeated imperial nation and a fledgling external resistance movement that, initially at least, lacked funds, proven leaders, and territory. Churchill was perfectly willing to ignore, exclude, or humiliate de Gaulle's supporters if it seemed strategically expedient to do so. De Gaulle, in turn, worked to end Free France's military and financial reliance on Britain in the long term while strenuously denying any such dependency in the short term. The tensions between these two leaders, their ministers, and military commanders were always sharpest within colonial territory. The same could be said of the undeclared state of war between the Vichy regime and its Free French nemesis. The competing rhetoric of 'Frenchness' articulated by Vichy and the London 'Gaullists' were strongly inflected with imperialist language. And while collaboration and resistance were acts (or processes) typically identified with life under occupation in metropolitan France, each was refracted colonially. Vichy's widening collaboration with the fascist powers, and its eventual descent into abject collaborationism, as well as the Free French struggle to expand their overseas dominion through the ouster of Vichy's colonial governments, were expressed in competing rhetorics of empire. More basically, the exactions imposed on Vichy by its Axis occupiers were quickly extended to the imperial territories still under Pétainist control. Equally, the material demands of Gaullist participation in an Allied war effort imposed staggering demands on the peoples of the rival Free French Empire.[4] Fighting World War II—and winning the undeclared civil war between the competing Vichyite and Gaullist empires—took French imperial rhetoric to new extremes. Ironically, though, each of these warring French parties often invoked Britain as the villain of the piece.

PHONEY WAR, PHONEY RHETORIC?

As the probability of renewed war with Germany increased in the late 1930s, some French colonial lobbyists admitted the failure of their efforts to convert their

---

[4] Eric Jennings, *La France Libre fut Africaine* (Paris: Perrin, 2014), troisième partie; Martin Thomas, 'Resource War, Civil War, Rights War: Factoring Empire into French North Africa's Second World War', *War in History*, 18:2 (2011), 225–48.

countrymen and women into self-confident imperialists. In March 1937, a con-
tributor to the journal *Outre-Mer*, mouthpiece of the training academy for empire
bureaucrats, the *École Coloniale*, was particularly acerbic: '"France, a nation of 104
million inhabitants"? That's a joke, because France has no imperial mentality.'[5] It
was not without irony, then, that imperialist rhetoric scaled new heights as first the
threat and then the reality of war struck home. It became a stock-in-trade of
ministers, colonial administrations, and imperial strategists that the empire's contribution to the impending conflict would surpass the flow of goods, money and,
above all, soldiers and factory workers that had helped secure victory twenty years
earlier.[6] This nostalgia for imperial grandeur, though, was more a search for solace
than any Damascene conversion to empire causes. It was typified in the public
mind by the concept of a '*répli impérial*', or 'imperial fallback', on to reservoirs of
colonial manpower and strategic raw materials. These, it was hoped, might obviate
the growing imbalance in population and economic capacity between France and
Nazi Germany.[7] Algeria's Governor Georges Le Beau exemplified this trend.
Confident that France's premier colony was returning to budgetary surplus after
a decade spent in the economic doldrums, Le Beau told Algeria's Supreme Advisory
Council in a high-profile speech on 23 November 1939 that the colony could
afford to provide further investment in local railway infrastructure in addition to a
140 million franc credit to help fund metropolitan rearmament. The solidity of
Algeria's export trade with Britain, the main purchaser of the colony's iron ore,
encouraged Le Beau to go further.[8] To the delight of his audience of mainly settler
politicians, the governor mused that the French and British empires, together
covering 31 per cent of the Earth's landmass and comprising some 600 million
(mainly Indian) souls, were bound to emerge victorious from war.[9]

Unsurprisingly perhaps, on the eve of the Third Republic's ignominious collapse, the government's imperial rhetoric became more overtly martial than at any
point since the infant Republic's first wave of colonial conquests in the late
nineteenth century. Parliamentary resolve to protect France's overseas possessions
was unanimous.[10] Imperial greatness was invoked in everything from sporting
achievement (a forerunner to the Paris–Dakar rally began in spring 1939) to
cinematic production—three of the year's biggest box-office successes were heroic

[5] J. Fayet, 'Un programme de propagande impériale', *Outre-Mer*, 9:1 (1937), 21.
[6] See, for example, General Maxime Weygand, 'L'Armée Coloniale 1914–1918', *Le Monde
Colonial Illustré*, 180 (June 1939), 112–15.
[7] Marc Michel terms this rediscovery of imperial pride a 'conscience impériale', see his 'La
puissance par l'Empire: Note sur la perception du facteur imperial dans l'élaboration de la défense
nationale (1936–1938)', *Revue Française d'Histoire d'Outre-Mer*, 69:254 (1982), 35; Charles-Robert
Ageron, 'A propos d'une prétendue politique de "répli imperial" dans la France des années 1938–39',
Revue d'Histoire Maghrébine, 12 (1978), 228–37; for the actual strategic balance, see Peter Jackson,
France and the Nazi Menace: Intelligence and Policy-Making, 1933–1939 (Oxford: Oxford University
Press, 2000), 318, 333.
[8] AN, F60/187, dossier A2, Rapports du Gouvernement Général, Algérie, 'Situation économique
et commerciale de l'Algérie en 1938', no date, 1939.
[9] AN, F60/187, dossier A2, Discours prononcé par Georges Le Beau, Session extraordinaire du
Conseil Supérieur de l'Algérie, 23 November 1939.
[10] Ageron, 'Les colonies devant l'opinion publique française (1919-1939)', 67–71.

tales of patriotic valour amid the Saharan forts of the Foreign Legion. On 14 July 1939, the 150th anniversary of the French Revolution, columns of Moroccan and West African troops formed the centrepiece of the Bastille Day festivities in the largest parade of colonial troops in Paris since the victory parades of 1919.[11] This colourful attempt to reassure a nervous French public was soon borne out by numbers. After full mobilization in October 1939, the tens of thousands of colonial soldiers in French uniform represented 11 per cent of total army strength.[12]

Underlying the parliamentary rhetoric and theatrical displays was a simple fact: the primary role of these colonial levies in war was not to protect the colonial inheritance but to supplement the battle-line in France. Indeed, the imperial strategists on the French general staff warned of three yawning gaps in the empire's defences as France went to war. The Indochina Peninsula was indefensible against Japanese attack by land and sea. Key naval bases from Tunisia to South Vietnam were still unprepared for war, lacking anti-aircraft defences, repair facilities, or functioning coastal batteries.[13] Finally, the requirements of home defence had denuded several colonies of the garrison strength necessary for self-defence against external invasion or internal disorder.[14] One reason for the success of subsequent Free French takeovers in sub-Saharan African territories from Chad to New Caledonia was that in-house military coups were easily accomplished in the absence of large garrisons to oppose them.[15]

A few weeks after the outbreak of war in September 1939, an official decree was published in France, forbidding written or spoken criticism of the British Empire.[16] The British government in general preferred less formal methods of censorship—and had deployed them pre-war to blunt press attacks on the Nazis—but there was probably at any rate little need in the UK for this type of proscription.[17] We can speak with a degree of confidence about popular attitudes, because this was now the era of public opinion research, as pioneered by Gallup and Mass-Observation (MO) from 1937, and subsequently sponsored by the wartime state in the form

[11] Marc Michel, '"Mémoire officielle", discours et pratique coloniale: Le 14 juillet et le 11 novembre au Sénégal entre les deux guerres', *Revue Française d'Histoire d'Outre-Mer*, 77:287 (1990), 150–3; for discussion of differing ideological responses to Bastille Day celebrations, see Joan Tumblety, '"Civil Wars of the Mind": The Commemoration of the 1789 Revolution in the Parisian Press of the Radical Right, 1939', *Journal of Contemporary History*, 30:3 (2000), 389–429.

[12] Henry Dutailly, 'Weaknesses in French Military Planning on the Eve of the Second World War', in B. J. C. McKercher and Roch Legault (eds), *Military Planning and the Origins of the Second World War in Europe* (Westport, CT: Greenwood Press, 2001), 93.

[13] B. Q., 'Japon. Le marche vers les mers du sud', *Revue Française d'Outre-Mer*, 766 (May 1939), 139–40; O. Louis, 'De Bizerte à Mers el-Kebir: les bases navales d'Afrique du Nord dans l "entre-deux-guerres", *Revue Historique des Armées*, 4 (1999), 36–7; Hervé Coutou-Bégarie and Claude Huan (eds), *Lettres et notes de l'Amiral Darlan* (Paris: Economica, 1992), 28–9, 49–53.

[14] Michel, 'La puissance par l'Empire', 38–41.

[15] Geraud Letang, 'Rallying Free France: Imperial Disobedience and National Dilemmas in a World at War (1940-1943)', paper at University of Strathclyde conference, *France and the Second World War in Global Perspective*, 3 July 2015; Rhodes House Library, MSS Afr. S.1334(10), J. Hoskyns Abrahall, 'Mission to the Free French, July 1940'.

[16] 'No French Criticism of Britain', *Manchester Guardian*, 28 September 1939.

[17] See Richard Cockett, *Twilight of Truth: Chamberlain, Appeasement and the Manipulation of the Press* (New York: St Martin's Press, 1989).

of the Ministry of Information's Home Intelligence Reports (between 1940 and 1944).[18] The French themselves were little loved. An MO survey in the spring of 1939 showed they were held in lower regard than the Germans. The stereotypical view of the Frenchman, perpetuated in cartoon and music hall representations, was of 'a voluable, excessively excitable, often slightly bearded, and somewhat lecherous personality'. Stories were commonly told of French selfish or uncooperative behaviour during the Great War. According to MO:

> At the same time, as war approached their prestige as a state steadily increased, partly owing to the large amount of newsreel and press photograph publicity for French tanks, guns and defences. The mental picture of a mighty army and an impregnable country became an extremely significant factor in the mental outlook of a great many Britons—and presently a major factor in the complacency of their war outlook.

Thus, respect for France was predicated more on its supposed military efficiency than on feelings of community with the French people. Simultaneously, though, 'there was the general feeling that France was another "democracy", and therefore a natural colleague'.[19]

Opinions about the French Empire do not seem to have been recorded, from which we may cautiously conclude both that it was not a priority for the investigators and that it did not tend to generate strong spontaneous emotions among the public. Indeed, it is notable that an official advertising campaign in the autumn of 1940, promoting the British Empire in terms of a 'New Magna Charta' and 'Democratic Imperialism', evoked relatively little interest.[20] This suggests not so much apathy towards British and European empire so much as acceptance of it as an unremarked fact of life. In spite of the cracks in the British imperial façade in the interwar years, and the (partially realized) pressures for reform, there was no sense of an impending watershed. This is not to say that there was no domestic criticism; among a left-wing minority this was already quite vocal. One might even hazard that the British people were more prone to express scepticism about their own empire than they were to show hostility to the French one, which evoked little interest or comment—in contrast, for example, to the humanitarian campaign against Belgian abuses in the Congo that had achieved prominence before World War I.

Chamberlain's government, during the Phoney War period, put relatively little effort into propaganda stressing Franco-British unity, but efforts were made to cement strategic and economic connections between the two empires. In the spring of 1940, Colonial Secretary Malcolm MacDonald held talks with Georges Mandel, his French opposite number. This resulted in the creation of machinery for liaison both between the colonial ministries in Paris and London and between those

---

[18] MO, in particular, presents scholars with methodological problems, but it is nonetheless an astonishingly rich source of information. See Penny Summerfield, 'Mass-Observation: Social Research or Social Movement?' *Journal of Contemporary History*, 20:3 (1985), 439–52.

[19] Mass Observation Archive, 'Public Opinion About the French', File Report 566, 1 February 1941.

[20] Mass Observation Archive, 'The Empire Crusade Campaign', File Report 528, 18 December 1940.

French and British colonies that neighboured one another.[21] After the fall of France, a French Colonial Intelligence Section was created within the Colonial Office to continue these liaison arrangements with the Free French Empire.[22]

In a speech in April 1940, the Dominions secretary, Anthony Eden, prophesied that the two empires would pull ever closer together. This was only possible, he said, because 'these two systems, with their many superficial divergences, are built on the same solid foundation of freedom and spontaneous growth'. Drawing an explicit contrast with the repressive imperialism of the German Reich, Eden cast the British and French empires as wise, tolerant, civilizing, humane, and even egalitarian. He emphasized—and this was a crucial dimension of official wartime rhetoric—the *spontaneous* decision of the peoples of the empire to leap to Britain's side the defence of liberty (blithely ignoring the fact that 340 million Indians were taken into war at the stroke of their viceroy's pen). Having little of substance to say about the French Empire, Eden simply cast it in the image that he fashioned for the British one.[23] This freedom trope recurred after France's collapse. A few days after the French armistice, a *Times* leader argued: 'The French Empire is a free empire like our own; and this means that, just as the essential British faith is as firmly held and as clearly expressed in Montreal or Canberra as in Westminster, so there are men who can speak or fight for France in every part of her scattered dominions.'[24]

A few months later, the colonial expert Margery Perham noted in the same newspaper that the French policies of centralization and assimilation contrasted with British plans for 'local self-development and self-government'. However: 'There is room in the world for both policies, because both are based on a belief in the potential equality of the races, but there can never be any compromise between this belief and the revived tribalism of our enemies.'[25] Incidentally, France's rhetorical commitment to assimilation may have contributed to the view, which was from time to time expressed by liberal voices in Britain, that 'The French Empire puts us to shame' by its (supposed) freedom from racial intolerance.[26]

THE FALL OF FRANCE AND AFTER

It is unlikely that any admiration for French colonial administrative practice affected British governmental choices as France stood on the brink of collapse in

---

[21] HC Deb, 21 March 1940, vol. 358, cols 2125–6.

[22] HL Deb, 17 December 1940, vol. 118, col. 129.

[23] 'Imperialism: A Contrast', *The Times*, 18 April 1940. On 'spontaneity', see also, for example, Malcolm MacDonald, 'Talks for Sixth Forms: Questions of Empire: 3', BBC Home Service Broadcast, 2 February 1940, text in Margery Perham Papers, 346/5, Bodleian Library, Oxford, and the 1941 Ministry of Information short 'From the Four Corners', available at <http://www.iwm.org.uk/collections/item/object/1060021299> accessed 17 October 2014. The film makes clear that empire soldiers are *not* to be regarded as having answered 'the Motherland's call to arms'—a view which is portrayed as patronising.

[24] 'After The Armistice', *The Times*, 26 June 1940.

[25] Marjery Perham, '"Free France" in Africa', *The Times*, 14 September 1940.

[26] 'The Colour Bar', *Manchester Guardian*, 4 September 1943.

June 1940. But the future of empire certainly did. In a desperate last effort to prevent France's surrender, the British government made a grand play. Devised with the help of Charles de Gaulle and Jean Monnet, it offered a 'Franco-British Union', whereby the two nations would be merged into a single entity, with common citizenship, and their parliaments would be combined into one body. An earlier message had proclaimed 'the indissoluble union of our two peoples and of our two Empires'.[27] During the War Cabinet meeting that approved the final proclamation, Arthur Greenwood, one of the Labour members, urged the need to make clear 'that the Union included the whole British Commonwealth of Nations and the French Empire'; yet the declaration as adopted did not clarify this point. By contrast, the draft version stated that 'All customs are abolished between Britain and France. There shall not be two currencies, but one.' However, ministers objected that a single currency was impracticable and that the proposal to abolish customs would cut across the 1932 Ottawa trade agreements and create problems with Britain's Dominions. A vague statement about unified economic and financial policies was therefore included instead.[28] Leo Amery, the Conservative secretary of state for India, wrote in his diary: 'I sent my amended version across and heard later that the more rhetorical and less practical Monnet one was accepted almost unchanged.'[29]

That, though, was probably the point. Many of those involved undoubtedly believed sincerely in the pragmatic benefits of the union proposal, but its primary significance was as a splendid, public, rhetorical gesture. It was intended to 'revive the flagging energies of the French and invigorate our own people'.[30] It appealed to Churchill's sense of the dramatic.[31] France could not be saved by acts such as this, however generous or impressive, but the move served to establish British good faith in the public record at a time when—not least on account of the retreat to Dunkirk—many French people were increasingly inclined to call it into question.

If the period after the French surrender was marked by mutual recriminations and protestations of wounded innocence, perhaps its more salient characteristic at the time was confusion. The harshness of the German peace terms was not known straightaway, and hopes persisted that the French fleet might make a dash for British ports and that the French Empire as a whole would carry on the fight. Even when the worst was known, some commentators continued to express trust in Marshal Philippe Pétain, the armistice signatory soon to be invested as Vichy head of state. A World War I hero of almost legendary status, Pétain was perceived by some to be resisting the demands of the more extreme collaborationists.[32]

---

[27] TNA, CAB 65/7/60, WM(40)165, Cabinet Minutes, 13 June 1940.

[28] TNA, CAB 65/7/64, WM(40)169, Cabinet Minutes, 16 June 1940.

[29] John Barnes and David Nicholson (eds), *The Empire at Bay: The Leo Amery Diaries, 1929–1945* (London: Hutchinson, 1988), 624 (entry for 16 June 1940).

[30] John Colville, *The Fringes of Power: Downing Street Diaries, 1939–1955* (London: Hodder and Stoughton, 1985), 159 (entry for 16 June 1940).

[31] For which, see Jonathan Rose, *The Literary Churchill: Author, Reader, Actor* (New Haven, CT: Yale University Press, 2014).

[32] See, for example, 'Notes of the Week', *The Economist*, 18 April 1942.

In these conditions, British official attitudes towards de Gaulle and his incipient Free French movement were necessarily ambivalent. It required Churchill's express approval before the relatively obscure general was allowed to deliver his 'flame of French resistance' broadcast from London on 18 June.[33] De Gaulle's famous *Appel* over the airwaves of the BBC is commemorated as the first definitive statement of the Gaullist creed of grandiloquent, unstinting patriotism, but it was his follow-up broadcast a day later that was the more politically significant. Less a stirring call to arms than a blunt statement of intent, it specified de Gaulle's assumption of authority under the mantle of Free France. Neither broadcast resonated with the majority of the French people at the time. Few heard either one; among those that did, other preoccupations dominated.[34] Furthermore, on 20 June Foreign Secretary Lord Halifax withheld access to the BBC lest de Gaulle complicate Britain's last-ditch efforts to dissuade the French government in Bordeaux from surrendering everything through the impending armistice accords with Germany and Italy. (The decision was reversed once the armistice accords were signed a week later.)[35] What bears emphasis is that one of the British government's major contributions to public discourse surrounding France and her empire was its facilitation of, and attempted influence over, de Gaulle's own rhetoric—and also his travel arrangements. British ministers tried to use their control of access to the airwaves to ensure that de Gaulle's messages conformed to their own wishes. They could not, however, control all of de Gaulle's public statements, which they frequently found infuriating.

De Gaulle's attempts to establish the Free French movement on a secure footing suffered a body blow with the British destruction of the French battleship squadron at anchor in the Algerian naval base of Mers el-Kébir at the port of Oran on 3 July. The volley of shells fired by a Royal Navy flotilla, led by the emblematic battleship HMS *Hood*, killed 1,297 French sailors. Churchill later recalled that the choice to launch an attack against the forces of a country that had so recently been an ally had been a 'hateful' one.[36] With the Commons in an atmosphere of 'tense excitement' that rivalled its mood at the outbreak of war in 1914, the prime minister delivered a powerful speech justifying British actions.[37] Without any verbal flourishes, Churchill explained the background to the decision and related how events had unfolded on the day: 'with the most dramatic effect and yet with the most superb composure, he narrated as a historian this vivid passage of history'.[38] Although the

---

[33] François Kersaudy, *Churchill and De Gaulle* (London: Collins, 1981), 77–8.

[34] Writing years after the event, and with more than a hint of disdain for supposed French defeatism, de Gaulle's British confidant, Edward Spears, explained the muted reaction to de Gaulle's 19 June broadcast thus: 'These fine words expressing both an assumption of authority and the will to fight were lost in France, drowned in the clatter of weapons thrown away, running feet, in the clamour of tear-drenched voices from Bordeaux [to which the French government had retreated] enjoining resignation.' St Antony's College Middle East Centre Archive, Oxford, Major-General Edward Spears papers, Box IX/file 1, extracts from book manuscript on relations with de Gaulle, 1.

[35] Spears papers Box IX/file 1, extracts from manuscript on relations with de Gaulle, 2.

[36] Winston S. Churchill, *The Second World War Vol. II: Their Finest Hour* (London: Reprint Society, 1951), 198.

[37] Lord Harmsworth diary, 4 July 1940, Cecil Harmsworth Papers, University of Exeter.

[38] James Leutze (ed.), *The London Observer: The Journal of General Raymond E. Lee 1940–1941* (London: Hutchinson, 1971), 12 (entry for 4 July 1940).

MPs' enthusiastic response may have been partially orchestrated by the Conservative chief whip, Churchill scored a major personal triumph, helping to win over a Tory Party still resentful at the treatment of his predecessor, Neville Chamberlain.[39] Perhaps most importantly from our perspective, Churchill's speech made clear that the naval action was intended partly as a symbolic or even rhetorical act, serving to disprove German propagandists' claims that the British meant to enter peace talks.[40]

Rachel Chin has noted that official British descriptions of Mers el-Kébir consistently portrayed the action 'as inevitable, removing actual agency from British policy makers'. Thus 'the policy was depicted as having constructed itself only in response to French actions', although specific individuals were not singled out for blame. Moreover, although officials considered claiming that the assault had been undertaken in the interests of restoring the French Empire, this was not reflected in the government press releases actually issued.[41] The decision to play down the imperial dimension may have been the result of cautious discretion. For the British to argue openly that it had been necessary to attack the French in order to restore their greatness (destroying the village in order to save it, as it were) would have provided Pétain and his supporters—who justified the armistice in the interests of salvaging the French Empire—with a tempting rhetorical opportunity. As it was, while the French government railed against British treachery in word, print, newsreels, and other propaganda, Pétain's Cabinet also conceded that the bombardment freed France from any residual attachments to its erstwhile alliance with Britain. Priority could be given to securing Germany's agreement to relax the armistice restrictions imposed on defeated France.[42]

Because of the violence involved, it was certainly harder for the British authorities to justify the attack before world opinion than it was for its opponents to condemn it.[43] The problem of justification, pressing before the bombardment occurred, was even more difficult to evade after it. As the poster in Fig. 5.1 indicates, for the propagandists of the Vichy regime, the place-names Mers el-Kébir and Oran would become a shorthand for British treachery.

[39] Richard Toye, *The Roar of the Lion: The Untold Story of Churchill's World War II Speeches* (Oxford: Oxford University Press, 2013), 62–3.

[40] Speech of 4 July 1940. Unless otherwise stated, all Churchill's speeches cited are to be found in Robert Rhodes James (ed.), *Winston S. Churchill: His Complete Speeches, 1897–1963*, 8 vols (New York: Chelsea House, 1974).

[41] Rachel Chin, 'A Rhetorical Construction of Anglo-French Clashes at Mers el-Kébir: July 3, 1940', in Martin Thomas and Richard Toye (eds), *Rhetorics of Empire: Languages of Colonial Conflict after 1900* (Manchester: Manchester University Press, forthcoming).

[42] MAE, Guerre 1939–1945, Vichy-Levant, série E, vol. 1, Foreign Ministry note on 'Politique générale', 5 July 1940. For vivid evidence of Vichy reactions and its manipulation of opinion through cinema newsreels, see Brett C. Bowles, ' "La tragédie de Mers el-Kébir" and the Politics of Filmed News in France, 1940–1944', *Journal of Modern History*, 76:2 (2004), 348–51, 355–73.

[43] Although three months after the event, Mers el-Kébir was lead item on the inaugural screening of *France-Actualités-Pathé-Gaumont*, Vichy's authorized broadcaster in France's unoccupied Southern Zone and its empire, see: Brett Bowles, 'Newsreels, Ideology, and Public Opinion under Vichy: The Case of *La France en Marche*', *French Historical Studies*, 27:2 (2004), 427.

Fig. 5.1. 'N'oubliez pas Oran!' (Remember Oran). A widely circulated Vichy propaganda poster depicting a French sailor in the aftermath of the 3 July 1940 attack.

Mary Evans Picture Library, image 11002303

On 30 June, Admiral Dudley North, commander of Britain's North Atlantic fleet at Gibraltar, convened a meeting of his fellow captains and flag officers aboard HMS *Hood*, his flagship. Everyone present opposed the use of force against former French allies.[44] North's reiteration of his opposition to the attack on Oran in the days after it took place earned him Churchill's lasting contempt.[45]

Free French supporters joined the condemnation of Churchill's government, not for bombarding the ships at Mers el-Kébir but for failing to publicize its reasons for doing so—which was arguably unfair in the light of Churchill's speech.[46] The preceding negotiations with French naval commander, Admiral Marcel Gensoul, were poorly explained, it was said; so, too, the underlying British fear that the French Navy was no longer a free agent but beholden to German demands.[47] Admiral Georges Muselier, the one senior (albeit recently retired) naval officer in the Free French movement, was especially critical. But the force of his arguments diminished as he antagonized one after another of his Free French colleagues. By mid-August the British liaison mission to de Gaulle's French National Committee in London were casting around for ways to put safe distance between Muselier and any important decision-making centres. One of the less outlandish proposals emanated from Admiral Gerald Dickens who, as the Admiralty's liaison officer to client navies, found himself to be Muselier's principal contact. Dickens suggested that Muselier be designated head of a nominal force, but one with a suitably grand rhetorical ring to it (Dickens favoured the 'Muselier Marines'). This force might then be landed 'somewhere in Africa'; Dickens didn't seem bothered about where. As he put it, 'It would be an example of ruthless warfare which even the Germans would envy. The physical effect might not be very great, but as the man is such a crushing bore it would wear down the nerves of even the stoutest Touaregs.'[48] An amusing vignette, but also indicative of the off-hand way in which the still-nascent Free French movement was apt to be treated in the aftermath of Mers el-Kébir when disdain for French sensibilities ran deep.

FREE FRANCE AND THE FUTURE OF EMPIRE

Muselier was not, in fact, dispatched on some quixotic African mission (although he was briefly thrown in jail in Brixton after being falsely accused of treachery), but

[44] TNA, ADM 1/19177, Admiral North, Gibraltar, to Admiralty Secretary, J. S. Barnes, 4 July 1940. Arthur J. Marder's classic account captures the officers' reservations: *From the Dardanelles to Oran: Studies of the Royal Navy in War and Peace, 1915–1940* (Oxford: Oxford University Press, 1974). For French and international reactions, see Martin Thomas, 'After Mers el-Kébir: The Armed Neutrality of the Vichy French Navy, 1940–43', *English Historical Review*, 112:447 (1997), 643–70.

[45] TNA, ADM 1/19177, J. S. Barnes to North, 17 July 1940, Churchill to First Lord of the Admiralty, A. V. Alexander, 20 July 1940; ADM 1/19178, Alexander to First Sea Lord, 15 July 1940.

[46] Spears papers Box 1/file II, note on 'Admiral Muselier', 11 July 1940.

[47] These complaints were reiterated by several Vichy naval personnel captured during the British takeover of Madagascar in 1942, see: TNA, FO 898/210, M. Mangeot report, 'The Action at Mers el-Kébir', no date, September 1942.

[48] Spears papers, Box I/file II, Admiral Dickens to Spears, 13 August 1940.

the poor treatment he received was symptomatic of something deeper. Britain's political leaders were anxious to avoid pledging themselves to any restoration of the French Empire. In mid-July—a few days after the Vichy regime was formally established—the War Cabinet, in the prime minister's absence, considered a draft letter from Churchill to de Gaulle. Chamberlain (who, for the time being, remained in the Cabinet as Lord President of the Council) 'said that he felt anxious about the concluding words of the letter' which 'gave a guarantee that after victory had been gained by the Allied army we would restore the independence and territorial integrity of France and of the French Empire. This was a very big undertaking.' Accordingly, the War Cabinet put on record its view that no such commitment was necessary.[49] Although the British never faced serious pressure to make the promise, in the absence of a guarantee, suspicions could easily be raised (not least in the mind of de Gaulle) that Britain coveted French imperial territory for itself. This necessitated a rhetoric of reassurance that on the one hand spoke in glowing terms about the rebirth of France, and on the other stopped short of any concrete undertaking to underwrite her colonial future.

Writing in *The Spectator*, the Russian-born research chemist Michael Zventzigov, whose wartime service included work for the Foreign Office and the BBC, took the view that the Pétainist commitment to the preservation of the sacred soil of France involved a reactionary repudiation of the vision of greater France. He argued: 'The collapse of French prestige in the French Empire is directly due to this renunciation of the supranational value of the French civilisation, which is a worldwide heritage; this means that the Empire will be lost.'[50] More generally, though, most commentators and policymakers in Britain seem to have been working on the operational assumption that the French Empire—still regarded as essentially benign—would in due course be restored. There was, however, a limited apprehension that 'whatever may happen to the French colonial empire elsewhere, it is hardly conceivable that Indochina will remain a French domain'.[51]

De Gaulle, for his part, was judged chiefly by what he could add to the strength of the anti-Nazi forces, thus, in effect, by how much of the French Empire he could win over to his cause. The British tendency to take up Free French cudgels only when strategically convenient was compounded by mutual misunderstandings between the vast bureaucracy of wartime British government and the skeletal staff of the Free French 'National Committee' in London. The original agreement of 7 August 1940 by which Churchill's government recognized de Gaulle as the legitimate voice of 'Free France' was pivotal here. Its wording was rhetorically powerful, but legally obscure. British ministers, civil servants, and colonial administrators were left uncertain about the status of those working for the wider Free French movement. The institution of a Free French National Committee went some way to dispel the confusion, but not far enough. Rhetorically, de Gaulle retained the power to define Free France as the impersonal extension of his singular

---

[49] TNA, CAB 65/8/14, WM(40)202, Cabinet Minutes, 13 July 1940.
[50] Michael Zveginzov, 'France and Ourselves', *The Spectator*, 22 August 1940.
[51] ' "Greater East Asia": From a Correspondent Lately in Japan', *The Times*, 1 April 1941.

personal beliefs.[52] Indicative of this, the general reacted furiously to a joint Foreign Office and Ministry of Information proposal in July 1941 suggesting that all pro-Allied governments-in-exile endorse the idea of a 'Party of Liberation' to rally support for resistance within their occupied homelands.[53] The general dismissed British arguments about the rhetorical advantage of a single rallying point, noting tersely that it already existed: namely, Free France. It was left to Maurice Dejean, appointed at British suggestion in February 1941 as Free French liaison to both Duff Cooper's Ministry of Information and the BBC, to smooth the Whitehall feathers ruffled by this latest icy blast from de Gaulle's office.[54]

The blurred line between Britain's support for de Gaulle and its endorsement of the Free French movement continued to generate confusion. The Foreign Office was forced to correct the American government, which, following the Allied landings in North Africa in November 1942, presumed that Churchill's Cabinet already recognized the Free French National Committee as a prospective government. Not so: the British authorities regarded Free France solely as exercising *provisional* sovereignty over those parts of the French Empire under their control.[55] Only with the creation in 1943 of an Algiers-based French Committee of National Liberation (FCNL), *de facto*, if not *de jure* tantamount to a Free French government-in-exile, was this problem minimized, albeit never entirely overcome.[56] Formal British recognition of the FCNL came hedged with the proviso that the committee was *not* recognized as the government of France but 'as having *de facto* sovereign rights over the territories which acknowledge its administration'.[57] This was hardly a ringing endorsement.

Major-General Louis Spears, Churchill's appointee as delegate to Charles de Gaulle's nascent Free French executive at Carlton Gardens in St James', London, became the lightning rod through which both the prime minister's and the Frenchman's demands were conducted. Highly opinionated and supremely self-confident, Spears would trace an arc from ardent faith in de Gaulle to visceral loathing. It was a trajectory that mirrored the vicissitudes of Spears' wartime career from favoured intermediary in 1940–1 to peripheral outsider as thoughts turned to the post-war reconstruction of Franco-British relations in 1944–5.[58] Spears was also an author who shared Churchill's fondness for pithy rhetoric. He repeatedly warned the Cabinet, the service chiefs, the prime minister's intelligence advisors, and anyone

[52] Spears papers Box II/6, 'Note by Major Desmond Morton on Relations with the Free French', 6 January 1942.
[53] MAE, Guerre 1939–45, Comité National Francais (CNF) Londres, vol. 191, no. 4873/AP, Maurice Dejean to de Gaulle, 9 July 1941.
[54] MAE, Guerre 1939–45, Comité National Francais (CNF) Londres, vol. 193, Duff Cooper letters to de Gaulle and Dejean, 25 February and 27 March 1941; vol. 191, no. 2098A, De Gaulle (Brazzaville) to Dejean, 15 July 1941.
[55] TNA, CO 968/87/7, FO circular to overseas embassies, 'North Africa', 17 January 1943.
[56] Martin Thomas, 'The Discarded Leader: General Henri Giraud and the Foundation of the French Committee of National Liberation', *French History*, 10:1 (1996), 86–111.
[57] TNA, T 160/1233/F17400/06, Treasury Trading with the Enemy Department to Patrick Dean, FO, 18 September 1943.
[58] Max Egremont, *Under Two Flags: The Life of Major-General Sir Edward Spears* (London: Weidenfeld & Nicolson, 1997), 257–62.

who would listen to him in Whitehall that it would be disastrous folly to follow the American lead in tolerating Vichy while sidelining Free France. Hitler, he warned, had used Vichy 'as a dissolvent of the French Empire', dividing a once great empire against itself.[59]

Spears' lobbying, laced with stirring rhetorical appeals to Anglo-Free French unity, was one reason why, in late September 1940, Churchill's government endorsed the abortive effort to sway the loyalty of French West Africa by ferrying de Gaulle to Dakar, the administrative hub of this vast colonial federation. An attempted landing of Gaullist envoys was cut short by firing from Dakar's coastal artillery on the Royal Navy ships lying offshore. Through a lingering sea mist that precluded any larger-scale assault, it became glaringly obvious that Dakar's Vichyite garrison was not about to change sides. Chance played its part too. Fatally, the Royal Navy had previously intercepted a Vichy cruiser squadron that was making for Gabon to pre-empt any further Gaullist seizures of power in French Equatorial Africa. This forced the Vichy ships to seek refuge in Dakar.[60] Fiercely anti-British after the Mers el-Kébir attack, the presence of these vessels and their crews stifled support for de Gaulle within Dakar's civil administration.[61]

So it was that the British naval flotilla withdrew. De Gaulle was shipped away without setting a foot on Senegalese soil. Vichy's French West Africa governor, the fiery General Pierre Boisson, a one-legged *mutilé de guerre*, celebrated the defence of Dakar as affirmation of 'the cohesion, the complete understanding, and the team-spirit' among the port's defenders.[62] Although Boisson represented the action as a British defeat, Gaullist embarrassment was deepened by two additional elements, each of them rendered obvious by what had transpired. The first was that, contrary to Gaullist rhetoric since July, Vichy *was* considered legitimate, at least by those within the French colonial military prepared to fight for it. The second was that Free French claims of colonial popularity were discredited. At best, their intelligence gathering was flawed; at worst, Gaullist propaganda was misleading.[63] De Gaulle's confidence that the local Vichy forces could be induced to switch sides seemed laughable. Initially a highly popular figure with the British public, Dakar damaged his prestige, although this was afterwards somewhat restored by Churchill's willingness to speak well of him publicly.[64]

[59] TNA, FO 892/65, Spears memo. for Morton committee, 'The Free French, Vichy, and ourselves', 10 February 1941.

[60] Service Historique de la Marine (SHM), Vincennes, Fonds privés, Sous-série GG2/Papiers Amiral Sacaze, no. 51, EM-3, Contre-Amiral Bourragué, commandant Force Y, memo., 16 September 1940.

[61] SHM, Fonds privés, Sous-série GG2/Papiers Amiral Sacaze, no. 3, EM-2/S, Vice-Amiral Lacroix, Dakar memo., 25 January 1941.

[62] SHD-DAT, 1P34/D4, Boisson report to Secretariat for Colonies, 'A/S: attaque Dakar du 23 au 25 Septembre 1940'.

[63] Spears papers, Box II/4, unpublished Spears memoir on Free France and the Levant, 14 April 1954.

[64] Mass Observation Archive, 'Public Opinion About the French', File Report 566, 1 February 1941.

The prime minister, however, rationed his praise of the general with strategic parsimony. In October he made a broadcast to the French people—the speech went out to the colonial empire in addition to metropolitan France. There was neither commendation of de Gaulle, nor condemnation of Pétain, who tended to be portrayed in British propaganda as 'a venerable, though unfortunate statesman unable to resist Axis pressure'.[65] Churchill read the speech in English before repeating it in French—in rehearsal with the translator beforehand he had 'relished the flavour of some words as though he was tasting fruit'.[66] His broadcast emphasized that Hitler and Mussolini both wanted 'to carve up France and her Empire as if it were a fowl; to one a leg, to another a wing or perhaps part of the breast'. At the urging of his personal assistant, Major Desmond Morton, he also denied the Nazi claim 'that we English seek to take your ships and colonies'.[67] Eden, now secretary of state for war, reiterated the point at the Free French HQ in Cairo a few days later.[68]

According to a British assessment of the French radio response to Churchill's speech: 'The reply is that England intends "to save France against the will of the French" and there follows a series of references to the past, ranging from the deportation of Napoleon to the evacuation of Dunkirk and the bombing of Dakar, each undertaken "to save France".'[69] Churchill's words seem to have resonated with many French listeners even so.[70] The Foreign Office, meanwhile, was as keen to maintain its contacts with Vichy as it was to keep news about these liaisons out of the press.[71] The British may not have questioned the future of the French Empire as such, but they were unconvinced of the Free French movement's capacity to act as its custodians. They were no more committed to the Free French as the future governors of France itself.[72]

Thus, Churchill's public assurance to de Gaulle that 'you embody the hope of millions of Frenchmen and Frenchwomen who do not despair of France and the French Empire' was not much of an assurance at all.[73] It was as replete with ambiguity as was Eden's pledge that 'Britain is firmly resolved to restore France'.[74]

[65] Mark Abrams Papers, ABMS 1/2/1, 'Propaganda Research Papers 3A Week No. 60: Broadcasts in French During Week 21st–27th October', 30 October 1940. See also TNA, FO 800/312, Lord Halifax to Lord Stanhope, 19 August 1940.

[66] '"A Day With Churchill" by Michel Saint-Denis', broadcast on the BBC Home Service, 30 November 1959. Transcript in the Michel Saint-Denis Archive, British Library MS. Add. 81159.

[67] Churchill Papers, CHAR 9/176B/116, broadcast of 21 October 1940; Kathleen Hill to Winston Churchill, 20 October 1940; Churchill Papers, CHAR 9/145/34, draft of broadcast of 21 October 1940.

[68] 'France Will Be Restored', *The Times*, 28 October 1940.

[69] Mark Abrams Papers, ABMS 1/2/1, 'Propaganda Research Papers 3A Week No. 60: Broadcasts in French During Week 21st–27th October', 30 October 1940.

[70] Martyn Cornick, '"Fraternity Among Listeners". The BBC and French Resistance: Evidence from Refugees', in Hanna Diamond and Simon Kitson (eds), *Vichy, Resistance, Liberation: New Perspectives on Wartime France* (Oxford: Berg, 2005), 101–13, at 106.

[71] See TNA, FO 800/312, Lord Halifax to Lord Camrose, 11 November 1940.

[72] Martin Thomas, 'France and its Colonial Civil Wars, 1940–1945', in Evan Mawdsley and Joe Maiolo (eds), *The Cambridge History of the Second World War*, vol. 2 (Cambridge: Cambridge University Press, 2015), 581–93.

[73] 'Premier's Message to De Gaulle', *The Times*, 7 April 1941.

[74] 'France Will Be Restored', *The Times*, 28 October 1940.

De Gaulle might well have been forgiven for doubting British sincerity, for it was quite clear that he and they interpreted things differently. British lines of communication to Vichy were not entirely cut. For one thing, the Canadian government, with an eye to its large francophone community, maintained limited diplomatic representation and, with it, a British imperial backchannel to Vichy. For another, several of Churchill's Whitehall military advisors, among them Major-General F. H. N. Davidson, director of intelligence at the War Office, acknowledged that Britain could ill afford to antagonize Vichy's senior colonial administrators. Most Vichy governors, including the former chief of French general staff, Maxime Weygand, were clearly anti-Nazi in sentiment.[75] Weygand in particular, who remained Vichy's North African generalissimo for most of 1941, was not a card to be thrown away lightly.[76]

In mid-October 1940, ten days before Pétain's formal affirmation of collaboration during his meeting with Hitler at Montoire, the Foreign Office Political Warfare Executive, responsible for devising propaganda and psychological warfare in enemy-occupied territories, turned its attention to French Algeria. Not only was the territory still under Vichy's control, it would soon be Weygand's administrative home. A three-pronged rhetorical strategy emerged. To serving officials the message was menacingly simple: Vichy was a creature of the Axis, so serving Vichy was serving the enemy—and would be judged as such. To Algeria's settlers the message was of economic self-interest: Vichy francs were unconvertible and valueless; Germany would milk Algeria's European community dry, riding roughshod over their rights to land and property. To Algeria's Muslims the message contrasted Allied good with Axis evil: by allowing unprecedented exploitation of Algerian resources for the Nazi war effort, Vichy proved itself a bad imperial ruler. Britain, by contrast, governed its empire in the interest of its constituent peoples.[77]

A fortnight later Admiral Darlan turned this British logic on its head. Vichy's navy minister would soon take on additional responsibilities as deputy-premier, effectively a prime ministerial office as Pétain's role as Vichy head of state was more presidential. Darlan justified closer collaboration with Germany, not as subservience to evil but as ethically expedient, a means to regain the military freedom necessary to protect the French Empire and its peoples from Allied depredation.[78] The admiral's imprint was clear in the grandiose renaming of the small naval squadrons that the German Armistice Commission duly permitted the Vichy

[75] Simon Kitson, *The Hunt for Nazi Spies: Fighting Espionage in Vichy France* (Chicago, IL: University of Chicago Press, 2008), 141–5.
[76] Liddell Hart Centre for Military Archives, King's College, London, General F. H. N. Davidson papers, 1941 Diary, fo. 35, entry for 6 January 1941; MAE, PAAP288/Papiers Maurice Dejean, vol. 25, 'La situation politique en France et le problème de l'Afrique du Nord', 26 April 1941.
[77] TNA, FO 898/126, Valentine Williams/PWE memo., 'Propaganda—Algeria', 13 October 1940. A week earlier, Pétain advised General Weygand, whom he appointed civil-military governor of Vichy North Africa, of the need to resuscitate the Maghreb economies lest their populations turn against Vichy rule: Service Historique de la Défense-Département de l'Armée de Terre (SHD-DAT), Vincennes, box 1P89/D1, Pétain, 'Instruction de mission pour Général Weygand', 5 October 1940.
[78] Service Historique de la Marine (SHM), Vincennes, Série TT: Guerre 1939–1945, box TTA2, no. 138, Darlan message to Weygand, 7 November 1940.

authorities to maintain as convoy escorts for the shipping of supplies between Vichyite colonies and mainland France.[79]

Weygand, meanwhile, was careful to distance himself from Vichy's turn to collaboration. In a well-publicized message to his administrative staff in Algiers on 21 May 1941, the general refused to endorse the deal recently finalized between the Vichy government and the German Armistice Commission. The so-called May accords marked the tangible extension of collaboration to the French Empire, increasing the extraction of colonial resources to serve the Nazi war economy in return for modifications to the armistice, notably limited releases of older French POWs with large families. Weygand acknowledged that such collaboration allevi-ated the armistice 'diktat', but he insisted that his North African mission remained unchanged: he would defend France's three Maghreb territories against all attack-ers.[80] At one level, this was rhetorical sophistry, leaving unsaid whether heightened economic extraction constituted 'an attack'. At another level, though, it confirmed Weygand's role as Vichy's most powerful internal critic and thus, potentially, as an Allied asset.

Darlan, by now Weygand's most voluble opponent inside the Vichy govern-ment, drew his rhetorical dagger on 24 September 1941. The Admiral was then at the height of his powers within Vichy's shifting governmental hierarchy, serving not only as prime minister but as foreign minister and head of Vichy's service ministries as well. In this capacity he signed off on a new oath of loyalty required of serving French military personnel. The oath pledged fidelity to Marshal Pétain personally, promising to obey his every command 'for the good of the armed services and the success of French arms'. The wording was significant, echoing Pétain's earlier oath as head of state to dedicate himself to 'France' and connecting such service to military victory. The question of victory over whom was left unanswered, allowing Vichy service personnel to claim they served only French interests in all circumstances.[81] In the event, Darlan clarified this issue in a decisive report sent to Pétain on 8 November 1941 to justify General Weygand's removal as Vichy plenipotentiary in North Africa. The nub of Darlan's argument was simple, if disingenuous: collaboration enabled France to survive as a nation. Its sovereignty was better assured by steering a course between neutrality and limited cooperation with the Axis Powers (Darlan's preferred alternative) than by leaning towards non-cooperation in the vain hope that the Allies would eventually come to the rescue (Weygand's preferred alternative). Anyone serving Vichy had to accept Darlan's option or face dismissal.[82]

[79] SHM, box TTA102, FMF-3 memo., 'La Marine depuis l'armistice', 17 March 1941. Notionally, these *Forces Coloniales Océaniques* formed part of an integrated imperial fleet headed by the *Force de Haute Mer*, or High Seas Fleet, that, in practice, never left its home port of Toulon before its eventual scuttling in late November 1942.

[80] SHD-DAT, box 1P89, 'Communication verbale du Général Weygand aux Haut Fonctionnaires, Alger', 21 May 1941.

[81] SHM, Série TT: Guerre 1939–1945, box TTA2, no 57/CAB, Secrétariat d'Etat à la Marine circulaire, 24 September 1941.

[82] SHD-DAT, 1K496/Dossier: Débarquement en Afrique du Nord, Darlan memo., 'Rapport au Maréchal de France', 8 November 1941.

Powerless to prevent Vichy's slide into deeper collaboration, the French National Committee in London was at least able to contest the regime's stronger rhetorical defence of such collaboration as a means to ease armistice restrictions. On 13 January 1941, de Gaulle asked his senior advisors to comment on the line to be taken. The most emphatic response came from Admiral Georges Thierry d'Argenlieu, a near-fanatical Gaullist devotee later to serve a catastrophic term as high commissioner of French Vietnam. D'Argenlieu ruled out any contact, official or unofficial, with Vichy, insisting that it was vital to depict Free France as its diametric opposite. Vichy lost all legitimacy by signing the armistice; Free France won legitimacy by rejecting it. Vichy dishonoured the French nation; Free France offered its salvation. Because Free France served a higher ethical purpose it should not stoop to any personal attacks on Pétain.[83] This rhetorical restraint would also set Free France above the vicious, anti-Semitic propaganda that Vichy spewed out.

The problem was that Gaullist propaganda, no matter how well it played to the growing number of resistance sympathizers in France, made little impact on British opinion, high or low. Such was the depth of *mésentente* between Britain and Free France that, as 1941 drew to a close, the Cabinet's advisory Committee on Foreign (Allied) Resistance stepped in. Often described eponymously as the Vansittart Committee in recognition of the former Foreign Office head who chaired it, its core task was to recommend actions and propagandist messages likely to foster popular opposition to Axis rule in occupied Europe. To that end, the committee considered measures designed to increase understanding of Free France within the British Empire.[84] Committee chair, Sir Robert Vansittart, maintained close links with the French National Committee in London. A noted anti-appeaser and Germanophobe during his time as Foreign Office permanent under-secretary in the 1930s, Vansittart was even willing to broadcast Free French statements on the BBC Home Service. In one such statement on 16 August 1941, for instance, Vansittart attacked a recent government reshuffle at Vichy as evidence of the regime's closer collaboration with the Nazis.[85]

It was always likely, then, that Vansittart's committee would take the lead in trying to build public support for Free France. Focused on 'increased information by radio and in print', its proposals challenged the prevailing British imperial stereotypes about France and its people. The widespread belief that the French had 'let us down' in 1940 was to be counteracted by a rhetorical insistence on the singular bravery evinced by the Free French determination to fight on. The received wisdom that the French people remained hopelessly divided at home and imperially would be countered by constant reminders that Churchill's government recognized Free France and only Free France. The committee did not follow Spears' recommendation of a stronger condemnation of the Vichy leadership to back up

---

[83] SHM, Sous-série TTC, Forces Navales, France Libre, box TTC1, D'Argenlieu letter to de Gaulle, 6 February 1941.

[84] Spears papers, Box II/5, CFR(41)200, 'Improvement in Anglo-French Relations', 4 December 1941.

[85] MAE, PAAP288/Papiers Dejean, vol. 31, Dejean-Vansittart correspondence, 15 and 16 August 1941.

d'Argenlieu's propaganda plans.[86] But Vansittart and his colleagues acknowledged the need for more government statements and press releases designed to weaken the public perception that de Gaulle's cause was unpopular in the United States. The committee concluded by expressing the vain hope that any Gaullist military triumphs in Africa or elsewhere should be celebrated in the media in the same way that British victories were cheered.[87] There was, though, an air of tokenism to these deliberations. More than that, Vansittart's proposals were out of kilter with the coolness towards Free France evident in British Cabinet pronouncements in late 1941. As we shall see in Chapter 6, there was one overriding reason for this: renewed tensions over the most hotly contested region in Franco-British imperial history—the Middle East.

[86] Spears papers, Box II/5, Spears 'Memorandum on Propaganda to the French', 27 May 1941. Spears justified his argument on the grounds that the senior Vichy figures that had signed up to the Franco-German armistice could never be induced to take up arms again.

[87] Spears papers, Box II/5, CFR(41)200, 'Improvement in Anglo-French Relations', 4 December 1941.

6

World War as Imperial Crisis, II
Allies in Conflict, 1941–5

MIDDLE EASTERN CLASHES

In June 1941, British imperial forces backed by Free French troops ousted the Vichy regime from control of the Levant states. France had held Syria and Lebanon since the early 1920s as League of Nations mandates. Foreign Office monitoring of French public opinion confirmed in mid-June that Darlan's government had tried but failed to whip up anti-British sentiment over what was by some margin the largest Anglo-Gaullist attack of the war against a Vichy-held territory. The French premier even neglected to mention the Syrian situation at all in a succession of policy pronouncements earlier that month.[1]

Darlan gave an equally lacklustre performance in a later radio broadcast appealing to Free French troops to change sides and support General Fernand Dentz's defending garrison. In a subsequent message to Vichy's embassies overseas, the French premier noted that the Syria armistice was perfunctory—an interim arrangement to cover a temporary Allied military occupation. He also told Vichy's ambassadors that the British were noticeably disdainful of their supposed Gaullist 'allies', a motley crew who had 'rebelled against their country'.[2] For Vichy, this was standard fare. Darlan, his government internally divided over the feasibility of fighting on in Syria, was going through the motions, nothing more.[3] The same could not be said of de Gaulle's Free French. In a telegram sent from Cairo on 29 June, de Gaulle expressed his reservations about the material—and symbolic—dangers of what lay ahead:

> The manner in which British policy develops towards Syria will be a criterion of very great importance. It is the first time that British forces united to those of Free France are penetrating into a territory submitted to French authority . . . If, to the satisfaction of Vichy, Berlin and Rome, our common action in Syria and Lebanon seems to result in diminution of the position of France and [the] introduction there of tendencies and action which are purely British, I am convinced that the effect on the opinion of my country will be disastrous. I must add that my own effort, which consists in

---

[1] TNA, FO 892/84, FO intelligence report 39, 16 June 1941.
[2] MAE, Guerre 1939–45, Comité National Francais (CNF) Londres, vol. 39, Darlan circular to embassy staff, 18 July 1941.
[3] TNA, FO 892/84, FO intelligence report 40, 24 June 1941.

maintaining, morally and materially, French resistance at the side of England against our enemies would be gravely compromised.[4]

The general had a point. Although trailled, and to some degree conducted, as a joint Anglo-Free French 'liberation' of the Vichy-held Levant states, Operation Exporter was anything but.[5] The troops most directly engaged were Australian and Indian, the great majority of the defending Vichy garrison fought bitterly, and for neither Syrians nor Lebanese did the transition from one variant of French imperial administration to another represent any kind of liberation.[6] It transpired that the defending Vichy forces, mainly career colonial soldiers and Foreign Legionnaires, had no idea that Free French troops were involved in the assault. Few, if any, had heard de Gaulle's statement, transmitted from Brazzaville, capital of Free French Equatorial Africa, lambasting the Vichy authorities' latest treachery in permitting Axis units to use Syrian air bases.[7] Most, by contrast, had heard Pétain's radio broadcast refuting the Allied pretext for the attack; 'there isn't a single German soldier in Syria or Lebanon' he assured them.[8]

Gaullist suspicions that the British intended to pull the imperial strings in Beirut and, more especially, Damascus, were matched by local politicians' hopes that their roads to national independence might be smoothed by precisely this outcome.[9] Both the armistice terms agreed with Dentz's vanquished government and British refusal to cede military or strategic authority to General Henri Catroux's incoming Free French administration seemed to confirm Gaullist and Syrian nationalist suppositions—increasing the probability of conflict between the two.[10] So venomous were the resultant arguments between de Gaulle, Spears, and Oliver Lyttelton, recently appointed as minister of state in the Middle East, that in late July Spears and Lyttelton drew up plans to drop de Gaulle entirely. As Spears confided to his diary after a stormy meeting with the general in Cairo on 21 July: 'If it comes to a punch we could dispose [of] him and nominate Catroux, notifying all in the Free French movement that all pay and emoluments will be made through Catroux.'[11]

---

[4] Spears' papers, Box IA/Pre-Syria armistice telegrams, no. 2031, de Gaulle to Churchill, 29 June 1941.

[5] MAE, Guerre 1939–45, CNF Londres, vol. 39, CNF direction des affaires politiques communiqué, 8 June 1941.

[6] For background, see: Aviel Roshwald, *Estranged Bedfellows: Britain and France in the Middle East during the Second World War* (Oxford: Oxford University Press, 1990); Andrew B. Gaunson, *The Anglo-French Clash in Lebanon and Syria, 1941–1945* (Basingstoke: Palgrave, 1987).

[7] MAE, Guerre 1939–45, Comité National Francais (CNF) Londres, vol. 39, 'France Libre communiqué', 16 May 1941.

[8] MAE, Guerre 1939–45, CNF Londres, vol. 39, CNF direction des affaires politiques, 'Note sur l'intervention alliée en Syrie', 2 July 1941.

[9] St Antony's College Middle East Centre Archive, Oxford, Major-General Edward Spears' papers, box 1, Syrian Committee telegrams, Spears (Cairo) to FO, 17 July 1941.

[10] MAE, Guerre 1939–45, CNF Londres, vol. 39, CNF direction des affaires politiques, 'Mémoire concernant l'administration des états de Syrie et du Liban', 5 July 1941. De Gaulle, who met Spears in Cairo on 20 July 1941 to discuss the change of administration in Syria and Lebanon, was infuriated by the armistice terms, which allowed French troops of the defeated Levant Army to return to France by sea from Beirut, an offer taken up by the overwhelming majority: Spears papers, box 1, 1941 diary, entry for 20 July 1941.

[11] Spears papers, box 1, 1941 diary, entry for 21 July 1941.

Hardly surprising, then, that the question of how and by whom Syria was to be governed provoked the most poisonous rhetorical exchanges of the entire war between the British and Free French authorities. When the British finally provided him with transportation to Damascus in late July 1941, de Gaulle's one high-profile speech in the Syrian capital breezily affirmed Free French willingness to end the mandate regime and negotiate a treaty of 'alliance' (not 'independence') with Syria. But his speech dwelt at much greater length on the permissible limits to British military jurisdiction in the Levant—evidently, the general's real preoccupation.[12] The Gaullist press meanwhile raged against the British decision to allow the repatriation of Vichy's garrison troops.[13] This, it claimed, was a deliberate ploy to reduce the number of potential converts to Free France, thereby ensuring the numerical dominance of British imperial occupation forces in Syria and Lebanon.[14] At a tempestuous Downing Street meeting held less than two months after Operation Exporter's conclusion, de Gaulle insisted that Britain's actions in the Levant 'made him doubt British sincerity'. Churchill responded by accusing the general of leaving 'a trail of Anglophobia' behind him wherever he went.[15]

Viewed from a juridical standpoint, it was impossible to resolve these differences. Free France, a political movement with no recognized status as a sovereign authority under international law, was legally powerless either to serve as the mandatory power in Syria and Lebanon or, conversely, to negotiate an end to that mandate. Any declaration that the Free French or their British clients intended to enact Syrian or Lebanese independence also risked handing a propaganda victory to Vichy, which maintained its claim to be the sole legally authorized ruler of the Levant states.[16] Free France's lack of governmental authority was, if anything, amplified inside Lebanon and Syria where the acute shortage of Gaullist administrators was matched by the paucity of their security forces.[17] Each was far outnumbered by their British imperial counterparts. British military commanders and civilian officials were, in turn, beholden to a government more anxious to conciliate wider Arab opinion in the Middle East than to ease the Gaullists' juridical dilemmas.[18] More significantly, nationalist leaders in Damascus and Beirut moved

---

[12] MAE, Guerre 1939–45, Vichy-Levant, vol. 25, Jean Helleu, Istanbul, 'Bulletin de renseignements no. 110', 12 August 1941. (The Vichy embassy in neutral Turkey monitored events in Syria closely throughout the war.)

[13] SHD-DAT, 1P20/Sous-dossier: Troupes de Levant, no. 13216/EMA, War Ministry note, 1 October 1941. Most repatriated soldiers were, in fact, demobilized, excepting North African professional troops and specialist anti-aircraft gunners.

[14] MAE, Guerre 1939–45, Vichy-Levant, vol. 25, Jean Helleu, Istanbul, 'Bulletin de renseignements no. 110', 12 August 1941.

[15] Spears papers, box II/4, record of a meeting between the prime minister and General de Gaulle, 12 September 1941.

[16] Spears papers, box II/4, note of a meeting between the prime minister, Oliver Lyttelton, and General de Gaulle at 10 Downing Street, 1 October 1941.

[17] TNA, WO 201/950, CC/58, Jerusalem Control Commission, daily progress return, 9 August 1941. British-supervised repatriations of Vichy French military personnel continued meanwhile, with 4,384 troops embarking from Lebanon on 7 August alone. Four further troop ship convoys were scheduled to ferry French troops from Beirut on 15, 20, 27, and 30 August 1941. Figures from TNA, ADM 199/180.

[18] Spears papers, box II/5, no. SS/30, Spears to Lyttelton, 25 November 1941.

quickly to proclaim national independence, which, after all, had been underwritten by pre-war treaties negotiated with the French Popular Front government in late 1936 and only postponed, first by the war's outbreak and then by France's 1940 defeat. By late November 1941, Catroux, as Free French governor in the Levant, found himself cornered into endorsing these national proclamations while stipulating that their enactment should wait until the war was won.[19]

Catroux's halfway house declaration satisfied nobody, least of all the population of Beirut, which reportedly reacted 'at best with cynical apathy and at the worst with active disapproval'.[20] As Free French representative, rather than official plenipotentiary, Catroux had declared the mandate at an end without the legal authority to do so. Whereas Churchill believed that Britain and Free France were jointly committed to making this independence real, de Gaulle's supporters refused to make good on the pledge, and they resented what they perceived as British interference.[21] Few of Catroux's Free French colleagues had any intention of turning rhetorical support for Lebanese and Syrian independence into reality.[22] Forcible Free French removal of the Lebanese government in November 1943 made this shockingly clear, provoking another Anglo-Gaullist crisis over the Levant that barely subsided despite successful British pressure for the release and reinstatement of the Lebanese ministers.[23]

Meanwhile, political alignments between Syrian politicians and the rival governments in Jordan and Iraq became part of the broader struggle to ensure Syria's independence. King Abdullah of Jordan nursed ambitions to lead a Greater Syria, a project deeply offensive to the country's nationalists. Syrian President Shukri al-Quwatli's National Bloc duly secured Saudi and Egyptian support for a quick transition to independence to block King Abdullah's plans. Further Syrian and Lebanese ministerial trips to Baghdad, Cairo, and Riyadh between January and March 1944 underlined the potential for a Greater Syria scheme to destroy the inter-Arab cooperation then taking shape in the formative discussions of the Arab League. Since the preservation of British interests in Egypt and Palestine led Churchill's government outwardly to support the Arab unity movement, in French eyes the connection was easily made between Syrian and Lebanese diplomacy and shadowy British regional planning.[24] In this instance, it was the absence of rhetorical claims—or indeed of any unequivocal policy statements—that allow

---

[19] MAE, Guerre 1939–45, CNF Londres, vol. 39, France Libre Délégation générale au Levant, 'Chronologie des événements politiques au Liban', no date, 1943; Spears papers, Box IC/Spears Mission telegrams, 1941–2, tel. 3588 to FO, 15 November 1941.

[20] Spears papers, box IC/Spears Mission telegrams, 1941–2, tel. 3760, Spears to FO, 29 November 1941.

[21] Churchill Archives Centre, Cambridge, Duff Cooper papers, DUFC 4/3, Winston Churchill to Duff Cooper, 17 August 1944.

[22] Spears papers, box II/6, Levant Staff Office (Intelligence), 'The Free French and Syria', 18 August 1942.

[23] The severity of the covert conflict between French and British security personnel in the Levant states is revealed in Meir Zamir, *The Secret Anglo-French War in the Middle East: Intelligence and Decolonization, 1940–1948* (Abingdon: Routledge, 2015).

[24] This paragraph draws on Martin Thomas, 'Divisive Decolonization: The Anglo-French Withdrawal from Syria and Lebanon', *Journal of Imperial & Commonwealth History*, 28:3 (2000),

tensions to fester between British and French representatives throughout the Middle East. Neither the Foreign Office Middle Eastern Department nor Herbert Morrison's Palestine Planning Committee, the main architect of revised British Cabinet schemes for a new Middle East partition, cared to advertise the extent of their involvement in the region's affairs. But partial knowledge of the complexities of Anglo-Arab diplomacy led de Gaulle's regional envoys, including General Paul Beynet, Catroux's more combative replacement as Delegate-general in Beirut, to resent their exclusion still more.[25]

So bad did relations become between the British and French within the two Levant states that General Bernard Paget, the British Army's theatre commander, issued a statement to his junior officers reminding them that rhetorical attacks on Free French behaviour whether made in public or in face-to-face discussions, could prejudice local security. Yet even Paget couldn't resist a few digs at the Gaullists: their actions in Lebanon were not only unjustifiable, but illegal; their presence in Beirut was entirely thanks to Britain's eviction of the Vichy administration; and 'such powers as [the] French possess here devolve on them by our goodwill'.[26] Paget was no doubt expressing a widely held British imperial viewpoint. With a Gaullist-led provisional government in prospect in Paris after the city's liberation in August 1944, British—and Syrian—fears grew that de Gaulle's supporters intended to impose martial law in the Levant as soon as the opportunity presented itself.[27]

THE AMERICAN FACTOR

The issue of where President Roosevelt's administration stood in relation to France and its empire helps explain why the Free French behaved in ways that appeared to the British as insanely provocative and inconsistent with the realities of French power. Morton recalled: 'there was certainly a period when Winston, who was kept informed of all that was going on, would have given an eye-tooth, if he had any left, to depose de Gaulle'.[28] The situation was further complicated by the divergent Anglo-American attitudes towards Pétain's regime. Vichy had made skilful propaganda appeals to US public opinion based on America and France's shared republican and revolutionary heritage.[29] The British and the Americans clashed

75–6. See also: Roshwald, *Estranged Bedfellows*, 209–12; Bruce Maddy-Weitzman, 'Jordan and Iraq: Efforts at Intra-Hashimite Unity', *Middle Eastern Studies*, 26: 1 (1990), 65–6.

[25] TNA, CO 733/461/23, P(M)(43)29, Ministerial Committee on Palestine draft report, 20 December 1943; William Roger Louis, *The British Empire in the Middle East, 1945–1951: Arab Nationalism, the United States and Postwar Imperialism* (Oxford: Oxford University Press, 1984), 147–56.

[26] TNA, WO 201/1007, 9A/574/GSI, 9th Army Command statement, 'Anglo-French Relations and the Lebanese Crisis', 5 December 1943.

[27] Spears papers, box II/6, Spears letter to FO, 15 August 1944.

[28] Violet Bonham Carter Papers 294, f. 166, Bodleian Library, Oxford, Desmond Morton to Bonham Carter, 13 June 1968.

[29] See, for example, AN, Philippe Pétain Papers, 2AG/439, 'Déclaration du Maréchal aux Américains', 30 July 1940.

repeatedly over the question of blockading Vichy, and Roosevelt never overcame his visceral distrust of de Gaulle.[30] America's entry into the war after Pearl Harbor did little to improve her relations with the Free French. Notably, it was Vichy that eventually severed diplomatic relations with the USA (in November 1942), not the other way round.

For their part, the more the Free French leadership were excluded from Allied counsels, the greater their inclination to strike out alone. The venom injected into an otherwise insignificant incident illustrated both tendencies in action. On Christmas Eve 1941, without warning to Britain or the USA, Gaullist forces seized control of St Pierre and Miquelon, two small islands off the coast of Newfoundland, until then under Vichy rule. With the rhetorical battles over Syria and Lebanon still raging, de Gaulle, it seemed, had turned the tables, shutting out the British and Americans from a different imperial venture. The State Department was furious; the White House arguably more so.[31] British public opinion split between those who were angry at American 'attempts at appeasement towards Vichy' and those who expressed 'astonishment that General de Gaulle should have countenanced such piracy without the sanction of the Allies'.[32] Privately, Churchill pressured the general to compromise with the Americans and became frustrated at his stubbornness—although the Free French held on to the islands and the incident faded from memory. Publicly, though, the prime minister gave his strongest denunciation yet of 'the men of Vichy', and handed out liberal praise to de Gaulle, in the course of his famous speech at the Canadian parliament in Ottawa on 30 December 1941.[33]

Churchill rationalized his tactics to the Americans by presenting them as part of a conscious Anglo-US division of rhetorical labour, which kept different options open. 'You're being nice to Vichy,' he said to Roosevelt, 'we're being nice to de Gaulle.'[34] Still digesting news from St Pierre and Miquelon, Roosevelt continued to put his faith in General Weygand. Roosevelt's yuletide message on 27 December 1941 comforted the general, who was still smarting from his removal as Vichy's delegate-general in Algiers: 'I am conscious of your courage and devotion in maintaining in so far as possible under the armistice limitations the integrity of the French Empire.'[35]

Roosevelt's words—or rather, those of the State Department, which drafted the message—were indicative of an inconsistency in American attitudes to empire. There was a strong strand of US hostility to imperialism. Whether or not Roosevelt genuinely shared this, which is more than debatable, he at least successfully

[30] Mario Rossi, 'United States Military Authorities and Free France, 1942–1944', *Journal of Military History*, 61:1 (1997), 49–64.

[31] Martin Thomas, 'Deferring to Vichy in the Western Hemisphere: The St Pierre and Miquelon Affair of 1941', *International History Review*, 19:4 (1997), 789–808.

[32] TNA, INF 1/292, 'Home Intelligence Weekly Report No. 65', 31 December 1941.

[33] Speech of 30 December 1941.

[34] François Kersaudy, *Churchill and De Gaulle* (London: Collins, 1981), 175.

[35] Franklin D. Roosevelt to Maxime Weygand, 27 December 1941, in United States Department of State, *Foreign Relations of the United States: The Conferences at Washington, 1941–1942, and Casablanca, 1943* (Washington, DC: US Government Printing Office, 1968), 244.

cultivated a reputation for doing so.[36] In August 1941, before America entered the war, he had secured British agreement to Point 3 of the Atlantic Charter, under which the two governments acknowledged 'the right of all peoples to choose the form of government under which they will live'.[37] (Churchill and his Cabinet took the view that this did not apply to the British Empire.)[38] Yet the president's own officials had recently assured Vichy that 'the United States had no other interest in the French Empire territories than their preservation for the French people'.[39] The pledge to maintain the integrity of the French Empire was made to de Gaulle's National Committee in London too.[40] In other words, it seemed to be *British* imperialism that the Americans found particularly problematic. As criticism of Britain heated up in the autumn of 1942, much stimulated by the violent suppression of the 'Quit India' movement, the influential American journalist Dorothy Thompson observed: 'I have not seen in a single paper any attack on the Dutch Empire or on the French Empire, all of which we claim we intend to recover. It is only our fighting British allies whose Empire we attack, and to make it laughable, Martinique radio, part of Vichy's Empire, is now attacking the British with quotations from our own press.'[41]

Soon after Thompson made her comments, Wendell Willkie (the defeated Republican candidate in 1940), called for the 'orderly' abolition of colonialism.[42] In a well-known speech at the Mansion House, delivered shortly after the famous British victory at El Alamein, Churchill offered what was surely intended as a riposte to this demand. 'We mean to hold our own', he said. 'I have not become the King's First minister in order to preside over the liquidation of the British Empire.' It is striking, however, that these words came after a section in which the prime minister praised both de Gaulle and Henri Giraud (the latter another, more senior general who was now a rival for the leadership of the Free French), and offered words of reassurance as to Britain's geopolitical intentions:

> For ourselves we have no wish but to see France free and strong, with her Empire gathered round her and with Alsace-Lorraine restored. We covet no French possession; we have no acquisitive appetites or ambitions in North Africa or any other part of the world. We have not entered this war for profit or expansion, but only for honour and to do our duty in defending the right.[43]

---

[36] Foster Rhea Dulles and Gerald E. Ridinger, 'The Anti-Colonial Policies of Franklin D. Roosevelt', *Political Science Quarterly*, 70:1 (1955), 1–18; Andrew Preston, 'Franklin D. Roosevelt and America's Empire of Anti-Imperialism', in Martin Thomas and Richard Toye (eds), *Rhetorics of Empire*: Languages of Colonial Conflict Since 1900 (Manchester: Manchester University Press, forthcoming).

[37] The text of the Atlantic Charter is reprinted in 'Declaration by United Nations', Cmd. 6388, London, 1942.

[38] Richard Toye, *Churchill's Empire: The World That Made Him and the World He Made* (London: Macmillan, 2010), 214.

[39] 'Final US Warning to Vichy', *The Times*, 6 June 1941.

[40] See memorandum by Samuel Reber, 12 January 1942, United States Department of State, *Foreign Relations of the United States: Diplomatic Papers, 1942, Vol. II: Europe* (Washington, DC: US Government Printing Office, 1962), 502–3.

[41] 'Britain and India', *Manchester Guardian*, 12 October 1942.

[42] 'Commonwealth of the World', *The Times*, 28 October 1942.

[43] Speech of 10 November 1942.

Thus Churchill hit back at the American critics of empire (and British ones too) while soothing the French at the same time. However, his language and emphasis—especially his insistence on using the term 'empire', with its connotations of exploitation, rather than 'Commonwealth', which had overtones of partnership—were at odds with the official British propaganda line.[44]

Ironically, the US government in the end gave more specific guarantees than the British did about the territorial integrity of the French Empire. This was the case even though Roosevelt opposed the restoration of French sovereignty in Indochina (which faced greater Japanese encroachment from 1941).[45] The situation suited Churchill, who made clear to Lord Halifax, Britain's Washington ambassador:

> I do not at all mind the various statements that have been made by the President and others near him about restoring the French Empire and territory, because it is very difficult to see how this line can be taken by the State Department about France and at the same time a policy of liquidating the British Empire pursued. You should not therefore labour to get these assurances to France withdrawn.[46]

The Roosevelt administration's subtle distinctions between British and French imperialism were cold comfort to the Free French envoys in Washington working to secure a seat at the Allies' top table. Typical in this regard was Maurice Dejean, a longstanding member of the Free French mission in the US capital. In February 1942, frustrated by the State Department's continuing indulgence towards Vichy, Dejean made the case for Gaullism by using the rhetorical device of contrasting alternatives. American policy, timid and contingent as it was, was unbefitting a great nation: Washington tolerated Vichy lest Pétain and his associates make this or that concession to the Axis Powers. British support for Free France was, by contrast, striking in its boldness and far-sighted in its recognition that partnership between the Western democracies was the only solid foundation for a just and peaceful world.[47] Underpinning Dejean's annoyance was a deeper truth: the Roosevelt administration simply did not attach the high priority to French affairs that de Gaulle and others presumed it should.

This observation was confirmed by a study of hostile foreign propaganda in French North Africa produced on 1 June 1942 by Vichy's political intelligence unit, General Henri Roux's Governmental Information Centre. Roux's assessment ranked American propaganda of least importance, noting how little was produced. Even British governmental criticism seemed stuck in a rhetorical rut, harping on about Vichy's powerlessness and worsening local economic conditions without explaining how support for a Gaullist alternative would improve matters. The Free French themselves had said virtually nothing of relevance to North Africa's

---

[44] See, for example, 'Answering You No. 81 (Two-Way Series No. 20)', BBC North American Service broadcast, 7 February 1943, transcript in Perham Papers, 346/7.

[45] TNA, CAB 66/53/44, WP 44(444), Anthony Eden, 'Indo-China', 13 August 1944; Eric Jennings, *Vichy in the Tropics: Pétain's National Revolution in Madagascar, Guadeloupe, and Indochina, 1940–1944* (Stanford, CA: Stanford University Press, 2001), 140–1.

[46] Churchill Papers, CHAR 20/106/47, Churchill to Halifax, 10 February 1943.

[47] TNA, FO 892/197, Dejean memo., 'Washington et Vichy', 4 February 1942.

Muslim majority, confining their appeals to the European administrative elite. Far more damaging were the activities of German propagandists, whether attached to the Armistice Commission in Morocco or providing broadcast time to various Maghreb nationalists and Islamist groups on Radio Berlin and the French-language Nazi radio station *Paris Mondial*.[48]

Roux's observations about Free France's inability to connect with North Africans resonated more strongly still in Indochina. Admiral Jean Decoux's Hanoi government perhaps went furthest in implementing the racist authoritarianism of Vichy's national revolution despite working under the shadow of a likely Japanese takeover. This eventually came in March 1945.[49] For all that, as the Free French Information Commissariat conceded in August 1942, Indochina presented the hardest rhetorical challenge to Gaullist propagandists. The basic problem was credibility. Gaullist radio broadcasts from Hong Kong, Singapore, and Manila were all casualties of Japan's southward advance through Asia.[50] But what could they have said anyway? As Roosevelt was apt to point out, French colonial rule seemed administratively hollow and morally bankrupt in the face of rampant inflation, chronic foodstuff shortages, and, later, devastating famine.[51] Yet Free France—or any kind of France for that matter—could never 'liberate' Vietnam, Cambodia, or Laos without American, British, or Chinese support.[52] The only serious 'resistance' to Japanese incursion and Vichy racism came from the Communist-led Vietminh coalition, the sole movement backed by America's Office of Strategic Services. De Gaulle's supporters would remain conspicuously silent about French Indochina until the prospect of Allied intervention became real in the war's final months.[53] Even then, de Gaulle's provisional government said nothing about incoming reports of famine in Northern Vietnam but chose instead to respond to a statement from the Tokyo authorities on 25 August 1944, declaring Indochina 'an autonomous province of the Japanese Empire'.[54]

Evidence of Free French irrelevance to the concerns of North Africans and Vietnamese was well understood in Washington, where it was increasingly clear

---

[48] SHD-DAT, 1P45, CIG, General Roux memo., 'Étude sur les propagandes étrangères en Afrique du Nord', 1 June 1942.

[49] Jennings, *Vichy in the Tropics*, 142–61, 188–98; Pierre Brocheux and Daniel Hémery, *Indochina: An Ambiguous Colonization, 1858–1954* (Berkeley, CA: University of California Press, 2009), 340–9, MAE, Guerre 1939–45, CNF, vol. 73, Bulletin de renseignements 64, Text of Decoux speech to Hanoi government council, 16 December 1942.

[50] MAE, Guerre 1939–45, CNF, vol. 70, Commissariat National à l'Information, 'Propagande sur l'Indochine', 8 August 1942.

[51] Britain, too, oversaw appalling wartime famine conditions in its Asian Empire, see: Sugata Bose, 'Starvation Amidst Plenty: The Making of Famine in Bengal, Honan and Tonkin, 1942–45', *Modern Asian Studies*, 24:4 (1990), 699–727.

[52] MAE, Guerre 1939–45, CNF, vol. 73, no. 327, 'A/S de l'Indochine et les opérations futurs dans le Pacifique', 2 March 1943.

[53] Martin Thomas, 'Free France, the British Government, and the Future of French Indo-China, 1940–45', *Journal of Southeast Asian Studies*, 28:1 (1997), 137–60; for Vietnamese and international perspectives, see Stein Tønnesson, *The Vietnamese Revolution of 1945: Roosevelt, Ho Chi Minh and de Gaulle in a World at War* (Oslo: PRIO, 1991).

[54] MAE, Guerre 1939–45, Vichy, Série E: Vichy Asie, vol. 255, Vichy/Libre, 'Une déclaration du GPRF à propos de l'Indochine', 30 August 1944.

by late 1942 that American, not French, military actions were more likely to determine the fate of these peoples in the immediate future. Only in late September 1942, as part of their joint planning for American-led landings in North Africa in November—code-named TORCH—did Britain's Political Warfare Executive (PWE) persuade the US State Department and Office of Strategic Services to devise a combined psychological warfare scheme for France and its North African territories. Starting from the proposition that psychological warfare was 'a planned process of influencing the will and so directing the actions of peoples in enemy-occupied territories', in rhetorical terms the resultant programme approached metropolitan France and its dependent territories quite differently. The PWE French Section attached foremost importance to proving that a change of regime in French North Africa would become the 'standard bearer' of France's re-entry to the war. This alone might persuade what remained of the French Mediterranean fleet in port at Toulon to come over to the Allied side.[55] Determined to prove to the French that the Allies had no designs on France's imperial assets, emphasis was laid on the Maghreb's pivotal role as a staging post for the liberation of France. As for other colonial administrations, Vichy West Africa uppermost, 'the main objective is to persuade French possessions that both their duty and their self-interest demand that they should cast in their lot with the Allies'.[56]

Unusually—indeed, uniquely—the PWE also suggested that the Free French might be publicly endorsed as a worthy government-in-waiting for liberated North Africa. But who might head such an administration? According to the PWE French Section, British propaganda, couched in suitably stirring rhetoric, might serve to kill two birds with one stone—facilitating a Free French takeover but ensuring that General Henri Giraud, a higher-ranking officer than de Gaulle, headed it:

> General de Gaulle should get due credit for having been the first in his refusal to accept defeat. On the other hand, he should be invited to implement his repeated pledge that he would be willing to place himself at the service of any senior officer untainted by the Bordeaux-Vichy plot. General Giraud, if he could be secured, would fit this role perfectly. Any refusal by General de Gaulle in such circumstances will necessarily put him in an impossible position, not only before French public opinion, but before the rest of his supporters.[57]

THE NORTH AFRICAN LANDINGS AND FRENCH LEADERSHIP STRUGGLES

As the PWE analysis predicted, Operation TORCH forced the underlying problems in the triangular British-French-American relationship to the surface. As was often the case, empire provided the territory, but not the agenda, for

[55] TNA, FO 898/132, Colonel Sutton, PWE French Section, memo., 30 September 1942.
[56] TNA, FO 898/129, 'Joint American-British Plan of Psychological Warfare Plan for France and French Empire', 23 September 1942.
[57] TNA, FO 898/132, Colonel Sutton, PWE French Section, memo., 30 September 1942.

debate.[58] To put it another way, arguments about events that clearly concerned the future French Empire were conducted without much talk about empire and imperialism per se.

With the Americans directing the North African landings, it was little wonder that de Gaulle's supporters, entirely excluded from TORCH planning, got no mention in the ceasefire accords that General Dwight Eisenhower's force commanders reached with Admiral Darlan. Ironic as it was that America's first decisive contribution to the war in the Mediterranean should keep in office a collaborator who had stepped into Weygand's shoes as civil-military overseer of French North Africa, rhetorically the deeper significance of the ceasefire accords lay elsewhere. Missing from their clauses was even a cursory nod to local opinion or the form of colonial government expected to replace Vichy rule after Allied liberation. Leaving Darlan in office left North Africa's 'liberation' looking hollow at best. (Fig. 6.1).[59]

Even so, the Vichy governmental reaction to the TORCH landings expressed mock outrage over this latest Allied 'betrayal'. If the indignation was contrived, the sense of betrayal was not. On 9 November, Pétain replied to Roosevelt's official confirmation that American forces had landed in North Africa with palpable disbelief. Dismissing American claims that French North Africa was slipping into Axis control, Pétain chided the president: 'You invoke pretexts which nothing justifies. You attribute to your enemies intentions which have not even been manifested in acts.'[60] Real or not, the annoyance of the Vichy authorities was at least logically predictable. Five months earlier, loyal Pétainists in unoccupied France staged vociferous, sometimes violently Anglophobic demonstrations in response to news of a similar takeover of Vichy-controlled colonial territory—Madagascar.[61]

Few Vichy supporters expected any better of the British, but there was genuine shock at the American decision to seize the North African heart of France's empire. With a complete Axis occupation looming and the Vichy regime commensurately reduced to vassal status, official protests from within mainland France cut little ice in Washington or London. Gaullist reactions—and their rhetorical expression—were more problematic insofar as they demanded some form of inter-Allied response. Darlan's ceasefire orders, issued from Algiers 'in the name of the Marshal' on 10 November, stressed that all Vichy commanders and colonial officials in North Africa would retain their posts.[62] The admiral was later confirmed as Pétain's designated successor by the North African administration's Imperial Council, which accepted

---

[58] Thomas, 'France and its Colonial Civil Wars', 582.
[59] TNA, FO 898/129, 'Amendments to Psychological Warfare Plan for France and French Empire', 2 October 1942; draft outline plan, 14 October 1942.
[60] TNA, FO 898/132, Washington tel. 5511, 9 November 1942.
[61] SHM, Guerre 1939–45, box TTA3, no. 100/CAB, Maritime Prefect report on disturbances in Toulon, 13 May 1942.
[62] SHD-DAT, 5P49/D1, copy tel. Darlan to Generals Juin, Noguès and Barré, 10 November 1942. US forces briefly took Darlan into 'protective custody' before releasing him, despite the Admiral's refusal of General Mark Clark's request that he meet Giraud face to face. See: TNA, WO 193/842, Eisenhower tel. to Combined Chiefs of Staff, 10 November 1942; Gibraltar Command to ABFOR, 11 November 1942.

THE MANCHESTER GUARDIAN, WEDNESDAY, DECEMBER 9, 1942

"NOW MAKE HIM DISAPPEAR"
(By arrangement with the "Evening Standard.")

Fig. 6.1. 'Now make him disappear', a cartoon by David Low, first published in *The Evening Standard* on 8 December 1942 depicting Foreign Secretary Eden and Secretary of State Cordell Hull elevating Darlan as 'chief of the French' to ironic calls from roving US Republican statesman, Wendell Willkie, seated alongside de Gaulle and Soviet Ambassador Ivan Maisky.

Mary Evans Picture Library, image 10914048

Darlan's argument that the German occupation of Vichy France on 11 November legitimized the admiral's assumption of full powers on Pétain's behalf.[63] As Free French supporters (and British newspapers) were soon complaining, Darlan's continued presence cast doubt on what exactly TORCH had accomplished.[64]

Churchill, caught between the pragmatism of the Americans and the fulminations of the Free French, vented his feelings about de Gaulle in a secret House of Commons session. He disabused MPs, concerned about the Darlan affair, of the idea that de Gaulle was a good friend of Britain. De Gaulle, the prime minister

[63] TNA, ADM 199/843, tel. 1208, Eisenhower to Combined Chiefs of Staff, 4 December 1942.
[64] TNA, ADM 199/180, FO to Lord Halifax (Washington), 6 January 1943.

insisted, was an Anglophobe, and he reminded MPs of an August 1941 *Chicago Daily News* interview 'in wh[ich] he suggested that Britain coveted the African colonies of France'.[65] Churchill also blocked de Gaulle from making a broadcast, to which Eden (now foreign secretary) had previously agreed.[66] In the event, the mutual recriminations were cut short when a young Gaullist resister gunned Darlan down in Algiers on Christmas Eve 1942. Partly, it appears, to avoid embarrassing questions about British and Gaullist secret service involvement in the killing, the eighteen-year-old assassin was hastily executed days later.

In the weeks before Darlan's death, the London Gaullists' anger at being shut out from TORCH crystallized, not around the ill-fated admiral, but on the figure of Henri Giraud. The French general had escaped from detention in Germany earlier in 1942. His lengthy incarceration ensured that he was untainted by Vichy, easing his path to adoption by Eisenhower's military administration in North Africa as putative head of a unified overseas French resistance movement: Fighting France. News of Eisenhower's declaration of support for Giraud on 10 November 1942, galvanized de Gaulle's supporters in London and Washington. Adrien Tixier and André Philip, pre-war Socialists who headed the Free French diplomatic mission in Washington, rushed out a press statement underlining 'the absolute necessity' for the Allied Powers to respect 'the unity of French resistance', meaning, in practice, a resistance led by de Gaulle.[67] It was to no avail. The following day American public radio and the East Coast press repeated almost verbatim information supplied by Washington extolling Giraud's war record, his North African expertise, and his unique ability to unite the people of France and its empire.[68]

The American propaganda wave surging behind Giraud stirred the Free French foreign affairs commission in London into action. In his investiture speech as French commander-in-chief in North Africa, Giraud stated that the primary responsibility of all French military personnel was to chase Axis forces from the Maghreb as the prelude to liberating France.[69] Free French circulars appeared forty-eight hours later, commenting on Giraud's manifest failure to 'rally' anyone, French or otherwise, in Algeria.[70] Much was made five days later of a letter of support, purportedly written by Giraud to Pétain following the general's escape from prison in May 1942.[71] Messages from various internal resistance movements in France endorsing de Gaulle were republished meanwhile, amplifying the contrast

[65] Churchill Papers CHAR 9/187B/193, notes for speech of 10 December 1942. The passage was excised when Churchill's secret session speeches were published after the war, and was at last published in Kersaudy, *Churchill and De Gaulle*, 227–8. For further details, see Richard Toye, *The Roar of the Lion: The Untold Story of Churchill's World War II Speeches* (Oxford: Oxford University Press, 2013), 154–6.

[66] Elisabeth Barker, *Churchill and Eden at War* (Basingstoke: Macmillan, 1978), 65–6.

[67] MAE, Guerre 1939–45, CNF Londres, vol. 130, tel. 965, Tixier to de Gaulle, 10 November 1942.

[68] MAE, Guerre 1939–45, CNF Londres, vol. 130, tel. 925, Tixier to de Gaulle, 11 November 1943.

[69] SHD-DAT, 5P49/D1, 'Opérations en Front Tunisien—journal de marche, 1942–43'.

[70] MAE, Guerre 1939–45, CNF Londres, vol. 130, Diplo/12 1471, Affaires étrangères circular, 12 November 1942.

[71] MAE, Guerre 1939–45, CNF Londres, vol. 130, no. 12439b, Affaires étrangères to overseas governors, 17 November 1942.

between the two generals' respective capacities as leaders. Among these were three 1942 editorials in the newspaper *Libération*, two issues of the monthly journal *Combat* from March and August calling on its readers to get behind de Gaulle, and even two further commentaries in the Communist resistance organ *Franc Tireur* appealing for unity of command.[72]

Perhaps inevitably, when, on 17 December 1942, de Gaulle at last secured a meeting with a senior official in Roosevelt's administration—Admiral Harold Stark, the commander of US naval forces in Europe—he grasped the opportunity to lecture the American, and through him the Washington government, on their errors in dealing separately with various French authorities in mainland France and francophone Africa.[73] 'All French, whether in France or in the colonies,' de Gaulle insisted, 'look to some central symbolic authority.' So there was but one political and moral choice to be made: between either him or Pétain. Giraud's failure to win any support in North Africa proved the point—de Gaulle's so-called rival for power was, in fact, 'nothing'. The Americans had mistakenly presumed that France, as a former Republic with numerous subordinate colonial administrations, shared the United States' approach to the diffusion of power between federal and state governments. This could not be further from the truth. Imperial France might be comprised of numerous colonies but all were singly responsible to one centralized authority. The essential question was whether that central power should be Vichy or Free France, to which, of course, there could be only one answer.[74] It was a remarkable rhetorical performance, dismissing Vichy, Giraud, and Rooseveltian foreign policy without pausing for breath. Needless to say, de Gaulle's remarks did not go down well with Stark's superiors, especially as they came accompanied with a request for face-to-face talks at the White House.

Events in mainland France lent weight to de Gaulle's claims to unique political legitimacy, however. As already mentioned, on 11 November 1942 German forces had occupied the whole of metropolitan France, violating the armistice. With the remnants of Vichy sovereignty gone and Darlan out of the picture, the Gaullists' prior decision to focus their rhetorical attacks on Giraud made increasing sense. His plea for an invitation to Washington still unanswered, in a New Year statement released by the Free French press service on 2 January 1943, de Gaulle lamented the worsening political confusion in Algiers and Dakar in the wake of the TORCH landings and Darlan's assassination. The cause of this mess in the administrative hubs of French North and West Africa, he said, was as simple as the remedy was obvious. With France now wholly occupied, Vichy's claim to imperial authority lacked credibility or purpose. 'The great force of [French] national fervour' lay elsewhere: with Fighting France, an authority already waging war alongside the Allies and the sole legitimate ruler of the French Empire.[75] Fighting France, the

---

[72] MAE, Guerre 1939–45, CNF Londres, vol. 130, Resistance press reprint extracts, 18 November 1942.

[73] MAE, Guerre 1939–45, CNF Londres, vol. 130, record of Admiral Stark's conversation with de Gaulle, 17 November 1942.

[74] Ibid.

[75] TNA, FO 892/174, French press service communiqué no. 34, 2 January 1943.

new designation for Free France devised to accommodate Giraud's supporters, also conveyed an implicit rhetorical message: the Gaullist movement could contribute more to the Allied war effort from a secure political base in North Africa.

The American government had little option in these changed circumstances but to concede de Gaulle a role in the post-TORCH summitry. At the Casablanca Conference of early 1943, Roosevelt and Churchill successfully pressured de Gaulle and Giraud to work together. Once Giraud took over as high commissioner in North Africa following Darlan's killing, de Gaulle lent his public support to an 'enlarged provisional authority' in Algiers—meaning, of course, a *de facto* government including Free French representation. Giraud was 'saluted' but not explicitly endorsed as its leader.[76] Giraud, for his part, stressed his credentials as a compromise candidate, someone uniquely capable of reconciling Free French supporters with the thousands of former Vichy administrators and military personnel in North and West Africa.[77] This de Gaulle could never hope to do.

Still closely advised by d'Argenlieu, de Gaulle remained guarded at Casablanca. His joint pronouncements with Giraud were confined to military accords promoting a common war effort prosecuted by Gaullist black Africa and Giraudist North Africa.[78] Politically astute, and more strongly backed by resistance movements in France and its empire, de Gaulle held the upper hand. Over the six months from January to June 1943 he marginalized his ineffectual competitor.[79] Much of this was accomplished through words rather than deeds.

The Gaullists' relentless rhetorical assault on Giraud's capabilities did nothing to endear Fighting France to its Casablanca partners. Days after the conference concluded, de Gaulle told a meeting of 200 Free French military personnel at Queensbury Place in London that the ceasefire agreement concluded with Darlan's Algiers administration after the TORCH landings was crassly irresponsible. The allies' willingness to deal with discredited collaborators was 'liable to provoke civil war in France'.[80] So irritated was the Foreign Office with Free French complaints of insufficient Anglo-American support for de Gaulle that, a few days after the general's inflammatory remarks at Queensbury Place, plans were made to stifle the Gaullists' London newspaper *La Marseillaise* by withholding the necessary supplies of paper to print it.[81] As for the Americans, it was left to Eisenhower as supreme Allied commander in North Africa to vent Washington's frustration. Angry that the Gaullist-Giraudist contest rumbled on despite the formation of a supposedly unified FCNL on 3 June 1943, Eisenhower issued a remarkably pointed rebuke via the Associated Press three weeks later. With major Allied

[76] MAE, Guerre 1939–45, Comité National Francais (CNF) Londres, vol. 133, Anglo-Foreign Information Bureau, 'The Whitehall Letter', 1 January 1943.

[77] MAE, Guerre 1939–45, CNF, vol. 133, Guy Ramsey interview, 'Giraud Explains Why He Has Not Cleared Out Vichy Men', *News Chronicle*, 1 February 1943.

[78] MAE, Guerre 1939–45, CNF, vol. 132, tel. 665, CNF press release, 27 January 1943.

[79] MAE, Guerre 1939–45, CNF, vol. 133, CNF Affaires Politiques, 'Note sur le mouvement Giraudiste', no date, 1943.

[80] MAE, PAAP288/Papiers Maurice Dejean, vol. 25, 'Réunion du 3 Février 1943'.

[81] TNA, FO 898/210, PWE note, 13 February 1943.

operations looming (the impending invasion of Italy could not, for security reasons, be mentioned explicitly), the US commander had secured Washington's authorization to take 'whatever steps he may find necessary to eliminate any threat to success' created by the political controversy between the warring French generals. French politicking would no longer be tolerated, although quite what this threat amounted to was left unspecified.[82]

Roosevelt meanwhile kept above the fray. Only when Martinique, Vichy's last outpost in the Americas finally came over to the Allies in July 1943, did the president reflect at length on US policy towards the competing French authorities. During a White House press conference on 16 July, Roosevelt conceded a little disingenuously that America's refusal to involve itself in the political rivalries of competing groups had provoked 'all kinds of curious propaganda' directed against the State Department in particular. In fact, the president recollected, 'The US Government had had a consistent policy since the fall of France, that policy being the preservation of the French fleet and the prevention of French naval and air bases from falling into Axis hands.' Military strategy, in other words, trumped political machination. As far as politics was concerned, 'The US had been working in close co-operation with all Frenchmen everywhere who were patriotically resisting the Axis Powers and it had been working to encourage the people of France to keep thoroughly alive to the principles of liberty and freedom. So far it had worked pretty well.'[83] Disingenuous indeed: but also a neat rhetorical means to praise Gaullist and other French resistance without endorsing the Free French or de Gaulle explicitly.

DISCORDANT ALLIES

As the Americans and Free French edged towards a loveless marriage of convenience during 1943, in the Levant states the political temperature rose dangerously high. An array of women's groups in both Syria and Lebanon, for instance, turned the Free French rhetoric of citizens' rights to resist unjust government against the Gaullist administration, demanding enfranchisement and improved economic and social rights for working women and mothers.[84] In two late February radio broadcasts one week apart, Catroux promised the restoration of constitutional government, first in Lebanon and then in Syria. Pressed hard by the Spears mission to do so, Catroux effectively pledged an accelerated transition to self-rule in the two French mandates. Any beneficial effects in both countries were soon undone. For one thing the Lebanese government refused to cooperate in this new transitory scheme. For another thing, the force of civil unrest was getting stronger. Seven died

[82] MAE, Guerre 1939–45, CNF Londres, vol. 132, Reuters press release issued in New York, 28 June 1943.
[83] TNA, CAB 122/216, tel. 3269, Lord Halifax (Washington) to FO, 16 July 1943.
[84] Elizabeth Thompson, 'Gender, War, and the Birth of States: Syrian and Lebanese Women's Mobilization during World War II', in Nicole Ann Dombrowski (ed.), *Women and War in the Twentieth Century* (New York: Routledge, 2004), 271–84.

during food riots in Damascus in protest at harsher rationing restrictions introduced days before Catroux's announcement.[85]

Much as in 1941, competition in the Middle East remained the most combustible ingredient in Anglo-French imperial relations. It also generated commensurately inflammatory rhetoric from both sides. Underlying everything was the obvious Free French foot-dragging over the commitments made to Syrian and Lebanese independence two years earlier. Few were surprised when a Lebanese parliament was elected and a government returned that was unequivocally hostile to Catroux's administration. The Gaullists, in turn, suspected Spears and the British of stirring up popular feeling against them. When the parliament moved to abrogate France's mandate and declare complete independence, the French reacted by arresting both the prime minister and the president. More repression ensued after demonstrators took to the streets of Beirut.[86] Eventually, at the insistence of the British, the imprisoned leaders were released, a climb-down that only underlined the bankruptcy of Free French rule in the Levant states.

Harold Macmillan, the British minister-resident in the Middle East, acknowledged privately that both the British and the French handled the situation badly. 'Spears wants a Fashoda; and I do not', he told his diary.[87] A cartoon by David Low in the *Evening Standard* portrayed Macmillan searching for agreement on the common ground of 'Present necessity' between the extremes of the 'French Mandate Attitude' and the 'Lebanese Independence Attitude'.[88] Another, by Leslie Illingworth in the *Daily Mail*, showed the prostrated figure of Lebanon being stabbed through the heart with a French flag marked 'Liberté, Egalité, Fraternité'.[89] Churchill—with *chutzpah* to rival that of the *Mail*—told Roosevelt that France's behaviour was 'entirely contrary to the Atlantic Charter'.[90] In the Commons, the left-wing Labour MP Aneurin Bevan asked pointedly: 'Is it intended that we should extend our enthusiasm for self-government to the British Empire, or will it be only at the expense of the French Empire?'[91]

At the end of 1944, Churchill did at last sack his old friend Spears, although he was later forced to deny in public that Spears was recalled to please de Gaulle.[92] The Free French, meanwhile, were increasingly preoccupied by the consolidation of their imperial control, both in the war's final stages and on into the peace. The resulting shift in the rhetorical emphasis of Gaullist pronouncements neither revealed much confidence nor inspired it. As Martin Shipway has shown, Gaullist preparations for a January 1944 conference at Brazzaville, trumpeted as a forum for the planning of post-war colonial reforms in French black Africa, actually laid bare the innate

---

[85] TNA, FO 600/35, Spears tells. to FO, 19 and 20 March 1943; E2151/27/89, Spears letter to Eden, 1 April 1943.

[86] Jean Lacouture, *De Gaulle: The Rebel, 1890–1944* (London: Collins Harvill, 1990), 496.

[87] Harold Macmillan, *War Diaries: The Mediterranean 1943–1945* (London: Papermac, 1985), 297 (entry for 19 November 1943).

[88] *Evening Standard*, 15 November 1943.   [89] *Daily Mail*, 17 November 1943.

[90] Churchill to Roosevelt, 13 November 1943, in Warren F. Kimball (ed.), *Churchill and Roosevelt: The Complete Correspondence II: Alliance Forged, November 1942–February 1944* (Princeton, NJ: University Press, 1984), 599.

[91] HC Deb, 23 November 1943, vol. 393, cols 1451–2.   [92] Speech of 5 June 1945.

conservatism of the politicians and imperial administrators involved.[93] The FCNL, in its contribution to the process, devoted greater energy to the resurrection of imperial protectionism and the political dangers of any empire-wide extension of citizenship status than it did to plans for reform, rhetorical or otherwise.[94] The provisional government's 'essential task', the committee advised de Gaulle, would be to match any programme of reforms to the modest means available to achieve them in black Africa. Anything more ambitious was bound to fail, drawing accusations that France's loyal colonial subjects had been deliberately deceived. Far better to focus on pragmatic measures to improve the quality of life for French Africans in the short term than to make impossible promises for the long term.[95]

For all the talk at Brazzaville and elsewhere of an empire reunited after France's liberation, during the war's final months concerns grew within the provisional government that its imperial rhetoric had made no impression on North African opinion. Restored to Gaullist control, the Moroccan residency, for instance, found its November 1944 announcement of welfare reforms and an extended Muslim franchise dismissed outright by the country's leading nationalist movement, the Istiqlal, as nothing but *belles phrases*.[96] Residency officials in Rabat suggested that Morocco's nationalists were transfixed by the quicker pace of change within the British and American empires. British talk of a transition from empire to Commonwealth, its apparent support for Libyan trusteeship, plus Foreign Office willingness to deal with the Arab League in Cairo, left French reformist rhetoric seeming unambitious and tired. The Americans, meanwhile, had already promised independence to the Philippines while, closer to home, their network of consuls across Morocco were encouraging Sultan Mohammed V to press Morocco's claims to self-rule.[97]

French suspicions were soon realized. In March 1945 the Istiqlal seized on the opening of the inaugural United Nations conference in San Francisco to lobby for Morocco's independence, citing the continued political upheaval, not just in Morocco but also in Syria, Lebanon, and Vietnam as proof of the bankruptcy of French imperial oversight. The notion of imperial France as 'protector' of Moroccans (or as mandate holder in Syria and Lebanon for that matter) was a sick joke.[98] De Gaulle wasn't listening. So ingrained was his suspicion of British intentions in the Arab world by this point that the general even suggested that the May 1945 uprising in eastern Algeria, in many ways the precursor to Algeria's

[93] Paul Isoart, 'Les aspects politiques, constitutionnels et administratifs des recommandations', in Institut Charles de Gaulle, *Brazzaville, Janvier-Février 1944: Aux sources de la décolonisation* (Paris: Plon, 1988), 79–96.

[94] AN, F60/889, Dossier: Conférence de Brazzaville, January 1944: CFLN Secretariat, 'Note concernant la politique coloniale du Comité', 13 January 1944.

[95] AN, F60/889, Dossier: Conférence de Brazzaville, January 1944: CFLN Secretariat note for de Gaulle, 5 January 1944.

[96] AN, F60/837, Dossier: Maroc, no. 685, Résidence générale to Catroux, sends copy of Istiqlal memo., 'Au sujet des recentes réformes marocaines', 28 December 1944.

[97] AN, F60/835, Dossier: Activité politique étrangère en AFN, Colonel Materne report, 'Les propagandes Anglo-Saxonnes', 24 October 1944; tel. 1706, Chalres Mast (Tunis) to Georges Bidault, 13 November 1944.

[98] AN, F60/885, Dossier: Agitation nationaliste au Maroc, tel. 324, Gabriel Puaux to Georges Bidault, 22 March 1945.

subsequent war of independence, was actually a part of the same foul British plot to oust the French from Syria by mobilizing Arab support against them.[99]

Meanwhile in Tunisia, French North Africa's other protectorate administration acknowledged its error in locking up the nationalist leaders of Neo-Destour in late 1943, despite their bravery in opposing the preceding German occupation.[100] Such was the gravity of this error that it drove the perennially divided 'Old' and 'New' wings of the Destour movement to put aside their factionalism. In March 1945 the two groups merged into a united 'People's Party', itself a rhetorical tool that evoked their popular legitimacy in the face of government repression.[101] Another concern was that Free French pronouncements had long since been eclipsed by the virulent Islamist nationalism of the Arabic radio broadcasts organized by the Nazi government in Berlin. Variously targeted at audiences in French North Africa and, more particularly, at Maghreb prisoners of war housed in labour camps in France, these broadcasts were, to a degree, counteracted by Vichy's own Arabic-language radio service. But this, too, had served only to divide North African opinion further, undermining residual loyalty to France, at least according to the War Ministry's Muslim affairs service.[102]

Gabriel Puaux, a long-serving colonial administrator restored to the position of Morocco's resident-general, squarely addressed the problem, albeit not until the war was safely over. Speaking on 9 August 1945 before the provisional government's North Africa Committee, a standing advisory group whose proceedings were widely reported in the colonial press, Puaux conceded that neither constitutional reforms nor political concessions, no matter how well presented, were likely to register much impact with ordinary Moroccans. The real challenge was to raise living standards—and quickly, without undermining the protectorate's foundations in the process. Political rhetoric unmatched by tangible socio-economic change, in other words, was substantially pointless.[103]

By then the force of Puaux's argument had already been made clear in Syria. At the end of May 1945, British troops moved in to restore order in Damascus. This was in response to a French bombardment of the capital's central districts beginning on 29 May, which the garrison commander, General Oliva-Roget, justified as a punitive action against pro-independence demonstrations.[104] The death toll ran into hundreds, the callousness of the action attracting the United Nations' first ever official criticism of an act of colonial repression weeks after the General Assembly was established. Worse from de Gaulle's martial perspective, Oliva-Roget's troops were forcibly confined to barracks by the much larger British

---

[99] Jean-Pierre Peyroulou, 'La politique algérienne du Général de Gaulle (1943–1946)', in Maurice Vaïsse (ed.), *De Gaulle et l'Algérie, 1943–1969* (Paris: Armand Colin, 2012), 30.

[100] AN, F60/883, Exposé du Général Mast au Comité de l'Empire Francais, 20 June 1945.

[101] AN, F60/883, Service des affaires musulmanes resnseignement, 'Etat d'esprit des Tunisiens', no date, March 1945.

[102] AN, F60/837, Service des affaires musulmanes, bulletin de renseignements, 30 January 1945.

[103] AN, F60/885, Dossier: Agitation nationaliste au Maroc, Comité de l'Afrique du Nord, 'Exposé de Gabriel Puaux', 9 August 1945.

[104] SHD-DAT, 4H360/D1, Commandement Supérieur des Troupes du Levant, no. 1591/2S, 1 June 1945; Thomas, 'Divisive Decolonization', 81.

military garrison in Syria, the French authorities having failed to control urban protests that their original crackdown was designed to stifle.[105] Although this move was in fact unwelcome to Churchill, de Gaulle saw it in conspiratorial terms as a scheme humiliate France and to present Britain as the Arabs' protector.[106] In the Commons—in one of his final contributions before parliament dissolved for the forthcoming general election—Churchill emphasized:

> We have done our utmost to preserve calm, to prevent misunderstandings and to bring the two sides together. My promise to General de Gaulle to withdraw all our troops as soon as satisfactory arrangements were made which would prevent disorder in Syria and the Lebanon was a serious step in policy and ought completely to have removed from the French mind the idea that we wished to supplant them or steal their influence.[107]

No such luck. It so happened that Churchill had just been on the receiving end of some effusive praise from a broadcaster in Spain, which clearly would not have happened without the Franco regime's approval. This provided part of the context for a Radio France broadcast by Claude Henri Lecompte, who described the British actions as 'a surprise blow against French economic interests in the Middle East', specifically against the Office de Céréales Panifiables—the politics of grain supply being a matter of much controversy in Syria. Lecompte declared:

> We Frenchmen would like to conserve in a sort of inward pantheon made of gratitude and immortality the Churchill who is unique and, above all, integral; and not the Winston Churchill in whom the attack on the Cereales Panifiables Francaises of the Levant lives side by side with the Entente Cordiale, and who can reconcile the high-sounding anti-Hitlerite phrases of the Atlantic Charter with the applause of the hangmen of Spain.[108]

It would be easy to write off such outpourings as paranoia, and so in part they were. But reflection shows why Churchill's consistent assurances that Britain did not wish to steal France's territory or influence might not have seemed so reassuring after all. It was perfectly true that the British were not out to perform a land-grab in Lebanon and Syria; but in fact they were quite complacent about the decline of French imperial power. As they made clear, they were happy to allow France a special position in the Levant—on condition that the Syrian and Lebanese governments were prepared to grant this by treaty. Yet as the policymakers in Whitehall well knew, there was no real chance of this happening. For the British to wrap all this up in the language of the Atlantic Charter—which they were not willing to apply to their own colonies—might well have seemed somewhat nauseating. On this basis, it becomes easier to understand de Gaulle's frustration during the Syrian

[105] TNA, FO 371/45580, E5800/8/89, War Office, 'Historical record—Levant 29 May–11 June 1945'.
[106] Kersaudy, *Churchill and De Gaulle*, 402–9.
[107] Speech of 5 June 1945.
[108] Daily Report, Foreign Radio Broadcasts, 7 June 1945, Foreign Broadcast Information Service, FBIS-FRB-45-136.

crisis when he raged to the British Ambassador in Paris that 'he would not allow France to be put into the dock before the Anglo-Americans'.[109] Just a few months earlier, using very similar language, Churchill had himself protested to Stalin and Roosevelt about what he feared would be excessive interference in colonial matters by the UN: 'I will have no suggestion that the British Empire is to be put into the dock and examined by everybody to see whether it is up to their standard.'[110]

CONCLUSION

The rhetorical polemics over the Syrian crisis meant that Franco-British imperial relations ended the war at a political low-point unseen since the Chanak crisis. If the French had good reason to claim a victory of sorts in that earlier contest, it was difficult to see much cause for celebration in May 1945. Algeria was in revolt. Syria was in meltdown. Indochina remained in the hands of Japanese occupiers against whom the doggedness of Vietnamese resistance pointed to a still larger anti-colonial war to come. Bitter rivals, even enemies, in the Middle East, they may have been, but the fact remained that Britain and France were co-imperialists. They would face comparable crises of contested decolonization, many of which were foreshadowed in their earlier wartime clashes. The experience of global war, its obvious propagandist dimensions, and the unique dilemmas thrown up by France's defeat, lent even greater potency to political rhetoric, an essential tool in a conflict impelled as much by ideological causes as by geopolitics.

At the outset of the war, the French Empire appears to have been treated by the British as part of the natural order of things. There was no notable hostility in Britain to the French Empire, no great store of resentment of the kind that fed the myth of 'perfidious Albion'; there was, perhaps, an attitude of benign neglect that derived from the consciousness of Britain's relative imperial strength. Equally, after the fall of France, her empire's restoration seemed necessary in order 'to restore France itself to its former role in Europe, and to restore Europe to its place in a world of free and friendly peoples'.[111] Yet in spite of Churchill and Eden's 'rhetoric of reassurance', the limitations of the British commitment were palpable from 1940 onwards. If there was little criticism of French imperialism as such, there was a willingness to speak the language of self-determination (selectively) at France's expense. This may have indicated the dawning of a perception that old-style European imperialism was on the way out—without, of course, an attendant awareness of the likely implications this would have for Britain.

[109] John Julius Norwich (ed.), *The Duff Cooper Diaries, 1915–1951* (London: Weidenfeld and Nicolson, 2005), 369 (entry for 26 May 1945).
[110] James F. Byrnes, *Speaking Frankly* (New York: Harper & Brothers, 1947), x.
[111] 'French North Africa—I', *The Economist*, 21 November 1942.

7

Suez, 1956

The Anglo-French invasion of Egypt in 1956 was a conspiracy on a grand scale. Gamal Abdul Nasser's Egyptian government nationalized the Suez Canal in July, in the wake of the USA's announcement that she would not fund the proposed Aswan High Dam. Nasser's *demarche* prompted outrage from Britain and France, and military preparations followed; but there was no immediate action. Instead, there were months of effort to create an international climate of opinion against Egypt, with a view either to paving the way either for the use of force or to securing a 'compromise' solution that would leave Nasser humiliated and fatally weakened.[1] In October, British and French representatives made a secret agreement with the Israelis for the latter to invade Egypt. Britain and France would then intervene, ostensibly in an international police action to 'separate the combatants', but in reality to seize control of the canal.

Within days the plan was launched. A complex, multi-pronged assault, as indicated in Map 7.1, militarily the invasion was a success. Politically, it spelt disaster. In the face of global condemnation, Britain and France were forced to withdraw, making way for a UN force, and British Prime Minister Anthony Eden quickly resigned, nominally on the grounds of his genuine ill health. The condemnation operated transnationally thanks, in part, to the speed with which speeches and other statements were transmitted around the word and thanks also to the growing influence of fora such as the UN, the Non-Aligned Movement executive, multinational non-governmental organizations, and other anti-colonial pressure groups. Much of the British rhetoric on Suez plumbed the depths of deceit in an attempt to disguise the nature of the collusion with Israel; the French, being less embarrassed, were less hypocritical, although even they echoed some of the internationalist rhetoric on which their British allies put such emphasis.

[1] Jonathan Pearson, in his book *Sir Anthony Eden and the Suez Crisis: Reluctant Gamble* (Basingstoke: Palgrave, 2003), has offered a challenge to the idea that Eden was determined from July onwards to use force no matter what. It is certainly plausible to think that Eden would have preferred a peaceful solution, but for political reasons he could only have accepted an agreement of a type that would cause Nasser to lose face. In other words, Britain and France had to be seen as heading an effort by the international community to *impose its will* on Egypt, whether by force or otherwise. By the same token, Nasser was willing to compromise only insofar as his claim to have defied 'the imperialists' would not be prejudiced. In other words, both Eden's and Nasser's condition for making a deal was that it be politically unacceptable to the other side. For the domestic constraints and internal opponents that Nasser faced, see Barnaby Crowcroft, 'Egypt's Other Nationalists and the Suez Crisis of 1956', *Historical Journal*, 59:2 (2016), 253–85.

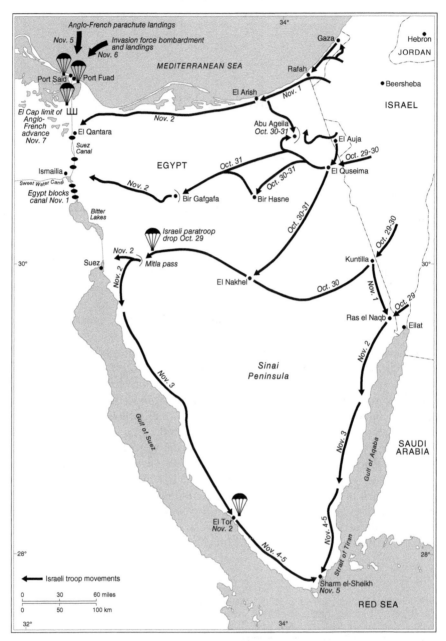

Anglo-French parachute landings
Nov. 5
Nov. 6 Invasion force bombardment and landings
MEDITERRANEAN SEA
Gaza
Hebron
JORDAN
Port Said •Port Fuad
Rafah
Nov. 1
El Arish
Beersheba
ISRAEL
El Cap limit of Anglo-French advance *Nov. 7*
Nov. 2
•El Qantara
Abu Ageila *Oct. 30-31*
El Auja
Oct. 29-30
Suez Canal
EGYPT
Oct. 31
Oct. 30-31
El Quseima
Ismailia•
Nov. 2
Sweet Water Canal
Bir Gafgafa
•Bir Hasne
Egypt blocks canal *Nov. 1*
Bitter Lakes
Oct. 30-31
Oct. 29-30
Israeli paratroop drop *Oct. 29*
Suez•
Nov. 2
Nov. 2 •Mitla pass
El Nakhel
Kuntilla•
-30°   30°-
Oct. 30
Ras el Naqb
•Eilat
Oct. 29
Nov. 1
Nov. 3
Sinai Peninsula
Nov. 2
SAUDI ARABIA
Gulf of Suez
Nov. 3
Gulf of Aqaba
Nov. 4-5
El Tor *Nov. 2*
Strait of Tiran
-28°   28°-
← Israeli troop movements
Nov. 4-5
Sharm el-Sheikh *Nov. 5*
RED SEA

0   30   60 miles
0   50   100 km
32°   34°

Map 7.1. The invasion of Egypt, 1956

Although there is a high level of awareness that lies were told, the historical literature has much less to say about the competing appeals that drove the Suez debate in both countries throughout the course of the crisis. Tony Shaw's work on British propaganda during Suez is invaluable, especially on efforts to appeal to American opinion.[2] What we lack, though, is analysis of the ways in which this last gasp of empire was justified (or indeed opposed) in imperial or post-imperial terms. What is striking is the way in which the latter-day imperialists couched their actions in internationalist rhetoric reminiscent of the Gladstone government's justifications for intervention in 1882, albeit reframed for a new world environment radically changed by the advent of the UN, the Cold War, the state of Israel, and Third World nationalism, as well as by Britain's weakened power status. These changed conditions helped ensure that Eden's use of use of liberal—or rather, conservative internationalist—language was driven not only by domestic considerations but also by the awareness that a more naked case based on national self-interest would have been politically impossible at the global level.[3] In terms of rhetoric, then, he was Gladstone's inheritor rather than Salisbury's, and this fact was accompanied by a capacity for righteous self-deception on his part equivalent to the Grand Old Man's most spectacular efforts.

Turning briefly to the French government's rhetorical inheritance, it is difficult to argue that members of the recently elected centre-left Republican Front coalition led by Socialist leader Guy Mollet considered themselves the republican scions of Léon Gambetta. Quite the contrary: where Gambetta had discovered a stronger interest in colonial affairs in recognition of their implications for wider international stability, the Republican Front eventually subordinated international considerations to staunchly nationalistic arguments about French interests in North Africa. Not only does this provide a nice counterpoint to the British case, it also confirms the extent to which French Socialists eventually spurned internationalism more generally under the stresses of France's contested decolonization.

BRITAIN

On 26 July, Nasser announced the nationalization of the canal in a lengthy speech at Alexandria, in which he excoriated both 'imperialism' and Israel, 'the stooge of imperialism'.[4] The crisis this action triggered had a complex background. Within Egypt, nationalist sentiment ran high, and there had been sporadic anti-British

[2] Tony Shaw, *Eden, Suez and the Mass Media: Propaganda and Persuasion during the Suez Crisis* (London: I.B. Tauris, 1996). On the media, see also Jeff Hulbert, 'Right-Wing Propaganda or Reporting History? The Newsreels and the Suez Crisis of 1956', *Film History*, 14:3/4, (2002), 261–81.

[3] For the origins of British conservative internationalism, see George Egerton, 'Conservative Internationalism: British Approaches to International Organization and the Creation of the League of Nations', *Diplomacy & Statecraft*, 5:1 (1994), 1–20.

[4] Nasser's speech of 26 July 1956, in 'Summary of World Broadcasts Part IV: The Arab World, Israel, Greece, Turkey, Persia', 28 July 1956. These summaries can be found at the BBC Written Archives Centre, Caversham. We consulted copies at the Arab World Documentation Unit, University of Exeter.

violence in Ismailia and other canal-zone cities in the early 1950s. Prior to this, British and American attempts to court Nasser with promises of aid in exchange for an Arab-Israeli settlement failed, and in addition there were fears that he was turning towards the Soviet bloc. Britain's weakening position in the Middle East as a whole, symbolized by the dismissal of General John Glubb from command of Jordan's Arab Legion in March 1956, must also be taken into account. So must Eden's political problems at home, both in the form of the implacably imperialist Suez Group of Tory MPs and of a more general sense of political drift.[5] To the disgust of the Suez Group, the 1954 Anglo-Egyptian agreement (negotiated by Eden as foreign secretary) culminated in the withdrawal of British troops from the canal zone just a few weeks before Nasser's nationalization speech.

The British government was caught between the need to take a firm line in order to retain its credibility and the risk that doing so would discredit it as 'imperialist' in the eyes of, in particular, American opinion. The Cabinet's discussion the day after the nationalization announcement both prefigured the line the government would take consistently in public and laid bare the inherent tensions within its position:

> The Cabinet agreed that we should be on weak ground in basing our resistance on the narrow argument that Colonel Nasser had acted illegally. The Suez Canal Company was registered as an Egyptian company under Egyptian law; and Colonel Nasser had indicated he intended to compensate the shareholders at ruling market prices. From a narrow legal point of view, his action amounted to no more than a decision to buy out the shareholders. Our case must be presented on wider international grounds. Our argument must be that the Canal was an important international asset and facility, and that Egypt could not be allowed to exploit it for a purely internal purpose. [...] The Canal was a vital link between the East and the West and its importance as an international waterway, recognised in the Convention signed in 1888, had increased with the development of the oil industry and the dependence of the world on oil supplies. It was not a piece of Egyptian property but an international asset of the highest importance and it should be managed as an international trust.[6]

The acknowledgement that the legal case against nationalization was weak segued seamlessly into the claim that the canal was an international asset over which Egypt could not rightfully take control. But this claim was one that could itself only be plausibly justified with reference to arguments based to a substantial extent on law. The seeming move away from 'legal quibbles' actually led directly back to the 1888 convention and thus to an argument based on highly contestable legal assumptions.[7] Whereas Britain might have had an arguable case had she chosen to take it to the International Court of Justice, this did not mean that it was legal for her to use

---

[5] The literature on Suez and its origins is immense. Essential starting points are Keith Kyle, *Suez: Britain's End of Empire in the Middle East* (London: I.B. Tauris, 2011), and W. Scott Lucas, *Divided We Stand: Britain, the US and the Suez Crisis* (London: Hodder & Stoughton, 1991). For a comparison of Britain's and France's respective roles, see Martin Thomas, *Fight or Flight? Britain, France, and their Roads from Empire* (Oxford: Oxford University Press, 2014), 164–89.

[6] TNA, CAB 128/30, Cabinet Minutes, CM (56) 54th conclusions, 27 July 1956.

[7] TNA, PREM11/1098, Anthony Eden to Dwight D. Eisenhower, 27 July 1956.

force against Egypt.[8] But the government consistently made its case in (pseudo) legal terms, and the perceived need to maintain a façade of legality was the determinant of the specific scenario in which force was actually used.

Yet the government's emphasis on international law served a function beyond the attempt to establish that the use of force would be technically permissible. In his initial Commons statements, Eden did not speak of the empire and made only passing reference to the Commonwealth; rather, he spoke of the canal as 'this great international waterway', and to the Canal Company as 'an international organization of the highest importance and standing'. Nor did he speak of 'British interests', but rather of the 'interests of international shipping' and of the need to safeguard, in any future arrangements, 'the legitimate interests' of Egypt herself.[9] After Eden had opened the first major Suez debate on 2 August, the Suez Group MP Viscount Hinchingbrooke approvingly described his speech as offering 'a grand design of the internationalisation of the Canal for all time' to be established by 'by diplomacy and [by] force if necessary'.[10] So on the one hand this was a language that was congenial even to the most bellicose; on the other, it allowed Eden to stand somewhat above the fray, and to distance himself from the more overtly hawkish attitude that he was privately encouraging the press to take.[11] Others followed his lead. Notwithstanding the rather embarrassing activities of the fringe League of Empire Loyalists, it was a rare Tory politician who explicitly invoked the concept of 'duty to the British Empire'.[12] Mainstream Conservatives were much more likely to raise the standard of international law or even of 'international morality' (a notion that would have induced conniptions in most of their Victorian predecessors).[13] A few weeks into the crisis, one writer in the left-wing weekly *Tribune* explicitly invoked the memory of 1882, in an article headlined 'Is Sir Anthony Going to Do a Gladstone?'[14]

Eden's language may have reflected his awareness of the likely proclivities of British public opinion. Polls in August and September showed large majorities disapproving of Nasser's action and in favour of the government's handling of the crisis but also in favour of international, UN-centred solutions; economic and political action was preferred to the use of force. A somewhat higher proportion of Conservative voters than others were inclined to insist that Egypt be forced to

[8] See, for example, the analysis provided by R. Y. Jennings, Whewell Professor of International Law at Cambridge, in his August–September 1956 correspondence with Gwilym Lloyd-George in TNA, FO 371/118812. The Foreign Office's legal advisers were themselves deeply unhappy at the invasion: Lewis Johnman, 'Playing the Role of a Cassandra: Sir Gerald Fitzmaurice, Senior Legal Adviser to the Foreign Office', in Saul Kelly and Anthony Gorst (eds), *Whitehall and the Suez Crisis* (London: Frank Cass, 2000), 46–63.

[9] HC Deb, 30 July 1956, vol. 557, cols 918–21; HC Deb, 2 August 1956, vol. 557, cols 1602–9.

[10] HC Deb, 02 August 1956, vol. 557, cols 1636–40.

[11] Shaw, *Eden*, 24–30. On press attitudes see also Guillaume Parmentier, 'The British Press in the Suez Crisis', *Historical Journal*, 23:2 (1980), 435–48, and Ralph Negrine, 'The Press and the Suez Crisis: A Myth Re-examined', *Historical Journal*, 25 (1982), 975–84.

[12] Speech of Lord Windlesham: HL Deb, 13 September 1956, vol. 199, cols 816–18. For the LEL and official Conservative attempts to marginalize it, see Mark Pitchford, *The Conservative Party and the Extreme Right 1945–75* (Manchester: Manchester University Press, 2011), 78–82.

[13] 'MP Accuses Mr. Dulles of "Betraying" Premier', *Manchester Guardian*, 6 October 1956.

[14] John Marullus, 'Is Sir Anthony Going to Do a Gladstone?', *Tribune*, 17 August 1956.

accept 'international control' of the canal, but support for referral of the problem to the UN (at over 80 per cent) did not vary according to party allegiance.[15] This high figure may have reflected both a high level of civil society support for the UN and a sunny assumption that a just system of international arbitration would naturally result in a victory for the British position, without force being necessary. Equally importantly, internationalist language of the type Eden used was acceptable to many within the Labour Party. Hugh Gaitskell, the Labour leader, strongly echoed it in his reply to Eden on 2 August. This speech has been noted for its comparison of Nasser with Mussolini and Hitler, a trope that was to be used freely by Conservatives too.[16]

It is also striking that Gaitskell, unlike Eden, at this point used the language of 'prestige', in a passage, which, he noted in his diary, was disliked by left-wingers. Equally comment-worthy was his acceptance of Eden's principle of 'international control'; yet at the same time he issued an important reservation. He noted Britain's membership of the UN and her commitment to international law, and said that it would be 'wrong to get into a position where we might be denounced in the Security Council as aggressors'.[17] (Chancellor of the Exchequer Harold Macmillan described this in his diary as 'quite a helpful speech—except the last part, wh[ich] was against the use of force and will weaken the broad position'.)[18] In his own speech, former Labour Foreign Secretary Herbert Morrison—who had failed to swing the Attlee government in favour of force during the Iranian crisis of 1951— articulated the Labour case for international control more vividly. He presented Egypt's action as the individualistic and 'anarchic' action of a 'modern nationalist, hysterical State, determined to act on its own irrespective of the interests of the rest of the world'. Such behaviour, furthermore, could be

> just as much an evil and a danger to world well-being as was the old imperialism and the old jingoism. I spent much of my life, when I was young, in denouncing imperialism and I have no reason to regret it; in denouncing jingoism, and I have no reason to regret it; and in denouncing excessive nationalism, and I have no reason to regret it. What worries me is the way in which some people, having spent many years in denouncing that in respect of our own country, and having enjoyed its advantages, are now spending their spare time in praising countries like Egypt, which are doing the very thing that Britain and other imperialist countries were doing a hundred years ago.[19]

[15] The key exhibits are polls published in the *News Chronicle* on 10 August and 11 September 1956; these, and other valuable material, can be found in PREM 11/1123, TNA. Useful qualitative evidence, in the form of letters from members of the public, can be found in FO 371/118808–118829. See also Anthony Adamthwaite, 'Suez Revisited', *International Affairs*, 64:3 (1988), 449–64, at 455–7.

[16] Philip M. Williams, *Hugh Gaitskell: A Political Biography* (London: Jonathan Cape, 1979), 422. Eden continued to press the parallel in retirement. See Peter Beck, 'Politicians versus Historians: Lord Avon's "Appeasement Battle" against "Lamentably, Appeasement-Minded" Historians', *Twentieth Century British History*, 9 (1998), 396–419.

[17] HC Deb, 2 August 1956, vol. 557, cols 1609–17. For the genesis of the speech, see Philip M. Williams (ed.), *The Diary of Hugh Gaitskell 1945–1956* (London: Jonathan Cape, 1983), 563–70 (entry for 2–3 August 1956).

[18] Peter Catterall (ed.), *The Macmillan Diaries: The Cabinet Years 1950–1957* (London: Macmillan, 2003), 581 (entry for 2 August 1956).

[19] HC Deb, 2 August 1956, vol. 557, cols 1653–61.

In this analysis, then, Nasser's anti-imperialist credentials were phoney; international progress required transcending chaotic nationalist impulses, which conflicted with morality and promoted conflict.

These concerns were shared to some degree even by Aneurin Bevan, the prominent left-winger who, like, Morrison, had fought Gaitskell for the leadership in 1955, and was now the shadow spokesman on colonial affairs. As a renowned advocate of nationalization of domestic industry, he was almost bound to support Egypt's right to nationalize the canal; and yet he also took the view that 'all waterways like the Suez Canal should come under international control, and not only the Canal itself'.[20] (The Panama Canal was the other obvious major example, and this potentially impinged on American sensitivities.) Writing in *Tribune*, which was widely seen as a Bevanite mouthpiece, he both asserted that Egypt's case on nationalization was indisputable *and* that she would be ill advised to stand on her sovereign rights in unmodified form. 'It is no answer to say that the Suez Canal was an imperialist project from the beginning and that it has been exploited ever since', he claimed. 'That does not establish Egypt's right to exploit the Canal in her own narrow national interests.'[21] This, however, was at odds with *Tribune*'s editorial line, and 'caused a storm' among Bevan's own supporters.[22]

There was therefore a fault line between the Labour advocates of international control and those who took a more overtly anti-colonial and pro-Nasser line. Crucially, however, *both* arguments were cast in terms of anti-imperialism and internationalism, and at the same time Nasser's sympathizers did not shy away from talking about British interests. In the view of the backbench MP William Warbey, for example, it was necessary to recognize not only that there were 'hundreds of millions in Asia and Africa who are now quite determined that they shall not live in the ways of imperialism', but also that British interests could now only be protected 'by recognising and not over-riding the legitimate interests of the people of other countries'.[23] Overall, Eden's language of international control simultaneously helped him secure a substantial measure of support from Labour's most important figures, and sowed confusion in the ranks of the opposition. At the same time, the Commons debate may have led Eden to become too sanguine about the degree of backing he had, although it must be said that he seems to have been wilfully blind to Gaitskell's evident unwillingness to support force in the absence of further provocation by Nasser.[24]

In addition, Eden's language was calculated to play well in the United States. John Foster Dulles, the US secretary of state, was prone to discourse on the role of 'moral force' in international politics.[25] There was also traditional American

[20] Williams, *Gaitskell Diary*, p. 565 (entry for 2–3 August 1956).

[21] Aneurin Bevan, 'It Must Not Be All "Take," Colonel Nasser', *Tribune*, 10 August 1956.

[22] 'Mr. Bevan Differs from Bevanites', *The Times*, 10 August 1956; Janet Morgan (ed.), *The Backbench Diaries of Richard Crossman* (London: Book Club Associates, 1981), 508 (entry for 5 September 1956).

[23] HC Deb, 2 August 1956, vol. 557, cols 1641–9.

[24] Ian Waller, 'Will Suez Cause a Split in Labour's Ranks?', *Evening Times*, 10 August 1956.

[25] James Reston, *Deadline: A Memoir* (New York: Random House, 1991), 227–35; 'Dulles Predicts "Moral Force" Will Solve Suez Canal Crisis Without Use of Troops', *News and Courier* (Charleston, SC),

hostility to British imperialism to be taken into account. Although this attitude was openly criticized by some Tory MPs as a double standard, Eden needed to be more tactful.[26] 'International control' might get Britain the substance of what she wanted without her appearing to be engaged in old-fashioned colonialism. The celebrated US columnist Walter Lippmann opposed the use of force and rejected 'the restoration of the old [imperial] relationship'; but even he (like Bevan) conceded that 'national interests in the Middle East will have to be based not on vested rights but on contracts and agreements arrived at by the calculation of mutual advantages'.[27] Eden's best hope for winning over US public opinion lay in presenting Nasser as an offender against the international community and Britain as an upholder of that community's rights, not of its own historic interests.

In Egypt, by contrast, the concept of international control was strongly rejected. This was partly because Eden's assertion that Britain could not tolerate the canal remaining under the unfettered control of a single power seemed to imply that Britain had never meant to allow the concession to revert to Egypt after its expiry in 1968.[28] In Nasser's view, moreover, the type of solution proposed by the British and French was inherently objectionable: 'I consider the international control they talk about [to be] a new kind of imperialism—collective imperialism.'[29] 'Collective imperialism' (alternatively 'collective colonialism') became an important theme of Egyptian propaganda, and indeed Eden's way of proceeding did little to dispel the idea that his efforts at international consultation were a façade. As Dulles commented privately, the 'essential difference' between the UK and the USA 'was that, while the United States considered that all possible efforts should be made to reach a satisfactory solution by collective consultation, the United Kingdom regarded such efforts as a matter of form'.[30] French Foreign Minister Christian Pineau let the Anglo-French cat out of the diplomatic bag when, ignoring such reservations, he waxed lyrical in public about 'the willingness of the United States to bring about a solution resulting in the internationalisation of the Suez Canal, that is to say, a solution contrary to the principles of Colonel Nasser'.[31] For Eden, as for him, the precise terms of the solution were less important than that it should be objectionable to the Egyptians, and the rhetoric adopted was a means of cloaking the attempted humiliation of the weaker power in the language of liberal internationalism. The point here is not that Eden had already decided irrevocably on the use of force, but rather that for him a diplomatic solution was acceptable only if it was imposed on Egypt—and was seen to

4 August 1956; Andrew Preston, *Sword of the Spirit, Shield of Faith: Religion in American War and Diplomacy* (New York: Anchor Books, 2012), chapters 21 and 23.

[26] See, notably, the speech of Sir John Hall: HC Deb, 2 August 1956, vol. 557, cols 1649–53.

[27] Quoted in TNA, FO 371/120313, UK Washington embassy, 'Weekly Political Summary, 4–11 August 1956', 11 August 1956.

[28] See Cairo radio's quotation of an article by Anwar al-Sadat, 1 August 1956, in 'Summary of World Broadcasts Part IV', 2 August 1956.

[29] Nasser's broadcast of 12 August 1956, in 'Summary of World Broadcasts Part IV', 14 August 1956.

[30] TNA, FO 371/119090, record of a meeting held in the foreign secretary's room, Foreign Office, August 1, 1956.

[31] TNA, FO 371/119095, British Embassy, Paris, to Foreign Office, 3 August 1956.

be imposed—by a resolute international community under British leadership. Nasser could not be granted a compromise that he would find acceptable but had to be obliged to knuckle under, and for this to be possible it was necessary that the threat of force always remained implicit in British rhetoric.

While military preparations were set in train, Britain's diplomats concentrated on arranging an international conference to be held in London in order to discuss the canal's future. On 8 August, Eden made a broadcast in order to help prepare the ground. Historically, much of the strategic significance of the canal had lain in the fact that it served as Britain's route to India, but India had gained independence in 1947. Now, its importance lay increasingly in its role in transporting oil to Europe. Thus, although Eden noted that the canal 'has always been the main artery to and from the Commonwealth', he placed greater emphasis on Europe's dependence on it for fuel. 'This is a matter of life and death to all of us', he said. Yet, while he thus brought home the gravity of the situation to the British people, he did not claim that Britain's interest in the canal was qualitatively different to that of other countries. (He did subsequently suggest, though, that Britain's position as the canal's principal user gave it a natural role as a diplomatic leader on the issue.) In trying to build a coalition Eden presented the problem as one that affected Western Europe as a whole, as well as America and Australasia, and Eastern countries such as India, Pakistan, and Ceylon.[32]

In a broadcast the following week, Selwyn Lloyd, the foreign secretary, made a similar argument.[33]' This speech, like Eden's, had a global audience, or rather audiences. With some Middle Eastern papers carrying the full text in Arabic, it was actually better reported there than in London: Lloyd's highly personal attack on Nasser as a dictator seems to have gone down badly.[34] In Egypt, one newspaper ridiculed 'Sheikh Selwyn Lloyd' for his expression of sympathy with Muslims: 'Abdul Nasser's cause was not a religious but a national cause embracing the entire Arab world. It was a creed which had dug [a] grave for collective colonialism and inspired [the] struggle of free men against it'.[35] It is striking that, in contrast with 1882, discussion of Islam as a political force was quite limited in the British debate. It is equally noteworthy that Lloyd, like Eden, did not dwell at any length on the threat to Britain's world position, but rather chose to emphasize Nasser's lawlessness, untrustworthiness, and aggrandizing tendencies, while keeping open the option of using force against him. It fell to Australian Prime Minister Robert Menzies, in a broadcast given the day before Lloyd's, to assert more explicitly that world peace required 'that the British Commonwealth and, in particular, its greatest and most experienced member, the United Kingdom, should retain power, prestige

---

[32] 'Britain Not Seeking Suez Solution by Force', *The Times*, 9 August 1956. For Eden's comments on Britain as 'the party most concerned in the business', see HC Deb, 12 September 1956, vol. 558, col. 8.

[33] 'Mr. Selwyn Lloyd on Threat to Life of Britain', *The Times*, 15 August 1956. One official had successfully reminded Lloyd 'to include some general and non-committal reference to the United Nations' as this was 'a point on which many highbrows in this country and elsewhere feel strongly'. TNA, FO 371/119111, J. H. A. Watson, 'Secretary of State's Speech', 11 August 1956.

[34] TNA, FO 371/119109, UK Beirut Embassy to Foreign Office, 16 August 1956.

[35] TNA, FO 371/119109, *Akhbar*, quoted in UK Cairo Embassy to Foreign Office, 16 August 1956.

and moral influence'.[36] Perhaps Menzies, acting as a kind of proxy or surrogate for the British government, felt able to say openly what Eden and Lloyd could not. But even he—who had a legal background—placed most of his emphasis on the legal issue and the sanctity of contractual obligations.[37]

Some of the problems inherent in talking too much about British prestige were highlighted in a letter written several weeks later to the Foreign Office by Bernard Burrows, UK ambassador to Bahrain. 'Is it possible for less prominence to be given to the line:—"If Nasser gets away with it we are finished in the Middle East"?' he asked. 'I do not myself believe that the proposition is true, but the best way to make it come true is to go on saying it publicly.' (At the stage that Burrows wrote it seemed quite likely that Nasser would 'get away with it' in the sense of avoiding the use of force against him.) Burrows argued that if the British went on wringing their hands and declaring that all was lost unless dramatic action was taken against Nasser, they would in fact succeed in building him up, and others would be tempted to imitate him.[38] The French probably didn't help here insofar as they were already arguing that Nasser was an Arab kingpin (and kingmaker) who needed to be eliminated. The Foreign Office response was that Burrows was basically right, that the British propaganda line nonetheless avoided the pitfalls he had highlighted, but that the press, which was hard to control, was a different matter.[39] This was true enough insofar as ministers emphasized the threat to living standards, not to Britain's position in the Middle East. Yet Eden was certainly not trying to rein in the press enthusiasts for force; rather the government hoped to use them to build up momentum for military action even while ministers said nothing in public that directly advocated it.[40] He doubtless relished, for example, the *Times* editorial of 27 August, which defended Britain against cries of 'colonialism', took sideswipes at Communist imperialism, and concluded that the British people 'still want Britain great'.[41]

Ultimately, though, Eden's public relations strategy made it difficult for him to back down from the use of force, even in the absence of a viable scenario for its use: the pressure to act ended up operating against *him* as much as it did against Nasser. As we shall see, Mollet's government didn't face the same risk of being trapped by their own rhetoric largely because they were more at ease with threatening and using force. For them the more problematic issue was how to massage the fact that Israel was to do most of the dirty work.

The London conference held in August resulted in a set of proposals for international control of the canal, which were presented to Nasser by a mission headed by Menzies early in September. He rejected them. Meanwhile, the waters were muddied by an American-inspired plan for a Suez Canal Users' Association (SCUA; CASU in its first iteration), which would collect shipping dues and operate the canal with its own pilots. The Americans saw this as a way of slowing down the

---

[36] 'Need for "Firm and Robust" Views', *The Times*, 14 August 1956.

[37] W. J. Hudson, *Blind Loyalty: Australia and the Suez Crisis, 1956* (Carlton, Victoria: Melbourne University Press, 1989), 63–4.

[38] TNA, FO 371/119156, Bernard Burrows to Harold Beeley, 1 October 1956.

[39] TNA, FO 371/119156, P. F. Grey to Bernard Burrows, 11 October 1956.

[40] Shaw, *Eden*, 46.   [41] 'Escapers' Club', *The Times*, 27 August 1956.

British and French impetus towards war; the British accepted it (as did the French, more reluctantly) because they saw it as a way of laying the groundwork for the use of force.[42] Deeply sceptical about the SCUA, Mollet's government left it to their senior diplomat, Hervé Alphand, who was at the time preparing to take up his post as Washington ambassador, to mollify his American hosts. Speaking to the American Club in Paris on the eve of his departure in early September, Alphand declared that France and the United States shared the same attachment to democracy and could be credited with refining its modern form. Aware that Georges Picot, director-general of the Suez Canal Company was also in the audience, Alphand reassured him that true democracies would always unite in opposite to unilateral violations of international law.[43]

Back in Britain, the annual Trades Union Congress had passed a resolution endorsing the London conference proposals, acknowledging Egypt's sovereign rights, and calling on the Egyptian government 'to exhibit world statesmanship which recognises world needs above a narrow conception of national sovereignty'. The debate revealed tensions between strong anti-Nasserites and those who wished to reserve the brunt of their criticism for the government's imperialist tendencies.[44] Nonetheless, internationalism provided a standard around which the Labour movement could unite, however awkwardly. (When the Labour Party conference met a few weeks later, Gaitskell found himself in the unusual position of replying to a motion that complimented the actions of the parliamentary party.)[45] Thus, when parliament reconvened on 12 September, Eden would have been able to avoid the opposition triggering a vote had he promised to take the issue to the UN.[46] Instead, he opened the debate by emphasizing that 'What Colonel Nasser has done is to "de-internationalise" the Canal' and outlining the SCUA proposal. He appeared to suggest that if Egypt did not cooperate with it, force would be used against her.[47] 'This led to an outburst in the House, the Tories cheering wildly and the Labour people shouting "Resign" and "Warmongers!"'[48] Eden's provocative stance prompted Dulles to clarify, in a press conference, that the USA did not intend to 'shoot our way through' the canal—news of which statement came through to MPs later in the debate.[49] Such national unity as had existed at the start of the crisis was now in tatters, and Eden's diplomatic strategy was breaking down too. The Labour MP Richard Crossman surmised that the prime minister emerged from the debate 'boxed, cribbed and confined'.[50]

[42] Kyle, *Suez*, 223–4.

[43] '"Il s'agit, pour les démocraties, de mettre un terme à des actes unilatéraux" déclare M. Hervé Alphand à l'American-club', *Le Monde*, 7 September 1956.

[44] *Report of Proceedings at the 88th Annual Trades Union Congress, September 3 to 7, 1956* (London: TUC, 1956), 433–41.

[45] *Report of the 55th Annual Conference, October 1 to October 5, 1956* (London: Labour Party, 1956), 70–8.

[46] Anthony Eden, *The Memoirs of Sir Anthony Eden: Full Circle* (London: Cassell, 1960), 481–2.

[47] HC Deb, 12 September 1956, vol. 558, cols 2–15.

[48] Nigel Nicolson (ed.), *Harold Nicolson: Diaries and Letters 1945–62* (London: Collins, 1968), 309 (entry for 12 September 1956).

[49] Kyle, *Suez*, 246.

[50] Morgan, *Crossman Diaries*, p. 515 (entry for 14 September 1956).

But how were concepts of empire, Commonwealth, and imperialism/colonialism used during the debate? The divisions were not straightforward. Some Labour MPs, such as Maurice Edelman, stuck to the line favoured by Morrison, i.e. that Third World nationalism could be as 'sinister and dangerous in its purposes, and as inimical to the peace of the world, as were the policies of the old imperialists'.[51] Were they alluding only to Nasser here or to others as well? A greater number, like Crossman, inclined to a more standard condemnation of 'Kipling' style imperialism.[52] There were no Tories to be found who would admit they were in favour of that, or any other variant. Rather, they denied that the government's policy amounted to imperialism, while pointing the finger at others. Hence Eden's derision of Soviet criticisms of 'alleged colonialism', coupled with his observation that 'Soviet Russia had in the years since the war enormously extended its territorial boundaries and increased the number of its subject peoples'.[53] Hence also, the efforts of other Conservatives to suggest that Nasser was aiming at an empire of his own. Given that Egypt had previously renounced her claims to the Sudan, this argument did not seem as plausible as it might have done once, but there was always the potential to suggest that these claims would be revived if Nasser was not faced down.[54] 'If Nasser gets away with this act, British prestige, which has suffered many blows since the war, will be completely eliminated from the Middle East' said Patrick Wall MP, 'Our friends will fall away from us and Nasser will, I believe, have a very good opportunity of creating his dream empire, which will stretch from Casablanca to the Caspian.'[55]

Gilbert Longden was another who suggested that Nasser might be aiming at 'the establishment of an Arab empire [. . .] no doubt with himself as the new Caliph'.[56] Such comments were effectively skewered by Tony Benn, a Labour MP who was a prominent member of the Movement for Colonial Freedom: 'What is the first complaint against Colonel Nasser? It is that he dreams of empire. The party opposite objecting to dreams of empire! What about Cecil Rhodes who dreamed of controlling Africa from the Cape to Cairo? What about Disraeli?'[57] However, it had actually been Gaitskell who had started this particular line of criticism, in his speech of 2 August, when he noted 'that Colonel Nasser has repeatedly boasted of his intention to create an Arab empire from the Atlantic to the Persian Gulf'; and Lloyd took care to quote the Labour leader back at him.[58] Still, Benn was surely right to note that there was a particular oddity in Conservatives using such reasoning. That they did so is suggestive of what a dirty word 'empire' now seemed to be. Indeed, its very disreputableness was enhanced by the closeness with which

[51] HC Deb, 12 September 1956, vol. 558, cols 107–14.
[52] HC Deb, 12 September 1956, vol. 558, col. 95.
[53] HC Deb, 12 September 1956, vol. 558, col. 7.
[54] This exact argument was not made during the debate in question, but see TNA, FO 371/119111, J. H. A. Watson, 'Secretary of State's Speech', and enclosed draft passages, 11 August 1956.
[55] HC Deb, 12 September 1956, vol. 558, cols 47–52.
[56] HC Deb, 13 September 1956, vol. 558, cols 256–65.
[57] HC Deb, 13 September 1956, vol. 558, cols 219–26.
[58] HC Deb, 2 August 1956, vol. 557, col. 1612; HC Deb, 13 September 1956, vol. 558, col. 162.

the British and French were now working together. As Attlee put it in the Lords, 'in Africa and Asia to-day France is regarded as the last protagonist of the old colonialism, and therefore it is unfortunate that we should go forward in association with them'.[59] Some suggested that allowing French troops to be stationed in Cyprus as part of the military build-up was especially unfortunate, taking this to in some way imply potential support for France in the Algerian war.[60]

If Conservative parliamentarians had all but ceased to use 'empire' in a positive sense, neither did they rush to embrace the language of Commonwealth. Neither the imperial stress on bonds between kith and kin, nor the language of equity and partnership that characterized Commonwealth pronouncements, were applicable in an Egyptian context. The French, by contrast, could claim that acting against Nasser was indirectly safeguarding almost a million European residents in Algeria as well as the substantial settler communities still present in anti-Nasserite but newly independent Morocco and Tunisia. True, Wall presented Nasser's putative empire as a threat 'to the Commonwealth, and to the world as a whole'. He suggested: 'if Egypt and her new empire became dominated by the Soviet Government, India might go the same way'.[61] But he was an exception. Labour MPs deployed arguments about the Commonwealth far more often than their opponents did. Their key claims were as follows. First, the government's actions, far from defending the Commonwealth, threatened to weaken or even split it: the use of force was likely to be fatal in this regard. Second, the Conservatives did not really believe in the Commonwealth anyway. These themes were combined in the following exchange, during a speech by Bob Mellish:

> If war should come with Egypt it could not end there. [...] Perhaps Russia, and certainly India, would take a view which would lead to the possible destruction of much of the Commonwealth which many of us on these benches have supported. [An HON. MEMBER: 'Since when?'] The trouble with hon. Members opposite is that they talk in terms of the Empire. We on this side of the House like to talk in terms of the Commonwealth.[62]

The argument here was that Labour, which had far-sightedly (it was claimed) launched the policy of decolonization when in power in 1945–51, had a modern vision of a multiracial Commonwealth. The Conservatives, it was suggested, were deeply uncomfortable with this, and had effectively given up on an institution that was no longer dominated by whites. For example, Julian Snow MP suggested that the government had been listening too much to the traditionally imperialistic Beaverbrook press, which 'for a long time now has been pleading the idea of a Commonwealth based on a white European element'.[63] This narrative of Conservative hostility to the New Commonwealth (i.e. the non-white section) had been developing since before the 1955 general election, and would continue to be

[59] HL Deb, 13 September 1956, vol. 199, cols 727–34.
[60] See, for example, the speech of Julian Snow: HC Deb, 13 September 1956, vol. 558, col. 280.
[61] HC Deb, 12 September 1956, vol. 558, cols 49–50.
[62] HC Deb, 12 September 1956, vol. 558, col. 76.
[63] HC Deb, 13 September 1956, vol. 558, col. 281.

important during the early 1960s debates about membership of the European Economic Community (EEC).[64] The Conservative government's endorsement of the Central African Federation post-1953—and their willingness to allow *de facto* South Rhodesian domination of it—lent weight to these criticisms. In some cases, Labour Commonwealth-cum-internationalist rhetoric took on a messianic tone, as in the peroration offered by Konni Zilliacus MP:

> Above all, we should learn to think in terms of giving leadership through the United Nations in new techniques of international relations. Imperialism will not work. We are a third-class Power in that field. But we could be the leaders of all mankind if the political genius of the British people, which has shown itself in the Mother of Parliaments and in the free Commonwealth, would also show itself through the United Nations in working for the development of the United Nations into a system of world government based on the equal rights of all nations.[65]

Zilliacus was notorious as a fellow traveller of the Soviet Union, but he did sometimes articulate ideas that had a wider resonance within the Labour Party. Even Gaitskell—to his own surprise—thought this 'quite a reasonable speech'.[66]

Aside from pooh-poohing the idea that their own policies were imperialistic, Tories made few efforts to counteract Labour's narrative by making positive claims about their own faith in the Commonwealth. There was a certain amount of genuine Conservative Commonwealth idealism, and those who subscribed to it were uncomfortable with the government's policy. Sir Evelyn Wrench, founder of the English-Speaking Union and a supporter of an empire of self-governing peoples, wrote to *The Times* drawing attention to the government's failure to consult other members of the Commonwealth after the failure of the Menzies mission. He asked: 'In the last analysis is it not better to save the Commonwealth than to save the Suez Canal?'[67] After the invasion, the Conservative Party historian Keith Feiling lamented the way that Canada and India had been cold-shouldered and deplored the government's Commonwealth policy as 'short-sighted, ungrateful, and politically imbecile'.[68]

Yet the majority of Conservatives, who supported the government, failed to recruit the Commonwealth into their own arguments in meaningful ways. Perhaps the party's MPs were sensitive to the need to avoid mentioning 'empire' but believed that their more atavistic supporters were uncomfortable with Commonwealth multiracialism, exactly as Labour alleged. The Conservative Party conference in October gave evidence of the strength of feeling against Nasser at the grassroots. After it passed a resolution condemning both Egypt and Labour's alleged efforts to divide the nation on the issue, one delegate suggested that the

[64] Labour Party Research Department, *Speakers Handbook 1954* (London: Labour Party, 1954), 331–2; Richard Toye, 'Words of Change: The Rhetoric of Commonwealth, Common Market, and Cold War, 1961–3', in Larry Butler and Sarah Stockwell (eds), *The Wind of Change: Harold Macmillan and British Decolonization* (Basingstoke: Palgrave Macmillan, 2013), 140–58.
[65] HC Deb, 12 September 1956, vol. 558, cols 125–31.
[66] Williams, *Gaitskell Diary*, 603 (entry for 14 September 1956).
[67] 'Parliament's Role', *The Times*, 18 September 1956.
[68] 'Landings In Egypt', *The Times*, 6 November 1956. See also Adamthwaite, 'Suez Revisited', 456.

words of the motion might be 'written in blood'. Although he did add 'but God forbid!' this may not have been quite the tone that Eden was looking for.[69] In his own speech the prime minister confined himself to denying that the dispute had anything to do with colonialism—the *Manchester Guardian* suggested that this might have been intended as a dig at Dulles, who had appeared to suggest in public that it did—and asserting that it was 'the sanctity of contracts' that was at stake.[70] By this point, Britain and France had referred the issue to the UN Security Council, in a further effort to establish their credentials as upholders of international law.

At the same time, Eden was planning covert actions that radically undermined such claims and which would, soon enough, destroy his own reputation. The day after making his conference speech he met with the French representatives Maurice Challe and Albert Gazier, who proposed to him the plan for colluding with Israel to attack Egypt. Eden received the idea with enthusiasm, triggering the chain of events that led to the invasion not much more than two weeks later. When the Commons learned of the Anglo-French 'ultimatum' in response to the Israeli action, there were scenes of uproar and confusion. Over the first few days of November, as the British and French attacks on Egypt started, and as allegations of collusion surfaced, the government struggled to provide a coherent account of its actions. Notoriously, Eden observed that a technical state of war did not exist; rather, 'we are in an armed conflict'.[71]

Labour, at this point, was able to deploy a new argument: that the attack on Egypt had weakened Britain's moral credibility when it came to criticizing the near-simultaneous Soviet aggression towards Hungary.[72] The ramifications in France of Soviet suppression of the Hungarian uprising in October 1956 were more complex. Events in Budapest disarmed the French Communists, members of the one French political party consistently and noisily opposed to the Suez operation. But the linkage that was made at the United Nations as well as within the Eisenhower administration between Soviet repression and French actions—not just in Egypt, but in Algeria too—embarrassed the main parties in government: the Socialists and the Radicals, all to the long-term benefit of de Gaulle's supporters.[73] There was also a Cold War dimension to former Colonial Secretary Jim Griffiths' indictment of the Suez invasion, in which he linked the question of the 'uncommitted', i.e. neutralist, world to that of Britain's post-imperial mission. (The Bandung conference, a celebrated moment in the history of the Non-Aligned Movement, had taken place the previous year.) Griffiths argued:

> For the people in the Commonwealth and the Colonies—and in the uncommitted world—this will be an attack by a powerful white country on a weak country of coloured

---

[69] Speech of Charles Stuart Hallinan (a leading figure in Cardiff politics), 11 October 1956, Conservative Party annual conference report, 1956, 32.

[70] 'Sanctity of Contracts at Stake: Not Colonialism', *Manchester Guardian*, 15 October 1956.

[71] HC Deb, 1 November 1956, vol. 558, col. 1641.

[72] See Gaitskell's comments: HC Deb, 3 November 1956, vol. 558, col. 1861.

[73] Lázló J. Nagy, 'La politique algérienne de De Gaulle vue de Hongrie', in Maurice Vaïsse (ed.), *De Gaulle et l'Algérie, 1943–1969* (Paris: Armand Colin, 2012), 124–5.

people. When one reads the pronouncements in the Press of the Commonwealth and Colonies it becomes increasingly clear that, by the action taken this week, we may very well have destroyed this great venture, this Commonwealth, towards which we have been working. And it is a Conservative Government, it is the party which regarded the Empire almost as a branch of the Conservative Party, whose members talk about it as if it belonged to them—they are the Government who are breaking up the Commonwealth at this time.[74]

These were claims that gained much credence from the fact that the majority of Commonwealth countries were hostile to Britain's action; the support given to her by Australia and New Zealand was conspicuous for its isolated nature. On the Conservative side, there was again little attempt to make a virtue of the Commonwealth.[75] Rather, Tory MPs justified the government's actions in terms of support for the United Nations.

The maverick Labour MP S. N. Evans, who was soon to resign his seat on account of his support for the invasion, declared in the Commons that the UN was 'at best a political eunuch and at worst a fraud, a snare and a delusion'.[76] Conservatives might have agreed with him, but they certainly dared not say so. Rather, they went to lengths to emphasize that the invasion was in support of international order, consistent with the values of the UN, and was necessitated because the organization was not (as yet) in a position to act so as to make those values real. This approach was taken even by some well to the right of the parliamentary party. Hinchingbrooke twitted the Labour Party with its alleged opposition to all forms of military activity: 'They should realise in time that when these actions have ceased there will be established the kind of international order which they basically favour, that is to say, the placing of international commerce in an international political setting.'[77] Such claims need to be seen in the context of much older claims that the Empire/Commonwealth could act as the core, or prototype, around which a wider international order might develop. 'In fact the league of nations has begun', Lloyd George had said in 1918. 'The British empire is a league of nations.'[78] In his Suez broadcast, Eden did not make the link so explicit—in fact, he said that there had not been enough time to consult 'Our friends inside the Commonwealth', a studiously ambiguous phrasing—but he did, like Gladstone, claim to have been labouring in the cause of peace. He declared: 'I have been a League of Nations man and a United Nations man, and I am still the same man, with the same convictions the same devotion to peace.'[79] Gaitskell's argument, by contrast, was that there was 'nothing in the United Nations Charter which justifies any nation appointing itself as world policeman'—ironically an

[74] HC Deb, 1 November 1956, vol. 558, cols 1631–9.
[75] Exceptionally, John Biggs-Davidson claimed that he was 'desperately anxious to make a reality of the British Commonwealth of the twentieth century'. HC Deb, 31 October 1956, vol. 558, col. 1545.
[76] HC Deb, 1 November 1956, vol. 558, cols 1681–6.
[77] HC Deb, 31 October 1956, vol. 558, col. 1464.
[78] Speech of September 1918, quoted in Mark Mazower, *Governing the World: The History of an Idea* (London: Allen Lane, 2012), 128.
[79] Anthony Eden, 'The Government's Policy in the Middle East', *Listener*, 8 November 1956.

echo, albeit in rather different circumstances, of Bonar Law's famed comment at the time of Chanak.[80]

The invasion came to an end within days, in the face of a combination of world hostility and the seeming prospect of a collapse of Britain's financial reserves. At one level, the government's insistence on the importance of the UN and of international-al law rendered it obviously vulnerable to charges of hypocrisy, as the Labour Party, now almost wholly united, adopted the slogan 'Law, not War', accompanied by the symbol of the UN flag.[81] Furthermore, the claim that Britain and France were acting on the UN's behalf made it very hard to resist demands for their withdrawal from Egypt when a United Nations Emergency Force was rapidly constituted to undertake a peacekeeping role in their place. On the other hand, though, a fig leaf was provided to cover Britain and the Conservative Party's humiliation, even as Eden met his personal Waterloo. It has to be remembered that, even though the fact of collusion was obvious to many, it was not definitively proven for some years.

Fig. 7.1. Manchester demonstration against British involvement in the Suez crisis, 2 October 1956.

Mary Evans Picture Library, image 10281996

[80] HC Deb, 30 October 1956, vol. 558, col. 1347.
[81] Ruth Winstone (ed.), *Tony Benn: Years of Hope: Diaries, Papers and Letters 1940–1962* (London: Hutchinson, 1994), 198 (entry for 2 November 1956).

Fig. 7.2. 'Wipe Suez Out', graffiti in North Kensington, London.
Mary Evans Picture Library, image 10294325

It is therefore not inconceivable that some Conservative MPs genuinely believed the official explanations that they parroted, and very probable that a considerable body of public opinion did too. Tory Suez rebel Nigel Nicolson—whose principled stand led to him being deselected as an MP—recalled that he and his fellow dissenters dared not make reference to what they knew about collusion when they justified themselves in public, because they thought they would be laughed out of court if they did.[82] The strength of British feeling for and against the Suez venture is captured in Figs. 7.1 and 7.2.

FRANCE

Guy Mollet's coalition government reacted to news of the Suez nationalization with predictable outrage. Predictable because Nasser was already a hate figure for the Republican Front, a left-of-centre administration whose support derived from the Socialists, the Radicals, the UDSR (Union Démocratique et Sociale de la Résistance), and Jacques Chaban-Delmas' Social Republicans. Outrage even so because, in

---

[82] Nigel Nicolson, *Long Life: Memoirs* (New York: G.P. Putnam's Sons, 1998), 156–7.

seizing unilateral control of the canal, Nasser appeared to confirm French charac-
terizations of the Egyptian leader as a dangerous ideological fanatic, kingpin of the
Arab world, and master-manipulator of circumstance.[83] Nasser, so the Parisian
rhetoric went, was the real imperialist.[84] His support for pan-Arab solidarity was
reverberating throughout north-west Africa. This mattered because the region
remained a French sphere of influence, despite Morocco and Tunisia having
secured independence earlier in the year. Nasser's political vision, ostensibly anti-
colonialist and internationally non-aligned, was, according to Mollet, his Foreign
Minister Christian Pineau, and others, a new form of Egyptian empire-building,
transnational in its propagandizing to be sure, but one whose fulfilment depended,
in practice, on surreptitious Soviet backing.

The Egyptian leader, then, was a dictator in all but name, one whose expansionist
ambitions it now fell to France and Britain to expose. As a result, it was what French
historians term the 'Munich syndrome' (sometimes, rather confusingly, described
by the French press as the 'anti-Munich syndrome', but meaning the same thing) that
completed this rhetorical jigsaw. Eighteen years previously, so the argument went, the
entente partners had failed to their cost either to unite or to react in time to thwart
fascist aggrandizement. France, even more than Britain, had learned from bitter
experience that it was fatal to appease dictators who professed only to be reclaiming
their sovereign rights. On 29 July 1956, only forty hours after the crisis erupted,
Pineau reassured his opposite number Selwyn Lloyd that 'the French Government
were ready to go with us to the end in dealing with Nasser'.[85] Indeed they were.

By July 1956 the French intelligence services and the Ministry of National
Defence had been monitoring Nasser's deepening relationship with Algeria's
nationalist fighters for the best part of a year. So the rhetorical flights of fancy
that greeted the announcement of canal nationalization were conditioned, above
all, by knowledge of widening Egyptian influence in Algeria's war of independence.
Senior figures in government, in the military and in the security services were, as a
result, predisposed to seize the opportunity for a killer blow. By 3 August there was
talk in the French Cabinet of 'liquidating' the Egyptian leader.[86] Similarly ominous
pledges to reverse the Suez nationalization figured when French Cabinet members
spoke in the National Assembly debate on the developing crisis in Egypt later that
day. A dramatic turn of events; a violent, uncompromising use of language: yet also
misleading as an evidential source. Why? Because to focus on the French *Conseil
des ministres*, or full Cabinet, as the principal source of French governmental
discussion—and consequent pronouncements—about the Suez crisis, is to miss
an essential point. In narrowly French political terms, the real significance of the

[83] Albert Mousset, 'France le progrès de Lyon: le début des complications', *Le Monde*, 14 August
1956.

[84] Neither Mollet's government nor the French press seem to have been aware of the plurality of
opinions within Egyptian domestic politics at the time, about which, see: Crowcroft, 'Egypt's Other
Nationalists', 267–79.

[85] Christopher Brady, 'The Cabinet System and Management of the Suez Crisis', *Contemporary
British History*, 11:2 (1997), 84.

[86] Martin Evans, *Algeria: France's Undeclared War* (Oxford: Oxford University Press, 2012), 183.

Arguing about Empire

way that Nasser's actions were first depicted and then defied was to expose the disfunctionality intrinsic to the policymaking process in the Fourth Republic.

When it came to the management of crises in which French global interests were at stake, decision making was appropriated by a select few within France's civil-military elite. This discomfiting tendency was evident from the regime's long, difficult birth during the interregnum between the Liberation of Paris in August 1944 and the ratification of a new constitutional settlement in late 1946. In May of that year the National Assembly first voted on the French Union. Substantially drafted by colonial parliamentary representatives, this was a post-war constitutional settlement for France's empire that promised a fundamental redistribution of imperial power. A small group of ministers and senior colonial policy officials came together in response to thwart it. It was they who formulated the less ambitious French Union redraft that secured National Assembly approval in October 1946.[87]

Over the next twelve months, equally crucial decisions about whether, when, and how to fight the developing Communist-led insurgency in French Vietnam were similarly arrogated to two discrete groups of French policy insiders, one in Paris, the other in Saigon.[88] Everything from the distribution of sensitive political intelligence to the exchange of basic information about the prospects for negotiation with Ho Chi Minh's Hanoi regime was channelled via Saigon High Commission staff to a select group of ministers, generals, and security service officials. Those known to favour a policy of confrontation were kept well informed. Those desperate to keep talking with Hanoi were shut out. In consequence, from 1947 onwards vital strategic decisions to fight the Indochina War were taken outside the *Conseil des ministres* within the confines of an 'Inter-Ministerial Committee on Indochina'. It was this inner cabinet that took the fatal steps towards escalation and international-ization of the conflict in French Vietnam. The outcome was disastrous. For all that, in mid-1956, barely two years after the violent end of France's colonial presence in South East Asia, imperial policymaking was, yet again, hijacked by a closed group of like-minded insiders within government, the military, and the security services.

The most notable casualty of this bureaucratic infighting was the Quai d'Orsay. Maurice Faure, Pineau's deputy at the Foreign Ministry, typified the Arabist sensibilities of his diplomatic staff. Speaking before a rural audience at Gourdon in the Lot on 29 August, Faure took the opportunity to call for moderation. 'France,' he said, 'contrary to what certain malicious propaganda is claiming, has no wish to impose any solution on the Egyptian people at odds with their national honour or their vital interests . . . Nor does France plan to seize any pretext to exact some sort of "revenge" against Arab nationalism. Let me solemnly reaffirm here that

---

[87] Martin Shipway, 'Thinking Like an Empire: Governor Henri Laurentie and Postwar Plans for the Late Colonial French "Empire-State"', in Martin Thomas (ed.), *The French Colonial Mind: Mental Maps of Empire and Colonial Encounters*, vol. 1 (Lincoln, NE: University of Nebraska Press, 2011), 219–50; James I. Lewis, 'The MRP and the Genesis of the French Union, 1944–1948', *French History*, 12 (1998): 276–314.

[88] The fullest account of this process is now Stein Tonnesson, *Vietnam 1946: How the War Began* (Berkeley, CA: University of California Press, 2010).

our policy is not imperialist.'[89] Soothing French words—and disclaimers of any imperialistic intent much like those emanating from Eden's government—were all very well. The problem, though, lay less in mollifying hostile foreign opinion than in persuading other branches of government in Paris impatient with the Foreign Ministry's conciliatory line.

The principal doubters were inside the French Defence Ministry. From there, the pre-eminent duo of Defence Minister Maurice Bourgès-Maunoury and his secretary-general, Abel Thomas, did more than anyone else to reorient French Middle Eastern policy—and consequent official rhetoric—in 1956.[90] Senior commanders in Algeria, as well as Interior Ministry staff in Paris and their Algiers government cousins—together, jointly responsible for managing the war in Algeria day by day—were also eager to strike at Nasser in a bid to transform their Algerian prospects. And it was this inner core of politicians, officials, and military commanders that were taking charge of Suez crisis management.[91] Two days after Faure's speech, Mollet's Cabinet approved the dispatch of French troops to Cyprus to prepare for a joint intervention with their British counterparts. Government sources let slip to the press that Mollet and his senior colleagues retained little faith in any diplomatic solution, further noting that, should it come to military action, they expected the Americans to acquiesce.[92]

We need, therefore, to frame French decision-making during the Suez crisis—as well as the rhetorical justifications produced to justify it—within the context of a dysfunctional political system in which secrecy, misinformation, and the exclusion from key decisions—not just of individual ministers, but of entire branches of government—had become the norm. Put differently, while historians of Britain's Suez crisis have criticized both Anthony Eden and a style of government typified by the 'Egypt Committee', which served as something between a war cabinet, an inner cabinet, and, on occasion, a sounding board for prime ministerial preferences, this proclivity to rule by cabal pales alongside its French equivalent.[93] What, in the British case, might be understood as a dangerous tendency towards uncritical analysis of policy choices, or 'group think', was in its French iteration closer to political subversion and systematic deception of fellow ministers, overseas allies, and the wider public in France.

---

[89] 'Le gouvernement français ne saurait accepter que la négociation s'enlise dans d'éternelles palabres déclare M. Maurice Faure', *Le Monde*, 30 August 1956.

[90] Maurice Vaïsse, 'France and the Suez Crisis', in William Roger Louis and Roger Owen (eds), *Suez 1956: The Crisis and its Consequences* (Oxford: Clarendon, 1989), 134; Zach Levey, 'French-Israeli Relations, 1950–1956: The Strategic Dimension', in Simon C. Smith (ed.), *Reassessing Suez 1956: New Perspectives on the Crisis and its Aftermath* (Aldershot: Ashgate, 2008), 88, 95, 99.

[91] Michèle Battesti, 'Les ambiguités de Suez', *Revue Historique des Armées*, 4:1 (1986), 11–12.

[92] Raymond Barrillon, 'La détermination et l'unanimité du gouvernement français demeurent inchangée', *Le Monde*, 1 September 1956.

[93] Christopher Brady argues that the Cabinet Egypt Committee did not represent any constitutional abuse of Cabinet government but did tend towards 'tunnel vision' about Nasser, see his 'The Cabinet System', 87–9. For a harsher view of committee procedure and, especially, of Macmillan's adventurism within it, see Howard J. Dooley, 'Great Britain's "Last Battle" in the Middle East: Notes on Cabinet Planning during the Suez Crisis of 1956', *International History Review*, 11:3 (1989), 486–501.

Moving beyond the realm of government, at least five other discrete factors conditioned French political debate about the Egyptian regime, the Suez Canal nationalization, and eventual collusion with Israel and Britain. First among them, as we have seen, was the looming presence of the Algerian conflict.[94] What began in late 1954 as an anti-colonial rebellion mushroomed over the course of 1956 into a massive conflagration, involving the largest deployment of French forces outside Europe since World War I. The ethical parameters of French political choices and the territorial limits of French military action collapsed in the process. Such is well known. What remains harder to explain is why a Socialist-led government not only acquiesced in this descent into the Algerian abyss, but propelled it forward. Mollet, after all, came into office promising to put a stop to 'this imbecilic and unending war'.[95] In fact, his government, the longest-lasting coalition in the Fourth Republic's twelve-year lifespan, did precisely the opposite. The point did not go wholly unnoticed in Britain. Writing in *Tribune* in September 1956, the French Socialist Lucien Weitz observed: 'Suez is a diversion from the tragedy of Algeria. Stumbling on from pitfall to pitfall, the Government wants to retrieve its failure in Algiers by striking in Cairo.'[96]

Linked to this was a second factor: the emergence of more militant voices in opposition to French imperial ventures. Typically associated with the anti-imperialist intellectualism of figures such as Jean-Paul Sartre and Simone de Beauvoir, the chic ultra-leftism of the Parisian Left Bank was, during 1956, less significant than the widespread public unease over the use of national servicemen on the Algerian frontline.[97]

The dispatch of conscripts and, equally important, of older army reservists to North Africa was a recent development. It was agreed as part of the 'Emergency Powers' legislation passed by the National Assembly on 12 March 1956 by an overwhelming vote of 455 to 76. The purpose was to crush the Algerian rebellion with the sheer force of French numbers. But Mollet's government rode to electoral victory in January 1956 promising to end the Algerian war through dialogue, not military saturation. As the French premier told a packed Chamber of Deputies in the Special Powers debate on 9 March, adopting such sweeping legislation would change the entire thrust of Algeria policy. But, he insisted, the objective remained the same: peace in Algeria, albeit necessarily after order was restored.[98] Addressing himself to the government's Socialist supporters, Mollet

---

[94] Raymond Barrillon, 'Le gouvernement français lie toujours étroitement la question algérienne à l'affaire de Suez', *Le Monde*, 3 September 1956.

[95] Sabine Jansen (ed.), *Les grands discours parlementaires de la Quatrième République de Pierre Mendès France à Charles de Gaulle* (Paris: Armand Colin, 2006), 219.

[96] Lucien Weitz, 'When Socialists become Small Town Jingoes', *Tribune*, 14 September 1956.

[97] Mireille Conia highlights the depth of local reaction to the dispatch of national servicemen to Algeria in the context of one provincial *département*, Haute-Marne. See her: 'La Haute-Marne: berceau des actions de solidarité envers les soldats', in Raphaëlle Branche and Sylvie Thénault (eds), *La France en guerre: Expériences métropolitaines de la guerre d'indépendance algérienne* (Paris: Autrement, 2008), 58–69.

[98] Martin Thomas, 'Order before Reform: The Spread of French Military Operations in Algeria, 1954–1958', in David Killingray and David Omissi (eds), *Guardians of Empire* (Manchester: Manchester University Press, 1999), 198–200, 207–9.

affirmed that reinforcing the army in Algeria was meant to restore security and public confidence in two absolute certainties: that France would never leave and that, in consequence, a negotiated settlement was the best that Algeria's nationalist fighters could achieve.[99]

Turning to the government's bitterest opponents, the anti-parliamentary extreme-rightists of Pierre Poujade's *Union de défense des commerçants et artisans*, the prime minister reminded them that the Socialists had a prouder record of defending France than the hard right. This was a sensitive topic, and not just because of the unhealed wounds of the Vichy past. Barely a month earlier the 'Poujadists', always closer to an anti-republican protest movement than a responsible political party, had staged inflammatory demonstrations inside and outside the National Assembly. On 14 February, at the height of the National Assembly disturbances, shots—mercifully only blanks—were fired from the spectators' gallery.[100] Ostensibly, their complaint was against a constitutional court ruling that invalidated certain election results involving a dozen of the fifty-six Poujadist deputies elected in January. But the Poujadists' tactics and their vitriolic anti-republicanism were redolent of the well-orchestrated settler demonstrations in Algiers that, famously, compelled Mollet to reverse course over the war a few days beforehand.[101] Underpinning the Poujadists' poisonous rhetoric was the suspicion that the Republican Front was intent on an Algerian 'sell-out', leaving Algeria's poor white settlers—always an assured reservoir of Poujadist support—to their fate. In was no coincidence that Mollet's final act in the 9 March debate was to focus on the Poujadists' noisiest parliamentary ally, the young deputy and Indo-china War veteran, Jean-Marie Le Pen. Algeria's settlers, Mollet told him, would be protected; there would be no repetition of France's recent defeat in Vietnam.[102]

By the time a revised Operation Musketeer, the joint invasion of Egypt, began in late October, Operation Valmy, the far-larger offensive against Algeria's FLN (Front de Libération Nationale), was backed up by almost half a million French troops.[103] The largest sustained colonial operation of the twentieth century, this was more than imperial counter-insurgency. It was total colonial war. The human costs were brought home as casualties mounted over the summer and autumn—just as the Suez crisis peaked. Algerian civilian casualties far outstripped French losses. But it was the death of conscripts and reservists, reluctant warriors compelled by an unforeseen change in the law to serve in North Africa, that resonated most powerfully in France.[104]

---

[99] Guy Mollet, 'La France sans l'Algérie, ce ne serait plus la France', 2ème séance du 9 Mars 1956, in Jansen (ed.), *Les grands discours*, 220–2.

[100] Preface and 'Séance du 10 Février 1956', in Jansen (ed.), *Les grands discours*, 205–9.

[101] Evans, *Algeria*, 148–51.

[102] Guy Mollet, 'La France sans l'Algérie, ce ne serait plus la France', 2ème séance du 9 Mars 1956, in Jansen (ed.), *Les grands discours*, 222–4.

[103] SHD-DAT, 1H1374/D3, fiche 'Situation des effectives des trois Armées en Algérie', n.d. 1956; Vincent Joly, *Guerres d'Afrique: 130 ans de guerres coloniales: L'expérience française* (Rennes: Presses Universitaires de Rennes, 2009), 270.

[104] Raphaëlle Branche, *L'embuscade de Palestro: Algérie 1956* (Paris: Armand Colin, 2010), 42–3, 55–60.

On 23 May 1956, Pierre Mendès France, the most dynamic figure in the French Radical Party and the politician credited with negotiating definitive pull-outs from Indochina, Morocco, and Tunisia, resigned his post as minister without portfolio. He had voted for the Emergency Powers, but only as part of a wider Algerian solution in which social reforms and fundamental constitutional changes were implemented alongside the military surge. That balance, he complained, was gone. An important loss, although not a decisive one, Mendès France's departure was indicative nonetheless.[105] Although it held together, Mollet's Republican Front was accused of ignoring its original mandate for government. Uncompromising in its support for an extended war, increasingly outspoken in its defiance of domestic and international opinion, the Mollet coalition seemed to have cast itself adrift from its ethical moorings, forgetting its professed liberalism and thereby sacrificing much of its core constituency in the centre-left of French politics. In July, 45 per cent of those interviewed by French opinion pollster IFOP (Institut français d'opinion publique) indicated their support for Algerian independence.[106] The coalition—and the Socialist Party in particular—was leeching support by the time that Nasser acted over Suez.

This brings us to a third factor: the nature of party political opposition in the Fourth Republic. This was in notable contrast to Britain. Although the notion that there was a British 'post-war consensus' is much contested, the two-party system was undoubtedly stable.[107] But from its beginnings in 1944 to its suicidal end in May 1958, France's restored democracy was hamstrung by its opponents on the left and right of the political spectrum. At one end stood the French Communist Party. Nominally Stalinist and avowedly anti-colonial, although actually more equivocal on both counts, Party leaders were always ready to exploit signs of government distress to enhance Communist support.[108] Opposing them was the Gaullist RPF (Rassemblement du Peuple Français). Intrinsically hostile to what they decried as the Fourth Republic 'system', the RPF was a populist movement-cum-party united by its messianic belief in the restorative powers of a de Gaulle presidency. This would culminate eighteen months after the October 1956 invasion of Egypt in an Algiers coup whose ruthless implementation brought the Fourth Republic to its knees. Put differently, the rhetoric of French government in 1956 was not simply a matter of promoting national or even party political interest. It was a struggle to maintain the legitimacy of the republican regime against powerful opponents who vilified not just the government in office but the way the Fourth Republic did—or did not—work.

The issue of legitimacy is central to the fourth and fifth factors as well. For the tropes that recurred most frequently in French decision-makers' rhetoric throughout

---

[105] Evans, *Algeria*, 167; Pierre Mendès France, *Gouverner, c'est choisir, 1954–1955* (Paris: Gallimard, 1986), 181–9; Robert Frank, 'Pierre Mendès France: au miroir du Moyen-Orient, une certaine vision du monde (1956–1957)', in *Pierre Mendès France et le rôle de la France dans le monde* (Grenoble: Presses Universitaires de Grenoble, 1991), 275–6.

[106] Charles-Robert Ageron, 'L'opinion française à travers les sondages', in Jean-Pierre Rioux (ed.), *La guerre d'Algérie et les Français* (Paris: Fayard, 1990), 27.

[107] Richard Toye, 'From "Consensus" to "Common Ground": The Rhetoric of the Postwar Settlement and its Collapse', *Journal of Contemporary History*, 48:1 (2013), 3–23.

[108] Jacques Fauvet, 'L'affaire de Suez offre une nouvelle occasion de conflit entre les communistes et M. Guy Mollet', *Le Monde*, 6 August 1956.

the Suez crisis related governmental choices to two things: avoiding the mistakes of 1930s appeasement and rekindling the against-the-odds bravery of wartime resistance. The attempt to tie France's actions in 1956 to a resistance heritage was made easier by the simple fact that the majority of those 'inside' the decision-making circles of French government boasted resistance credentials.[109] And this fourth conditioning factor helps account for the fifth and final one, which was France's closer strategic alignment with the state of Israel. An obvious point perhaps, but what bears emphasis is that, from the French standpoint, the decisive ally in 1956 was neither Britain, nor the United States; rather, it was an Israeli regime of which France had, in the short term at least, become the foremost military backer.[110] Despite abiding mutual suspicions of one another's motives, on 23 June French and Israeli defence and security service officials met outside Paris to sign off an US$80 million arms supply contract. Its headline item was seventy-two Dassault Mystère 4A jet fighters, enough to assure Israel's aerial supremacy over Egypt.[111] Indeed, one could read official approval on 27 July of the Mystère arms sale as the first meaningful French reaction to news of the Suez nationalization.[112]

Again, a cautionary word needs to be added here. The Franco-Israeli partnership was a strategic marriage of convenience, and a tenuous one at that. It flew in the face of residual French support for Syria and never really dented the abiding Israeli determination to consolidate American support.[113] But there was another, less calculable quality that helped sustain the Franco-Israeli cohabitation. Israel's leaders, like their French counterparts, drew their political legitimacy from a resistance heritage of their own, one that was shaped by the struggle against Nazism, against the British presence in mandate Palestine, and against warring Arab states. For both partners the demonization of Nasser and the reversion to secret plotting that followed marked less of a departure than might be imagined. As French historian Maurice Vaïsse suggests, 'It was a veritable contest of collective memory in which the Frenchmen most intimately involved in the preparations literally immersed themselves in the resistance atmosphere, and even recaptured the reflexes of clandestine action.'[114] Much like their Israeli partners, the French political leadership, in other words, viewed the Suez crisis in a fundamentally different strategic context than that preferred by their 'Anglo-Saxon' allies. What for Britain and the

---

[109] The complexities and contradictions of former resisters overseeing the repression of anti-colonial resistance in Algeria have been explored by, among others, Martin Evans, *The Memory of Resistance: French Opposition to the Algerian War (1954–1962)* (Oxford: Berg, 1992); and Bertrand Hamelin, 'Les Résistants et la guerre d'Algérie (1954–1962): quelques jalons problématiques', in Branche and Thénault, *La France en guerre*, 138–42.

[110] DDF, 1956, vol. 1: January–June 1956 (Paris: Imprimerie Nationale, 1988), docs. 86, 235, 258, 401; Abel Thomas, *Comment Israël fut sauvé: Les secrets de l'expédition de Suez* (Paris: 1978), 25–6; also cited in Vaïsse, 'France and the Suez Crisis', 132.

[111] Levey, 'French-Israeli Relations', 102.

[112] Vaïsse, 'France and the Suez Crisis', 134. It is worth recording, though, that Foreign Minister Pineau did not dwell on Franco-Israeli relations in his first communiqué to the British after the Suez nationalization, see: DDF, 1956, vol. II: July–October 1956 (Paris: Imprimerie Nationale, 1989), doc. 84.

[113] Levey, 'French-Israeli Relations', 87–9, 103–6.

[114] Vaïsse, 'France and the Suez Crisis', 134–5.

USA were primarily imperial or geopolitical calculations were for France and Israel reducible to a more existential question: could French Algeria and the state of Israel survive the consolidation of Nasserism throughout the Arab world?

France's senior serving soldier, chief of general staff, General Paul Ély, reflecting in his 1969 memoirs on the Algerian conflict, explained French actions in 1956 as an effort to protect Algeria, North Africa, even the African continent, from the ideological clutches of the USSR and Nasser's pan-Arabism, in short, from world-views at variance with Western values.[115] Revealingly, anxious CIA and US State Department officials, who tried to disentangle French rhetorical bluster from the more realist calculations behind it, ultimately concluded that no such distinctions could be made. Where British government members clearly adjusted their language both to win over doubters at home and to mollify allies and longstanding imperial partners overseas, the French, the CIA concluded, simply meant what they said. A briefing paper prepared for Eisenhower's National Security Council in early September 1956 got to the heart of the matter:

> UK and French governments . . . have almost certainly estimated that a compromise with Nasser on the principle of international control of the canal would greatly weaken their position in the Middle East and Africa. They may believe that use of force would produce less undesirable consequences than would such a compromise. Therefore, even without further provocation, they might resort to force if convinced that negotiations were not going to produce a prompt settlement satisfactory to them. In these circumstances, they would attempt to document Nasser's refusal to negotiate such a settlement, and to dramatize it before world opinion as justification for the use of force.[116]

Significantly, when Kermit Roosevelt, a leading CIA Middle East specialist, met a delegation of Egyptian government insiders in New York on 4 October 1956, he found the Egyptians wholly preoccupied with working out just how serious the British were about intervention. The French, it seemed, were already judged to be deaf to compromise.[117]

RETRACING THE PATH TO COLLUSION

Within France, however, there was less certainty that the government's mind was made up. The supporters of intervention had been reassured by the government's uncompromising stance announced to the National Assembly after the Cabinet meeting on 3 August. But over the six weeks that followed, doubts about the coalition's (and, more especially, the Socialists') stomach for confrontation began to surface. Mollet's apparent acquiescence in the Americans' SCUA scheme, and the

---

[115] Général d'Armée Paul Ély, *Mémoires: Suez . . . le 13 Mai* (Paris: Plon, 1969), 54–66.

[116] CIA Intelligence in the Middle East, online archive, no. 189, CIA director, National Intelligence Estimate 30-4-56, 'Probable Repercussions of British-French Military Action in the Suez Crisis', 5 September 1956.

[117] CIA Intelligence in the Middle East, online archive, CIA memorandum, report of conversation on Suez with certain Egyptians, New York, 4 October 1956, 9 October 1956.

claims made during the London conference in early September about 'defusing' and 'depoliticizing' the Suez crisis, went down poorly with supporters of the Defence Ministry's harder line.[118] So, too, did Mollet's insistence on returning to Paris that government actions were animated, not by colonial concerns, but by what he dubbed the '*antimunichois*' complex. On the one hand, by following Anglo-American initiatives, the French premier clouded the essential justification for French actions: namely, that a poisonous Egyptian regime was supporting an illegitimate rebellion in Algeria, which, after all, was sovereign French territory. On the other hand, the incontestable lesson of Munich was that allowing a dictator to get away with small territorial infractions only opened the door to wider conflict in future.[119] Mollet, according to his nationalist critics at home, should be more robust, not less.

The Senator Leo Hamon was among the first to take issue with Mollet's new rhetorical line. Lauded for his wartime involvement in French Jewish resistance networks, Hamon took a particular interest in imperial affairs, aligning himself with a number of cross-bench parliamentarians (the *Indépendants d'Outre-Mer*) hailing from overseas territories. Writing in *Le Monde* on 6 September, Hamon pleaded for greater realism—and realpolitik. The fact was that, whereas Britain could afford to take a more dispassionate approach, placing alleged violations of international law and obstacles to trade at the heart of its case against Nasser, the French position was different. No one was silly enough to think that toppling the Cairo regime would end the Algerian war. But it was equally naïve to pretend that no connection existed. Allowing Nasser's star to rise unchecked would, by extension, enhance the FLN's influence both inside Algeria and globally while, at the same time, destabilizing the fledgling governments of Morocco and Tunisia that were basically favourable to French interests.[120]

The French prime minister felt obliged to retort, and, in the process, showed how close to the British he had moved. The London conference, he confirmed, revealed the 'quasi-unanimity' of views among the users of the canal over their rights of access, something that Australian Premier Robert Menzies had made clear to Nasser. Should the colonel refuse to respect these rights, the consequences would be grave. Mollet made a formal statement to waiting journalists on 10 September. He was anxious to restore public confidence that the government's unequivocal hostility to the nationalization, defined in the National Assembly debate on 3 August, remained unchanged: 'Without any showy bragging (*vaines rodomontades*) I affirm, simply but firmly, that these [3 August] declarations are still valid. Since there has been so much tendentious speculation here and there, let me repeat that, even if there was no Algerian dimension to consider, our attitude would be exactly the same.'[121]

---

[118] 'Les Ministres français et britanniques voudraient "dépolitiser" l'affaire de Suez L'O.N.U. serait seulement "informée" de la situation', *Le Monde*, 12 September 1956.

[119] Jacques Fauvet, 'Le gouvernement ne définira qu'à la fin du mois le futur statut politique de l'Algérie', *Le Monde*, 6 September 1956.

[120] Leo Hamon, 'Lutter contre Nasser? Oui, mais comment?', *Le Monde*, 6 September 1956.

[121] 'M. Guy Mollet: la crise de Suez montre la nécessité de disposer de nouvelles sources d'énergie', *Le Monde*, 11 September 1956.

As was becoming usual, however, whenever the hardliners appeared to have the upper hand, the Quai d'Orsay tried to leave French options open. On the evening of 16 September, Foreign Minister Pineau used a national radio broadcast to denounce what was characterized as a campaign that pitched the supporters of force against those, like himself, who favoured continued talks. With a disingenuousness that was surely easier before a radio microphone than a TV camera, Pineau maintained that the government had not resolved on war and was in fact using every means at its disposal to avoid it. 'Peaceful coexistence' was the watchword of French foreign policy. This did not affect France's right to demand that binding international obligations be respected even so. With a hint of menace Pineau added that global peace was best assured by taking steps to thwart 'dictators' whose unilateral actions disrupted the international system. It was a curious performance, the studied ambivalence of which exemplified Pineau's public statements throughout the Suez affair. It paid some lip service to the British rhetorical line in echoing Eden's stress on international rights. But this was blended with a 'lessons from recent history' approach designed to play better with the Defence Ministry hawks at home.

A day later Mollet weighed in again. This time he sought to reassure the French people that the bluster of the Suez crisis and the fog of the Algerian war were not distracting the government from its foremost task: bringing domestic inflation under control.[122] Perhaps unsurprisingly, the combination of Pineau's zigzagging and Mollet's reordering of policy priorities only added to the scepticism about Foreign Ministry preferences and Socialist Party inclinations among those who favoured Nasser's removal. And this was soon to take a new rhetorical turn.[123]

During the last ten days of September, pressure mounted on Mollet's government not to waver in its original commitment to reverse the Suez nationalization by whatever means necessary. On the one hand, leading Radicals, among which figured the governing coalition's staunchest hardliners, joined their erstwhile coalition partners, the Christian Democrats of the MRP (Mouvement Républicain Populaire), in expressing their anxieties lest the seemingly unending cycle of conferences, UN discussions, and other diplomatic exchanges induce Mollet to give ground. The implication here was that the premier might yet bend to Foreign Ministry advice regardless of the secret military planning for war. On the other hand, Algeria's governors, past and present, warned the prime minister against pursuing any decisive reforms in the colony unless and until Nasser was brought to heel. Their logic was simple. Making fewer concessions, if any, to Algeria's Muslims over citizenship rights and social spending would be much easier were Nasser first overthrown.[124] Ejecting Nasser from power, then, was less about delivering a knock-out blow to the FLN—always a highly dubious proposition—and more about decisively slowing the

---

[122] 'Suez et Algérie ne font pas oublier le niveau des prix', *Le Monde*, 18 September 1956.

[123] 'M. Pineau: le gouvernement français non seulement ne se résout pas à la guerre, mais recherche tous les moyens de l'éviter', *Le Monde*, 17 September 1956.

[124] Jacques Fauvet, 'M. Guy Mollet veut conclure un "nouveau contrat" avec l'Assemblée', *Le Monde*, 5 Octobre 1956.

momentum for Algerian political reform that was always central to the Socialists' justification for ceding special powers to the army.[125]

The MRP, the strongest supporters of intervention on the opposition benches, applied the strongest pressure. The Party executive agreed on 19 September to send a delegation to the Hotel Matignon to seek assurances from the prime minister that government policy was unchanged. Writing in the National Assembly journal, MRP veteran Maurice Schumann meanwhile took a sideswipe at Pineau's Quai d'Orsay, suggesting that the French public were confused and discouraged by the labyrinthine course that Suez diplomacy had taken.[126] It was time to get back to a more basic message: the lessons of Munich had been learned and a dictator's advance was being stopped. Schumann's party colleague, François de Menthon, another former minister boasting exemplary Resistance credentials, took up the charge. On the same day that the MRP executive was meeting in Paris, de Menthon repeated Schumann's message almost word for word to a Limoges gathering of party activists from Haute-Vienne, the Corrèze, and la Charente. Two months of international negotiation had yielded 'derisory' results, which undermined the original clarity of French government statements and, worst of all, risked confronting France with a *fait accompli* if some sort of deal were done with Cairo.[127] Hours later, Schumann let rip again, telling reporters that 'the Suez crisis is far from over. By remaining firm, the day will soon come when our allies will thank us for having thrown the first roadblock across the road to Munich'.[128]

It was at this point that the first voice from within Mollet's government joined the chorus. Minister of Education René Billères, whose roots lay in the Radical Party fiefdom of the Hautes-Pyrénées, adopted a more apocalyptic tone with his local Party supporters. 'The destiny of peace is being played out in Africa', he began. It was for the West to demonstrate that freedom was the best guarantee for the improvement of living standards in the developing world; otherwise there would be war. And while Billères rejected foreign accusations that France was prosecuting a 'war of religion' in North Africa, he acknowledged that the outcome of the Suez crisis would determine whether France would sink to the level of a 'second-rank' country.[129]

Set against this background, the National Assembly debate on Suez on the afternoon of 17 October was stormy, but short. Coming less than a week before the in-flight arrest of four members of the FLN executive en route from Rabat to Tunis on 22 October, the shadow of Algeria—although not yet of a decisive

[125] For background, see: Philippe Bourdel, *La Dernière chance de l'Algérie française: Du gouvernement socialiste au retour de De Gaulle, 1956–1958* (Paris: Albin Michel, 1996); Étienne Maquin, *Le Parti socialiste et la guerre d;Algérie* (Paris: L'Harmattan, 1990).
[126] 'Le M.R.P. demande si les objectifs du gouvernement restent les mêmes', *Le Monde*, 21 September 1956.
[127] 'M. de Menthon (M. R. P.): l'acceptation du fait accompli aurait des conséquences exceptionnellement graves', *Le Monde*, 25 September 1956.
[128] 'M. Maurice Schumann (M.R.P.): sans un prompt redressement, les alliances de la France recevraient un coup fatal', *Le Monde*, 25 September 1956.
[129] 'M. Billères (Radical): l'evolution de la crise décidera si la France est un pays de deuxième ordre', *Le Monde*, 25 September 1956.

breakthrough—pervaded the session. The most decisive intervention came from the Communist Roger Garaudy. He was a man well acquainted with Algeria, having been imprisoned by the Vichy regime at Djelfa for much of World War II. Piece by piece, Garaudy dismantled the case for intervention in Egypt built up by Mollet's government over preceding months. Any suggestion that Suez nationalization, an exercise of sovereign rights within a sovereign state, was remotely comparable to Hitler's march into the Sudetenland was ridiculous. And the Communists, the one French party uniformly opposed to the Munich settlement in 1938 (loud applause from the Communist benches), deserved to be taken seriously on that score. As for the claim that French or Western interests were somehow threatened by Nasserism, this, too, was to mistake the rising power of anti-colonialism for a generic hostility to 'the West' in the Arab world. The former was a legitimate cause; the latter was a figment of French nationalist imagination. Such paranoid self-deception was nurtured by the corruptive effects of the Algerian conflict. One manifestation of the war's distortive impact on French politics was that it allowed the government to make hay with the claim that, not only the capability, but the reputation of the French Army were somehow threatened by Egypt's actions. Nonsense—how could this possibly be true? The entire governmental case for action, in other words, was based on false analogy and a cynical inflation of the dangers presented by leaving Nasser unchallenged.[130]

It was unfortunate that this, a meticulous and logical refutation of the case for 'firmness' that government members had repeatedly laid out since its original iteration on 3 August 1956, was made by a controversial figure at the extreme left of the political spectrum. It was too easy to dismiss Garaudy as a leftist fellow traveller with strongly pro-Arab sympathies. At the very moment that Garaudy was attacking governmental double-dealing, the Finance Ministry was taking steps to protect the franc during the impending war by securing authorization to draw on International Monetary Fund reserves.[131] Once Operation Musketeer Revise rolled into action, the French diplomatic establishment, orchestrated by Foreign Minister Pineau, maintained that French actions were guided by respect for the UN Charter and the tenets of international law. Invasion was a matter of upholding legitimate rights of access to the Suez Canal, not the removal of a troublesome Arab foe.[132]

Indeed, perhaps the more remarkable feature of French political debate as the crisis reached its denouement is the muffled, low-level volume of the few voices raised in opposition to the government's actions. The Council of Ministers emerged from a late morning session on 1 November exuding confidence. Despite

---

[130] André Ballet, 'Le débat sur Suez a tourné court à l'Assemblée', *Le Monde*, 18 October 1956. Garaudy's later career was stormier still. A fierce critic of Soviet suppression of the 1968 Prague Spring, resultant expulsion from the PCF in the early 1970s heralded his shift towards militant pro-Arabism. He converted to Islam in 1982 and, in 1996, published a book, later translated as *The Founding Myths of Modern Israel*, which cost him a suspended jail sentence and a 240,000 franc fine for Holocaust denial.

[131] Dooley, 'Great Britain's "Last Battle" in the Middle East', 509–10.

[132] DDF, vol. III, 1956, doc. 77, Pineau circular to French ambassadors overseas, 31 October 1956.

short-term delays to joint military operations—variously attributed to logistical difficulties, the complexity of diplomatic messaging, and last-minute American demarches in London—there was no sign, in public at least, that Mollet and his colleagues were either internally divided or under crushing pressure from Washington or elsewhere.[133] The prime minister's standing with the French public was further consolidated in the days ahead, the consensus view—or, at least, the government's stated interpretation of it—being that French policy had remained consistent since 3 August. Nasser's action had to be challenged or worse would follow. An Egyptian-Israeli confrontation was, anyway, unavoidable. So it was better to act now in support of a trusted ally against an inveterate dictator.[134]

This air of unruffled calm persisted even as the invasion of Egypt stalled. Visited by numerous party delegations in the second week of November, Mollet kept to the line that the government was simply following through on its long-declared policy. Along with chief hardliner, Defence Minister Bourgès-Maunoury, the prime minister suggested that it was too soon to declare intervention a failure, still less to reach definitive conclusions about the original thinking behind it. Why not celebrate the offensive capability of the French forces deployed and the massive logistical effort that made the invasion possible?[135] Ironically, only the opposition MRP continued to back the government as the full extent of both the failure and the flawed thinking became clearer in the days ahead. Others were less sanguine. Two former premiers took the lead. Ironically, one was Paul Reynaud. Ironic because as prime minister in the final days of the battle of France in June 1940, he had accepted Churchill's famous, unfulfilled proposal of a Franco-British Union to keep France fighting. Sixteen years later Reynaud laid into Mollet's government, accusing it of maladministration, misinforming the French public, and misman-aging the war against Egypt. As Pineau later commented, Reynaud, having himself presided over imminent defeat, seemed to take pleasure in the misfortunes of others.[136] The other elder statesman to turn on the government was René Pleven. As defence minister, he had presided over France's final Vietnamese defeat at Dien Bien Phu in 1954. Pleven now accused Mollet's government of blundering into war alongside Britain. France's position in Algeria would suffer. The likelihood of UN condemnation was much increased.[137]

Admittedly, there were still influential supporters of intervention prepared to defend its logic. François Charles-Roux was one of them. President of the Suez Canal Company since 1948, his hostility to nationalization might safely be taken for granted. But Charles-Roux was also distinguished by an illustrious diplo-matic career that culminated in his appointment to the top job of Quai d'Orsay

---

[133] Jacques Fauvet, 'Le gouvernement espère que l'intervention aura des effets politiques tant en Égypte qu'en Algérie', *Le Monde*, 2 November 1956.

[134] 'Les événements consolident la position de M. Guy Mollet, Mardi déclaration de M. Pineau à l'Assemblée', *Le Monde*, 6 November 1956.

[135] For concise details of the French intervention, see Philippe Masson, 'Origines et bilan d'une défaite', *Revue Historique des Armées*, 4:1 (1986), 52–4.

[136] Christian Pineau, *1956/Suez* (Paris: Robert Laffont, 1976), 198.

[137] 'Les parlementaires tirent les leçons des derniers événements', *Le Monde*, 13 November 1956.

secretary-general, albeit at an unpropitious moment: May 1940. He called on this diplomatic expertise in late November 1956, telling an audience at the Académie des sciences morales et politiques that the legality of Nasser's actions had to be contextualized in terms of the Cairo regime's arbitrary methods and the 'fanaticism' it cultivated. Confining oneself to a narrow reading of international law missed the point: it was the Egyptian leader who first sought confrontation.[138]

François-Roux's 'he started it' reasoning ignored the fact that the 'narrow' reading of international law he so detested was actually the correct one. His arguments cut no ice with the government's two most stinging critics, each of whom had turned from allies to bitter opponents of the Republican Front. First was Pierre Mendès France, the self-appointed moral conscience of France's liberal left in matters of empire. Speaking to an 800-strong audience at Bordeaux's Saint-Augustin *salle des fêtes*, the Radical Party politician lambasted intervention as unethical, ineffectual, and deeply stupid. The Americans were needlessly antagonized, the UN alienated, and France's residual claims to any 'right to rule' in North Africa undermined. These blunt truths did not go over well. In addition to a chorus of boos and whistles, firecrackers, stink bombs, and rotten apples were hurled towards the stage in an effort to shut the outspoken politician up.[139]

If Mendès France's outspokenness hinged on issues of morality and power projection, his fellow critic, André Philip, targeted his attacks on the damage done to French socialism by the coalition's action over the preceding year. An acknowledged financial specialist who prided himself in his role in steering French reconstruction as minister of national economy in the immediate post-war years, Philip had been out of sympathy with the Socialist Party leadership for years. His definitive break with the Socialists would come in January 1958. But it was clearly foretold in his analysis of the Republican Front's misadventures in Algeria and Egypt during 1956. Having won the January elections promising peace and dialogue in Algeria, Mollet's government not only expanded that war but started another on the banks of the Nile. Leaving the Socialist Party morally bankrupt was bad enough, but the invasion of Egypt also spelt strategic disaster at a time when Socialists ought to have been capitalizing on the divisions opened in Communist ranks by the brutality of Soviet actions in Budapest. As it was, the toxic Algeria-Suez cocktail had denied the Socialists their best opportunity since the PCF's (Parti Communiste Français) creation in 1920 to win back Communist supporters disillusioned by their leaders' doctrinaire loyalism to Moscow.[140] For a true Socialist, then, Suez was particularly tragic. Philip had no quarrel with Mendès France's criticism of North African policies that were as ethically reprehensible as they were internationally damaging.[141] But what stopped Philip short was that the

[138] 'M. François Charles-Roux évoque à l'Académie des sciences morales et politiques la nationalisation de Suez', *Le Monde*, 20 November 1956.

[139] 'M. Mendès-France: Français et Anglais sont intervenus trop tard', *Le Monde*, 20 November 1956.

[140] 'M André Philip reproche au gouvernement sa politique au Moyen-Orient et en Algérie', *Le Monde*, 22 November 1956.

[141] Ibid.

Republican Front's new-found imperialism had ensured that the debilitating rupture within the French left would continue for years.[142] It was this, he would later claim, that left the door ajar to opponents of the Fourth Republic to overthrow the regime during the May crisis of 1958.[143]

CONCLUSION

As the invasion of Egypt began, the CIA sent a short briefing paper to President Eisenhower summarizing global reactions to the unfolding crisis. With a curt incisiveness, it repeated what was by then a long-held view inside 'the Agency', namely that, since early August, the French decision to intervene was a foregone conclusion:

> Internationally, except for Israelis, people most pleased with developments seem to be [the] French. National Assembly gave Mollet less extensive support for intervention, however, that [*sic*] it gave last August, when only Communists opposed a strong policy. [It] seems generally accepted in Paris that French have been planning move with Israel and Britain for some weeks.[144]

The appearance of a nation unperturbed by the failure of intervention in Egypt was superficially correct, but it was profoundly misleading all the same. By the end of November, Mollet's Socialist Party was in open revolt against the premier. Party rebels alleged that the disastrous attempt to topple Nasser was the logical consequence of the unethical adventurism that had come to define Republican Front actions in North Africa as a whole. Little wonder that the Algerian public celebrated the against-the-odds 'victory' of Nasser, champion of Third Worldism.[145] Mollet, the convinced Anglophile, was cut adrift from London, finding sanctuary in a welcoming West German embrace as the finalization of plans for the European Community offered solace for Middle Eastern humiliation.[146] More significant in the short term, the French political fallout from Suez rekindled the mistrust between civilian authorities in Paris and professional army commanders in Algeria. Even Christian Pineau, whose memoir of Suez sought to demythologize the supposed French connection between deposing Nasser and winning in Algeria, found it difficult not to place the escalating colonial war at the heart of his narrative.[147] Mollet's government, had begun 1956 by cementing a new bond between civil government and the officer corps with 'special powers' legislation that

[142] Maurice Vaïsse, 'Post-Suez France', in Louis and Owen, *Suez 1956*, 337.

[143] Philip published this fierce critique of his former Party as *Le Socialisme trahi* (*Socialism Betrayed*) in 1958. The moral crisis in the French Socialist Party triggered by Algeria, and exacerbated by Suez, is nicely described by Benjamin Stora, *La gangrène et l'oubli. La mémoire de la guerre d'Algérie* (Paris: La Découverte, 1991), 74–9.

[144] CIA Intelligence in the Middle East, online archive, CIA briefing paper, 'Near East-Crisis', 31 October 1956.

[145] Masson, 'Origines et bilan d'une défaite', 58.

[146] Vaïsse, 'Post-Suez France', in Louis and Owen, *Suez 1956*, 336–7.

[147] See Pineau, *1956/Suez*, 25–9, 37–41, 139–47, 189–91.

offered military commanders unprecedented means to crush the Algerian rebellion. Ministers ended the year with the prospect of fatal army indiscipline in Algiers only months away.

The British rhetoric of support for international law may perhaps have helped the Conservatives recover domestically once Eden was out of the way. The 1959 Conservative manifesto, on the back of which Harold Macmillan won a landslide election victory, emphasized the party's commitment to the UN, while also making thirteen references to the Commonwealth, whereas the language of 'empire' and 'colonies' had disappeared.[148] ('Empire' had rated ten mentions in 1955, as against twenty-two for 'Commonwealth' and fourteen for 'colonies'/'colonial'.)[149] Suez may have been a national/imperial disaster for Britain and a personal one for Eden, but some nimble rhetorical footwork helped ensure that, in terms of the Conservatives' electoral chances, it was barely even a setback. It might even be said that although Suez finished Eden's career, it was much less problematic for the Conservative Party as a whole than a failure to act would have been.

Both countries denied that they were being 'imperialistic'. Although the British would always have distanced themselves from this word, prior to World War II there had been a much greater level of comfort in talking about 'empire'. For the French, that term had always had overtones of Napoleon III and was therefore problematic; it was necessary to talk instead about 'colonies' and, after 1945, 'union'.

The British strategy during the crisis involved presenting Britain as the principled leader of a morally based international community (although that exact term was not much in use at the time) and as the upholder of international law. To some extent they inveigled Mollet and Pineau into echoing this language even though their hard-line critics depicted the Frenchmen's use of such conciliatory language as a sign of weakness.

The French experience reminds us that, however one reads the rhetoric of empire emanating from Paris and London throughout 1956, it makes more sense to interpret the Suez disaster, not just as a crisis of liberal democracies at war, but of very different democratic systems in operation. Anthony Eden was ultimately brought down by a parliamentary system that functioned, combined with a British public sphere that accommodated harsh criticism of government misdeeds. Britain's imperial presence in the Middle East survived; its all-important transatlantic connections were soon rebuilt. In France, the exact reverse applied. Guy Mollet's Republican Front both survived the Suez humiliation—not least by blaming British inconsistency—and, if poll evidence is to be credited, emerged with stronger public endorsement than before.

The Suez crisis laid bare the dysfunctional core of the Fourth Republic's parliamentary system even so. And wider public engagement with the crisis was skewed by the overwhelming preoccupation with the Algerian war. Thus, where the

---

[148] There was, however, a reference to 'misrepresentation about British "colonialism"': Conservative Manifesto 1959, in F. W. S. Craig (ed.), *British General Election Manifestos 1918–1966* (Chichester: Political Reference Publications, 1970), 188–96.

[149] Conservative Manifesto 1955, in Craig, *Manifestos*, 156–76.

consequences of Suez for governmental structures and overseas power projection were generally more limited in the British case than typically assumed, in the French case they were seismic. French international standing in the Arab world hit a low from which it only recovered in the wake of the Six-Day War in 1967. Perhaps more significant, the Fourth Republic limped from one Algeria-induced crisis to another until its final unlamented collapse eighteen months later. What was a crisis of prestige for Britain was a fatal crisis of regime for France.

Conclusion

This book began with a notorious episode of Western imperialism. Britain's 1882 occupation of Egypt was conducted in opposition to local proto-nationalist forces, which appeared (or which were claimed) to threaten Britain's financial and strategic interests. As shown in Chapter 1, although the French also had considerable economic interests in the country, and were already acting jointly with the British to control Egyptian finances, France in the end held back from participating in the invasion. As we have seen, the style and consequences of France's intervention in Tunisia the year before had much to do with this. Deepening involvement in Tunis not only set material limits to French actions in Egypt, but also conditioned French rhetoric in relation to the 1882 crisis.

The book ended, in Chapter 7, with another notorious episode in the same region. In the wake of the Nasser regime's nationalization of the Suez Canal in 1956, the British again invaded. This time France did participate, both nations being in secret collusion with Israel, which agreed to attack Egypt. Israel's military engagement provided the pretext that the British and French used to intervene to 'stop the conflict from spreading'. On this occasion, although the military operation was again a success, the political and diplomatic consequences were catastrophic. Global opinion was almost uniformly hostile and the USA asserted political and financial leverage to force the occupiers to withdraw.

The 1882 and the 1956 crises, which generated such heated debate in both Britain and France, were, in fact, interconnected; rhetorically enmeshed, even. Comparing how the British and French argued about these issues, and also examining how the rhetoric of the later crisis contrasted with the earlier one, teaches important lessons about the two nations' respective imperial cultures. Specifically, the latter-day imperialists Anthony Eden and Guy Mollet couched their actions in internationalist rhetoric. Eden's language was reminiscent of the Gladstone government's justifications for intervention in 1882. Mollet's claims that the wider stability of North Africa was at stake evoked French justifications for intervention in Tunis in 1881. Each claimed their actions were taken both to uphold better standards of governance and to restore regional order. At the rhetorical level, if not at the practical one, imperialism was eschewed. For all that, the British and French governments viewed their Egyptian problems through the lens of wider overseas interests. For Britain, Middle Eastern relationships, Commonwealth connections and global trading prospects were called into question. For France in 1956, as in 1882, the question of whether to intervene or not in Egypt was beholden to other, nearby crises that remained unresolved. France's annexation of Tunisia in 1881 cast a long shadow over decisions made about Egypt a year later, setting the agenda for domestic political debate. In this sense, the continuing fallout from one imperial venture inflected the rhetoric surrounding another. A similar point could be made about France and Suez in 1956. Here it was the Egyptian regime's support for nationalist rebels fighting for independence in the colony of Algeria (a problem, ironically, that was further complicated by Tunisia's achievement of sovereign independence four months before the Suez nationalization) that drove both the decisions made and their depiction to domestic and global audiences.

There were, however, differences as well as similarities. The crises Britain experienced in 1882 and 1956 hinged on the intangible, but nonetheless vital issue of prestige—not only national prestige, but, perhaps more importantly, prime ministerial and governmental prestige. At stake were two connected perceptions, one of strategic capability, the other of ethical probity. These could be safeguarded politically not by military intervention alone, but by intervention in combination with the rhetoric of liberal order. But what were crises of prestige for Britain were crises of regime for France—neither of which could be overcome through rhetoric—and in the case of 1956 the disease quite quickly proved fatal. The domestic political arguments triggered in 1881–2 by action in Tunis and inaction in Alexandria raised fundamental questions about the Third Republic's increasing self-identification as an 'imperial' regime. Virulent criticism from the republican left and the anti-republican right was set to increase as further costly colonial ventures were pursued in Vietnam and, later, the East African headwaters of the Nile. In 1956 the failure of French efforts to overthrow a more powerful Egyptian regime amplified the Fourth Republic's ineffectiveness as its governing coalitions flailed about in search of a solution to the deepening crisis in Algeria. In these respects, the late nineteenth-century expansion and the twentieth-century collapse of the British and French empires were not only surprisingly alike but also mutually entangled in hitherto unsuspected ways.

Direct confrontations between Europe's two pre-eminent colonial powers, typified by the 1898 Fashoda crisis, were, of course, matched by uneasy accords, as evidenced in the Moroccan crises of the early 1900s. But the recurring invocation of 'crisis', apparent again during the profound Franco-British *mésentente* over nationalist Turkey's 1920s resurgence—the Chanak crisis—points to another aspect of these imperial entanglements. Whether in the process of expansion, or when faced with external challenges, internal violence, and ultimate contraction, the British and French empires rose and fell together. Sometimes one imperial power conspired against the other; sometimes the two empires were ostensibly united. Sometimes conflict and cooperation went hand in hand, as was the case during World War II. One factor remained consistent throughout: governments, oppositions, and publics on both sides of the Channel argued intensely about the meaning and purpose of imperial intervention. Rhetoric was not just critical to the defence of imperial action—or, in some cases, inaction; it defined the ways in which colonial crises were constructed and understood.

Of course, 1956 was not the end of the story for either empire any more than 1882 had been the beginning. Historians now tend to stress that, in the British case, Suez was not a sharp rupture. G. C. Peden has argued that the crisis reinforced rather than created British dependence on the USA, and also that Whitehall policymakers were reluctant in the immediate post-Suez years to accept the necessity for alteration in the UK's world role.[1] British policymakers were much better able to perceive the inevitability of French imperial decline—greater distance, it seemed, brought looming decolonization into better focus.[2] All the same, all but the most diehard Conservatives were by now aware that it would not be possible to sustain the formal empire indefinitely. The same might be said for a wide ideological spectrum of French political leaders. Abiding official disdain in Paris and francophone colonial capitals for the post-war British imperial vocabulary of 'self-government' and Commonwealth 'partnership' was matched by a realization that Britain's contracting imperial presence in the Middle East and Africa was bound to affect the restructuring of France's colonial relationships.[3] The transnational networks integral to anti-colonial nationalists before and after 1945 drew on precedents observed in other dependent territories. Indeed, the rhetoric of anti-colonialism was as influenced by local developments in different empires in much the same way that French and British imperialists found themselves compelled to respond to decisive reforms or transitions to independence in neighbouring colonies.[4]

In Britain, as the 1950s came to a close, Labour and the Tories were in bitter dispute over the speed of African decolonization and the terms on which it would be granted—but both parties assumed that it was going to come.[5] Even radical left-wingers still presumed that, in addition to bequeathing viable institutions to the successor nations, the populations of British Africa should still be inculcated with the norms and values of their former motherland. Note, for example, the comment of Labour MP Barbara Castle as she denounced the brutal treatment of Mau Mau detainees: 'if there is one thing we must hand on to the Africans in Kenya, it is a profound respect for British justice'.[6] In this account, decolonization was to be not merely a legal handover but an active process by which international relations were to be morally reshaped under British leadership.

The theme of moral leadership can also be seen in Harold Macmillan's famous 'wind of change' speech, delivered in tense circumstances in Apartheid South Africa in 1960. 'In that speech, Mr. Macmillan said nothing startling or novel', claimed John Wyndham, one of his former private secretaries, a few years later. 'Indeed, one

---

[1] G. C. Peden, 'Suez and Britain's Decline as a World Power', *Historical Journal*, 55 (2012), 1073–96.

[2] Martin Thomas, 'A Path Not Taken: British Perspectives on French Colonial Violence after 1945', in L. J. Butler and Sarah Stockwell (eds), *The Wind of Change: Harold Macmillan and British Decolonization* (Basingstoke: Palgrave-Macmillan, 2013), 162–5.

[3] Frederick Cooper, *Citizenship between Empire and Nation: Remaking France and French Africa, 1945–1960* (Ithaca, NY: Cornell University Press, 2015), 291–4, 301–2, 375.

[4] Johanna Bockman, 'Socialist Globalization against Capitalist Neocolonialism', *Humanity*, 6:1 (2015), 109–10; Amzat Boukari-Yabara, *Africa Unite! Une histoire du panafricanisme* (Paris: La Découverte, 2014), 115–18, 125–30, 137–40.

[5] See Sir Arthur Benson, 'Set Pattern Of Advance', *The Times*, 30 November 1959.

[6] HC Deb, 16 June 1959, vol. 607, col. 300.

of the most effective passages was a quotation from a speech made five months earlier by the Foreign Secretary at the United Nations.'[7] Another former private secretary, T. J. Bligh, also took this line, noting that the 'wind of change' phrase itself had been used by Macmillan earlier in his African tour without attracting attention: 'so it was not new in Cape Town but the setting and the occasion and the audience set it off'.[8] Macmillan's contribution thus needs to be seen as a masterly rhetorical dramatization of what was already established policy, albeit one that helped establish something approaching a cross-party consensus at home on imperial issues of the type that had been so conspicuously lacking since Suez.

Yet the emphasis on continuities should not be taken too far. Of course, Anglo-French political and economic involvement in the affairs of former colonial territories may be presented, often with strong foundation, as forms of neo-imperialism. (Such involvement, it should be added, often took place with the active collaboration of the newly independent governments.) Yet, undeniably, something significant had changed, and changed very rapidly. Between 1958 and 1962 there were developments in both Britain and France that made clear not only that the two empires were coming to an end, but that they were doing so more dramatically and on quite different terms from those that many had envisaged just a few years before.

In France, more imminent signs of an end of the Algerian connection were intimately bound up with the terminal collapse of the Fourth Republic, which finally came during yet another imperial crisis—that of May 1958. A highly orchestrated pro-imperial protest movement in Algiers would achieve one short-term objective, General de Gaulle's return to office as head of a new, presidential Republic, only to witness its longer term goal, the conservation of Algeria's white settler minority regime, spurned by its putative saviour: de Gaulle himself.[9] For all his complicity in it, de Gaulle was acutely embarrassed by the Fifth Republic's reactionary origins in the conspiratorial insurrectionism of Algeria's settlers and the military commanders they lionized. The general's shift towards negotiation and withdrawal from Algeria was prefigured in ceasefire proposals in 1958–9 but only slowly enacted over four more years of bitter colonial war.[10] Powerfully opposed by the loose coalition of settlers and senior soldiers that did so much to propel him back to power, de Gaulle's turn away from Algeria was punctuated by feats of lugubrious rhetorical brilliance—radio broadcasts and, increasingly, television

[7] Lord Egremont [formerly John Wyndham], 'The Wind of Change Myth', *Sunday Times*, 10 May 1964.
[8] TNA, PREM 11/4937, T. J. Bligh to Lord Egremont, 26 May 1964. On the speech generally, see Butler and Stockwell, *The Wind of Change*.
[9] Odile Rudelle, *Mai 1958, de Gaulle et la République* (Paris: Plon, 1988), 103–10; Jean Charlot, *Le Gaullisme d'opposition, 1946–1958* (Paris: Fayard, 1983), 347–60.
[10] Maurice Vaïsse, *La Grandeur: Politique étrangère du Général de Gaulle, 1958–1969* (Paris: Fayard, 1998), chapters 1 and 7; Irwin M. Wall, *France, the United States, and the Algerian War* (Berkeley, CA: University of California Press, 2001), 192–228; Jeffrey James Bryne, 'Négociation perpétuelle: de Gaulle et le FLN, 1961–1968', in Maurice Vaïsse (ed.), *De Gaulle et l'Algérie, 1943–1969* (Paris: Armand Colin, 2012), 299–304.

addresses, which carried the French public and its service personnel along with him.[11] His Algerian nationalist opponents in the FLN meanwhile won victory after victory in the propaganda war waged before domestic and global audiences, persuading the world of the bankruptcy of French colonialism.[12] Ironically perhaps, the outcome of this terrible North African conflict, devastating for Algerian society, was determined as much by words as by deeds.

In Britain, by contrast, there was again no 'crisis of regime', and yet between 1959 and 1961 African decolonization accelerated rapidly during Iain Macleod's reforming tenure as colonial secretary. It was not the case, as is often asserted, that the British, consciences stung by revelations about atrocities in Kenya and Nyasaland, suddenly realized that their imperial game 'was finally up'.[13] Rather, Macmillan, who would have preferred to retain the harder-line Alan Lennox-Boyd at the Colonial Office, probably did not realize the full policy implications when he appointed Macleod. But although contingency and personality played their parts, there were structural factors at work too. As Macmillan rightly observed in Cape Town, African nationalism had by now reached a critical mass—and there was no obvious geopolitical or electoral benefit in attempting to resist it. Of course, the retreat required more than a little linguistic finesse. David McCourt makes the point that Britain remained committed to maintaining its global influence, well beyond its late 1960s departure from its 'East of Suez role'—a conception which, he suggests, was itself a latter-day rhetorical construction, created out of a 'diverse set of remnants from Britain's Imperial past'.[14]

Britain's 1960s turn towards Europe raises questions about the depth of the country's commitment towards the Commonwealth. Grandiose statements about its continuing salience to the British global mission, could, of course, be deployed opportunistically for domestic political reasons and internationally to smooth the sensibilities of the Commonwealth countries themselves. At the same time, they provided a rhetorical weapon to de Gaulle, as he sought to bar British entry to the EEC. In his famous 1963 'veto' press conference, he declared: 'England in effect is insular, she is maritime, she is linked through her exchanges, her markets, her supply lines to the most diverse and often the most distant countries; she pursues essentially industrial and commercial activities, and only slight agricultural ones.

---

[11] Serge Berstein, *The Republic of de Gaulle, 1958–1969* (Cambridge: Cambridge University Press, 1993), 47–50; Julia Heinemann, 'De la parole diffuse à la parole confisquée: la transmission de la parole gaullienne aux militaires en guerre d'Algérie, 1958–1962', in Vaïsse, *De Gaulle et l'Algérie*, 205–11.

[12] Matthew Connelly, 'Rethinking the Cold War and Decolonization: The Grand Strategy of the Algerian War of Independence', *International Journal of Middle East Studies*, 33:2 (2001), 223–41; Charles-Robert Ageron, 'Un aspect de la guerre d'Algérie: la propaganda radiophonique du FLN et des états arabes', in Ageron, *La guerre d'Algérie et les Algériens, 1954–1962* (Paris: Armand Colin, 1997), 245–59.

[13] R. W. Johnson, 'By Any Means Necessary', *Sunday Times*, 9 January 2005; Richard Toye, 'Arguing about Hola Camp: The Rhetorical Consequences of a Colonial Massacre', in Martin Thomas and Richard Toye (eds), *Rhetorics of Empire* (forthcoming).

[14] David M. McCourt, 'What was Britain's "East of Suez Role"? Reassessing the Withdrawal, 1964–1968', *Diplomacy & Statecraft*, 20 (2009), 453–72, at 454.

She has in all her doings very marked and very original habits and traditions.'[15] The general could delay British membership—he wielded a second veto four years later—but, as we know, he could not frustrate it indefinitely. Arguably, his presentation of Britain as 'uncontinental' distracted attention from those abiding imperial interests which Britain and France continued to pursue, whether in common or in competition.

In contrast to the profound scars left by the Algerian war, the Fifth Republic, in particular, showed no hesitation in cultivating long-term relationships with postcolonial regimes in francophone Africa, some of them highly autocratic one-party states.[16] These ties were nurtured by de Gaulle's chosen African political fixer, Jacques Foccart. A shadowy *eminence grise* inside the Elysée Palace for a decade from the mid-1960s, Foccart shunned open political discussion, let alone the back-and-forth rhetorical arguments once characteristic of French colonial affairs.[17] In discursive terms, a corner had been turned in the way France did business in Africa. For a while at least, this lack of rhetorical engagement was no barrier to burgeoning neocolonial influence. From military base agreements and intelligence cooperation to trade deals and inward investment, the French imprint in much of black Africa was deeper than its British equivalent. Even in Algeria, the nemesis of French colonialism, military, police, and security service connections were quietly rebuilt in the mid-1960s, some of which subsist to the present day.[18]

In other areas, though, lingering echoes of imperial rhetoric after empire were to be found. Such was particularly the case where the former imperial rivals rubbed up against one another. As Joanna Warson has argued with respect to France's attitude to Britain's Rhodesian crisis, 'The rhetoric employed on both sides of the Channel to describe Anglo-French relations over Rhodesia and African affairs in general underscores the importance of Franco-British partnership in the minds of the French and the British engaged in Rhodesian business.'[19] Her broader point is that the Anglo-French relationship over such issues was based on a mixture of competition and cooperation, categories that coexisted and overlapped rather than being mutually exclusive.[20] This, in turn, raises the interesting question of whether

---

[15] Press conference held by General de Gaulle, 14 January 1963, text at <http://www.cvce.eu/> accessed 29 October 2015.

[16] Rachel Utley, 'Not to Do Less but to Do Better'...: French Military Policy in Africa', *International Affairs*, 78:1 (2002), 130–1; Bruno Charbonneau and Tony Chafer, 'Peace Operations and Francophone Spaces', *International Peacekeeping*, 19:3 (2012), 276–7.

[17] Jean-Pierre Bat, *Le syndrome Foccart: La politique francaise en Afrique de 1959 à nos jours* (Paris: Gallimard, 2012), parts I & II; Jean-Pierre Bat, 'Jacques Foccart, *eminence grise* for African Affairs', in Tony Chafer and Alexander Keese (eds), *Francophone Africa at Fifty* (Basingstoke: Palgrave-Macmillan, 2013), 135–45.

[18] MAE, Direction des Affaires Politiques, Service de liaison avec l'Algérie, 1957–66, carton 16: evolution de la coopération technique en Algérie, 1962–7, especially 'A/S conversation avec le Capitaine Gourine: organisation d'un S.D.E.C.E. algérien', 6 October 1967.

[19] Joanna Warson, 'Beyond Co-operation and Competition: Anglo-French Relations, Connected Histories of Decolonization and Rhodesia's Unilateral Declaration of Independence, 1965–80', *Historical Research*, 88 (2015), 740–64, at 745.

[20] For background, see Gordon D. Cumming and Tony Chafer, 'From Rivalry to Partnership? Critical Reflections on Anglo-French Cooperation in Africa', *Review of International Studies*, 37:5 (2011), 2439–63.

or not there was a distinctive Anglo-French postcolonial *sonderweg*, the pragmatic and rhetorical roots of which lay deep in the co-imperialist past.

That, perhaps, is too broad a question be answered definitively here, but it is worth noting a comment made by former Foreign Secretary Douglas Hurd at the time of the 2011 Libyan conflict: 'The British and the French are the only countries in the European Union with the instinct to intervene... We are always looking for different playing fields.'[21] And from Operation Palliser, the British peace enforcement action in the latter stages of Sierra Leone's civil war in 2000, to Operation Serval, the French military deployment against the Islamists of northern Mali between 2012 and 2014, the post-imperial interventionism of Britain and France has acquired a humanitarian complexion.[22] In the French case especially, gone is the Foccart-era preference for murky dealings with favoured clients. President François Hollande's African policy rhetoric exemplifies an unabashed liberal interventionism unafraid to make connections between France's imperial past and its current regional priorities.[23] Tellingly, West Africa's twenty-first-century war zones have nurtured deepening Franco-British security partnerships typified by logistic support and intelligence-sharing.[24] At the time of writing—in the wake of the Islamic State (IS) attacks in Paris in November 2015—a new wave of intervention in Syria appears to be in prospect. (It is worth noting that IS uses the slogan 'Death to Sykes–Picot!') This is not to say that longstanding sources of Franco-British tension have been forgotten or that they have disappeared, as concurrent debates over the future of the European Union demonstrate. In this book we have shown that Britain and France acted as long-term co-empires but that, at least at the conscious level, their politicians, administrators, and commentators had a weak sense of imperial solidarity with their British or French counterparts. In more than one way, the Anglo-French co-interventionists of the early twenty-first century may have more in common with their co-imperialist predecessors than any of them would be willing to admit.

[21] Comments made on 16 June 2011, quoted in Peter Hennessy, *Distilling the Frenzy: Writing the History of One's Own Times* (London: Biteback Publishing, 2013), 23. For discussion of the nature of the humanitarian intervention in Libya, see Roland Paris, 'The "Responsibility to Protect" and the Structural Problems of Preventive Humanitarian Intervention', *International Peacekeeping*, 21:5 (2014), 569–603.

[22] This is not to deny the nineteenth-century imperial origins of humanitarian interventionism, both in revised concepts of just war and in the codification of standards of civilizational conduct in international law. See Alexis Heraclides and Ada Dialla, *Humanitarian Intervention in the Long Nineteenth Century: Setting the Precedent* (Manchester: Manchester University Press, 2015), 14–16, 31–8.

[23] 'Francois Hollande's African Adventures'. *The Economist*, 19 July 2014.

[24] Charbonneau and Chafer, 'Peace Operations', 278.

Bibliography

ARCHIVES AND PRIVATE PAPERS (BRITAIN)

The National Archives, Kew, London (TNA)
Admiralty papers: ADM 1, ADM 199
Cabinet papers: CAB 23, CAB 24, CAB 37, CAB 65, CAB 66, CAB 122, CAB 128
Colonial Office papers: CO 968, CO 733
Foreign Office papers: FO 27, FO 141, FO 146, FO 371, FO 600, FO 800, FO 881, FO 892, FO 898
Ministry of Information papers: INF 1
Prime Ministers' papers: PREM 11
Domestic Records of the Public Record Office: PRO 30
Treasury papers: T 160
War Office papers: WO 106, WO 201

British Library, London
Lord Curzon papers
Charles Dilke papers
W. E. Gladstone papers
Michel Saint-Denis papers

Parliamentary Archives, London
David Lloyd George papers

Bodleian Library, Oxford
Violet Bonham Carter papers
Lewis Harcourt papers
Margery Perham papers

Liddell Hart Centre for Military Archives, King's College, London
General F. H. N. Davidson papers

Middle East Centre Archive, St Antony's College, Oxford
Edward Spears papers

University of Exeter
BBC Summaries of World Broadcasts, Arab World Documentation Unit, Research Commons
Cecil Harmsworth papers, University of Exeter Special Collections

Churchill Archives Centre, Cambridge
Mark Abrams papers
Duff Cooper papers

ARCHIVES AND PRIVATE PAPERS (FRANCE)

Ministère des Affaires étrangères (MAE)
23AD: Affaires diverses politiques, 1814–1897
1ADP: Affaires diverses, Afrique
17MD: Mémoires et documents
123CPCOM: Correspondance politique et commerciale, 1897–1918 (Afrique, questions
    générales/Commandant Marchand)
161CPCOM: Grande-Bretagne, Correspondance politique et commerciale, 1897–1918
178CPCOM: Madagascar, fondation de la colonie
179CPCOM: Maroc, Correspondance politique et commerciale, 1897–1918
Série E ed. Levant 1918–1929
Série Guerre 1939–45
Série Z Europe

Papiers d'agents—archives privées (PAAP)
Maurice Bompard papers (417PAAP)
Léon Bourgeois papers (29PAAP)
Maurice Dejean papers (PAAP288)
Edmond Doutte papers (PAAP65)
Charles de Freycinet papers (77PAAP)
Léon Gambetta papers (79PAAP)
Gabriel Hanotaux papers (189PAAP)
Edouard Herriot papers (89PAAP)
René Massigli papers (17PAAP)
Gabriel Puaux papers (252PAAP)

Archives Nationales (AN)
Série F^7: Interior Ministry, Police files
Série F^{60}: Prime Minister's Office files
Fonds Privés:
Louis-Hubert Lyautey papers
Paul Painlevé papers
Philippe Pétain papers

Service Historique de la Marine (SHM), Vincennes
Série TT: Guerre 1939–45
Sous-série TTA: Secrétariat à la Marine, Vichy
Sous-série TTC: Forces Navales, France Libre
Fonds privés, Sous-série GG2/Papiers Amiral Sacaze

Service Historique de la Défense-Département de l'Armée de Terre (SHD-DAT)
Série 1K: Archives privées
Série 1P: Deuxième Guerre Mondiale
Série 5P: Deuxième Guerre Mondiale—Défense nationale/empire

Archives Nationales d'Outre-Mer (ANOM)
Georges Mandel papers (PA18)

Marius Moutet papers (PA28)
Albert Sarraut papers (PA9)

Archives départementales de l'Aude, Carcassonne
Albert Sarraut papers

NEWSPAPERS AND PERIODICALS (BRITAIN)

Aberdeen Weekly Journal
Birmingham Daily Post
Blackwood's Edinburgh Magazine
Bristol Mercury and Daily Post
Daily Mail
Daily News
Dundee Courier & Argus
Economist
English Review
Evening Standard
Evening Times
Glasgow Herald
Illustrated London News
Leeds Mercury
Leicester Chronicle and the Leicestershire Mercury
Listener
Liverpool Mercury
Manchester Guardian
Morning Post
National Review
Nineteenth Century
Northern Echo
Observer
Pall Mall Gazette
Review of Reviews
Saturday Review
Speaker
Spectator
Standard
Sunday Times
Times
Tribune
Wasp
Western Times

NEWSPAPERS AND PERIODICALS (FRANCE)

L'Action française
L'Armée français
L'Aurore

Bulletin du Comité de l'Afrique française
L'Echo de Paris
Le Figaro
Le Gaulois
L'Intransigeant
L'Humanité
Le Journal des Débats
La Justice
La Lanterne
Le Matin
Le Monde
Le Monde Colonial Illustré
L'Ouest-Éclair
Outre-Mer
Le Petit Journal
Le Petit Journal Illustré
Le Petit Parisien
Le Petit Parisien Illustré
Le Temps

ELECTRONIC DATABASES AND WEBSITES

Churchill Papers Online
Foreign Broadcast Information Service
House of Commons Parliamentary Papers
Mass Observation Archive
W. L. Mackenzie King diary <http://www.collectionscanada.gc.ca/>

OFFICIAL PUBLICATIONS

Journal Officiel de la République française, Débats parlementaires
Chambre des Députés
Sénat
Hansard
House of Commons
House of Lords

PUBLISHED DOCUMENTS

Documents Diplomatiques Français (DDF) Paris: Imprimerie Nationale, 1997 *et seq*

BOOKS

Afflerbach, Holger, and David Stevenson, eds, *An Improbable War? The Outbreak of World War I and European Political Culture before 1914* Oxford: Berghahn, 2007.
Ageron, Charles-Robert, ed., *La guerre d'Algérie et les Algériens, 1954–1962* Paris: Armand Colin, 1997.
Allain, Jean-Claude, *Agadir 1911: Une crise impérialiste en Europe pour la conquête du Maroc* Paris: Publications de la Sorbonne, 1976.

Amrith, Sunil, *Migration and Diaspora in Modern Asia* Cambridge: Cambridge University Press, 2011.

Amrith, Sunil, and Tim Harper, eds, *Sites of Asian Interaction: Ideas, Networks and Mobility* Delhi: Cambridge University Press, 2014.

Andrew, Christopher M., *Théophile Delcassé and the Making of the Entente Cordiale* London: Macmillan, 1968.

Andrew, Christopher M., and A. S. Kanya-Forstner, *France Overseas: The Great War and the Climax of French Imperial Expansion* London: Thames & Hudson, 1981.

Barker, Elisabeth, *Churchill and Eden at War* Basingstoke: Macmillan, 1978.

Barnes, John, and David Nicholson, eds, *The Empire at Bay: The Leo Amery Diaries, 1929–1945* London: Hutchinson, 1988.

Bat, Jean-Pierre, *Le syndrome Foccart: La politique francaise en Afrique de 1959 à nos jours* Paris: Gallimard, 2012.

Bates, Darrell, *The Fashoda Incident of 1898: Encounter on the Nile* Oxford: Oxford University Press, 1984.

Berenson, Edward, *Hereoes of Empire: Five Charismatic Men and the Conquest of Empire* Berkeley, CA: University of California Press, 2012.

Berger, Stefan, and Chris Lorenz, eds, *Nationalising the Past: Historians as Nation Builders in Modern Europe* Basingstoke: Palgrave-Macmillan, 2010.

Berstein, Serge, *The Republic of de Gaulle, 1958–1969* Cambridge: Cambridge University Press, 1993.

Bickers, Robert, *The Scramble for China: Foreign Devils in the Qing Empire, 1832–1914* London: Allen Lane, 2011.

Bidwell, Robin *Morocco under Colonial Rule French Administration of Tribal Areas, 1912–1956* London: Frank Cass, 1973.

Blanchard, Pascal, and Sandrine Lemaire, eds, *Culture coloniale: La France conquise par son Empire, 1871–1931* Paris: Autrement, 2003.

Blanchard, Pascal, and Sandrine Lemaire, eds, *Culture impériale: Les colonies au coeur de la République, 1931–1961* Paris: Autrement, 2004.

Blondiaux, Loic, *La fabrique de l'opinion: Histoire sociale des sondages* Paris: Presses Universitaires de France, 1998.

Bloxham, Donald, *The Great Game of Genocide: Imperialism, Nationalism, and the Destruction of the Ottoman Armenians* Oxford: Oxford University Press, 2005.

Bonin, Hubert, Catherine Hodeir, and Jean-François Klein, eds, *L'esprit économique impérial (1830–1970): Groupes de pression et réseaux du patronat colonial en France et dans l'empire* Paris: Publications de la SFHOM, 2008.

Boukari-Yabara, Amzat, *Africa Unite! Une Histoire du panafricanisme* Paris: La Découverte, 2014.

Boyle, Peter G. ed., *The Eden-Eisenhower Correspondence, 1955–1957* Chapel Hill, NC: University of North Carolina Press, 2005.

Branche, Raphaëlle, *L'embuscade de Palestro: Algérie 1956* Paris: Armand Colin, 2010.

Branche, Raphaëlle, and Sylvie Thénault, eds, *La France en guerre: Expériences métropolitaines de la guerre d'indépendance algérienne* Paris: Autrement, 2008.

Brocheux, Pierre, and Daniel Hémery, *Indochina: An Ambiguous Colonization, 1858–1954* Berkeley, CA: University of California Press, 2009.

Bourdel, Philippe, *La Dernière chance de l'Algérie française: Du gouvernement socialiste au retour de De Gaulle, 1956–1958* Paris: Albin Michel, 1996.

Brower, Benjamin Claude, *A Desert Named Peace: The Violence of France's Empire in the Algerian Sahara, 1844–1902* New York: Columbia University Press, 2009.

Bryant, F. Russell, ed., *The Coalition Diaries of H.A.L. Fisher, 1916–1922: The Historian in Lloyd George's Cabinet Volume III1921–1922* Lampeter: Edwin Mellen Press, 2006.

Burk, Kathleen, *Old World, New World: The Story of Britain and America* London: Little, Brown, 2007.

Burke III, Edmund, *Prelude to Protectorate in Morocco: Precolonial Protest and Resistance, 1860–1912* Chicago, IL: University of Chicago Press, 1976.

Bury, J. P. T., *Gambetta and the Making of the Third Republic* Harlow: Longman, 1973.

Butler, L. J., and Sarah Stockwell, eds, *The Wind of Change: Harold Macmillan and British Decolonization* Basingstoke: Palgrave-Macmillan, 2013.

Byrnes, James F., *Speaking Frankly* New York: Harper & Brothers, 1947.

Cabanes, Bruno, *The Great War and the Origins of Humanitarianism, 1918–1924* Cambridge: Cambridge University Press, 2014.

Ceadel, Martin, *Semi-Detached Idealists: The British Peace Movement and International Relations, 1854–1945* Oxford: Oxford University Press, 2000.

Cain, P. J., and A. G. Hopkins, *British Imperialism: Innovation and Expansion 1688–1914* Harlow: Longman, 1993.

Carlton, David, *Britain and the Suez Crisis* Oxford: Blackwell, 1981.

Catterall, Peter, ed., *The Macmillan Diaries: The Cabinet Years 1950–1957* London: Macmillan, 2003.

Chafer, Tony, and Amanda Sackur, eds, *Promoting the Colonial Idea: Propaganda and Visions of Empire in France* Basingstoke: Palgrave-Macmillan, 2002.

Charlot, Jean, *Le Gaullisme d'opposition, 1946–1958* Paris: Fayard, 1983.

Chipman, John, *France in Africa* Oxford: Blackwell, 1988.

Chisholm, Anne, and Michael Davie, *Beaverbrook: A Life* London: Pimlico, 1993.

Churchill, Winston S., *The Second World War Vol. II: Their Finest Hour* London: Reprint Society, 1951.

Churchill, Winston S., *The World Crisis 1911–1918, Vol. I* New York: Barnes and Noble Books, 1993.

Clark, Bruce, *Twice a Stranger: How Mass Expulsion Forged Modern Greece and Turkey* London: Granta, 2006.

Clark, Christopher, *The Sleepwalkers: How Europe Went to War in 1914* London: Penguin Books, 2013.

Cockett, Richard, *Twilight of Truth: Chamberlain, Appeasement and the Manipulation of the Press* New York: St Martin's Press, 1989.

Cohrs, Patrick O., *The Unfinished Peace after World War I: America, Britain, and the Stabilisation of Europe, 1919–1932* Cambridge: Cambridge University Press, 2006.

Colville, John, *The Fringes of Power: Downing Street Diaries, 1939–1955* London: Hodder and Stoughton, 1985.

Connelly, Matthew, *A Diplomatic Revolution: Algeria's Fight for Independence and the Origins of the Post-Cold War Era* New York: Oxford University Press, 2002.

Cooke, James J., *French New Imperialism, 1880–1910: The Third Republic and Colonial Expansion* Hamden, CT: Archon, 1973.

Cooper, Frederick, *Citizenship between Empire and Nation: Remaking France and French Africa, 1945–1960* Ithaca, NY: Cornell University Press, 2014.

Cooper, Frederick, and Ann Laura Stoler, eds, *Tensions of Empire: Colonial Cultures in a Bourgeois World* Berkeley, CA: University of California Press, 1997.

Coutou-Bégarie, Hervé, and Claude Huan, eds, *Lettres et notes de l'Amiral Darlan* Paris: Economica, 1992.

Craig, F. W. S., ed., *British General Election Manifestos 1918–1966* Chichester: Political Reference Publications, 1970.

Crémieux-Brilhac, Jean-Louis, *La France libre. De l'appel du 18 juin à la libération* Paris: Gallimard, 1998.

Crosbie, Barry, and Mark Hampton, eds, *The Cultural Construction of the British World* Manchester: Manchester University Press, 2015.

Darwin, John, *The Empire Project: The Rise and Fall of the British World System, 1820–1970* Cambridge: Cambridge University Press, 2009.

Daughton, J. P., *An Empire Divided: Religion, Republicanism, and the Making of French Colonialism, 1880–1914* Oxford: Oxford University Press, 2006.

Dawson, Graham, *Soldier Heroes: British Adventure, Empire and the Imagining of Masculinities* London: Routledge, 1994.

Diamond, Hanna, and Simon Kitson, eds, *Vichy, Resistance, Liberation: New Perspectives on Wartime France* Oxford: Berg, 2005.

Dimier, Veronique, *Le gouvernement des colonies, regards croisés franco-britanniques* Brussels: Editions de l'Université de Bruxelles, 2004.

Dombrowski, Nicole Ann, ed., *Women and War in the Twentieth Century* New York: Routledge, 2004.

Dutton, David, *The Politics of Diplomacy: Britain, France and the Balkans in the First World War* London: I.B. Tauris, 1998.

Echenberg, Myron, *Black Death, White Medicine: Bubonic Plague and the Politics of Public Health in Colonial Senegal, 1914–1945* Portsmouth, NH: Heinemann, 2002.

Eden, Anthony, *The Memoirs of Sir Anthony Eden: Full Circle* London: Cassell, 1960.

Egremont, Max, *Under Two Flags: The Life of Major-General Sir Edward Spears* London: Weidenfeld & Nicolson, 1997.

Elliott, J. H., *History in the Making* New Haven, CT: Yale University Press, 2012.

Ély, Général d'Armée Paul, *Mémoires: Suez… le 13 Mai* Paris: Plon, 1969.

Evans, Martin, *The Memory of Resistance: French Opposition to the Algerian War (1954–1962)* Oxford: Berg, 1992.

Evans, Martin, *Algeria: France's Undeclared War* Oxford: Oxford University Press, 2012.

Ezra, Elizabeth, *The Colonial Unconscious: Race and Culture in Interwar France* Ithaca, NY: Cornell University Press, 2000.

Fathi Al Dib, Mohamed, *Abdel Nasser et la Révolution algérienne* Paris: L'Harmattan, 1985.

Fink, Carol, Axel Frohn, and Jürgen Heideking, eds, *Genoa, Rapallo and European Reconstruction in 1922* Cambridge: Cambridge University Press, 1991.

Fogg, Shannon L., *The Politics of Everyday Life in Vichy France: Foreigners, Undesirables, and Strangers* Cambridge: Cambridge University Press, 2009.

Footitt, Hilary, *War and Liberation in France: Living with the Liberators* Basingstoke: Palgrave-Macmillan, 2004.

Fromkin, David, *A Peace to End All Peace: The Fall of the Ottoman Empire and the Creation of the Modern Middle East* New York: Henry Holt & Co., 1989.

Gaunson, Andrew B., *The Anglo-French Clash in Lebanon and Syria, 1941–1945* Basingstoke: Palgrave, 1987.

Gershoni, Israel, and James P. Jankowski, *Redefining the Egyptian Nation, 1930–1945* Cambridge: Cambridge University Press, 1995.

Gifford, Prosser, and Wm. Roger Louis, eds, *France and Britain in Africa: Imperial Rivalry and Colonial Rule* New Haven, CT: Yale University Press, 1971.

Gilbert, Bentley Brinkerhoff Gilbert, *David Lloyd George: A Political Life. The Architect of Change, 1863–1912* Columbus, OH: Ohio State University Press, 1987.

Gilbert, Martin, ed., *Winston S. Churchill: Companion Volume IV* London: Heinemann, 1977.

Gilmour, David, *Curzon* London: Papermac, 1995.

Graham, B. D., *Choice and Democratic Order: The French Socialist Party, 1937–1950* Cambridge: Cambridge University Press, 1994.

Green, E. H. H., *Ideologies of Conservatism: Conservative Political Ideas in the Twentieth Century* Oxford: Oxford University Press, 2002.

Greenhalgh, Elizabeth, *Victory through Coalition: Britain and France during the First World War* Cambridge: Cambridge University Press, 2005.

Güçlü, Yücel, *The Question of the Sanjak of Alexandretta: A Study in Turkish-French-Syrian Relations* Ankara: Turkish Historical Society, 2001.

Guillen, Pierre, *L'Allemagne et le Maroc de 1870 à 1905* Paris: P.U.F., 1967.

Gwynn, Stephen, and Gertrude M. Tuckwell, *The Life of the Rt. Hon. Sir Charles W. Dilke, Bart., MP*, Vol. I, London: John Murray, 1917.

Harp, Stephen L., *A World History of Rubber: Empire, History, and the Everyday* Oxford: Wiley-Blackwell, 2015.

Harris, Ruth, *The Man on Devil's Island: Alfred Dreyfus and the Affair that Divided France* London: Penguin, 2010.

Hart, David M., *Tribe and Society in Rural Morocco* Abingdon: Routledge, 2000.

Hattersley, Roy, *David Lloyd George: The Great Outsider* London: Little, Brown, 2010.

Hayne, M. B., *The French Foreign Office and the Origins of the First World War, 1898–1914* Oxford: Clarendon Press, 1993.

Hennessy, Peter, *Distilling the Frenzy: Writing the History of One's Own Times* London: Biteback Publishing, 2013.

Heraclides, Alexis, and Ada Dialla, *Humanitarian Intervention in the Long Nineteenth Century: Setting the Precedent* Manchester: Manchester University Press, 2015.

Hoisington Jr, William A., *Lyautey and the French Conquest of Morocco* Basingstoke: Macmillan, 1995.

Howe, Stephen, ed., *The New Imperial Histories Reader* London: Routledge, 2010.

Hucker, Daniel, *Public Opinion and the End of Appeasement in Britain and France* Farnham: Ashgate, 2011.

Hudson, W. J., *Blind Loyalty: Australia and the Suez Crisis, 1956* Carlton, Victoria: Melbourne University Press, 1989.

Hughes, Matthew, *Allenby and General Strategy in the Middle East, 1917–1919* London: Frank Cass, 1999.

Hughes, W. M., *The Splendid Adventure: A Review of Empire Relations Within and Without the Commonwealth of Britannic Nations* London: Ernest Benn Ltd, 1929.

Hyam, Ronald, *Elgin and Churchill at the Colonial Office 1905–1908: The Watershed of the Empire-Commonwealth* London: Macmillan, 1968.

Hyam, Ronald, *Britain's Declining Empire: The Road to Decolonisation, 1918–1968* Cambridge: Cambridge University Press, 2006.

Irvine, William D., *Between Justice and Politics: The Ligue des Droits de l'Homme, 1898–1945* Stanford, CA: Stanford University Press, 2007.

Jackson, Julian, *France: The Dark Years, 1940–44* Oxford: Oxford University Press, 2001.

Jackson, Peter, *France and the Nazi Menace: Intelligence and Policy-Making, 1933–1939* Oxford: Oxford University Press, 2000.

Jackson, Peter, *Beyond the Balance of Power: France and Politics of National Security in the Era of the First World War* Cambridge: Cambridge University Press, 2013.

James, Robert Rhodes James, ed., *Winston S. Churchill: His Complete Speeches, 1897–1963*, 8 vols, New York: Chelsea House, 1974.

Jansen, Sabine, ed., *Les grands discours parlementaires de la Quatrième République de Pierre Mendès France à Charles de Gaulle* Paris: Armand Colin, 2006.

Jeffery, Keith, *The British Army and the Crisis of Empire, 1918–1922* Manchester: Manchester University Press, 1984.

Jeffery, Keith, *Field Marshal Sir Henry Wilson: A Political Soldier* Oxford: Oxford University Press, 2006.

Jennings, Eric, *Vichy in the Tropics: Pétain's National Revolution in Madagascar, Guadeloupe, and Indochina, 1940–1944* Stanford, CA: Stanford University Press, 2001.

Jennings, Eric, *La France Libre fut Africaine* Paris: Perrin, 2014.

Jennings, Jeremy, *Revolution and the Republic: A History of Political Thought in France since the Eighteenth Century* Oxford: Oxford University Press, 2011.

Johansen, Anja, *Soldiers as Police: The French and Prussian Armies and the Policing of Popular Protest, 1889–1914* Aldershot: Ashgate, 2005.

Joly, Vincent, *Guerres d'Afrique: 130 ans de guerres coloniales: L'expérience française* Rennes: Presses Universitaires de Rennes, 2009.

Kahler, Miles, *Decolonization in Britain and France: The Domestic Consequences of International Relations* Princeton, NJ: Princeton University Press, 1984.

Katz, Jonathan C., *Murder in Marrakesh: Émile Mauchamp and the French Colonial Adventure* Bloomington, IN: Indiana University Press, 2006.

Keiger, John F. V., *France and the First Origins of the World War* Basingstoke: Macmillan, 1983.

Keiger, John F. V., *Raymond Poincaré* Cambridge: Cambridge University Press, 2002.

Kelly, Saul, and Anthony Gorst, eds, *Whitehall and the Suez Crisis* London: Frank Cass, 2000.

Kersaudy, François, *Churchill and De Gaulle* London: Collins, 1981.

Khoury, Gérard D., *Une tutelle coloniale: Le Mandat français en Syrie et au Liban. Écrits politiques de Robert de Caix* Paris: Belin, 2006.

Killingray, David, and David Omissi, eds, *Guardians of Empire* Manchester: Manchester University Press, 1999.

Kimball, Warren F. Kimball, ed., *Churchill and Roosevelt: The Complete Correspondence II: Alliance Forged, November 1942–February 1944* Princeton, NJ: Princeton University Press, 1984.

Kitson, Simon, *The Hunt for Nazi Spies: Fighting Espionage in Vichy France* Chicago, IL: University of Chicago Press, 2008.

Knapp, Andrew, ed., *The Uncertain Foundation: France at the Liberation, 1944–1947* Basingstoke: Palgrave-Macmillan, 2007.

Koebner, Richard, and Helmut Dan Schmidt, *Imperialism: The Story and Significance of a Political Word, 1840–1960* Cambridge: Cambridge University Press, 1964.

Kyle, Keith, *Suez: Britain's End of Empire in the Middle East* London: I.B. Tauris, 2011.

Lacouture, Jean, *De Gaulle: The Rebel, 1890–1944* London: Collins Harvill, 1990.

Lawrence, Jon, *Electing Our Masters: The Hustings in British Politics From Hogarth to Blair* Oxford: Oxford University Press, 2009.

Lebon, André, *La Politique de la France en Afrique, 1896–1898: Mission Marchand—Niger—Madagascar* Paris: Plon, 1901.

Lebovics, Herman, *The Alliance of Iron and Wheat in the Third French Republic, 1860–1914: Origins of the New Conservatism* Baton Rouge, LA: Louisiana State University Press, 1988.

Le Sueur, James D., *Uncivil War: Intellectuals and Identity Politics During the Decolonization of Algeria* Philadelphia: University of Pennsylvania Press, 2001.

Leutze, James, ed., *The London Observer: The Journal of General Raymond E. Lee 1940–1941* London: Hutchinson, 1971.

Lewis, David Levering, *The Race to Fashoda: European Colonialism and African Resistance in the Scramble for Africa* London: Bloomsbury, 1988.

Lewis, Mary Dewhurst, *Divided Rule: Sovereignty and Empire in French Tunisia, 1881–1938* Stanford, CA: Stanford University Press, 2014.

Lieven, Dominic, *Empire: The Russian Empire and Its Rivals* New Haven, CT: Yale University Press, 2001.

Lloyd George, Frances, *The Years that are Past* London: Hutchinson, 1967.

Lockman, Zachary, *Contending Visions of the Middle East: The History and Politics of Orientalism*, 2nd edition, Cambridge: Cambridge University Press, 2010.

Louis, William Roger, *The British Empire in the Middle East, 1945–1951: Arab Nationalism, the United States and Postwar Imperialism* Oxford: Oxford University Press, 1984.

Louis, William Roger, and Roger Owen, eds, *Suez 1956: The Crisis and its Consequences* Oxford: Clarendon, 1989.

Lucas, W. Scott, *Divided We Stand: Britain, the US and the Suez Crisis* London: Hodder & Stoughton, 1991.

Lucy, Henry W., *The Balfourian Parliament 1900–1905* London: Hodder and Stoughton, 1906.

Macleod, Jenny, *Reconsidering Gallipoli* Manchester: Manchester University Press, 2004.

Macmillan, Harold, *War Diaries: The Mediterranean 1943–1945* London: Papermac, 1985.

Mahjoubi, Ali, and Hechmi Karoui, *Quand le soleil s'est levé à l'ouest: Tunisie 1881— impérialisme et résistance* Tunis: Cérès, 1983.

Manela, Erez, *The Wilsonian Moment: Self-Determination and the International Origins of Anticolonial Nationalism* Oxford: Oxford University Press, 2009.

Maquin, Étienne, *Le Parti socialiste et la guerre d'Algérie* Paris: L'Harmattan, 1990.

Marder, Arthur J., *From the Dardanelles to Oran: Studies of the Royal Navy in War and Peace, 1915–1940* Oxford: Oxford University Press, 1974.

Marr, David G., *Vietnamese Tradition on Trial, 1920–1945* Berkeley, CA: University of California Press, 1981.

Marsh, Peter T., *Joseph Chamberlain: Entrepreneur in Politics*, New Haven, CT: Yale University Press, 1994.

Matthew, H. C. G., ed., *The Gladstone Diaries with Cabinet Minutes and Prime Ministerial Correspondence Vol. X: January 1881–June 1883* Oxford: Clarendon Press, 1990.

Matthew, H. C. G., *Gladstone 1809–1898* Oxford: Clarendon Press, 1997.

Mawdsley, Evan, and Joe Maiolo, eds, *The Cambridge History of the Second World War*, vol. 2, Cambridge: Cambridge University Press, 2015.

Mayeur, Jean-Marie, and Madeleine Rebérioux, *The Third Republic from its Origins to the Great War, 1871–1914* Cambridge: Cambridge University Press, 1984.

Mayne, Richard, Douglas Johnson and Robert Tombs, eds, *Cross-Channel Currents: 100 Years of the Entente Cordiale* London: Routledge, 2004.

Mazower, Mark, *Governing the World: The History of an Idea* London: Allen Lane, 2012.

McAleer, John, and John M. MacKenzie, eds, *Exhibiting the Empire: Cultures of Display and the British Empire* Manchester: Manchester University Press, 2015.

McDowall, *A Modern History of the Kurds* London: I.B. Tauris, 1996.

McEwen, John M., ed., *The Riddell Diaries 1908–1923* London: The Athlone Press, 1986.

McKercher, B. J. C., and Roch Legault, eds, *Military Planning and the Origins of the Second World War in Europe* Westport, CT: Greenwood Press, 2001.

McKinstry, Leo, *Rosebery: Statesman in Turmoil* London: John Murray, 2005.

Mehta, Uday Singh, *Liberalism and Empire: A Study in Nineteenth-Century Political Thought and Practice* Chicago, IL: University of Chicago Press, 1999.

Mendès France, Pierre, *Gouverner, c'est choisir, 1954–1955* Paris: Gallimard, 1986.

Michel, Marc, *La Mission Marchand* Paris: Mouton/EPHE, 1972.

Mombauer, Annika, *Helmuth von Moltke and the Origins of the First World War* Cambridge: Cambridge University Press, 2001.

Morgan, Janet, ed., *The Backbench Diaries of Richard Crossman* London: Book Club Associates, 1981.

Morgan, Kenneth O., *Consensus and Disunity: The Lloyd George Coalition Government 1918–22* Oxford: Clarendon Press, 1979.

Murray, Williamson, and Jim Lacey, eds, *The Making of Peace: Rulers, States, and the Aftermath of War* Cambridge: Cambridge University Press, 2009.

Neilson, Keith, and Greg Kennedy, eds, *The British Way in Warfare: Power and the International System, 1856–1956* Farnham: Ashgate, 2010.

Nicolson, Nigel, ed., *Harold Nicolson: Diaries and Letters 1945–62* London: Collins, 1968.

Nicolson, Nigel, *Long Life: Memoirs* New York: G. P. Putnam's Sons, 1998.

Norwich, John Julius, ed., *The Duff Cooper Diaries, 1915–1951* London: Weidenfeld and Nicolson, 2005.

Ochonu, Moses E., *Colonial Meltdown: Northern Nigeria in the Great Depression* Athens, OH: Ohio University Press, 2009.

Orosz, Kenneth J., *Religious Conflict and the Evolution of Language Policy in German and French Cameroon, 1885–1939* New York: Peter Lang, 2008.

Owen, Roger, *The Middle East in the World Economy, 1800–1914* London: I.B. Tauris, 1993.

Pakenham, Thomas, *The Scramble for Africa 1876–1912* London: Weidenfeld and Nicolson, 1991.

Paris, Timothy J., *Britain, the Hashemites and Arab Rule: The Sherifian Solution* London: Frank Cass, 2003.

Passmore, Kevin, *The Right in France from the Third Republic to Vichy* Cambridge: Cambridge University Press, 2013.

Pearson, Jonathan, *Sir Anthony Eden and the Suez Crisis: Reluctant Gamble* Basingstoke: Palgrave, 2003.

Pedersen, Susan, *The Guardians: The League of Nations and the Crisis of Empire* Oxford: Oxford University Press, 2015.

Pellissier, Pierre, *Fachoda et la Mission Marchand, 1896–1899* Paris: Perrin, 2011.

Pineau, Christian, *1956/Suez* Paris: Robert Laffont, 1976.

Pitchford, Mark, *The Conservative Party and the Extreme Right 1945–75* Manchester: Manchester University Press, 2011.

Pitts, Jennifer, *A Turn to Empire: The Rise of Liberal Imperialism in Britain and France* Princeton, NJ: Princeton University Press, 2009.

Pollock, John, *Kitchener* London: Robinson, 2002.

Porter, Bernard, *The Absent-Minded Imperialists: Empire, Society, and Culture in Britain* Oxford: Oxford University Press, 2004.

Preston, Andrew, *Sword of the Spirit, Shield of Faith: Religion in American War and Diplomacy* New York: Anchor Books, 2012.

Pursell, Stuart Michael, *The French Colonial Lobby, 1889–1938* Stanford, CA: Hoover Institution Press, 1983.

Ramm, Agatha, ed., *Political Correspondence of Mr. Gladstone and Lord Granville, Vol. I: 1876–1882* Oxford: Clarendon Press, 1962.

Ramsden, John, *Man of the Century: Winston Churchill and His Legend Since 1945* London: HarperCollins, 2002.

Reardon, Terry, *Winston Churchill and Mackenzie King: So Similar, So Different* Toronto: Dundurn, 2012.

Reimer, Michael J., *Colonial Bridgehead: Government and Society in Alexandria, 1807–1882* Oxford: Westview Press, 1997.

Reston, James, *Deadline: A Memoir* New York: Random House, 1991.

Rioux, Jean-Pierre, ed., *La guerre d'Algérie et les Français* Paris: Fayard, 1990.

Rivet, Daniel, *Lyautey et l'institution du protectorat français au Maroc, 1912–1925* Paris: L'Harmattan, 1988.

Rivet, Daniel, *Le Maghreb à l'épreuve de la colonisation* Paris: Hachette, 2002.

Roberts, Andrew, *Lord Salisbury: Victorian Titan* London: Weidenfeld & Nicolson, 1999.

Robinson, Ronald, and John Gallagher, *Africa and the Victorians: The Official Mind of Imperialism* London: Macmillan, 1961.

Rodogno, Davide, *Against Massacre: Humanitarian Interventions in the Ottoman Empire, 1815–1914* Princeton, NJ: Princeton University Press, 2015.

Röhl, John C. G., *Wilhelm II: Into the Abyss of War and Exile, 1900–1941* Cambridge: Cambridge University Press, 2014.

Rose, Jonathan, *The Literary Churchill: Author, Reader, Actor* New Haven, CT: Yale University Press, 2014.

Rose, Sonya O., *Which People's War? National Identity and Citizenship in Wartime Britain, 1939–1945* Oxford: Oxford University Press, 2003.

Roshwald, Aviel, *Estranged Bedfellows: Britain and France in the Middle East during the Second World War* Oxford: Oxford University Press, 1990.

Rudelle, Odille, *Mai 1958, de Gaulle et la République* Paris: Plon, 1988.

Ruscio, Alain, *La question coloniale dans 'L'Humanité' (1904–2004)* Paris: La Dispute, 2005.

Said, Edward, *Orientalism* London: Routledge and Kegan Paul, 1978.

Said, Edward, *Culture and Imperialism* London: Vintage, 1994.

Schayegh, Cyrus, and Andrew Arsan, eds, *The Routledge Handbook of the History of the Middle East Mandates* Abingdon: Routledge, 2015.

Schneider, William H., *An Empire for the Masses: The French Popular Image of Africa, 1870–1900* Westport, CT: Greenwood Press, 1982.

Scott Lucas, W., *Divided We Stand: Britain, the US and the Suez Crisis* London: Hodder & Stoughton, 1991.

Sèbe, Berny, *Heroic Imperialists in Africa: The Promotion of British and French Colonial Heroes, 1879–1939* Manchester: Manchester University Press, 2013.

Shannon, Richard, *Gladstone: Heroic Minister 1865–1898* London: Allen Lane, 1999.

Shaw, Tony, *Eden, Suez and the Mass Media: Propaganda and Persuasion during the Suez Crisis* London: I.B. Tauris, 1996.

Shepard, Todd, *The Invention of Decolonization: The Algerian War and the Remaking of France* Ithaca, NY: Cornell University Press, 2006.

Shields, Sarah D., *Fezzes in the River: Identity Politics and European Diplomacy in the Middle East on the Eve of World War II* New York: Oxford University Press, 2011.

Smith, Simon, C., ed., *Reassessing Suez 1956: New Perspectives on the Crisis and its Aftermath* Aldershot: Ashgate, 2008.

Spiers, Edward M., ed., *Sudan: The Conquest Reappraised* London: Frank Cass, 1998.

Spurr, David, *The Rhetoric of Empire: Colonial Intercourse in Journalism, Travel Writing, and Imperial Administration* Durham, NC: Duke University Press, 1993.

Steele, David, *Lord Salisbury: A Political Biography* London: UCL Press, 1999.

Steiner, Zara, *The Lights that Failed: European International History, 1919–1933* Oxford: Oxford University Press, 2005.

Stevenson, David, *Armaments and the Coming War: Europe, 1904–1914* Oxford: Oxford University Press, 1996, reprint 2004.

Stoler, Ann Laura, *Along the Archival Grain: Epistemic Anxieties and Colonial Common Sense* Princeton, NJ: Princeton University Press, 2009.

Stora, Benjamin, *La gangrène et l'oubli. La mémoire de la guerre d'Algérie* Paris: La Découverte, 1991.

Strang, Bruce, ed., *Collision of Empires: Italy's Invasion of Ethiopia and its International Impact* Farnham: Ashgate, 2014.

Taithe, Bertrand, *The Killer Trail: A Colonial Scandal in the Heart of Africa* Oxford: Oxford University Press, 2009.

Tauber, Eliezer, *The Formation of Modern Syria and Iraq* London: Frank Cass, 1995.

Taylor, A. J. P., *The Struggle for Mastery in Europe 1848–1918* Oxford: Oxford University Press, 1954.

Thackeray, David, *Conservatism for the Democratic Age: Conservative Cultures and the Challenge of Mass Politics in Early Twentieth Century England* Manchester: Manchester University Press, 2013.

Thobie, Jacques, *Intérets et impérialisme français dans l'Empire ottoman, 1895–1914* Paris: Documentation française, 1977.

Thomas, Martin ed., *The French Colonial Mind: Mental Maps of Empire and Colonial Encounters* Lincoln, NE: University of Nebraska Press, 2011.

Thomas, Martin, *Fight or Flight: Britain, France, and their Roads from Empire* Oxford: Oxford University Press, 2014.

Thompson, Andrew S., ed., *Britain's Experience of Empire in the Twentieth Century* Oxford: Oxford University Press, 2011.

Thompson, James, *British Political Culture and the Idea of 'Public Opinion', 1867–1914* Cambridge: Cambridge University Press, 2013.

Tilley, Helen, with Robert Gordon, eds, *Ordering Africa: Anthropology, European Imperialism, and the Politics of Knowledge* Manchester: Manchester University Press, 2007.

Tombs, Robert, and Isabelle Tombs, *That Sweet Enemy: The British and the French from the Sun King to the Present* London: Heinemann, 2006.

Tønnesson, Stein, *The Vietnamese Revolution of 1945: Roosevelt, Ho Chi Minh and de Gaulle in a World at War* Oslo: PRIO, 1991.

Tønnesson, Stein, *Vietnam 1946: How the War Began* Berkeley, CA: University of California Press, 2010.

Toye, Richard, *Churchill's Empire: The World That Made Him and the World He Made* London: Macmillan, 2010.

Toye, Richard, *Rhetoric: A Very Short Introduction*, Oxford: Oxford University Press, 2013.

Toye, Richard, *The Roar of the Lion: The Untold Story of Churchill's World War II Speeches* Oxford: Oxford University Press, 2013.

Trentmann, Frank, *Free Trade Nation: Commerce, Consumption and Civil Society in Modern Britain* Oxford: Oxford University Press, 2008.

Trumball IV, George, *An Empire of Facts: Colonial Power, Cultural Knowledge and Islam in Algeria, 1870–1914* Cambridge: Cambridge University Press, 2009.

Tusan, Michelle, *Smyrna's Ashes: Humanitarianism, Genocide, and the Birth of the Middle East* Berkeley, CA: University of California Press, 2012.

Ullmann, Bernard, *Jacques Soustelle: Le mal aimé* Paris: Plon, 1995.

United States Department of State, *Foreign Relations of the United States: Diplomatic Papers, 1942, Vol. II: Europe* Washington, DC: US Government Printing Office, 1962.

United States Department of State, *Foreign Relations of the United States: The Conferences at Washington, 1941–1942, and Casablanca, 1943* Washington, DC: US Government Printing Office, 1968.

Vaïsse, Maurice, *La Grandeur: Politique étrangère du Général de Gaulle, 1958–1969* Paris: Fayard, 1998.

Vaïsse, Maurice, ed., *De Gaulle et l'Algérie, 1943–1969* Paris: Armand Colin, 2012.

Vanthemsche, Guy, *Belgium and the Congo, 1885–1980* Cambridge: Cambridge University Press, 2012.

Varley, Karine, *Under the Shadow of Defeat: The War of 1870–71 in French Memory* Basingstoke: Palgrave-Macmillan, 2008.

Walder, David, *The Chanak Affair* London: Hutchinson & Co., 1969.

Wall, Irwin M., *France, the United States, and the Algerian War* Berkeley, CA: University of California Press, 2001.

Waller, Philip J., ed., *Politics and Social Change in Modern Britain* Brighton: Harvester Press, 1987.

Watenpaugh, David, *Bread from Stones: The Middle East and the Making of Modern Humanitarianism* Berkeley, CA: University of California Press, 2015.

Williams, Philip M., *Hugh Gaitskell: A Political Biography* London: Jonathan Cape, 1979.

Williams, Philip M., ed., *The Diary of Hugh Gaitskell 1945–1956* London: Jonathan Cape, 1983.

Wilson, John, *CB: A Life of Sir Henry Campbell-Bannerman* London: Constable, 1973.

Wilson, Keith, ed., *The International Impact of the Boer War* Chesham: Acumen, 2001.

Wilson, Trevor, ed., *The Political Diaries of C. P. Scott, 1911–1928* London: Collins, 1970.

Winstone, Ruth, ed., *Tony Benn: Years of Hope: Diaries, Papers and Letters 1940–1962* London: Hutchinson, 1994.

Wolton, Suke, *Lord Hailey, the Colonial Office and the Politics of Race and Empire in the Second World War: The Loss of White Prestige* Basingstoke: Palgrave-Macmillan, 2000.

Wright, Patricia, *Conflict on the Nile: The Fashoda Incident of 1898* London: Heinemann, 1972.

Zamir, Meir, *The Secret Anglo-French War in the Middle East: Intelligence and Decolonization, 1940–1948* Abingdon: Routledge, 2015.

ARTICLES AND CHAPTERS IN BOOKS

Adamthwaite, Anthony, 'Suez Revisited', *International Affairs*, 64:3 (1988), 449–64.

Ageron, Charles-Robert, 'A propos d'une prétendue politique de "répli imperial" dans la France des années 1938–39', *Revue d'Histoire Maghrébine*, 12 (1978), 228–37.

Ageron, Charles-Robert, 'L'opinion française à travers les sondages', in Jean-Pierre Rioux, ed., *La guerre d'Algérie et les Français* (Paris: Fayard, 1990), 25–44.

Ageron, Charles-Robert, 'Les colonies devant l'opinion publique française (1919–1939)', *Revue Française d'Histoire d'Outre-Mer*, 77:286 (1990), 31–73.

Ageron, Charles-Robert, 'Un aspect de la guerre d'Algérie: la propaganda radiophonique du FLN et des états arabes', in Charles-Robert Ageron, ed., *La guerre d'Algérie et les Algériens, 1954–1962* (Paris: Armand Colin, 1997), 245–59.

Aldrich, Robert, and Stuart Ward, 'Ends of Empire: Decolonizing the Nation in British and French Historiography', in Stefan Berger and Chris Lorenz, eds, *Nationalising the Past:*

Historians as Nation Builders in Modern Europe (Basingstoke: Palgrave-Macmillan, 2010), 259–81.

Anderson, Warwick, 'Scientific Patriotism: Medical Science and National Self-Fashioning in Southeast Asia', *Comparative Studies in Society & History*, 54:1 (2012), 93–113.

Andrew, Christopher M., 'The French Colonialist Movement during the Third Republic: The Unofficial Mind of Imperialism', *Transactions of the Royal Historical Society*, Fifth Series, 26 (1976), 143–66.

Andrew, Christopher M., and A. S. Kanya-Forstner, 'The French "Colonial Party": Its Composition, Aims and Influence, 1885–1914', *Historical Journal*, 14:1 (1971), 99–128.

Andrew, Christopher M., and A. S. Kanya-Forstner, 'Gabriel Hanotaux, the Colonial Party and the Fashoda Strategy', in Ernest Penrose, ed., *European Imperialism and the Partition of Africa* (London: Frank Cass, 1975), 61–8.

Arnold-Forster, Mark, 'Chanak Rocks the Empire: The Anger of Billy Hughes', *Round Table*, 58 (1968), 169–77.

Arsan, Andrew, '"This is the Age of Associations": Committees, Petitions, and the Roots of Interwar Middle Eastern Internationalism', *Journal of Global History*, 7 (2012), 166–88.

Ashley, S. A., 'The Failure of Gambetta's *Grand Ministère*', *French Historical Studies*, 9:1 (1975), 105–24.

Austin, Gareth, 'Cash Crops and Freedom: Export Agriculture and the Decline of Slavery in Colonial West Africa', *International Review of Social History*, 54:1 (2009), 1–37.

Bat, Jean-Pierre, 'Jacques Foccart, *eminence grise* for African Affairs', in Tony Chafer and Alexander Keese, eds, *Francophone Africa at Fifty* (Basingstoke: Palgrave-Macmillan, 2013), 135–53.

Bate, Bernard, '"To Persuade Them into Speech and Action": Oratory and the Tamil Political, Madras, 1905–1919', *Comparative Studies in Society & History*, 55:1 (2013), 145–60.

Battesti, Michèle, 'Les ambiguités de Suez', *Revue Historique des Armées*, 4:1 (1986), 3–14.

Beck, Peter J., '"A Tedious and Perilous Controversy": Britain and the Settlement of the Mosul Dispute, 1918–1926', *Middle Eastern Studies*, 17:2 (1981), 256–76.

Beck, Peter J., 'Politicians versus Historians: Lord Avon's "Appeasement Battle" against "Lamentably, Appeasement-Minded" Historians', *Twentieth Century British History*, 9 (1998), 396–419.

Bell, Duncan, 'What is Liberalism?' *Political Theory*, published online before print 26 June 2014, doi: 10.1177/0090591714535103.

Berenson, Edward, 'Fashoda, Dreyfus, and the Myth of Jean-Baptiste Marchand', *Yale French Studies*, 111:1 (2007), 129–42.

Bockman, Johanna, 'Socialist Globalization against Capital Neocolonialism', *Humanity*, 6:1 (2015), 109–28.

Bose, Sugata, 'Starvation Amidst Plenty: The Making of Famine in Bengal, Honan and Tonkin, 1942–45', *Modern Asian Studies*, 24:4 (1990), 699–727.

Bowles, Brett C., '"La tragédie de Mers el-Kébir" and the Politics of Filmed News in France, 1940–1944', *Journal of Modern History*, 76:2 (2004), 347–88.

Bowles, Brett C., 'Newsreels, Ideology, and Public Opinion under Vichy: The Case of *La France en Marche*', *French Historical Studies*, 27:2 (2004), 419–63.

Boyle, Timothy, 'New Light on Lloyd George's Mansion House Speech', *Historical Journal*, 23:2 (1980), 431–3.

Brady, Christopher, 'The Cabinet System and Management of the Suez Crisis', *Contemporary British History*, 11:2 (1997), 65–93.

Bury, J. P. T., 'Gambetta and Overseas Problems', *English Historical Review*, 82:323 (1967), 277–95.

Byrne, Jeffrey James, 'Négociation perpétuelle: de Gaulle et le FLN, 1961–1968', in Maurice Vaïsse, ed., *De Gaulle et l'Algérie, 1943–1969* (Paris: Armand Colin, 2012), 299–312.

Cain, P. J., 'Character and Imperialism: The British Financial Administration of Egypt, 1878–1914', *Journal of Imperial and Commonwealth History*, 34:2 (2006), 177–200.

Cain, P. J., 'Empire and the Languages of Character and Virtue in Late Victorian and Edwardian Britain', *Modern Intellectual History*, 4:2 (2007), 249–73.

Chamberlain, M. E., 'Sir Charles Dilke and the British Intervention in Egypt, 1882: Decision-Making in a Nineteenth Century Cabinet', *British Journal of International Studies*, 2:3 (1976), 231–45.

Chamberlain, M. E., 'The Alexandria Massacre of 11 June 1882 and the British Occupation of Egypt', *Middle Eastern Studies*, 13:1 (1977), 14–39.

Chamberlain, M. E., 'British Public Opinion and the Invasion of Egypt, 1882', *Trivium*, 16 (1981), 5–28.

Charbonneau, Bruno, and Tony Chafer, 'Peace Operations and Francophone Spaces', *International Peacekeeping*, 19:3 (2012), 274–86.

Charle, Christophe, 'Les parlementaires: avant-garde ou arrière-garde d'une société en mouvement', in Jean-Marie Mayeur, Jean-Pierre Chaline, and Alain Corbin, eds, *Les Parlementaires de la Troisième République* (Paris: Publications de la Sorbonne, 2003), 49–60.

Chin, Rachel, 'A Rhetorical Construction of Anglo-French Clashes at Mers el-Kébir: July 3, 1940', in Martin Thomas and Richard Toye (eds), *Rhetorics of Empire: Languages of Colonial Conflict after 1900* Manchester: Manchester University Press, forthcoming.

Choate, Mark I., 'Identity Politics and Political Perception in the European Settlement of Tunisia: The French Colony versus the Italian Colony', *French Colonial History*, 8, (2007), 97–109.

Cockfield, Jamie, 'Germany and the Fashoda Crisis, 1898–99', *Central European History*, 16:3 (1983), 256–75.

Conklin, Alice L., 'Colonialism and Human Rights: A Contradiction in Terms? The Case of France and West Africa, 1895–1914', *American Historical Review*, 103:2 (1998): 419–42.

Conklin, Alice L., 'A Force for Civilization: Republican Discourse and French Administration in West Africa, 1895–1930', in Charles Becker, Saliou Mbaye, and Ibrahimi Thioub, eds, *AOF: réalités et héritages. Sociétés ouest-africaines et ordre colonial, 1895–1960*, 2 vols (Dakar: Direction des Archives du Sénégal, 1997), vol. 1, 283–302.

Conia, Mireille, 'La Haute-Marne: berceau des actions de solidarité envers les soldats', in Raphaëlle Branche and Sylvie Thénault, eds, *La France en guerre: Expériences métropolitaines de la guerre d'indépendance algérienne* (Paris: Autrement, 2008), 58–69.

Connelly, Matthew, 'Rethinking the Cold War and Decolonization: The Grand Strategy of the Algerian War of Independence', *International Journal of Middle East Studies*, 33:2 (2001), 223–41.

Conway, Stephen, '"Founded in Lasting Interests": British Projects for European Imperial Collaboration in the Age of the American Revolution', *International History Review*, 37:1 (2015), 22–40.

Cooke, James J., 'Lyautey and Etienne: The Soldier and the Politician in the Penetration of Morocco, 1904–1906', *Military Affairs*, 16:1 (1972), 14–18.

Cornick, Martyn, ' "Fraternity Among Listeners". The BBC and French Resistance: Evidence from Refugees', in Hanna Diamond and Simon Kitson, eds, *Vichy, Resistance, Liberation: New Perspectives on Wartime France* (Oxford: Berg, 2005), 101–13.

Cosgrove, Richard A., 'A Note on Lloyd George's Speech at the Mansion House, 21 July 1911', *Historical Journal*, 12:4 (1969), 698–701.

Crowcroft, Barnaby, 'Egypt's Other Nationalists and the Suez Crisis of 1956', *Historical Journal*, 59:2 (2016), 253–85.

Cumming, Gordon D., and Tony Chafer, 'From Rivalry to Partnership? Critical Reflections on Anglo-French Cooperation in Africa', *Review of International Studies*, 37:5 (2011), 2439–63.

Darwin, J. G., 'The Chanak Crisis and the British Cabinet', *History*, 65 (1980), 32–48.

Darwin, John, 'Imperialism and the Victorians: The Dynamics of Territorial Expansion', *English Historical Review*, 112:447 (1997), 614–42.

Darwin, John, 'An Undeclared Empire: The British in the Middle East, 1918–39', *Journal of Imperial & Commonwealth History*, 27:2 (1999), 159–76.

Datta, Venita, ' "L'appel au soldat": Visions of the Napoleonic Legend in Popular Culture of the Belle Epoque', *French Historical Studies*, 28:1 (2005), 1–30.

Daughton, J. P., 'A Colonial Affair?: Dreyfus and the French Empire', *Historical Reflections/ Réflexions Historiques*, 31:3 (2005), 469–83.

Daughton, J. P., 'Behind the Imperial Curtain: International Humanitarian Efforts and the Critique of French Colonialism in the Interwar Years ', *French Historical Studies*, 34:3 (2011), 503–28.

Derrick, Jonathan, 'The Dissenters: Anti-Colonialism in France, 1900–40', in Tony Chafer and Amanda Sackur, eds, *Promoting the Colonial Idea: Propaganda and Visions of Empire in France* (Basingstoke: Palgrave-Macmillan, 2002), 53–68.

Dooley, Howard J., 'Great Britain's "Last Battle" in the Middle East: Notes on Cabinet Planning during the Suez Crisis of 1956', *International History Review*, 11:3 (1989), 486–501.

Drayton, Richard, 'Where Does the World Historian Write From? Objectivity, Moral Conscience and the Past and Present of Imperialism', *Journal of Contemporary History*, 46:3 (2011), 671–85.

Duara, Prasenjit, 'The Discourse of Civilization and Pan-Asianism', *Journal of World History*, 12 (2001), 99–130.

Dulles, Foster Rhea, and Gerald E. Ridinger, 'The Anti-Colonial Policies of Franklin D. Roosevelt', *Political Science Quarterly*, 70:1 (1955), 1–18.

Durran, P. J., 'A Two-Edged Sword: The Liberal Attack on Disraelian Imperialism', *Journal of Imperial and Commonwealth History*, 10:3 (1982), 262–84.

Dutailly, Henry, 'Weaknesses in French Military Planning on the Eve of the Second World War', in B. J. C. McKercher and Roch Legault, eds, *Military Planning and the Origins of the Second World War in Europe* (Westport, CT: Greenwood Press, 2001), 89–102.

Edwards, E. W., 'The Franco–German Agreement on Morocco, 1909', *English Historical Review*, 78:308 (1963), 483–513.

Egerton, George, 'Conservative Internationalism: British Approaches to International Organization and the Creation of the League of Nations', *Diplomacy & Statecraft*, 5:1 (1994), 1–20.

Ehlers, Sarah, 'Europeanising Impacts from the Colonies: European Campaigns against Sleeping Sickness 1900–1914', in Matthieu Osmont et al., eds, *Europeanisation in the 20th Century: The Historical Lens* (Brussels: Peter Lang, 2012), 111–26.

Eldar, Dan, 'France in Syria: The Abolition of Sharifian Government, April–July 1920', *Middle Eastern Studies*, 29:3 (1993), 487–504.

Eubank, Keith, 'The Fashoda Crisis Re-examined', *The Historian*, 22:2 (1960), 145–62.

Fahmy, Ziad, 'Francophone Egyptian Nationalists, Anti-British Discourse, and European Public Opinion, 1885–1910: The Case of Mustafa Kamil and Ya'qub Sannu', *Comparative Studies of South Asia, Africa and the Middle East*, 28:1 (2008), 170–83.

Ferris, John R., ' "Far too Dangerous a Gamble"? British Intelligence and Policy during the Chanak Crisis, September–October 1922', *Diplomacy & Statecraft*, 14:1 (2003), 139–84.

Ferris, John R., 'The British Empire vs. the Hidden Hand: British Intelligence and Strategy and "The CUP-Jew-German-Bolshevik Combination", 1918–1924', in Keith Neilson and Greg Kennedy, eds, *The British Way in Warfare: Power and the International System, 1856–1956* (Farnham: Ashgate, 2010), 325–46.

Finel, Bernard M., and Kristin M. Lord, 'The Surprising Logic of Transparency', *International Studies Quarterly*, 43 (1999), 315–33.

Finlayson, Alan, and James Martin, ' "It Ain't What You Say . . . ": British Political Studies and the Analysis of Speech and Rhetoric', *British Politics*, 3 (2008), 445–64.

Fisher, John, 'Syria and Mesopotamia in British Middle Eastern Policy in 1919', *Middle Eastern Studies*, 34:2 (1998), 129–70.

Fisher, John, 'The Interdepartmental Committee on Eastern Unrest and British Responses to Bolshevik and Other Intrigues Against the Empire during the 1920s', *Journal of Asian History*, 34:1 (2000), 1–34.

Fitzgerald, Edward P., 'France's Middle Eastern Ambitions, the Sykes-Picot Negotiations, and the Oil Fields of Mosul, 1915–1918', *Journal of Modern History*, 66:4 (1994), 697–701.

Fitzmaurice, Andrew, 'Liberalism and Empire in Nineteenth-Century International Law', *American Historical Review*, 117:1 (February 2012), 122–40.

Frank, Robert, 'Pierre Mendès France: au miroir du Moyen-Orient, une certaine vision du monde (1956–1957)', in *Pierre Mendès France et le rôle de la France dans le monde* (Grenoble: Presses Universitaires de Grenoble, 1991).

Galbraith, John S., and Afaf Lutfi al-Sayyid-Marsot, 'The British Occupation of Egypt: Another View', *International Journal of Middle East Studies* (1978), 471–88.

Gelvin, James L., 'The Social Origins of Popular Nationalism in Syria: Evidence for a New Framework', *International Journal of Middle East Studies*, 26 (1994), 645–61.

Gerwarth, Robert, and Erez Manela, 'The Great War as a Global War: Imperial Conflict and the Reconfiguration of World Order, 1911–1923', *Diplomatic History*, 38:4 (2014), 786–800.

Ghosh, Durba, 'Another Set of Imperial Turns', *American Historical Review* (June 2012), 772–93.

Girault, René, 'La France en accusation à l'ONU, ou les pouvoirs d'une organisation internationale', *Relations Internationales*, 76:3 (1993), 411–22.

Gooch, John, ' "Building Buffers and Filling Vacuums": Great Britain and the Middle East, 1914–1922', in Williamson Murray and Jim Lacey, eds, *The Making of Peace: Rulers, States, and the Aftermath of War* (Cambridge: Cambridge University Press, 2009), 240–64.

Goold, J. Douglas, 'Lord Hardinge as Ambassador to France, and the Anglo-French Dilemma over Germany and the Near East, 1920–1922', *Historical Journal*, 21 (1978), 913–37.

Gouda, Frances, 'The Gendered Rhetoric of Colonialism and Anti-Colonialism in Twentieth-Century Indonesia', *Indonesia*, 55 (April 1993), 1–22.

Gouda, Frances, 'Languages of Gender and Neurosis in the Indonesian Struggle for Independence, 1945–1949', *Indonesia*, 64 (October 1997), 45–76.

Güçlü, Yücel, 'The Struggle for Mastery in Cilicia: Turkey, France and the Ankara Agreement of 1921', *International History Review*, 23:3 (2001), 580–603.

Guétant, Louis, *Marchand-Fachoda. La Mission Congo-Nil, Sa préparation. Ses pratiques. Son but. Ses résultats* Paris: Bureaux des Temps Nouveaux, 1899.

Guillen, Pierre, 'The Entente of 1904 as a Colonial Settlement', in Prosser Gifford and Wm. Roger Louis, eds, *France and Britain in Africa: Imperial Rivalry and Colonial Rule* (New Haven, CT: Yale University Press, 1971), 333–68.

Hacking, Ian, 'Making Up People', in *Historical Ontology* (Cambridge, MA: Harvard University Press, 2002), 99–114.

Halvorson, Dan, 'Prestige, Prudence and Public Opinion in the 1882 British Occupation of Egypt', *Australian Journal of Politics and History*, 56:3 (2010), 423–40.

Hamelin, Bertrand, 'Les Résistants et la guerre d'Algérie (1954–1962): quelques jalons problématiques', in Raphaëlle Branche and Sylvie Thénault, eds, *La France en guerre: Expériences métropolitaines de la guerre d'indépendance algérienne* (Paris: Autrement, 2008), 138–42.

Hanks, Robert K., 'Georges Clemenceau and the English', *Historical Journal*, 45:1 (2002), 53–77.

Harneit-Sievers, Axel, 'African Business, "Economic Nationalism," and British Colonial Policy: Southern Nigeria, 1935–1954', *African Economic History*, 23:1 (1995), 79–86.

Harrisson, Tom, 'What is Public Opinion?' *Political Quarterly*, 11 (1940), 368–83.

Heinnemann, Julia, 'De la parole diffuse à la parole confisquée: la transmission de la parole gaullienne aux militaires en guerre d'Algérie, 1958–1962', in Maurice Vaïsse, ed., *De Gaulle et l'Algérie, 1943–1969* (Paris: Armand Colin, 2012), 199–211.

Hinsley, F. H., 'International Rivalry, 1885–1895', in E. A. Benians, James Butler, and C. E. Carrington, eds, *The Cambridge History of the British Empire Vol. III: The Empire-Commonwealth 1870–1919* (Cambridge: Cambridge University Press, 1959), 255–91.

Hopkins, A. G., 'The Victorians and Africa: A Reconsideration of the Occupation of Egypt, 1882', *Journal of African History*, 27:2 (1986), 363–91.

Hughes, Matthew, 'The French Army at Gallipoli', *RUSI Journal*, 150:3 (2005), 64–7.

Hulbert, Jeff, 'Right-Wing Propaganda or Reporting History? The Newsreels and the Suez Crisis of 1956', *Film History*, 14:3/4, (2002), 261–81.

Imlay, Talbot, 'A Success Story? The Foreign Policies of France's Fourth Republic', *Contemporary European History*, 18:4 (2009), 499–519.

Isoart, Paul, 'Les aspects politiques, constitutionnels et administratifs des recommandations', in Institut Charles de Gaulle, *Brazzaville, Janvier-Février 1944: Aux sources de la décolonisation* (Paris: Plon, 1988), 79–96.

Jackson, Peter, 'Tradition and Adaptation: The Social Universe of the French Foreign Ministry in the Era of the First World War', *French History*, 24:2 (2010), 164–96.

Jeffery, Keith, and Alan Sharp, 'Lord Curzon and Secret Intelligence', in Christopher Andrew and Jeremy Noakes eds, *Intelligence and International Relations* (Exeter: Exeter University Press, 1987), 103–26.

Johnman, Lewis, 'Playing the Role of a Cassandra: Sir Gerald Fitzmaurice, Senior Legal Adviser to the Foreign Office', in Saul Kelly and Anthony Gorst, eds, *Whitehall and the Suez Crisis* (London: Frank Cass, 2000), 46–63.

Jones, Heather, 'Algeciras Revisited: European Crisis and Conference Diplomacy, 16 January–7 April 1906', EUI Working Paper, 2009, 1–16.

Karsh, Efraim, 'Reactive Imperialism: Britain, the Hashemites, and the Creation of Modern Iraq', *Journal of Imperial and Commonwealth History*, 30:3 (2002), 55–70.

Katz, Jonathan C., 'The 1907 Mauchamp Affair and the French Civilizing Mission in Morocco', *Journal of North African Studies*, 6:1 (2001), 143–66.

Keiger, John V. F., 'Omdurman, Fashoda and Franco-British Relations', in Edward M. Spiers ed., *Sudan: The Conquest Reappraised* (London: Frank Cass, 1998), 163–76.

Keiger, John V. F., 'How the Entente Began', in Richard Mayne, Douglas Johnson, and Robert Tombs, eds, *Cross-Channel Currents: 100 Years of the Entente Cordiale* (London: Routledge, 2004), 3–10.

Keiger, John V. F., 'Sir Edward Grey, France, and the Entente: How to Catch the Perfect Angler?' *International History Review*, 38:2 (2016), 285–9.

Kramer, Paul A., 'Imperial Histories of the United States in the World', *American Historical Review*, 116:5 (December 2011), 1348–91.

Larkin, Maurice, '"La République en danger"? The Pretenders, the Army and Déroulède, 1898–1899', *English Historical Review*, 100:394 (1985), 85–105.

Lebovics, Herman, 'The Discourse of Tradition in French Culture: The Rightist Social Science and Political Practice of Louis Marin, 1890–1945', *Historical Reflections*, 17:1 (Winter 1991), 45–75.

Levey, Zach, 'French-Israeli Relations, 1950–1956: The Strategic Dimension', in Simon C. Smith, ed., *Reassessing Suez 1956: New Perspectives on the Crisis and its Aftermath* (Aldershot: Ashgate, 2008), 87–106.

Lewis, James I., 'The MRP and the Genesis of the French Union, 1944–1948', *French History*, 12 (1998): 276–314.

Lewis, Mary Dewhurst, 'Geographies of Power: The Tunisian Civic Order, Jurisdictional Politics, and Imperial Rivalry in the Mediterranean, 1881–1935', *Journal of Modern History*, 80:4 (2008), 791–830.

Louis, O., 'De Bizerte à Mers el-Kebir: les bases navales d'Afrique du Nord dans l "entre-deux-guerres"', *Revue Historique des Armées*, 4 (1999), 31–45.

Maddy-Weitzman, Bruce, 'Jordan and Iraq: Efforts at Intra-Hashimite Unity', *Middle Eastern Studies*, 26 (1990), 65–75.

Manela, Erez, 'Imagining Woodrow Wilson in Asia: Dreams of East-West Harmony and the Revolt against Empire in 1919', *American Historical Review*, 111:5 (December 2006), 1327–51.

Masson, Philippe, 'Origines et bilan d'une défaite', *Revue Historique des Armées*, 4:1 (1986), 51–8.

Matthew, H. C. G., 'Rhetoric and Politics in Britain, 1860–1950', in P. J. Waller, ed., *Politics and Social Change in Modern Britain* (Brighton: Harvester, 1987), 34–58.

McCourt, David M., 'What was Britain's "East of Suez Role"? Reassessing the Withdrawal, 1964–1968', *Diplomacy & Statecraft*, 20 (2009), 453–72.

McGeoch, Lyle A., 'On the Road to War: British Foreign Policy in Transition, 1905–1906', *The Review of Politics*, 35 (1973), 204–18.

Merriman, John, *Massacre: The Life and Death of the Paris Commune of 1871* New Haven, CT: Yale University Press, 2014.

Meynier, Gilbert, 'Volonté de propaganda ou inconscient affiche? Images et imaginaire coloniaux français dans l'entre-deux-guerres', in Pascal Blanchard and Armelle Chatelier, eds, *Images et Colonies* (Paris: ACHAC, 1993), 41–8.

Michel, Marc, 'La puissance par l'Empire. Note sur la perception du facteur imperial dans l'élaboration de la défense nationale (1936–1938)', *Revue Française d'Histoire d'Outre-Mer*, 69:254 (1982), 35–46.

Michel, Marc, '"Mémoire officielle", discours et pratique coloniale: Le 14 juillet et le 11 novembre au Sénégal entre les deux guerres', *Revue Française d'Histoire d'Outre-Mer*, 77:287 (1990), 145–58.

Mikhail, Alan, and Christine M. Philliou, 'The Ottoman Empire and the Imperial Turn', *Comparative Studies in Society & History*, 54:4 (2012), 721–45.

Morgan, Kenneth O., 'Lloyd George's Premiership: A Study in "Prime Ministerial Government"', *Historical Journal*, 13:1 (1970), 130–57.

Munholland, J. Kim, 'Rival Approaches to Morocco: Lyautey and the Algerian-Moroccan Border, 1903–1905', *French Historical Studies*, 5:3 (1968), 328–43.

Myers, Frank, 'Harold Macmillan's "Winds of Change" Speech: A Case Study in the Rhetoric of Policy Change', *Rhetoric & Public Affairs*, 3 (2000), 555–75.

Nagy, Lázló J., 'La politique algérienne de De Gaulle vue de Hongrie', in Maurice Vaïsse, ed., *De Gaulle et l'Algérie, 1943–1969* (Paris: Armand Colin, 2012), 124–30.

Newsinger, John, 'Liberal Imperialism and the Occupation of Egypt in 1882', *Race & Class*, 49:3 (2007), 54–75.

Negrine, Ralph, 'The Press and the Suez Crisis: A Myth Re-examined', *Historical Journal*, 25 (1982), 975–84.

Nie, Michael de, '"Speed the Mahdi!" The Irish Press and Empire during the Sudan Conflict of 1883–1885', *Journal of British Studies*, 51:4 (October 2012), 883–909.

Nye, Robert A., 'Western Masculinities in War and Peace', *American Historical Review*, 112:2 (April 2007), 417–38.

O'Donnell, J. Dean, 'Cardinal Charles Lavigerie: The Politics of Getting a Red Hat', *Catholic Historical Review*, 63:2 (April 1977), 185–203.

Palti, Elías José, 'The "Theoretical Revolution" in Intellectual History: From the History of Political Ideas to the History of Political Languages', *History and Theory*, 53 (October 2014), 387–405.

Parmentier, Guillaume, 'The British Press in the Suez Crisis', *Historical Journal*, 23:2 (1980), 435–48.

Peden, G. C., 'Suez and Britain's Decline as a World Power', *Historical Journal*, 55 (2012), 1073–96.

Pedersen, Susan, 'The Impact of League Oversight on British Policy in Palestine', in Rory Miller, ed., *Britain, Palestine, and Empire: The Mandate Years* (Farnham: Ashgate, 2010), 39–64.

Paris, Roland, 'The "Responsibility to Protect" and the Structural Problems of Preventive Humanitarian Intervention', *International Peacekeeping*, 21:5 (2014), 569–603.

Perkins, Alfred, 'From Uncertainty to Opposition: French Catholic Liberals and Imperial Expansion, 1880–1885', *Catholic Historical Review*, 82:2 (1996), 204–24.

Perrenet, M., *Fachoda: L'épopée de Marchand* Limoges: M. Barbou, 1901.

Peyroulou, Jean-Pierre, 'La politique algérienne du Général de Gaulle (1943–1946)', in Maurice Vaïsse, ed., *De Gaulle et l'Algérie, 1943–1969* (Paris: Armand Colin, 2012), 28–37.

Pocock, J. C. A., 'The Concept of a Language and the *métier d'historien*: Some Considerations on Practice', in Anthony Pagden, ed., *The Languages of Political Theory in Early-Modern Europe* (Cambridge: Cambridge University Press, 1987), 19–38.

Preston, Andrew, 'Franklin D. Roosevelt and America's Empire of Anti-Imperialism', in Martin Thomas and Richard Toye, eds, *Rhetorics of Empire*, forthcoming.

Readman, Paul A., 'The 1895 General Election and Political Change in Late Victorian Britain', *Historical Journal*, 42:2 (1999), 467–93.

Readman, Paul A., 'The Conservative Party, Patriotism, and British Politics: The Case of the General Election of 1900', *Journal of British Studies*, 40:1 (2001), 107–45.

Reimer, Michael J. Reimer, 'Colonial Bridgehead: Social and Spatial Change in Alexandria, 1850–1882', *International Journal of Middle East Studies*, 20:4 (1988), 531–53.

Riker, T. W., 'A Survey of British Policy in the Fashoda Crisis', *Political Science Quarterly*, 44:1 (1929), 54–78.

Roberts, T. W., 'Republicanism, Railway Imperialism, and the French Empire in Africa, 1879–1889', *Historical Journal*, 54:2 (2011), 401–20.

Robertson, J. C., 'The Hoare-Laval Plan', *Journal of Contemporary History*, 10 (1975), 433–64.

Rodogno, Davide, 'The American Red Cross and the International Committee of the Red Cross' Humanitarian Politics and Policies in Asia Minor and Greece (1922–1923)', *First World War Studies*, 5:1 (2014), 82–99.

Roessel, David, 'Live Orientals and Dead Greeks: Forster's Response to the Chanak Crisis', *Twentieth Century Literature*, 36:1 (1990), 43–60.

Roi, Michael L., '"A Completely Immoral and Cowardly Attitude": The British Foreign Office, American Neutrality and the Hoare-Laval Plan', *Canadian Journal of History*, 29 (August 1994), 334–51.

Rossi, Mario, 'United States Military Authorities and Free France, 1942–1944', *Journal of Military History*, 61:1 (1997), 49–64.

Rutkoff, Peter M., 'The *Ligue des Patriotes*: The Nature of the Radical Right and the Dreyfus Affair', *French Historical Studies*, 8:4 (1974), 585–603.

Sales, Peter M., 'W. M. Hughes and the Chanak Crisis of 1922', *Australian Journal of Politics & History*, 17 (1971), 392–405.

Sanderson, G. N., 'The Origins and Significance of the Anglo-French Confrontation at Fashoda, 1898', in Prosser Gifford and W. Roger Louis, eds, *France and Britain in Africa: Imperial Rivalry and Colonial Rule* (New Haven, CT: Yale University Press, 1971), 285–331.

Satia, Priya, 'The Defense of Inhumanity: Air Control and the British Idea of Arabia', *American Historical Review*, 111:1 (February 2006), 16–51.

Schölch, Alexander, 'The "Men on the Spot" and the English Occupation of Egypt in 1882', *Historical Journal*, 19:3 (1976), 773–85.

Schultz, Matthias, 'Did Norms Matter in Nineteenth-Century International Relations? Progress and Decline in the "Culture of Peace" before World War I', in Holger Afflerbach and David Stevenson, eds, *An Improbable War? The Outbreak of World War I and European Political Culture before 1914* (Oxford: Berghahn, 2007), 43–63.

Shipway, Martin, 'Thinking Like an Empire: Governor Henri Laurentie and Postwar Plans for the Late Colonial French "Empire-State"', in Martin Thomas, ed., *The French Colonial Mind: Mental Maps of Empire and Colonial Encounters*, vol. 1 (Lincoln, NE: University of Nebraska Press, 2011), 219–50.

Simpson, Brad, 'The United States and the Curious History of Self-Determination', *Diplomatic History*, 36:4 (2012), 675–94.

Sluga, Glenda, 'Masculinities, Nations, and the New World Order: Peacemaking and Nationality in Britain, France, and the United States after the First World War', in Stefan Dudink, Karen Hagemann, and John Tosh, eds, *Masculinities in Politics and War: Gendering Modern History* (Manchester: Manchester University Press, 2004), 238–54.

Stanard, Matthew G., 'Interwar Pro-Empire Propaganda and European Colonial Culture: Toward a Comparative Research Agenda', *Journal of Contemporary History*, 44:1 (2009), 29–46.

Steele, E. D., 'Lord Salisbury, the "False Religion" of Islam, and the Reconquest of the Sudan', in Edward M. Spiers, ed., *Sudan: The Reconquest Reappraised* (London: Frank Cass, 1998), 11–33.

Stevenson, David, 'Militarization and Diplomacy in Europe before 1914', *International Security*, 22:1 (1997), 125–61.

Stoler, Ann Laura, 'Epistemic Politics: Ontologies of Colonial Common Sense', *Philosophical Forum*, 39:3 (2008), 341–69.

Stolte, Carolien, and Harald Fischer-Tiné, 'Imagining Asia in India: Nationalism and Internationalism (ca. 1905–1940)', *Comparative Studies in Society & History*, 54:1 (2012), 65–92.

Summerfield, Penny, 'Mass-Observation: Social Research or Social Movement?' *Journal of Contemporary History*, 20:3 (1985), 439–52.

Taithe, Bertrand, *Citizenship and Wars: France in Turmoil, 1870–1871* London: Routledge, 2001.

Taylor, A. J. P., 'Prelude to Fashoda: The Question of the Upper Nile, 1894–5', *English Historical Review*, 65:254 (1950), 52–80.

Thomas, Martin, 'The Discarded Leader: General Henri Giraud and the Foundation of the French Committee of National Liberation', *French History*, 10:1 (1996), 86–111.

Thomas, Martin, 'After Mers el-Kébir: The Armed Neutrality of the Vichy French Navy, 1940–43', *English Historical Review*, 112:447 (1997), 643–70.

Thomas, Martin, 'Free France, the British Government, and the Future of French Indo-China, 1940–45', *Journal of Southeast Asian Studies*, 28:1 (1997), 137–60.

Thomas, Martin, 'Deferring to Vichy in the Western Hemisphere: The St Pierre and Miquelon Affair of 1941', *International History Review*, 19:4 (1997), 789–808.

Thomas, Martin, 'Order before Reform: The Spread of French Military Operations in Algeria, 1954–1958', in David Killingray and David Omissi, eds, *Guardians of Empire* (Manchester: Manchester University Press, 1999), 198–220.

Thomas, Martin, 'Divisive Decolonization: The Anglo-French Withdrawal from Syria and Lebanon', *Journal of Imperial & Commonwealth History*, 28:3 (2000), 71–93.

Thomas, Martin, 'Anglo-French Imperial Relations in the Arab World: Intelligence Liaison and Nationalist Disorder', *Diplomacy & Statecraft*, 17:1 (2006), 1–28.

Thomas, Martin, 'Resource War, Civil War, Rights War: Factoring Empire into French North Africa's Second World War', *War in History*, 18:2 (2011), 225–48.

Thomas, Martin, 'A Path Not Taken: British Perspectives on French Colonial Violence after 1945', in L. J. Butler and Sarah Stockwell, eds, *The Wind of Change: Harold Macmillan and British Decolonization* (Basingstoke: Palgrave-Macmillan, 2013), 162–5.

Thomas, Martin, 'France and the Ethiopian Crisis, 1935–36: Security Dilemmas and Adjustable Interests', in G. Bruce Strang, ed., *Collision of Empires: Italy's Invasion of Ethiopia and its International Impact* (Farnham: Ashgate, 2014), 109–34.

Thomas, Martin, 'France and its Colonial Civil Wars, 1940–1945', in Evan Mawdsley and Joe Maiolo, eds, *The Cambridge History of the Second World War*, vol. 2 (Cambridge: Cambridge University Press, 2015), 581–603.

Thompson, Elizabeth F., 'Gender, War, and the Birth of States: Syrian and Lebanese Women's Mobilization during World War II', in Nicole Ann Dombrowski, ed., *Women and War in the Twentieth Century* (New York: Routledge, 2004), 266–87.

Thompson, Elizabeth F., 'Rashid Rida and the 190 Syrian-Arab Constitution: How the French Mandate Undermined Islamic Liberalism', in Cyrus Schayegh and Andrew Arsan, eds, *The Routledge Handbook of the History of the Middle East Mandates* (Abingdon: Routledge, 2015), 244–57.

Thorpe, Frederick J., 'The French Press and the Franco-Spanish Convention of 1904 on Morocco', *French Colonial History*, 3 (2003), 157–73.

Tombs, Robert, '"Lesser Breeds without the Law": The British Establishment and the Dreyfus Affair, 1894–1899', *Historical Journal*, 41:2 (1998), 495–510.

Toye, Richard, 'The Riddle of the Frontier: Winston Churchill, the Malakand Field Force, and the Rhetoric of Imperial Expansion', *Historical Research*, 84 (2011), 493–512.

Toye, Richard, 'From "Consensus" to "Common Ground": The Rhetoric of the Postwar Settlement and its Collapse', *Journal of Contemporary History*, 48:1 (2013), 3–23.

Toye, Richard, 'Words of Change: The Rhetoric of Commonwealth, Common Market, and Cold War, 1961–3', in Larry Butler and Sarah Stockwell, eds, *The Wind of Change: Harold Macmillan and British Decolonization* (Basingstoke: Palgrave Macmillan, 2013), 140–58.

Toye, Richard, 'Arguing about Hola Camp: The Rhetorical Consequences of a Colonial Massacre', in Martin Thomas and Richard Toye, eds, *Rhetorics of Empire* (forthcoming).

Tumblety, Joan, '"Civil Wars of the Mind": The Commemoration of the 1789 Revolution in the Parisian Press of the Radical Right, 1939', *Journal of Contemporary History*, 30:3 (2000), 389–429.

Tusan, Michelle, '"Crimes against Humanity": Human Rights, the British Empire, and the Origins of the Response to the Armenian Genocide', *American Historical Review*, 119:1 (2014), 47–77.

Tvedt, Terje, 'The Race to Fashoda: Robinson and Gallagher Revisited', *Forum for Development Studies*, 19:2 (1992), 195–210.

Utley, Rachel, 'Not to Do Less but to Do Better' . . . : French Military Policy in Africa', *International Affairs*, 78:1 (2002), 129–46.

Vaïsse, Maurice, 'France and the Suez Crisis', and 'Post-Suez France', both in W. Roger Louis and Roger Owen, eds, *Suez 1956: The Crisis and its Consequences* (Oxford: Clarendon, 1989).

Varnava, Andrekos, 'British and Greek Liberalism and Imperialism in the Long Nineteenth Century', in Matthew P. Fitzpatrick, ed., *Liberal Imperialism in Europe* (Basingstoke: Palgrave, 2012), 219–39.

Venier, Pascal, 'French Foreign Policy and the Boer War', in Keith Wilson, ed., *The International Impact of the Boer War* (Chesham: Acumen, 2001), 65–78.

Venier, Pascal, 'A Campaign of Colonial Propaganda: Gallieni, Lyautey and the Defence of the Military regime in Madagascar', in Tony Chafer and Amanda Sackur, eds, *Promoting the Colonial Idea: Propaganda and Visions of Empire in France* (Basingstoke: Palgrave-Macmillan, 2002), 29–39.

Villa, Luisa, 'A "Political Education": Wilfrid Scawen Blunt, the Arabs and the Egyptian Revolution (1881–82)', *Journal of Victorian Culture*, 17:1 (2012), 46–63.

Warson, Joanna, 'Beyond Co-operation and Competition: Anglo-French Relations, Connected Histories of Decolonization and Rhodesia's Unilateral Declaration of Independence, 1965–80', *Historical Research*, 88 (2015), 740–64.

Watenpaugh, David, 'The League of Nations' Rescue of Armenian Genocide Survivors and the Making of Modern Humanitarianism, 1920–1927', *American Historical Review*, 115:5 (December 2010), 1315–39.

Weinroth, Howard S., 'The British Radicals and the Balance of Power, 1902–1914', *Historical Journal*, 13 (1970), 653–82.

Weinroth, Howard S., 'British Radicals and the Agadir Crisis', *European History Quarterly*, 3:1 (1973), 39–61.

Weitz, Eric D., 'From the Vienna to the Paris System: International Politics and the Entangled Histories of Human Rights, Forced Deportations, and Civilizing Missions', *American Historical Review*, 113:5 (2008), 1313–43.

Werner, Michael, and Bénédicte Zimmermann, 'Beyond Comparison: Histoire Croisée and the Challenge of Reflexivity', *History and Theory*, 45:1 (2006), 30–50.

Wheatley, Natasha, 'Mandatory Interpretation: Legal Hermeneutics and the New International Order in Arab and Jewish Petitions to the League of Nations', *Past & Present*, 27 (May 2015), 206–35.

Wheatley, Natasha, 'The Mandate System as a Style of Reasoning: International Jurisdiction and the Parcelling of Imperial Sovereignty in Petitions from Palestine', in Schayegh and Arsan, eds, *The Routledge Handbook of the History of the Middle East Mandates* (Abingdon: Routledge, 2015), 106–22.

Wilder, Gary, 'From Optic to Topic: The Foreclosure Effect of Historiographic Turns', *American Historical Review*, 117:3 (2012), 723–45.

Wilson, Keith, 'The Agadir Crisis, the Mansion House Speech, and the Double-Edgedness of Agreements', *Historical Journal*, 15:3 (1972), 513–32.

Wolfe, Patrick, 'History and Imperialism: A Century of Theory, from Marx to Postcolonialism', *American Historical Review*, 102:2 (1997), 388–420.

Zamir, Meir, 'The "Missing Dimension": Britain's Secret War against France in Syria and Lebanon, 1942–45—Part II', *Middle Eastern Studies*, 46:6 (2010), 791–899.

Theses

Mackley, Simon, 'British Liberal Politics, the South African Question, and the Rhetoric of Empire, 1895–1907', unpublished PhD thesis, University of Exeter, 2016.

Morgan-Owen, David, 'The Invasion Question: Admiralty Plans to Defend the British Isles, 1888–1918', PhD thesis, University of Exeter, 2013.

Index